The Divorce of Lothar II

A volume in the series

Conjunctions of Religion and Power in the Medieval Past
Edited by Barbara H. Rosenwein

A list of titles in the series is available at www.cornellpress.cornell.edu.

The Divorce of Lothar II

CHRISTIAN MARRIAGE AND POLITICAL

POWER IN THE CAROLINGIAN WORLD

KARL HEIDECKER

Translated from the Dutch by Tanis M. Guest

Cornell University Press

Ithaca and London

The publication of this book was made possible by a publication grant from the Netherlands Organization for Scientific Research (NWO).

Original Dutch edition, *Kerk, huwelijk en politieke macht: de zaak Lotharius II (855–869)*, Amsterdam, 1997. Translated and revised for this first English-language edition.

English translation first published 2010 by Cornell University Press

Printed in the United States of America

Library of Congress Cataloging-in-Publication Data

Heidecker, Karl Josef.
  [Kerk, huwelijk en politieke macht. English]
  The divorce of Lothar II : Christian marriage and political power in the Carolingian world / Karl Heidecker ; translated from the Dutch by Tanis M. Guest.
      p. cm. – (Conjunctions of religion and power in the medieval past)
  Includes bibliographical references and index.
  ISBN 978-0-8014-3929-2 (cloth : alk. paper)
  1. Lothair II, King of Lorraine, ca. 825–869.   2. Lorraine (France)–Kings and rulers–Biography.   3. Divorce (Canon law)   4. France–History–To 987.   5. Lorraine (France)–History.   6. Marriage (Canon law)   7. Divorce–France–Lorraine–History.
I. Title.   II. Title: Divorce of Lothar the Second.   III. Series: Conjunctions of religion & power in the medieval past.
  DC655.2.H4513 2010
  944'.38014092–dc22

2009025600

Cloth printing   10 9 8 7 6 5 4 3 2 1

Contents

Preface   *vii*

Abbreviations   *ix*

Introduction   *1*

I. Preparing the Drama

I.1. Canonical Weapons: The Church's Regulations on Marriage
from the Eighth to the Mid-Ninth Century   *11*

I.2. A Cause Célèbre: The Divorce Case in the Sources   *36*

II. A Marital Drama in Six Acts

Act I. Lothar Ascends the Throne and Marries Theutberga,
855–857   *51*
The Accession: The Political Power of the King and Nobles   52
*Lothar's Marriage to Theutberga: Marriage as an Alliance between
Noble Families   59*

Act II. An Unsuccessful Attempt at Divorce, 857–859   *63*
The First Attempt at Divorce   65
Ermengarde's Family: The Marriage Alliance Continued in the Children   69

Act III. A Second Attempt at Divorce and the Involvement
of Hincmar of Reims, 859–860   *73*
The Legal Status of Marriage   77
The Powers of the Bishops   86
Hincmar's Rules in Their Political Context   92

Act IV. Lothar's Allies and His Marriage to Waldrada, 860–862   *100*

   The Legal Status of Marriage: The Arguments of Lothar's Bishops   105
   The Powers of the Bishops   128
   Lothar's Bishops in Their Political Context   130
   Alliances and Family Ties   135

 Act V. Pope Nicholas Intervenes and Theutberga Is Reinstated, 863–867   *149*

   Pope Nicholas and the Legal Status of Marriage   152
   The Powers of the Pope   159
   The Success of Nicholas's Claims to Power   164

Act VI. A New Pope and Lothar's Last Battle, 867–869   *173*

   Pope Adrian's Rules for Marriage and His Claims to Power   176
   Political Power and the Preservation of Lothar's Realm   179

Epilogue. Lothar's Reputation and His Descendants   *182*

Appendix 1. Map of Carolingian Europe in the Ninth Century   *189*

Appendix 2. Genealogies   *193*
   1. The Carolingians
   2. The Bosonids
   3. The Descendants of Gerard, Count of Paris, and Beggo
   4. The Etichonids
   *5. The Carolingians and Their Relatives, Present at the Treaty
      of Coblenz (860)*
   6. The Welfs

Appendix 3. Reigns of the Carolingian Kings   *201*

Selected Bibliography   203
Index   223

Preface

It may strike many readers as highly unusual to present a serious historical monograph in the form of a drama in six acts. As I investigated the tragic events that shaped the lives of Charlemagne's great-grandson King Lothar II and his wives, Theutberga and Waldrada, however, this approach seemed ever more compelling, and in the end proved too strong for me to resist. The book is based on an earlier Dutch-language version, *Kerk, huwelijk en politieke macht: De zaak Lotharius II (855–869)*. This English-language version has been revised to make the work accessible to a wider readership; new material has been added and some highly detailed pages have been removed. Readers who want a more exhaustive treatment of the subject and its source base should turn to the original version. One small section of the work was included in a paper, "Germanic Marriage: A Suitable Case for the Dustbin?" which I delivered at the 2001 International Congress on Medieval Studies in Kalamazoo, Michigan.

The actions described in this book involve a large number of individuals with often complicated family relationships. In order to help the reader grasp these relationships, I have included six genealogical tables in appendix 2 and a list of Carolingian kings in appendix 3. The reader should also be aware that there is no standard convention for the presentation of ninth-century personal names. Thus, in literature and even in contemporary sources, the same person can be found bearing names with different spellings and pronunciations. Thus, for example, Theutberga can appear as Tetberga, Tietberga, Teutberge, Tetburga, Theutburga, Dietburg, and all variations in between. I have here opted for the name found most often in the current Anglo-American historical literature. I have included a map of

Carolingian Europe to help orient readers to the places where Lothar's drama unfolded. This map is drawn in accordance with Kaj van Vliet's revisions to the borders of Lothar's kingdom[1] and Wolfert van Egmond's forthcoming work on the ethnogenesis of the Frisians.

The translation of this book was made possible by a publication grant from the Netherlands Organization for Scientific Research (NWO). The libraries of the École Normale Supérieure and the Institut Historique Allemand, Paris, offered me access to their collections. I benefited greatly from a grant from the French Ministry of Foreign Affairs and the hospitality of the Institut Néerlandais. Furthermore, the University of Amsterdam has provided generous support as I completed the project.

I express my deepest thanks to the following people, who have helped me with advice or information: Jan Smit, Loek Meijer, Peter van der Eerden, Jan Besteman, Kathleen Nieuwenhuisen, Bas de Melker, Cees Cappon, Mayke de Jong, Marco Mostert, Hans-Werner Goetz, Chris Coppens, Roger Reynolds, Abigail Firey, Ludger Körntgen, Wilfried Hartmann, Martina Stratmann, Philippe Depreux, Jérôme Belmon, and Véronique Frandon. Pierre Toubert facilitated my studies in Paris, received me warmly, and made important comments on a first draft of the work. Piet Leupen, director of my thesis, provided me with his support, guidance, and comments. My very special thanks go to Bert Demyttenaere, who has taught me and guided my work from the early days of my studies. He was present at the very "cradle" of the present work, and has commented on it throughout its long gestation. I regard him truly as my *maître*. I must also thank Tanis Guest, the translator of this work, Barbara Rosenwein, the editor of the Conjunctions of Religion and Power in the Medieval Past series, and John Ackerman, Cornell University Press director, for all their help in transforming my work into a book for an English-language readership. All errors that remain, of course, are mine.

In closing, I must pause to commemorate Inger Elzinga. She was a brilliant student, a most promising scholar, and a dear friend. For many years, ever since we started out as youngsters at the University of Amsterdam, we studied together, shared our fascination for scholarship, and wrote articles together. At a certain moment we both became involved in reflecting on the works of Georges Duby. The reader will recognize their importance for both the subject and the structure of this book. The opening sentences of the book that follows are Inger's.[2]

---

1. Kaj van Vliet, *In kringen van kanunniken: Munsters en kapittels in het bisdom Utrecht, 695–1227* (Zutphen, 2002), 132–35.

2. Inger Elzinga and Karl Heidecker, review of Georges Duby, "Ridder, vrouw en priester" (Dutch translation of *Le chevalier, la femme et le prêtre*), *Skript historisch tijdschrift* 8 (1986): 26–37.

Abbreviations

AASS	*Acta Sanctorum*
AASSB	*Acta Sanctorum Belgii*
AB	*Annales Bertiniani*
AESC	*Annales Économies Sociétés Civilisations*
AF	*Annales Fuldenses*
AHC	*Annuarium historiae conciliorum*
aᵒ	anno
AX	*Annales Xantenses*
Ben. Lev.	Benedictus Levita
BMGN	*Bijdragen en Mededelingen betreffende de Geschiedenis der Nederlanden*
c.	canon/caput/capitulum
CCSL	*Corpus Christianorum, Series Latina*
CCCM	*Corpus Christianorum, Continuatio Mediaevalis*
CSEL	*Corpus Scriptorum Ecclesiasticorum Latinorum*
col.	column
DA	*Deutsches Archiv für Erforschung des Mittelalters*
D Charles le Chauve	*Recueil des Actes de Charles II le Chauve, roi de France*
D Karl III	*Diplomata Karoli III*
D Lot.I	*Diplomata Lotharii I*
D Lot.II	*Diplomata Lotharii II*
D LD	*Diplomata Ludowici Germanici*
D LJ	*Diplomata Ludowici Junioris*
D Lud. II	*Die Urkunden Ludwigs II*
D Provence	*Recueil des Actes des rois de Provence*
Dach.	*Collectio Dacheriana* = *"Collectio antiqua canonum poenitentialium"*
De divortio	Hincmar of Rheims, *De divortio Lotharii regis et Theutbergae reginae*

Dion.-Hadr.	*Collectio Dionysio-Hadriana* = Dionysius Exiguus, *Codex canonum*
EME	*Early Medieval Europe*
Ep. Ben.	Benedict III, *Epistola*
Ep. Lot.	*Epistolae ad divortium Lotharii II. regis pertinentes*
Ep. Hadr.	Hadrian II, *Epistolae*
Ep. Hincm.	Hincmar of Reims, *Epistolae*
Ep. Joh. VIII	John VIII, *Epistolae*
Ep. Nic.	Nicholas I, *Epistolae*
FS	*Frühmittelalterliche Studien*
HJ	*Historisches Jahrbuch*
HZ	*Historische Zeitschrift*
lib.	liber
MA	*Le Moyen Age*
MGH	*Monumenta Germaniae Historica*
Cap.	*Capitularia regum Francorum*
Cap. episc.	*Capitula episcoporum*
Conc.	*Concilia*
Conc. 3	*Konzilien der karolingischen Teilreiche (843–859), MGH Concilia 3*
Conc. 4	*Konzilien der karolingischen Teilreiche (860–874), MGH Concilia 4*
DD	*Diplomata*
Epp.	*Epistolae*
Epp. Karol. aevi	*Epistolae Karolini aevi*
LL	*Leges*
SS	*Scriptores*
SS rer. germ. i.u.s.	*Scriptores rerum germanicarum in usum scholarum separatim editi*
MIÖG	*Mitteilungen des Instituts für Österreichische Geschichtsforschung*
ms.	manuscript
NA	*Neues Archiv der Gesellschaft für ältere deutsche Geschichtskunde*
PL	*Patrologiae Cursus Completus, Series Latina*
P&P	*Past and Present*
Ps.-Isid.	*Decretales Pseudo-Isidoriani*
QFIAB	*Quellen und Forschungen aus italienischen Archiven und Bibliotheken*
r.	reigned
RB	*Revue Bénédictine*
RDC	*Revue de Droit Canonique*
RH	*Revue Historique*
tit.	titulus
TvG	*Tijdschrift voor Geschiedenis*
WH	Wattenbach and Holtzmann, *Deutschlands Geschichtsquellen*
WL	Wattenbach and Levison, *Deutschlands Geschichtsquellen*
ZSRG	*Zeitschrift der Savigny-Stiftung für Rechtsgeschichte*
GA	*Germanistische Abteilung*
KA	*Kanonistische Abteilung*

The Divorce of Lothar II

Introduction

Who is there that was not born of the coming together of a man and a woman? And who, once born, is not part of a family? Only death is as universal as these simple social facts. Every society is faced with the task of devising a suitable framework for them. In the western Christian world the dominant framework is—or, perhaps I should say, was until recently—a clearly defined type of marriage: one man marries one woman, preferably from a different family, and once married if at all possible they stay married until separated by death. This is how it has been for a very long time, but it was not always so. Monogamous, indissoluble marriage has its own history. And this book will describe what is, in my view, a crucial episode in the evolution of this type of marriage, the Carolingian period as seen in the light of one specific case: that of Lothar II (855–69), king of the northern part of the Carolingian Middle Kingdom, later known after him as Lotharingia.

In 857, Lothar decided to divorce his wife, Theutberga. Today, he would go to see his lawyer, there would be a trial or a mediation, and, with the divorce granted, he would be free to remarry. In 857, however, divorce was not simply a legal matter. Lothar, though a king with a great deal of political power, nevertheless had to ask his bishops if he might divorce. He and they were not even sure that, if his divorce were valid, he might remarry. The "law" of divorce was entirely uncertain, and because of this it was a religious and political issue. This book is about the uncertainty of the law and how this uncertainty was exploited for political ends. It makes clear, as no other study has thus far done, how an event such as Lothar's divorce, which historians have hitherto treated as mainly a matter of law, may be best understood as an unusually well-documented model of the political machinations of the Carolingian world.

The divorce of Lothar was in its time a notorious case. It caused big waves, the more so because the parties involved sought to exploit public opinion to a maximal extent by slandering their opponents. Of course, this is not something nowadays totally unknown to politicians and their campaign managers, but the nature of the accusations in Lothar's divorce case was so far below the belt that it would probably make even the most hardened modern political manipulators blush. The notoriety of the case did not end with the death of its participants. It entered most prominently into the field of political argument (the kingdom of Lotharingia was a failure; the real kingdoms were France and Germany), legal precedent (one should never be allowed to divorce on those arguments), and even the popular imagination, becoming finally part of medieval folk legend. Inhabitants of the French Alpine town of Annecy still point out the dungeon of the towering old castle, rising high above the old lakeside town, in which the wicked King Lothar II held prisoner his noble wife, Queen Theutberga, and from which, one night, she secretly escaped, descending from her tower and then taking a small boat across the lake to freedom.

The case of Lothar II features prominently in much of the general literature on marriage in the early Middle Ages, but also in the general literature on many other subjects. A great many arguments have been based on it. Often, however, these derive from a superficial, and usually faulty, study of the case. To write about such a complicated subject as marriage in the Carolingian period, and to do so on the basis of a limited amount of often highly contradictory source material, is in itself no simple matter. Along with the difficulty of the sources, one of the problems that bedevil this subject lies in a number of misleading approaches to it. First, early medieval marriage is often described as though there existed one immutable standard model, the Christian monogamous union, with all other forms— often barbaric, pagan, or worse still, immoral—being deviations from this.[1] Second, there is the tendency toward an over-legalistic approach.[2] Non-Christian marriages especially, usually described as "Germanic," have been classified by historians or jurists according to strict criteria. A marital relationship in which the partners had gone through a particular procedure then became a particular type of marriage, for example, *Friedelehe* or

---

1. Rouche, "Mariages," and Rouche, "Early Middle Ages"; Gaudemet, *Mariage*; Devisse, *Hincmar archévêque*. The picture of the Carolingian period outlined by Wemple, *Women*, pp. 75–123, should be approached with caution; see the review by Nelson, *Women in Frankish Society*.

2. Kottje, "Ehe," and Kottje, "Eherechtliche Bestimmungen"; Konecny, *Frauen*.

Muntehe. Although classifications are useful, sometimes indispensable, in themselves they too often have been equated with the classifications used in the early Middle Ages and sometimes even with social reality. Some of these classifications, though, turn out to have been based on a very liberal interpretation of the sources,[3] while others are not the established norms they claim to be.[4] Forewarned is forearmed; and now it is time to introduce Lothar's case.

A Marital Drama

In 855 King Lothar II married Theutberga. A short time later he tried to repudiate her in order to marry Waldrada. But the intervention of Nicholas I, bishop of Rome, forced Lothar to keep Theutberga as his wife. This looks like a simple drama for four characters: Lothar, Theutberga, Waldrada, and Pope Nicholas in the role of judge. In fact, though, it was a long-drawn-out, stormy, and complicated extravaganza. The four characters had connections with many different groups, turning a simple affair into a complex political power struggle. Coalitions were made and broken, with threats, battles, promises, bribes, backbiting, intrigues, and manipulation the order of the day. Among the actors were educated men, clerics for the most part, who now and then constituted a sort of chorus and provided a commentary on the events—a commentary that consists of pious propaganda and does nothing to simplify matters. The chorus did not all keep to the same text, but spoke with many voices.

The vicissitudes of Lothar's marriage and divorce were clearly a political issue of the greatest importance. Among the nobility marriage was seen as a means of forging a bond not only between two individuals but between families, a means by which wealth, status, and power could be safeguarded—and, if possible, even increased—and perpetuated through one's descendants. Marriage, with its resultant relationships of blood and marriage, was certainly not the only way of forming mutual ties and securing power. Nor was it infallible. Just as matrimony did not guarantee enduring harmony between man and wife, neither did it guarantee enduring harmony between the families concerned. The marriage might be childless, or the fitness and legitimacy of any offspring might be called into question. Then any number of family members might get involved in the battle for power, preferably royal power. It's your own people you have to be wary of!

---

3. See pp. 119–23.
4. See pp. 16–17, 111–18, 186.

The Church's Rules on Marriage

His contemporaries' commentary on Lothar's matrimonial drama is far from unanimous. Lothar and his supporters argued that he was most definitely not married to Theutberga. Pope Nicholas said the opposite and ruled that Lothar and Theutberga had to remain joined in indissoluble matrimony. In discussing marriage, divorce, and remarriage in general and Lothar's marriage in particular, both parties put forward many, sometimes mutually contradictory, views. The most important commentators were senior clerics, abbots and especially bishops. But these religious leaders did not form a monolithic whole, united in heart and mind, proclaiming one single church doctrine on marriage. These eminent clerics could have different interests, depending on the political and social situation in which they found themselves. Often they did not have any scruples about changing their opinions when it was to their advantage to do so, although it must be said that they were not alone in this. People looked for arguments that would serve their own interests; when those interests changed, so very readily did the arguments. When it came to religious doctrine on marriage, the Bible, council texts, and church fathers—so far as they were known—did provide a certain general orientation, but not a clearly defined, concrete, and socially applicable set of rules.

The Political and Religious Background

The political and religious situation of the Carolingian empire in the middle years of the ninth century forms the setting for our matrimonial drama. When Lothar's grandfather, Louis the Pious, came to the throne in 814 as Charlemagne's sole heir, the empire roughly consisted of the present-day Benelux countries, most of France, northeastern Spain, Germany west of the Elbe, Switzerland, Austria, northern Italy, and parts of Hungary west of the Danube. Like their grandfather and all previous Frankish rulers, the sons of Louis the Pious saw the empire as an inheritance to which they could all lay claim. After the death of Louis the Pious his empire was eventually divided among his sons in 843. Lothar I received the central portion and the imperial title, Louis the German the eastern part, and Charles the Bald the western part. This division had been agreed on after bitter conflict, but neither the three brothers nor their descendants considered themselves bound by it. Time and again they tried to conquer one another's territory. In these attempts each of them was dependent on the support of the empire's magnates—the powerful nobles and the senior clergy—and of the other kings with whom they allied themselves in varying coalitions. This unremitting struggle for power between Charlemagne's descendants is the setting for the drama of Lothar's marriage.

The wielders of political and religious power all came from the same noble families. Moreover, they felt that together they were at the head of one and the same society—a society that was referred to sometimes as the "realm" (*regnum*; of the political province) or the "Church" (*ecclesia*; of the religious province), and other times, confusingly, as "Christendom" (*christianitas*; failing to distinguish between the two), though these were not established technical terms. According to Hincmar, the archbishop of Reims, one of the most prolific authors of the Carolingian period and the most important Frankish ecclesiastical politician of his time, even the partition of 843 did not change this situation: "one realm, one dove of Christ, namely the holy Church, under the law of one Christendom, one realm and one Church, though governed by various kings and various religious leaders."[5] Be that as it may, in every kingdom the bishops were involved in the government of the realm. They acted as advisers to the kings, were among the decision makers at diets, and performed diplomatic functions in the king's name; the royal chancelleries, staffed entirely by clerics, were headed by Church dignitaries. In the Carolingian empire, unlike the Roman, the bishops were seen as an essential constituent of political government.[6]

In practice, and in theory, realm and Church seemed to be telescoped into a single entity, governed by the kings on one side and the bishops on the other. It was stated that "the Church was so organized that it was governed by high priestly authority and by royal power."[7] But this did not mean that the spiritual and secular authorities were equal in every respect. There was a clear difference of task and function that was accepted by both sides. The bishop was acknowledged as the supreme leader in the liturgical service, and it was his duty as shepherd to watch over the flock of the faithful entrusted to him. In matters of Christian "belief" (religious doctrine and the liturgy) and "morality" (the conduct prescribed by the faith) they held a special responsibility. On the Day of Judgment the bishops—at least,

---

5. *De divortio*, p. 236: "Unum regnum, una Christi columba, videlicet sancta ecclesia, unius Christianitatis lege, regni unius et unius ecclesie, quamquam per plures regni principes et ecclesiarum presules gubernacula moderentur."

6. For the intertwining of Church and secular world in the Carolingian period, see Demyttenaere, "Mentaliteit," pp. 90–95; Nelson, "Kingship and Royal Government," pp. 388–92.

7. Council of Yütz near Diedenhofen (844) c. 2; in *MGH Conc.* 3, p. 31: "ita ecclesiam dispositam esse, ut pontificali auctoritate et regali potestate gubernetur."

so they claimed—would have to render account in these matters to God, who was described by Hincmar as the "Inspector of consciences," the "Shepherd of shepherds," and indeed also as the "King of kings."[8] On top of this, by virtue of their office as archbishop, bishop, or abbot, the religious leaders were also members of the clergy as a distinct organization with its own structures. The clergy had their own hierarchically structured systems for working together and their own territorial divisions, which did not coincide with those of the secular power.[9]

Pastors, Marriage, and Political Authority

Seen against this background the behavior of the religious leaders becomes more comprehensible. What the shepherds of souls said about marriage in general and Lothar's marriage in particular has to be taken in the political context in which they operated and of which they were part. To inspire and justify their precepts they undoubtedly needed to refer to the "traditional" teaching of the Church. But that teaching had come down to them in a mixture of heterogeneous and sometimes mutually contradictory rulings. This mixture offered scope for different interpretations, and consequently in the ups and downs of Lothar's marriage and divorce, and often depending on their political involvement, the bishops did indeed come up with different interpretations.

Who had authority to judge in matrimonial cases? Given the way in which political and religious responsibilities were intertwined, it is hardly surprising that this question gave rise to all manner of conflicts. The bishops might well be competent regarding "belief and morality," but where did belief and morality stop and politics begin?[10] The case concerned a marriage at the very highest level of society, and was therefore an issue of exceptional political importance. And the argument about competence was not only between the secular and spiritual leaders but between the spiritual leaders themselves. For example, in Pope Nicholas's view the authority of the bishops was rooted in and derived from papal authority, which he

---

8. *De divortio*, p. 111: "Inspectore conscientiarum . . . regi regum et pastori pastorum."

9. For example, the bishopric of Cambrai lay in Lothar's Middle Kingdom, but in the clerical hierarchy the bishop of Cambrai came under the archbishop of Reims, whose bishopric belonged to the West Frankish realm. This could lead to serious problems, as for instance when after the death of Theoderic (862) Lothar II appointed a new bishop of Cambrai whom Hincmar, the archbishop of Reims, refused to consecrate. See *Ep. Nic.*, nos. 13–15, pp. 279–81, and a letter to Hincmar from Lothar's bishops, ed. in *MGH Conc.* 4: p. 134.

10. On the difficulty of separating "matters of belief and morality" from "political matters" in social practice, see Demyttenaere, "Mentaliteit," 94–95.

considered to be superior even to that of the councils.[11] But a good many of his episcopal colleagues did not share his view on this. And so the whole business of Lothar's marriage and divorce became entangled with a long-running struggle for precedence between religious and secular rulers and among the religious leaders themselves.

The bishops' pronouncements on marriage were not made in a social vacuum, uninfluenced by current social practice. The Franks regarded marriage as a social institution, subject to the rules and customs of their society. Where the bishops went against deeply rooted customs they naturally found it difficult to lead their flock in the desired direction. Moreover, any change in marriage customs inevitably brought political complications. The attitude of the bishops, as well as the effectiveness of that attitude, cannot be seen in isolation from the actual political balance of power. If their pronouncements were vague and innocuous, or entirely advantageous, there was no problem. But a pronouncement that seemed prejudicial would not be accepted without question by the party concerned. Often such a pronouncement was contested by invoking different church rules or a different interpretation of the same rules. The success of such an action invariably depended on the ability to enforce it by political means.

The extravaganza surrounding Lothar's marital difficulties is thus a moment in the history, first, of ideas about the legal status of marriage; second, of competence to judge in such matters; and, third, of political power structures. And it is in terms of these three aspects that I shall look at it. What were the religious views on marriage advanced by the various parties in this case? Who was considered competent to judge in Lothar's case? What was the actual power structure that ensured that those judgments were pronounced and were, or were not, implemented?

I will summarize the events briefly in six successive acts, hoping in this way to provide the reader with an overall view of this complicated case. After each act I will discuss the questions it raises. In almost every act one or more actors in the drama put forward views on marriage. Some claim

---

11. Letter from Nicholas, in *AB* a° 863, p. 102, c.3: "The Apostolic See, in which their episcopal office has very clearly found its 'principium,' its starting point and basis" (Sede apostolica, unde eos principium episcopatus sumpsisse manifestum est). *Ep. Nic.* no. 29, to Radulf of Bourges, p. 296: "I ask you: what validity will your judgments have, if ours, which cannot be revoked, are in some way or other rendered impotent; and what force can your councils have, if the Apostolic See shall have lost its stability, without whose consent no council can be accepted, as we read?" (Quam rogo validitatem vestra poterunt habere iudicia, si nostra quomodolibet infirmantur de quibus nec retractari licet, vel quod robur concilia vestra optinere valebunt, si suam perdiderit sedes apostolica firmitatem, sine cuius consensu nulla concilia vel accepta esse leguntur?)

the authority to judge, others obey, and others resist. And in each of the six acts it will be apparent how all this connects up with the political situation at the time.

To understand the whole spectacle properly we first need some grasp of the Church rulings that could be, and were, invoked in Lothar's case. As I will explain in section I.1, these rulings were collected, systematized, and amplified mainly during the Carolingian drive for reform. Then, in section I.2, I will examine the various voices in the chorus that commented on Lothar's case, their degree of involvement, and their reliability. And finally, we must not forget that this marital drama is about people, people with ambitions and emotions. Was not the behavior of Lothar, Theutberga, and Waldrada also determined by the love or hate they felt for each other? Was not the affair of Lothar's marriage, for all its legal and political aspects, also simply a story of thwarted love, a true human drama? The outcome of their story, however, depended on one inexorable fact. The ultimate winners and losers in this affair would be determined by the ability to mobilize political power.

I PREPARING THE DRAMA

I.1
Canonical Weapons

*The Church's Regulations on Marriage
from the Eighth to the Mid-Ninth Century*

Around the middle of the eighth century Magingoz, bishop of
Würzburg (755–86), wrote to Lullus, bishop of Mainz, to ask for guidance
on the making and dissolving of Christian marriage and subsequent remarriage. Magingoz was particularly concerned about the question of
remarriage. With this he raised the issue that was socially the most important, since most of the conflicts in these matters were about remarriage. Divorce and rules about divorce mainly became a matter of discussion if one of the partners wanted to remarry, and thus discussion about
the rules of divorce and remarriage entailed discussion about the rightful
way of making a marriage. In Magingoz's time these rules were apparently
not yet clear and there was a need to clarify them prompted by, among other
things, these cases of remarriage. A century later, however, by the middle
of the ninth century, a group of churchmen had formulated a set of rules,
stating what according to them was the rightful way of making a marriage.
Here we shall see how this development took place.

Some of the traditional rulings on the subject were, it seemed to Magingoz, hard to reconcile with one another. With repeated rhetorical protesta-
tions of ignorance he addressed his colleague:

> We should be glad to receive the solution to a problem, one which is not easy
> given our limited knowledge, from you, Reverend Sir, who possess that
> knowledge in abundance. This we ask of you most urgently. Well then: it
> seems to us that the rules regarding the contracting and dissolving of mar-
> riage by Christians are formulated in so many different ways by the Church

fathers that for us with our limited knowledge it is difficult or impossible to derive a single consistent pronouncement from them.[1]

Magingoz was, as we have seen, particularly concerned about the question of remarriage. He started by wondering whether it was permitted to remarry one's former wife, if one has repudiated her on grounds of adultery:

> For Isidore [of Seville] and Jerome appear united in the assurance that an adulterous wife may be repudiated by the man to whom she was married when like a whore she entered into a relationship with someone else, since by wickedly dividing one flesh she has made herself unworthy of the honor of the conjugal state instituted by God and has alienated herself from it. According to them this is ordained and permitted by the Savior when he stated that a wife may not be put aside save by reason of adultery. Augustine, on the other hand, after close examination of the same pronouncement of the Savior in a long treatise, provides no clarification at all, or at least none that is intelligible to our unschooled mind, but at the end he says this: that the question of how this pronouncement of the Savior should be understood is still totally shrouded in obscurity. But . . . he says that there would be nothing wrong in her husband being reconciled with that woman, even though she had fallen into adultery.[2]

Magingoz correctly said that according to Jerome (†420) and Isidore (†636) the man must repudiate his adulterous wife, and of course he could not then remarry her. But according to Augustine (†430) he may, apparently after having repudiated her, take her back as his wife. And then Magingoz raised a second point: Could a woman remarry if her husband had been taken prisoner in war and there was no hope of his return? As Magingoz

---

1. Magingoz to Lullus, in *MGH Epp. Karol. aevi* 1: p. 420: "Quam ob rem solutionem questionis alicuius, quae videlicet infirmitatis nostrae cognitioni facilis non est, a dignitationis vestrae largitatae, id ipsum flagitantes multum, desideramus accipere. Itaque constitutio matrimonii christianorum in iungendo vel separando a patribus tanta diversitate, nobis videtur disponi, ut vix una et conpar sententia ipsorum nostrae pateat parvitati." For the manuscripts Magingoz may have consulted, see Bischoff and Hoffmann, *Libri*, p. 162.

2. Ibid., p. 420: "Videntur namque concorditur Essidorus ac Hieronimus adfirmare: non debere adulteram teneri a viro, cui sociata alteri se more meretricis adiungat; utpote quae, unam carnem nefariae dividens, indignam se et alienam ab honore conubii divinitus instituti reddiderit; et hoc esse preceptum vel permissum a salvatore, cum uxorem non demittendum absque fornicationis causa preciperet. Augustinus vero, cum sententiam eandem salvatoris diuturna tractatione ventilasset, nihil plane elucedationis, certe nostrae omnino teneritudini captabile, profert: sed hoc in extremo dicebat, quia, quomodo preceptum hoc salvatoris accipi debuisset, latebrosissimam adhuc superesse questionem, . . . dicit: non male illi viri mulieri licet in adulterium lapse conciliaretur." Magingoz is probably quoting from Isidore, *De ecclesiasticis officiis* II, xx, 11, pp. 93–94; Jerome, *Commentarius in Math.*, Lib. III, ad Mt. 19:9, p. 167, probably quoted via Isidore; Augustine, *De sermone in monte habito* I c. 14–16, pp. 41–56; see esp. c. 16, p. 48, which explains the last sentence of Magingoz.

wrote to Lullus, "The holy Pope Leo says: a woman whose husband has been captured by the enemy may, impelled by loneliness, marry another man without committing a sin when there is no hope of the prisoner returning."[3] According to Pope Leo (440–61), remarriage was permitted "on grounds of desertion of the wife," while according to Isidore and Jerome "infidelity to the matrimonial bond severs the marriage."[4] And now we come to Magingoz's problem: if one accepted the pronouncements both of Pope Leo *and* of Jerome and Isidore, what possibilities were available to the innocent parties in a divorce if they wished to remarry? They could not take back the adulterous spouse. If they did not want to live alone, what alternative had they but to marry someone else? "For otherwise what remains for the partner who finds himself in a state of helpless loneliness—if we are right in thinking that the pronouncements both of Isidore and Jerome and of Leo should be taken into account—save for him or her to marry someone else, I really do not know."[5] It was not "limited knowledge" that was responsible for Magingoz's intellectual struggles, but the vagueness, diversity, and inconsistency of an authoritative tradition made up of biblical texts, pronouncements by Church fathers, council decisions, and papal letters giving authoritative decisions on canon law—known as decretals. The difficulties were not confined to the issue of remarriage. There was also, for instance, the question of whether a man *could*, or *must*, repudiate his adulterous wife—a question that Magingoz left open. In any case the views of Jerome, and of Isidore following Jerome, went back to various and divergent Bible passages. Mark (10:2–12) stressed the indissolubility of marriage; for a husband to repudiate his wife (or vice versa, Mark 10:12) was unambiguously forbidden: "Whosoever shall put away his wife, and marry another, committeth adultery against her" (10:11).[6] In Matthew (19:3–9), on the other hand, it was stated, "Whosoever shall put away his wife, except it be

3. Magingoz to Lullus, in *MGH Epp. Karol. aevi* 1: p. 420: "Beatus vero Leo papa: feminam, capto ab hostibus marito, cogente solitudine inculpabitur alteri posse copulari, cum desperaretur captus." A reference to the decretal of Pope Leo to Nicetas, Leo the Great, *Epistolae*, col. 1136–37.

4. Magingoz to Lullus, in *MGH Epp. Karol. aevi* 1: p. 420: "Ibi notandum videtur, quod statim destitutio coniugis nubendi licentiam tribuit; apud Essidorum vero vel Iheronimum proditio foederis coniugalis matrimonium separat."

5. Magingoz to Lullus, in *MGH Epp. Karol. aevi* 1: p. 420: "Quid ergo supersit coniugi, quem vel quam solitudo perurguet, si et Hisidori val Hieronimi ac Leonis dercretum iuste creditur esse tenendum, nisi ut se matrimonio coniugant alterius, me fateor ignorare."

6. Ibid.: "Quicumque dimiserit uxorem suam et aliam duxerit adulterium committit super eam. Et si uxor dimiserit virum suum et alii nupserit, moechatur." The same view is found in Luke 16:18: "Omnis qui dimittit uxorem suam et alteram ducit, moechatur."

for fornication, and shall marry another, committeth adultery" (19:9).[7] Often, but by no means always, the passage from Mark was used to interpret Matthew as placing an absolute ban on remarriage. The phrase "except it be for fornication" would then refer solely to the repudiation of the spouse, which was sometimes, as in Augustine, understood as a possibility and sometimes, as in Jerome, as compulsory.[8] As for remarriage during the lifetime of the spouse, generally speaking there were two schools of thought: one that saw it as absolutely forbidden, and one that permitted it under certain circumstances.[9] Clearly, Magingoz belonged to the second group.

Bishops such as Magingoz and Lullus were part of a group of men from the Carolingian aristocracy, most but not all of them clerics, who were pursuing a comprehensive policy of Christian reform in an attempt to construct a uniform Christian realm; their concern with religious rules on marriage has to be seen as one aspect of this. They sought to assemble and circulate proper, that is, authoritative, rules, to standardize and systematize them and to interpret and modify them in the light of new ideas. The promulgation and accessibility of these rules was greatly aided by an important element of the Carolingian reforms: the development and dissemination of a new, easy-to-read script into which many manuscripts, including legislative and liturgical texts, were copied.[10]

In the liturgical field the reformers tried to restrict the proliferation of local usages somewhat by standardizing the liturgy, for instance by authorizing a specific version of a particular book known as a sacramentary, which contained the prayers to be spoken by the priest (including a nuptial benediction), and distributing numerous copies of it. In the field of church law they produced a great many dossiers of council rulings and papal decretals.[11]

7. Magingoz to Lullus, in *MGH Epp. Karol. aevi* 1: p. 420: "Quicumque dimiserit uxorem suam, nisi ab fornicationem et aliam duxerit moechatur et qui dimissam duxerit moechatur"; cf. Matthew 5:32: "Omnis qui dimiserit uxorem suam, excepta fornicationis causa, facit eam moechari, et qui dimissam duxerit, adulterat."

8. For this controversy see Gaudemet, *Mariage*, pp. 43–48; Van Tilborg, "Matheus 19, 3–12."

9. Among the Church fathers we find the latter view mainly in a work commonly ascribed to Ambrose (+397), which is actually by an unknown late-fourth-century author known since the sixteenth century as Ambrosiaster, who permits a husband to remarry after repudiating his wife for adultery, but forbids a wife in similar circumstances to do so: Ambrosiaster, *Commentarius in epistulas* 1 Cor.7:11, pp. 74–75. For the different patristic interpretations, see Gaudemet, *Mariage*, pp. 71–75, Philip Reynolds, *Marriage*, pp. 121–31, 173–12; for those of the fourth- and fifth-century Gallic councils, Gaudemet, *Mariage*, pp. 75–76; Demyttenaere, "Vrouw," pp. 253–54.

10. Ganz, "Preconditions," esp. pp. 26–28, 41–43; Ganz, "Book Production"; Bischoff, *Paläographie*, pp. 143–47, 151–60, and Bischoff, "Karolingische Minuskel," pp. 1–4.

11. For the attempts at standardization in various fields and their success or failure, see Kottje, "Einheit." He finds some positive results, but fewer than has generally been

These authoritative texts were then used in pronouncing judgments and establishing rules, which would then be circulated. This was done, for example, at formal assemblies of the high dignitaries of the Church, and especially of the bishops, convened usually by the Carolingian rulers. These gatherings or councils, known as *concilia* or *synodi*, varied considerably in scale.[12] They might consist of bishops from one church province or from one, or several, of the Carolingian kingdoms. The number of bishops attending also varied, from four at a council in Aachen in January 860 to forty-three at one in Savonnières in June 859. Those present often included not only bishops but also abbots, and often laymen. The involvement of this last group varied. Decisions were usually taken by the religious dignitaries, and sometimes these decisions were then ratified by the king. The subjects that the councils were convened to discuss also differed widely in nature. Sometimes the canons—the rules issued by the councils—concerned general issues of faith and morality and matters of church government. Sometimes they dealt with actual cases, on which judgment was pronounced as in a court of law. This judgment could be delivered in various ways: in a separate canon, in a legal document, in a letter, or in an official report that detailed the whole case before stating the judgment. The council's rulings were published, and on occasion a good deal of energy was devoted to their distribution.[13] Although the rules they formulated can certainly be regarded as laws of the Church, the division between religious and secular law is blurred. Moreover, the Carolingian princes incorporated many of the Church's laws into their legal, administrative, and religious-didactic decrees or *capitularia*.[14]

The bishop of Rome played a significant role in this process. The Carolingian princes derived much of their legitimacy from their links with Rome. It was with papal support that Mayor of the Palace Pippin III had deposed the last Merovingian king in 751 and had himself crowned king in his place; and it is hardly surprising that people often turned to the pope for "correct," authoritative liturgical texts and rulings on canon law.[15]

---

thought. See also McKitterick, *Carolingians and the Written Word*, p. 36. For the *Sacramentarium Gregorio-Hadrianum*, see also *Sacramentarium Gregorianum*, ed. Lietzmann, pp. XV–XVII, and *Sacramentaire grégorien*, ed. Deshusses 1: pp. 61–63. Fuhrmann, "Papsttum," is highly critical of the changes in canon law.

12. I make no distinction between a "council" and a "synod"; in the Carolingian period the terms *concilium* and *synodus* are used interchangeably, see Hartmann, *Synoden*, pp. 4–5.

13. Hartmann, *Synoden*, pp. 4–10.

14. See Mordek, "Kapitularien," col. 943–44.

15. Halphen, *Charlemagne*, pp. 72–40, Folz, *Couronnement*, pp. 48–52. For the Church of Rome as source of the "correct" tradition under the Carolingian rulers, see Mordek, "Kirchenrechtliche Autoritäten," pp. 238–43.

For convenience's sake I will divide the Carolingian reforms into three phases, in each of which the evolution of the Church's rules on marriage, divorce, and remarriage will be examined. I will focus mainly on the question of what in the Carolingian period, according to those rules, constituted a lawful marriage—a question that has preoccupied a great many historians over the past century.[16] The first phase runs from the middle of the eighth century into the first quarter of the ninth, or roughly the generations of Pippin (741–68) and Charlemagne (768–814); the second covers approximately the second quarter of the ninth century, or the generation of Louis the Pious (814–40); and the third the mid-ninth century, the generations of Louis' sons and grandsons. This third phase was crowned by a torrent of religious regulation, with the years 847–52 seeing the creation of an extensive collection of canons and capitularia. This torrent will merit special consideration.

Phase 1: ca. 740–814, Quantitative Expansion; Marriage Defined by Negatives

In the first phase we find mainly an expansion of the available stock of religious ordinances. As far as our subject is concerned, there are few changes in content.

In 742 the so-called Concilium Germanicum was held, the first major council in the Frankish empire in more than eighty years. Presided over by Mayor of the Palace Carloman, the Frankish bishops took a close look at the state of the Church and the world. Marriage was hardly mentioned.[17] Apparently it was not a major point of concern to them on that occasion. We do, however, see some—limited—interest in the subject in the conclusions of two councils held in the following two years, in 743 and 744. Here almost all the major points that we shall come upon many

16. For an overview and an opinion, see Mikat, *Dotierte Ehe*; for the controversy between Sohm and Friedberg: Sohm, *Recht*, esp. pp. 22–37, 59–66, 71–78, 100, and *Trauung*, as against Friedberg, *Recht*, esp. pp. 17–30, and *Verlobung*; Freisen, *Geschichte*, pp. 103–64; Esmein, *Mariage*. For the development of ideas on marriage in the Carolingian period in general, see Toubert, "Théorie"; Toubert, "Carolingian Moment," pp. 396–406, and Toubert, "Institution"; Gaudemet, *Mariage*, pp. 109–32; and Philip Reynolds, *Marriage*, pp. 152–55, 213–26, 386–412. See also Theodor Schieffer, "Eheschließung"; Konecny, *Frauen* and "Eherecht"; Kottje, "Ehe und Eheverständnis" and "Eherechtliche Bestimmungen"; De Clercq, *Législation*, 1: pp. 310–11, 2: pp. 398–99; Hartmann, *Synoden*, pp. 467–73; Guichard and Cuvillier, "Barbarian Europe"; Rouche, "Mariages"; Wemple, *Women*, pp. 75–96; Ritzer, *Formen*, pp. 262–87; Daudet, *Études*; Chélini, *Aube*, pp. 175–237; Brundage, *Law*, pp. 127–52, 169–75; Le Jan, *Famille*, pp. 280–85, 310–27.

17. *Concilium Germanicum*, in *MGH Conc.* 2: p. 3, c. 1, gives one ruling against lascivious and adulterous clerics.

times later are already present: the bans on incest, on unchaste behavior by priests, on marrying nuns, and on marrying a woman repudiated by her husband.[18]

These same rules are set out in a letter dated 2 January 747 from Pope Zachary to Mayor of the Palace Pippin III. Pippin had asked the bishop of Rome for advice on various matters concerning church discipline and social and moral issues. In reply Zachary sent him a letter and a dossier containing twenty-seven clauses.[19] He took the rulings in these clauses from the compilation of canon law then generally used in Rome, the *Collectio Dionysiana*, which comprised a collection of council decisions from late Antiquity and decretals. Of the twenty-seven rulings in Zachary's dossier one forbids marriage with relatives by blood or marriage; two forbid marrying a man or woman repudiated by someone else and remarriage by a man who has repudiated his wife for adultery; one forbids adultery; three forbid marriage with nuns; and three concern the marriage of clerics.[20]

Some years later, when Pippin, with the support of his followers and papal approval, had promoted himself to king, he issued a number of ordinances or capitularia. To this end he summoned assemblies of his great nobles at which these decrees were proclaimed. Among the provisions on marriage we find some of the topics from the earlier council decisions and Zachary's dossier, but with one important new element: marriages between free and unfree people are unlawful.[21] In addition, two linked texts deal with a number of circumstances in which divorce is permitted: entry into a

---

18. The Austrasian Council of Les Estinnes (743 or 744), in *MGH Conc.* 2: pp. 6–7, c. 1, 3. The Council of Soissons (744), headed by the Neustrian mayor of the palace Pippin (later King Pippin), in *MGH Conc.* 2: p. 35, c. 4, 8, 9.

19. *Codex Carolinus*, in *MGH Epp. Karol. aevi* 1: pp. 479–87. See also Fuhrmann, "Papsttum," pp. 425–27.

20. Respectively, c. 22, 12, 7, 25, 20, 21, 27, 11, 13 and 18. C. 12 is here numbered as *Concilium Africanum*, c. 69. This is the numbering not of the *Dionysiana* but of the more recent *Dionysio-Hadriana*. Fuhrmann, "Papsttum," pp. 433–34, argues that a *Dionysiana* with "*Hadriana* characteristics" must have already existed in Rome at that time. For the *Collection Dionysio-Hadriana*, see p. 18, below. See also the rulings of the Council of Rome of 743, headed by Zachary, with two rulings on incest, one on the abduction of nuns, one on marriages to Jews, and one on marriages of clerics: *Concilium Romanum*, in *MGH Conc.* 2: pp. 12–21, c. 6, 15, 7, 10, 1, respectively.

21. The Council of Ver (755) gives only the rather general ruling: "All lay persons must marry in public, both nobles and commoners" (Ut omnes homines laici publicas nuptias faciant tam nobiles quam innobiles). *Concilium Vernense* in *MGH Cap.* 1: p. 36, c. 15. For a detailed discussion of this text, with far-reaching conclusions, see Mikat, *Dotierte Ehe*, esp. pp. 22–32, 49–50, 74–77. At the Council of Dingolfing (ca. 770) we find rulings on marriage with nuns and unfree persons, *Concilium Dingolfingense*, in *MGH Conc.* 2: pp. 93–97, c. 4 and 10. For the rulings in the so-called Edicts of Compiègne and Verberie, see following note, 22.

convent or monastery, leprosy, captivity, the husband's long absence because of flight or obligations to his lord, and proven impotence.[22] The same
texts also contain rules on remarriage following divorce on grounds of incest. Remarriage is permitted after divorce because of kinship in the third
degree (probably according to the so-called Germanic-canonistic way:
counting back until and including the first common ancestor). Where the
reason for divorce was adultery with a relation by marriage the guilty party
cannot remarry, but the innocent party can.[23]

In 747 Pope Zachary had sent Pippin only a slim dossier of twenty-seven
capitula, but when Charlemagne visited Pope Adrian in Rome at Easter in
774 the pontiff gave him a whole book of rulings. This was a revised version of the *Collectio Dionysiana*, known as the *Collectio Dionysio-Hadriana*.[24]
With this volume the Carolingian reformers now had a complete "authorized" collection of council decisions and papal decretals up to and including Gregory II (715–31) to guide them in matters of canon law. Until 843 it
was mainly this *Collectio Dionysio-Hadriana* that was cited at Carolingian
councils.[25]

22. The so-called Edicts of Verberie (756?) and Compiègne (757). *Decretum Vermeriense*, in *MGH Cap.* 1, pp. 40–41, c. 4, c. 6–9, 13, 17, 19–21. *Decretum Compendiense* (757), in
MGH Cap. 1: pp. 37–39, c. 5, 6–9, 14, 16, 19, 21, 29. Opinions are divided as to the nature
of these Edicts of Compiègne and Verberie and their context, promulgation, and dating.
See esp. De Clercq, *Législation* 1: pp. 171–73, as against Hartmann, *Synoden*, pp. 73–79;
detailed comments: Heidecker, *Kerk*, pp. 21–22. The fact that many of their rulings are
framed to deal with specific cases explains not only the contradictions but also the highly
detailed and unique nature of some rulings.

23. *Decretum Vermeriense*, in *MGH Cap.* 1: pp. 40–41, c. 1, 2, 10–12, 18, *Decretum Compendiense*, in *MGH Cap.* 1: pp. 38–39, c. 10–11, 13, 17–18. For Carolingian rules on incest
and especially the problem of the degrees of kinship within which marriage was prohibited, see De Jong, "Unsolved Riddle," "Limits," and "Wat bedoelde paus Gregorius III?"

24. Fournier and Le Bras, *Histoire* 1: pp. 95–98. According to Fuhrmann, "Papsttum,"
pp. 433–34, this was not a compilation produced specially for the occasion but one that already existed in Rome, to which a clumsy poem of dedication was added. I know of no
modern edition of this collection; for want of a better: *PL* 67 col. 135–346: *Codex Canonum
ecclesiasticorum Dionysii Exigui sive codex canonum vetus ecclesiae Romanae.* According to
Mordek, *Kirchenrecht*, pp. 241–42, only the introduction and decretals of this edition accord with the *Dionysio-Hadriana*. De Clercq, *Législation* 1: p. 173, prefers Pithou's edition:
Codex Canonum Vetus Ecclesiae Romanae. As a consequence the reader should be aware that
references to the same councils and the numbers of their canons can be different. The lack
of modern editions is only part of the problem. The early tradition of canon law itself is
marred and quotations sometimes consist of bits and pieces put together, which are copied
and recopied. So the same council can bear different names and rulings can bear different
numbers.

25. Hartmann, "Zu einigen Problemen," p. 22. An important exception is the Council
of Arles (813), which relied on the *Collectio Hispana*; see Hartmann, *Synoden*, pp. 131–33,
304–5, 407–8. Of course, this does not mean that no other collections were known or used.
Mordek, "Kirchenrechtliche Autoritäten," pp. 244–50, argues that those attending would
have consulted earlier collections and compilations, some of them thematic, but would

Some of the rulings on marriage turn up again in the council decisions and capitularia of Charlemagne. The topics addressed remain largely the same.[26] In any case, the rulings on marriage make up only a very small part of the total, clearly indicating that other subjects attracted more attention. Again, a striking feature is the relatively large number of rulings prohibiting incest.[27] Two of these rulings are framed in practical terms, with the instruction that before the marriage the degree of kinship should be investigated by neighbors and distinguished persons and the priest informed of the result. If despite this careful investigation before marriage it should later turn out that the couple were in fact related, they must be divorced. They may, however, marry others if they had been unaware of their kinship.[28] The emphasis is consistently on the actions of the man. In the case of a divorce on grounds of adultery the reference is to a man repudiating his wife. That the reverse might be the case seems inconceivable to whoever compiled the text. A canon such as we find in Zachary's letter to Pippin does indeed speak of a woman repudiating her husband, but Charlemagne's great *capitulare* of 789, the so-called *Admonitio Generalis*, which refers back to this canon, omits this particular passage. In any case, according to the *Admonitio Generalis* neither the man who has repudiated his wife nor the repudiated wife may remarry.[29]

---

then quote the appropriate canon from the "correct," authentic *Collectio Dionysio-Hadriana*. See also Mordek, *Kirchenrecht*, pp. 151–60.

26. *Admonitio Generalis* (789), in *MGH Cap.* 1: p. 57, c. 51; *Capitulare missorum item speciale* (802?), in *MGH Cap.* 1: p. 103, c. 22; Council of Friuli (796/97), *Concilium Foroiulense* (796–97), in *MGH Conc.* 2: pp. 191–92, c. 8–11; *Capitulare missorum in Theodonis villa datum secundum generale* (805), in *MGH Cap.* 1: pp. 125–26, c. 22. *Concilium Cabillonense*, in *MGH Conc.* 2: p. 279, c. 30, 31. A capitulare for the Saxons punishes unlawful marriages with a fine: *Capitulatio de partibus saxoniae* (785, according to Ganshof, *Capitularia*, p. 106), in *MGH Cap.* 1: p. 69, c. 20. A Bavarian council simply repeats the ruling on public marriages from the Edict of Ver: *Statuta Rhispacensia, Frisingensia seu Salisburgensia* (799/800), in *MGH Cap.* 1: p. 230, c.46. For the rulings on incest, see next note.

27. Council of Friuli (796/97), *Concilium Foroiulense* (796–97), in *MGH Conc.* 2: pp. 191, c. 8; capitularia of 802, 805, and 813: *Capitulare missorum generale* (802) in *MGH Cap.* 1: p. 97, c. 33; *Capitulare missorum in Theodonis villa datum primum, mere ecclesiasticum* (805), in *MGH Cap.* 1: p. 122, c. 16; *Capitulare e canonibus excerpta* (813), in *MGH Cap.* 1: p. 174, c. 8; *Capitulare ecclesiasticum* (805–13), in Mordek, *Bibliotheca Capitularium*, p. 987, c. 21; *Capitulare generale* (813?), in Mordek, *Bibliotheca Capitularium*, p. 990, c. 5, the decisions of three councils of 813: *Concilium Arelatense* (813), in *MGH Conc.* 2: p. 251, c. 11; *Concilium Cabillonense* (813), in *MGH Conc.* 2: p. 279, c. 28, 29; *Concilium Moguntinense* (813), in *MGH Conc.* 2: pp. 272–73, c. 53–56.

28. *Concilium Foroiulense* (796–97), in *MGH Conc.* 2: p. 191, c. 8, a Bavarian council (dated to around 800 by Hartmann, *Synoden*, pp. 90, 472) in *MGH Conc.* 2: p. 53, c. 12; *Capitula Bavarica* (dated 813), in *MGH Cap. Episc.* 3: p. 197, c. 12.

29. The *Admonitio Generalis* (789), in *MGH Cap.* 1: p. 56, c. 43, states "in the same [African council], that neither the woman repudiated by her husband nor the man who repudiated her may remarry during the spouse's lifetime" (in eodem [concilio Africano], ut nec

The Carolingian reformers' efforts at standardization extended also to the liturgy, and thus also to the solemnization of marriage. Between 784 and 791, under Charlemagne, a copy of the so-called *Sacramentarium Gregorio-Hadrianum* was brought from Rome and used as an exemplar. The work was kept at Aachen and authenticated copies ("*ex authentico*") were made from it. This sacramentary included a nuptial blessing of the bride, which, in line with Roman usage, could be given only to virgins.[30]

Looking at all these rulings, we have to conclude that according to the canonical rules a lawful marriage is any marriage that is not unlawful. This may seem obvious, but it is crucial to understanding the Carolingian reformers' concerns regarding the legal status of marriage. Practically all these rulings do is label certain unions unlawful: marriages with relations by blood or marriage, with unfree persons, nuns, and those betrothed or married to other men (even when the latter are lawfully divorced). In fact, lawful marriage is defined by negatives. No constituent element that makes a union a lawful marriage is formulated.

The regulations on divorce and remarriage are as follows. The husband may repudiate his wife on grounds of adultery. Opinions differ about remarriage. After repudiation for adultery it is in principle not possible while the former spouse is still living. After compulsory divorce because of incest, remarriage by the innocent parties is sometimes permitted. The guilty parties, however, are barred from any further marital union. Not only must they divorce, they are forbidden to marry again. On this last point, though, there is no unanimity, with some authors allowing remarriage in such cases.[31]

---

uxor a viro dimissa alium accipiat virum vivente viro suo, nec vir aliam accipiat vivente uxore priore). This text is not a quotation but a contraction of the rubric to this canon in the *Dionysio-Hadriana* and the canon itself. Rubric and canon say different things: the rubric forbids remarriage by men who have repudiated their wives and vice versa—"De his qui uxores aut quae viros dimittunt, ut sic maneant" (Those who repudiate their wives or husbands must remain so)—while the canon forbids remarriage by the repudiated husband or wife—"Neque dimissus ab uxore, neque dimissa a marito alteri conjungantur, sed ita maneant aut sibi invicem reconcilientur" (Neither he who is repudiated by his wife, nor she who is repudiated by her husband may remarry, but they must remain so or be reconciled to each other). While making this contraction, however, the composers of this text also eliminated the "irrelevant" case of women repudiating their men. Cf. Migne, *PL* 67, col. 215–16, and the edition in *CCSL* 149, pp. 102, 218, 366.

30. *Sacramentaire Grégorien*, ed. Deshusses 1: pp. 61–63; Ritzer, *Formen*, pp. 173–81, 262–68; Stevenson, *Nuptial Blessing*, pp. 40–43; *Sacramentarium Gregorianum*, ed. Lietzmann, pp. XV–XVII; Metzger, *Sacramentaires*, pp. 57–80. The text of this blessing is in *Sacramentaire Grégorien*, ed. Deshusses 1: pp. 308–11, no. 200, and in *Sacramentarium Gregorianum*, ed. Lietzmann, no. 200, pp. 110–12; also in Ritzer, *Formen*, Anhang I.5, pp. 350–51; partial translation in Stevenson, *Nuptial Blessing*, pp. 245–46.

31. See above, *Decretum Vermeriense* c. 1, which allows those related in the third degree to remarry after divorce, and the same rule in the *capitula* of Haito of Basel c. 21, in *MGH Cap. Episc.* 1, p. 217. See n. 23, above, and n. 37, below.

Phase 2: 814–840, Systematization and Moralization

The second phase (the generation of Louis the Pious) is primarily one of consolidation. The most frequently cited collection was still the *Dionysio-Hadriana*, though this period also saw a systematization of the available texts. Where the content is concerned, in the capitularia and council decisions from the reign of Louis the Pious we initially find the same themes regarding marriage as in those of his father and grandfather. Marriage to relatives, abducted women, nuns, those married or betrothed to others, and the unfree is prohibited. Besides this, under Louis the Pious we find a significant addition to the content of the rules on marriage, namely, a moral justification.

The *Collectio Dionysio-Hadriana* provided the Carolingian reformers with an extensive collection of legal texts. A second collection, which became available to them at the end of the eighth century, was the *Collectio Hispana*.[32] In addition to the papal decretals, this originally Spanish collection also contained a far greater number of texts from Spanish, Gallic, North African, and other councils.[33] But although these two collections were arranged systematically, the arrangement was chronological and regional, not thematic, and thus anyone looking for rulings on a specific subject, such as marriage, had to work his way through every council and every decretal, making them far from practical to use. To make the *Hispana* more accessible, fairly extensive thematic indices were compiled in Spain in the second half of the seventh century, providing references to a number of canons in the collection for all manner of topics, including marriage.[34] In the early ninth century a few reformers continued this work. Using one of these indices, the *Collectio Hispana Sistematica*, they produced their own, entirely thematic collection, the *Collectio Dacheriana*, which was mostly made up of canons from the *Dionysio-Hadriana* supplemented with those not included in that from the *Hispana*.[35] Thus, they created an instrument of canon law

32. Fournier and Le Bras, *Histoire* 1: p. 98.

33. *Collectio Hispana*, in *PL* 84, here ascribed to Isidore of Seville; see also the as yet incomplete modern edition by Martinez Diaz.

34. The most important are the *Excerpta canonum* and the *Collectio Hispana sistematica*. Lib. V tit. I–VIII and XII relate to marriage. *Colección canonica Hispana*, ed. Martinez Diaz, vol. I, II.1, esp. pp. 25–38, 259–72; edition I, II.1, pp. 169–76, 381–87.

35. *Spicilegium: Collectio antiquae canonum poenitentialium*, ed. D'Achery and De La Barre, *Collectio Dacheriana* lib. 1, c. 52–93, pp. 525–29, relate to marriage. On its origins: *Colección canonica Hispana*, ed. Martinez Diaz, I, II.1, pp. 273–75; Fournier and Le Bras, *Histoire* 1: pp. 103–6. Firey, "Toward a History," pp. 112–94, and Roger Reynolds, "Organisation," p. 616, regard Florus of Lyon († ca. 860) as the work's compiler, as against

that was also relatively easy to consult. A great many copies were made of it: at least fifty-one manuscripts of the *Collectio Dacheriana* are known, the great majority of them from the West Frankish and Middle kingdoms.[36]

The so-called *Capitula* produced by bishops for the instruction of their priests give the same familiar rules. Marriage to relatives by blood or marriage, nuns, slaves, and divorced persons is not permitted. "Fornication," referring mainly to sexual contact with more than one partner, is forbidden. Divorce is not permitted, except on grounds of adultery; in that case, remarriage is forbidden to the adulterer. Then there is a further ban on "irrational" fornication, that is, sexual congress by men with each other or with animals. Remarriage following divorce due to kinship in the third degree is sometimes permitted. After divorce for fornication with a relative by marriage it is forbidden to remarry during the spouse's lifetime. Those guilty of fornication with a blood relative in the first or second degree are absolutely forbidden ever to marry again.[37] An unusual ruling is to be found in the so-called second *Capitulare* of Gerbald, bishop of Liège, with marriage against the will of the parents also forbidden.[38]

Generally speaking, the canon law regulations on marriage go no further than simply forbidding certain kinds of union. Naturally, clerical authors are also concerned with moral issues connected with sexuality. Some rulings also forbid fornication. Other, noncanonical, writings—penitentials for example—even devote a great deal of attention to the regulation of sexuality.[39] Marriage has a part to play in this, at least where laymen are concerned; the insistence on the indissolubility of marriage, except on grounds of fornication (or of vows of chastity), can be seen in this light. This demand is based on quotations from the gospels, so it is not particularly surprising that we come across it quite often.

But some substantive changes are discernible in the canonical rulings on marriage as we know them from the texts of this period. From about 800

Mordek, *Kirchenrecht*, pp. 259–63, and Mordek, "Kirchenrechtliche Autoritäten," pp. 247–50. An edition by David Zieman of one of the versions of the *Dacheriana* is forthcoming.

36. Mordek, *Kirchenrecht*, pp. 259–63, and Mordek, "Kirchenrechtliche Autoritäten," pp. 244–50.

37. Theodulf of Orléans, *Capitula* (798–818), in *MGH Cap. episc.* 1: p. 111, first capitulare c. 12, pp. 153–54, 161–64; second capitulare, c. II, 1–3, V, 2, 3, 5, 6, 8, VII, 1–10, VIII, 1–2. Haito of Basel, *Capitula* (806–23), in *MGH Cap. Episc.* 1: pp. 203–19, c. 21. Radulf of Bourges, *Capitula* (855–66), in *MGH Cap. Episc.* 1: pp. 245, 264–65, c. 16, 41, 42, c. 43: "fornicare irrationabiliter" (c. 41–43 taken from the penitential of Halitgar of Cambrai). Also the anonymous ninth-century *Capitula Franciae occidentalis* c. 13, in *MGH Cap. Episc.* 3: pp. 46–47.

38. Gerbald of Liège, second capitulare (802–9), in *MGH Cap. Episc.* 1, p. 27, c. 4.

39. For the penitentials, see Kottje, "Ehe und Eheverständis" and Meens, *Tripartite boeteboek*, pp. 276–84.

on leading figures of the Carolingian reform wrote what are known as "mirrors for laymen," moralistic texts aimed at the high aristocracy that explained to them how a layman should lead a good Christian life.[40] The role of marriage in most of these works lies in its usefulness for curbing lust and for begetting children.[41] The modern historian Pierre Toubert even argues that by means of marriage these works created an *ordo conjugatorum*, an order of married laymen, a third order alongside those of the secular clergy and of monks. A true Christian layman is bound by marriage just as is a priest or a monk by his vows. Thus, a meaningful place is created for the lay aristocracy within Christian social ideology.[42] This seems not to apply to all mirrors for laymen, however. Those of Alcuin (†804) and Hincmar of Reims (845–82) devote little space to marriage,[43] while that of Paulinus of Aquilea (†802) does not mention it at all. Very different, though, is *De institutione laicali* by Jonas, bishop of Orléans (818–41). Most of the second book of this work is devoted to a moralistic treatise on marriage, for which Jonas used writings by, among others, Augustine and Caesarius of Arles (502–42). Here marriage has a clear moral function, the nature and significance of which he discusses in detail. We have come a long way from the simple prohibitions listed above.

Jonas of Orléans was a major player at the council held in Paris in 829. His views are clear to see in the council's conclusions, which is not surprising, since he probably wrote them himself.[44] Again we find the ruling prohibiting the repudiation of a wife except for adultery. Even then it is better not to divorce, but remarriage is certainly not permitted. The more-or-less obligatory ban on incest is of course also included. But the document does not stop at repeating canons. It moralizes about marriage: it was instituted by God

40. Paulinus of Aquilea, *Liber exhortationis* (794–99); on the evils of the flesh, esp. c. 17, 25, 64–66, col. 210, 220–21, 225–26, 274–82 (see Brunhölzl, *Geschichte* 1: pp. 253–54); Alcuin, *De virtutibus et vitiis liber* (801–4); c. 16 *de castitate* col. 626–27, and c. 29 *de fornicatione* col. 633–34; covering letter to Count Wido in *Epp. Karol aevi* 2: pp. 464–65 (see also Brunhölzl, *Geschichte* 1: p. 280); Jonas of Orléans, *De institutione laicali* (pre-828), written for Count Matfrid, father of Engeltrude (see below, pp. 59, 71); esp. lib. II, c. 1–16, on marriage, col. 167–99; Hincmar of Reims, *De cavendis vitiis et virtutibus exercendis* (860–77), on lechery, pp. 143–47, inter alia on abstinence within marriage, pp. 216–22; see also Dhuoda, *Liber manualis* (841/43), esp. lib. IV c. 6, pp. 222–28, on fornication and abstinence. See Toubert, "Théorie"; Heene, *Legacy*, pp. 68–113; and esp. for Jonas of Orléans: Maccioni, "It is allowed neither to Husband."

41. See the above-mentioned works by Toubert and Heene. Heene discusses not only mirrors for laymen but also Carolingian sermons and hagiographies.

42. Toubert, "Théorie," pp. 252–54, 267–68, 276–82.

43. Alcuin, *De virtutibus et vitiis liber*, col. 627; Hincmar, *De cavendis*, pp. 220–22; in Dhuoda, *Liber manualis*, one brief phrase, p. 228. Toubert himself has some reservations: "Théorie," pp. 242–43.

44. De Clercq, *Législation* 2: pp.73–74, 79.

and its purpose is the begetting of children, not sensual pleasure. Virginity should be maintained until marriage. Within marriage, too, one should have sexual relations only with one's wife, and only for the aforementioned purpose. Consequently, it is forbidden for a man to keep concubines in addition to his wife.[45] Here, then, for the first time in Carolingian council texts, we find a moral recognition of marriage alongside the prohibitions.

During this period we come upon some other rulings not previously encountered at Carolingian councils. For example, at a council in Rome (826) it is forbidden to have sexual relations with another woman, whether wife or concubine, in addition to one's wife. This ruling may derive from the conclusions of the first Council of Toledo (397–400).[46] To be clear about this, what is forbidden is not keeping a concubine, but having two women at the same time. The ruling is thus against polygamy and adultery, against lasciviousness. Moreover, we also find here the ruling that a couple may divorce not only for adultery but also on religious grounds, provided that both partners agree, but only with the bishop's approval. The usual phrase for this is *conscientia episcopi*.[47]

In the early decades of the Carolingian reform, let us say up to the Council of Paris in 829, canon law regulations on marriage consist mainly of the prohibition on unlawful unions. But as of 829 we find ordinances on marriage accompanied by a moralizing commentary, drawn directly or indirectly from patristic writings, in which marriage is seen as a remedy for lasciviousness as well as an institution for the begetting of children. Prior to this ordinances had not indicated that clerics were to be involved in the conclusion of marriages in a far-reaching manner. Certainly, the priests had to ensure that no unlawful, and specifically no incestuous, marriages took place. Immoral behavior, such as fornication, adultery, and incest, had

---

45. Council of Paris (829), in *MGH Conc.* 2: pp. 670–71, c. 69.

46. *Concilium Romanum* (826), in *MGH Conc.* 2: p. 582, c. 37. In the first Council of Toledo, c. 17, to be found in: *Excerpta Hispana* lib. V, tit. VII, 3; *Hispana Sistematica* lib. V tit. VII, 1. This ruling derived originally from Roman law (*Sententia Pauli* II.21, 1) and was in turn included in the *Lex Romana Wisigothorum*, p. 368; in the *Breviarium Alaricianum*, p. 132. The ruling was repeated at the Council of Rome (853), in *MGH Conc.* 3: pp. 328–29, c. 37; a similar one at the Council of Mainz (852), in *MGH Conc.* 3: p. 251, c. 15, and also at the Council of Paris (829), *MGH Conc.* 2: p. 671.

47. *Concilium Romanum* (826), in *MGH Conc.* 2: p. 582, c. 36. This council also forbids incest, leaving one's wife (except for adultery), and remarriage. Ibid., pp. 582–83, c. 36–38. The ruling on divorce for adultery and remarriage is based on a paraphrase of Matthew 19:9 (see above, pp. 13–14) and 1 Corinthians 7:10–11 with all the latter's problems of interpretation. All the rulings are repeated and slightly expanded on at a council in Rome in 853, in *MGH Conc.* 3: pp. 328–29, c. 36–38. For the *conscientia episcopi*, see also below, pp. 88–89. Episcopal approval for contracting a marriage already appears in Ignatius of Antioch (ca. 100), Ritzer, *Formen*, p. 28.

to be prevented. But there was no canonical procedure that was obligatory for the conclusion of a marriage. Marriages were blessed, it is true, but this was not compulsory.[48] Where marriages were dissolved we find obligatory priestly involvement (the *conscientia episcopi*) stressed in cases of entry to a convent or monastery, that being a specifically religious occasion.

Phase 3: 840–869, Forgery and Blessing

In the third phase (the generation of Louis' sons) all the elements from the first two phases are again present: the familiar prohibitions and also some moralizing. One significant change, though, was a greater emphasis on the priest's role in the making of marriages. The *Dionysio-Hadriana* was still one of the collections consulted, but now the *Dacheriana* and *Hispana* were certainly used as well.[49] Finally, extensive collections of false rules were fabricated in cases where rulings were considered essential but could not be found anywhere: the so-called *Pseudo-Isidorian Forgeries*. These are so important that we shall look at them in more detail.

The councils held during the reign of Louis' sons for the most part repeat the familiar rulings on marriage. The abduction of virgins, widows, nuns, and those betrothed to other men is forbidden, as is the remarriage of an adulterous wife to her lover, even after her husband's death.[50] Also forbidden are marriages with unfree persons and with relatives, the marriage of priests, and the keeping of a concubine as well as a wife.[51] In the terms of the Treaty of Meersen, too, the three sons of Louis the Pious and their followers restate forcefully what relationships they will not tolerate: "an incestuous relationship with a kinswoman, with a nun, with an abducted woman, with an adulteress, whom he is not allowed to have there."[52] Some councils around

48. Vogel, "Rites," pp. 426, 432. Ritzer, *Formen*, pp. 171–73.

49. Hartmann, "Zu einigen Problemen," p. 22. For the use of the *Hispana*, esp. in the East Frankish kingdom, see Hartmann, *Konzil*.

50. Council of Meaux/Paris (845–46), in *MGH Conc.* 3: pp. 115–17, c. 64–69. C. 69 is difficult to translate. It concerns the case of a woman accused of adultery; her husband died and she then promptly married the man with whom she had supposedly committed adultery. In fact, both of them were sentenced to public penance and were allowed to remarry unless one or the other charge was proved. Council of Pavia (850), in *MGH Conc.* 3: p. 224, c. 10. Council of Quierzy (857), in *MGH Conc.* 3: p. 398, c. 5.

51. The *Edictum Pistense* of Charles the Bald (864), in *MGH Cap.* 2, p. 324, c. 31; Council of Mainz (847), in *MGH Conc.* 3: pp. 175–76, c. 28–30; reiterations of Mainz (813) c. 53, 54, 56, Chalons (813), c. 29, Hrabanus Maurus, *Poenitentiale*, c. 2; Council of Mainz (852), in *MGH Conc.* 3: pp. 247, 249, 251, c. 10, 15, 20; Council of Rome (853), in *MGH Conc.* 3: p. 136, c. 6, Council of Soissons (853), in *MGH Conc.* 3: p. 284, c. 11.

52. *Hlotharii, Hludowici et Karoli conventus apud Marsnam secundus* (851), in *MGH Cap.* 2: p. 73, c. 5: "Incestam propinquam suam aut sanctimonialem vel raptam sive adulteram, quam illic ei non licebat habere."

the middle of the ninth century, though, produced rulings on marriage that went beyond simple prohibitions.[53] There is strong disapproval of the fact that women are losing their virginity before marriage.[54] In the conclusions of a council at Mainz in 852 we find for the first time a positive criterion of what is and is not a lawful marriage. The case put to the council was apparently whether a man should have been allowed to marry a woman after he already had a prior partner, who was in this case called a concubine. Here a distinction is made between a concubine and a wife. The difference lies in the *desponsatio* or betrothal, the public ceremony in which binding vows for a future marriage were made: "If a man had a concubine who was not lawfully betrothed to him, and later, after sending away the concubine, he took a girl as his betrothed according to the rite, he may have her who was lawfully betrothed to him."[55] So the man was allowed to have and hold his second partner, since she was betrothed to him, and not the first one, provided of course he had sent away the first woman, since he was not allowed two partners at a time. The decision was supported by a reference to the letter of Pope Leo the Great (440–61) to Rusticus of Narbonne, much quoted in matrimonial cases. This letter, however, does not deal with a case that is exactly the same, for it refers to Roman law. The council rulings of the early church and the letters of the early popes, such as Leo, were influenced by the law of the state they were part of, the Roman Empire, hence by Roman law. Even after the fall of the Roman Empire collections of Roman law circulated in the Germanic kingdoms, where they were used by people who considered themselves Roman rather than Germanic. Thus, elements of Roman law appeared, albeit sometimes with a different meaning than had been intended by the Roman emperors, in councils of the Merovingian and Carolingian church. This is exactly what happened in 852 with the letter of Pope Leo to Rusticus. Entirely in line with the terminology of Roman law, Pope Leo distinguished between a wife (*uxor*) and a concubine (*concubina*). He equated the former with a free woman (*libera*), the latter with a slave (*ancilla*); the term "concubine" was reserved for an unfree woman. Thus, the concubine in this letter was, in the Roman sense of the word, a slave and Pope Leo's answer could therefore not be applied word for word.

53. Councils of Pavia (850), in *MGH Conc.* 3: p. 224, c. 9; of Mainz (852), in ibid., pp. 249, 251, c. 12, 15; of Rome (853), in ibid., pp. 328–29, c. 36–37.

54. Council of Pavia (850), in ibid., c. 9.

55. Council of Mainz (852), in ibid., p. 249, c. 12: "Quodsi quislibet concubinam habuerit, que non legitime fuit desponsata, et postea desponsatam rite puellam duxerit abiecta concubina, habeat illam, quam legitime desponsavit." See also the Council of Quierzy (857), in ibid., p. 398, c. 5, against the abduction of virgins and widows, that is, one must not approach them unless lawfully betrothed to them.

He says that "the woman should have been freed, lawfully provided with a *dos* or bridal gift and publicly married" in order to count as his wife.[56] By definition, a lawful betrothal between a free man and an unfree woman was impossible, both in Roman and Frankish times. This Council of Mainz, however, was probably dealing with the case of a free concubine and a free girl who was betrothed to the man in question. Emancipation was not at issue here, and consequently was not mentioned in this Mainz ruling, which—strikingly enough—replaced the elements of dotation and public marriage in the quote from Pope Leo with that of betrothal. Apparently the betrothal, and not the wedding or the bridal gift, was seen as the distinguishing mark for a lawful marriage.

As we saw, already in Charlemagne's reign an "authorized" sacramentary had been brought from Rome with a view to distributing it for use as the standard version. This *sacramentarium* contained a nuptial blessing of the bride, which, according to Roman practice, could be given only to virgins.[57] The question is, however, how often this blessing was used. We find very few traces of this blessing; the capitula containing the bishops' instructions to their priests make no mention of it.[58] Jonas of Orléans' *De institutione laicali* provides us with an example of a reformer's aims and how they contrast with social usage. People were supposed to remain chaste until they married, and could then be blessed by the priest, but alas, they deprived themselves of this blessing: "Hence the damnable custom prevails, that only very seldom are bride and bridegroom blessed during the celebration of a mass, according to the prescribed order."[59]

56. The council ruling itself refers to this decretal, Leo the Great, *Epistolae*, PL 54, col. 1205, "illa mulier et ingenua facta et dotata legitime et publicis nuptiis honestata," see also Mikat, *Dotierte Ehe*, pp. 34–38; Ritzer, *Formen*, p. 219. It probably dates to 458/59, the same time (458) when Emperor Maioranus promulgated a law making the *dos* compulsory; Gaudemet, *Mariage*, p. 104; Gaudemet, "Legs," pp. 150–54; Lemaire, "Origines"; Philip Reynolds, *Marriage*, pp. 162–67. The prohibition in Roman law on marriage between a slave and a free person in, for example, the *Breviarium Alaricianum*, p. 132.

57. See below, p. 20; *Sacramentaire Grégorien*, ed. Deshusses 1: pp. 61–63; Ritzer, *Formen*, pp. 171–81, 262–68; Stevenson, *Nuptial Blessing*, pp. 40–43; *Sacramentarium Gregorianum*, ed. Lietzmann, pp. XV–XVII; Metzger, *Sacramentaires*, pp. 57–80. The text of this blessing is in *Sacramentaire Grégorien*, ed. Deshusses 1: pp. 308–11, no. 200, and *Sacramentarium Gregorianum*, ed. Lietzmann, no. 200, pp. 110–12; partially translated in Stevenson, *Nuptial Blessing*, pp. 245–46; Vogel, "Rites," pp. 426, 432; Jonas of Orléans, *De institutione laicali*, col. 170–71.

58. Toubert, "Théorie," pp. 270–75. According to Toubert, the clerical reformers considered the customs surrounding marriage to be still so markedly secular that they were wary of giving them the approval of a Christian blessing. Nor is the effect of this standardization entirely clear; many variations with older blessings appear to have developed: Vogel, "Rites," pp. 440, 444.

59. Jonas of Orléans, *De institutione laicali* lib. II, c. 2, col. 170–71: "Unde etenim damnanda consuetudo inolevit, ut perraro sponsus et sponsa in missarum celebratione, secundum praemissum ordinem, benedicantur."

We do occasionally find the priestly nuptial blessing of the bride in the coronation rites of Carolingian queens, for instance in those of Judith (856) and Ermentrude (866), respectively the daughter and the first wife of Charles the Bald.[60] The *oratio* pronounced at Ermentrude's coronation is identical to the *benedictio* of the *Oratio ad sponsas velandas* in the *Sacramentarium Gregorianum*. This is clearly a blessing of the bride by a priest. The text can be interpreted in no other way: "bless you and your future wife."[61] But at that time Ermentrude and Charles had already been together for twenty-six years, Ermentrude hardly being his bride. In this case—and here we are dealing with the very highest level, that of the Carolingian reformers themselves and their circle—the blessing was used in a very special way. Here the blessing and crowning of the woman have one main purpose: to produce children. The preamble to the text of the coronation explains in so many words that Charles is in need of new heirs.[62] In general, one of the most important elements in the blessing of a marriage seems to be the prayer for the couple to be granted many children. Although it is occasionally mentioned that both bride and bridegroom are blessed, in most cases the stress seems to lie on the blessing of the bride, who in the rituals is described very much as the object of the transaction. The priest, however, by performing this blessing acquires an important role in promoting one of the main purposes of marriage: the begetting of children.[63]

The Torrent: Pseudo-Isidore

The canons in the extant collections of canon law do not include any obligation to have a religious marriage ceremony, although there was a religious ritual for blessing marriages. Some church reformers had formulated an ideology of marriage as an important moral and social element. However, they lacked the laws to regulate priestly involvement with nuptials; these established in the mid-ninth century. The regulation of marriage was, after all, only one fairly small part of a very large program that led in the years 847–52 to the fabrication of a whole collection of canons and capitularia setting out how, in the reformers' view, all religious matters should be regulated. This collection is known as the *Pseudo-Isidorian*

---

60. Editions in *MGH Cap.* 2: pp. 425–27, 453–55.

61. *Coronatio Hermintrudis reginae*, in *MGH Cap.* 2: pp. 454–55. "Benedicat te et futuram uxorem tuam." See also Ritzer, *Formen*, pp. 258–59.

62. *Coronatio Hermintrudis reginae*, in *MGH Cap.* 2: pp. 453–54.

63. The end of the decretal of Pseudo-Evaristus and various other texts also point in this direction, see below, pp. 30–34.

Forgeries, and consists of four strongly interdependent sections. Two of these are of interest to us: the collection of forged decretals supposedly by Isidore and the forged collection of capitularia by a man known by the pseudonym Benedict Levita (Benedict the Deacon).[64]

Benedict Levita's collection contains a great many capitularia, which differ widely in nature. Not all of them are forged, and often the forgeries are put together—as good forgeries should be—out of pieces of authentic text. At the forefront of many of Benedict Levita's capitula on marriage are the rulings on incest and the abduction of women.[65] But there are also some rulings that tell us more about how people should marry and when they could divorce and remarry.[66] To start with, the rulings of the Council of Paris in 829 forbidding remarriage after divorce on grounds of adultery are reiterated.[67] Divorce because of the husband's proven impotence was permitted and the wife could then remarry,[68] showing yet again the enormous importance attached to children. Also repeated is the ruling, derived from Roman law via the *Lex Romana Visigothorum* or the rulings of the Council of Toledo, against having a concubine as well as a wife.[69] Two rulings on the intrinsic nature of marriage, namely the duty of husband and wife to love and be faithful to each other and of the husband to provide for his wife, were taken from Jonas of Orléans' *De institutione laicali.*[70]

---

64. No consensus has yet been reached on where, exactly when, and by whom they were written; compare Fuhrmann, *Einfluß* 1, pp. 142, 147–50, 166, 191, whose conclusions have recently been revised by Zechiel-Eckes, "Verecundus," and Zechiel-Eckes, "Blick," who identifies the writer of the Pseudo-Isidorian works as Paschasius Ratpertus, the famous monk of Corbie, and refutes the chronological order of these works as put forward by Fuhrmann. Clearly, the aim of many of these forgeries is to support episcopal and papal authority, but many deal with other subjects. Further research is required. Regarding the forgeries on marriage see pp. 30–34; for a hypothesis about their composition see Heidecker, "Gathering." The first known author to use the Pseudo-Isidorian forgeries and hold them to be true is Hincmar of Reims (see act 3, p. 78, and Fuhrmann, *Einfluß* 1, 211–15). The first author to deem a Pseudo-Isidorian forgery to be false is also Hincmar of Reims (see act 5, n. 49), though it is only fair to add that in both cases he probably was confronted with a mixture of both Pseudo-Isidorian and genuine texts. Editions of the Pseudo-Isidorian decretals: *Decretales Pseudo-isidorianae et Capitula Angilramni* and Benedict Levita. New editions by the *MGH* are in preparation.

65. Ben. Lev., lib. I, c. 18–21, 91, 106, 165–60, 168, 180, 222–27, 232, 233, 238, 310, lib. II, c. 24–25, 36–37, 47–48, 55, 92, 95–96, lib. III c. 132, 179, 341, 381–82, 388, 395, 432–35, 470, Additio II, c. 23, Additio III, c. 54, 104, 115, 123–24, Additio IV, c. 75.

66. On marriage in Benedict Levita, see Ritzer, *Formen*, pp. 268–77.

67. Ben. Lev. lib. II. c. 230, 235; see also II. 63 and 91.

68. Ben. Lev. lib. II. c. 55 and 91: cf. *Decretum Vermeriense* c. 17.

69. Ben. Lev. lib. III. c. 336, see above, p. 24 and n. 46.

70. Ben. Lev. II. 432 is identical with the rubric of Jonas of Orléans, *De institutione laicali*, lib. II c. 5, col. 177, and Ben. Lev. lib. II. c. 433 with that of Jonas of Orléans, *De*

Thus far there is little that is new. But there are also a number of rulings that set out how a lawful marriage ought to be contracted. The first states that on the occasion of the marriage a bridal gift (*dos*) shall be given and that the wedding must take place in public.[71] The ruling on the *dos* again comes from Roman law via the *Lex Visigothorum*, that on marrying in public from the Council of Ver.[72] Thus we already have two fixed requirements, the bridal gift and public ceremony, both taken from Roman law. They also appear in the decretal of Pope Leo to Rusticus of Narbonne, also quoted here, which additionally required the emancipation of the prospective bride.[73] So far there have been no real fabrications. But this changes when we look at priestly involvement in marriage. Four capitula quote a text taken from the *Lex Visigothorum* or the twelfth Council of Toledo in 681 (the two are virtually identical) by which converted Jews were compelled to have their marriages blessed by a Christian priest, not to marry relatives, and to provide a bridal gift. Our forger simply replaces the word "Jews" with "Christians." He also adds that this applies to people marrying for the first time.[74]

A further ruling combines the requirement of a bridal gift, premarital chastity, and a blessing by a priest in the form laid down in the sacramentary.[75] Finally, there are two very detailed capitularia that bring all these requirements together.

The first of these begins by stating that marriages must take place in public. Our legislator's prime concern here is that there should be no sinful marriages, as does sometimes happen, he says, with marriages not held in public, such as those with abducted women. The sinful marriages cover the by now familiar groups of women whom a man is forbidden to marry, here neatly set out in a row: a kinswoman, another man's wife, another man's betrothed, an adulteress. And the consequences of such marriages are

---

institutione laicali, lib. II c. 4, col. 174. For Benedict's use of Jonas see Seckel, "Studien," VII, pp. 528–29.

71. Ben. Lev. lib. II. c. 133.

72. A *Novella* of 458 by Maioranus (VI. 9), in *Lex Visigothorum* III. 1, 9, pp. 131–32. In classical Roman law the *dos* was a bridal gift given to the bridegroom by the bride's family. Among the Germanic peoples, however, the *dos* was given by the bridegroom's family to the bride; see below, pp. 116–17. Probably the term *dos* had already changed its meaning in the late classical period during which the patristic texts used in Carolingian times were written; see Lemaire, "Origines de la règle," pp. 417–21. In any case it is clear that for the Carolingians, as for the Germanic peoples in general, the *dos* was a bridal gift to the bride from the bridegroom's family.

73. Ben. Lev., lib. III. c. 105, Leo the Great, *Epistolae*, *PL* 54, col. 1205; for the use made of this decretal, see above, pp. 26–27.

74. Ben. Lev. lib. II. c. 120, 327, 408, and Additio IV. c. 2. The last gives the most extensive text from the *Lex Visigothorum* XII 3, 8, pp. 435–36, and replaces "Jews" by "Jews and Christians." See for this Ritzer, *Formen*, pp. 228–29, 269–70.

75. Ben. Lev., lib. III. c. 389.

terrible: they lead to the birth of blind, lame, hunchbacked, or cross-eyed children.[76] Prior to the betrothal, therefore, the priest and "the people" of the parish must openly verify that no such prohibited union is involved. After that the bride must be betrothed with the priest's blessing and after consulting "good men," furnished with a bridal gift and handed over to the bridegroom by her parents.

The whole thing is bolstered by a quotation from Augustine that requires that a prospective bride be a virgin, be lawfully provided with a bridal gift, be handed over to her bridegroom by her parents, and be received by bridal attendants. After that she must "be received into a lawful marriage according to the law and the gospel after being honored by public nuptials."[77] Divorce is allowed if both partners wish it for religious reasons. To repudiate one's wife is not permitted, except if she has committed adultery and the man wishes it; but he is then forbidden to remarry during his wife's lifetime.[78] In fact, this entire quotation, with its precise description of the procedure for marriage, is a fabrication. Together with various other faked quotations from Augustine and Jerome it forms part of a collection of canon law probably compiled in Ireland around the end of the seventh century that survives mainly in a number of ninth-century Continental manuscripts.[79]

Benedict Levita follows this with some quotations from Leviticus and the decretals of Pope Gregory II, as well as the above-mentioned text from the *Lex Visigothorum* on the obligatory priestly blessing of marriage.[80] Once all this is in order, our author says, "then the woman, if she is a virgin, with the blessing of the priest as laid down in the sacramentary, and with the assent of many good men, shall be led openly, not secretly, to her marriage."[81] The reward for properly conducted nuptials is the prospect of healthy children, while the punishment for improper unions is the aforementioned lame, blind, crippled, or cross-eyed offspring.[82]

76. Ibid. c. 179

77. Ibid., "Secundum legem et evangelium publicis nuptiis honestata in coniugio licite sumenda."

78. Ibid.

79. *Liber XLVI de ratione matrimonii*, in *Die Irische Kanonensammlung*, ed. Wasserschleben, p. 185, c. 2; see Ritzer, *Formen*, pp. 248–51.

80. Leviticus 18:6, 20; *Concilium Romanum* (721) held under Pope Gregory II, c. 2–11, in *Sacrorum conciliorum collectio*, ed. Mansi 12: 261–66; Ritzer, *Formen*, pp. 271–72. See above, p. 30.

81. Ben. Lev., lib. III. c. 179: "Tunc, si virgo fuerit, cum benedictione sacerdotis, sicut in sacramentario continetur, et cum consilio multorum bonorum hominum publice et non occulta ducenda est uxor."

82. See n. 75 and n. 79, above. For the thinking on unlawful copulation and handicapped children, see Demyttenaere, "Cleric," p. 151.

The last major text on marriage in Benedict Levita—and the prize item for the degree of forgery—is a decretal falsely attributed to Pope Evaristus (99–107), a revered pope of the early church. It was also included in the collection of the false papal letters, the Pseudo-Isidorian decretals, where the forgers added a few lines at the end. This slightly extended version, which ' became the more popular one, runs as follows:

> We have it preserved and passed down to us that the wife must be joined with her husband in a lawful manner. A lawful marriage can only, as we have received it from the fathers and has been handed down by the holy apostles and their successors, take place in the following way: the woman is requested of those who have authority over that woman and under whose guardianship she is and she is betrothed by parents and kinsmen and is provided with a bridal gift according to the laws. And then, when the time has come, she is given—as custom teaches—a priestly blessing with prayers and offerings by the priest. And she is watched over and accompanied by bridal attendants, she is asked from her kinsmen at a proper time and is given and solemnly received according to the laws; and for two or three days they must pray and remain chaste, so that they shall bring forth sound children and please the Lord by their conduct. And in that way they will please the Lord and bring forth no bastards but lawful and heritable children.
>
> Therefore, beloved and rightly illustrious sons, know that marriages contracted thus with the help of the Catholic faith are lawful, but nonmarital unions contracted otherwise are without doubt no marriages, but adultery or cohabitation or shameful deeds or acts of fornication rather than lawful marriages, unless supported by their own will and founded on the lawful vows.[83]

A proper marriage, then, includes a number of elements: the betrothal by parents and kinsmen, the bridal gift, the blessing of the bride by the priest, the handing over of the bride by her attendants, and, finally, some nights

---

83. *Ps.-Isid.*, pp. 87–88: "Similiter custoditum et traditum habemus, ut uxor legitime viro iungatur. Aliter enim legitimum, ut a patribus accepimus et a sanctis apostolis eorumque successoribus traditum invenimus, non fit coniugium, nisi ab his, qui super ipsam feminam dominationem habere videntur et a quibus custoditur, uxor petatur et a parentibus propinquioribus sponsetur et legibus dotetur et suo tempore sacerdotaliter, ut mos est, cum precibus et oblationibus a sacerdote benedicatur et a paranimphis, ut consuetudo docet, custodita et sociata a proximis tempore congruo petita legibus detur et solemniter accipiatur; et biduo vel triduo orationibus vacent et castitatem custodiant, ut bonae soboles generentur et Domino suis in actibus placeant. Taliter enim et Domino placebunt et filios non spurios, sed legitimos atque hereditabiles generabunt. Quapropter, filii carissimi et merito inlustres, fide catholica suffragante ita peracta legitima scitote esse coniugia; aliter vero praesumpta non coniugia, sed aut adulteria aut contubernia aut stupra vel fornicationes potius quam legitima coniugia esse non dubitate, nisi voluntas propria suffragaverit et vota succurrerint legitima." Virtually the same text appears in the forged capitularia of Benedict Levita, lib. III, c. 463. There, however, the last part is lacking (from "Quapropter").

spent chastely in prayer. One possible model for the blessing and observance of chastity after the wedding may have been a canon from the so-called *Statuta Ecclesiae Antiqua* written around 500 by Gennadius of Marseilles. This canon was regarded as a ruling of the fourth Council of Carthage and included under that heading in the *Collectio Hispana* and the *Dacheriana*.[84] A sanction is immediately spelled out by the forger: if these rules are not adhered to, God will not bless the union with healthy children. The fabricator of this decretal is very firm in stating that all marriages not conducted according to this description are not marriages. But then at the end, almost casually, he introduces a reservation and writes that "they are not marriages, except when supported by their own will and lawful vows." Thus, marriages that comply only with these last two conditions are still lawful marriages. This is a baffling conclusion in view of what the author has just stated. He has set out in every last detail exactly how a marriage should be celebrated with the priestly blessing and associated fasting. He has impressed upon his audience that this was the only way of marrying that was lawful and pleasing to God, and that all other ways were shameful obscenities. And then he must have realized that in the actual social practice of his day a sizeable proportion, maybe even the majority, of marriages did not meet these requirements. So he backpedals and puts in that extra clause, "except when supported by their own will and lawful vows." Ultimately he ends up with only two absolute requirements, that the partners must want to marry and that lawful vows, probably meaning public vows, must be made in the presence of those concerned and of witnesses. Undoubtedly he is referring here to public betrothal, at which the families of the betrothed seal the agreement. Therefore, only a minimum requirement remains: the couple's consent and public betrothal with the approval of both families.

Benedict Levita's collection of capitularia was to be influential. They provided the basis for a few West Frankish episcopal capitularia. In these instructions to their priests the bishops thenceforth made the priestly blessing of marriages obligatory.[85]

---

84. For the *Statuta Ecclesiae Antiqua* c. 101, see, e.g., Vogel, "Rites," p. 429. Edition in *Concilia Galliae A.314–A.506*, pp. 184–85. In the *Collectio Hispana* lib. V, tit. I, c. 5, and in the *Collectio Dacheriana* lib. I, c. 61, it appears as the fourth Council of Carthage, c. 13.

85. Herard of Tours, *Capitulare* (858), in *MGH Cap. episc.* 2: pp. 130–55, c. 36, 38, 41, 42, 66, 67, 89, 110, 111, 124, 130, of which 89 (= Ben. Lev., lib. III. c. 463) and 130 (= Ben. Lev., lib. III. c. 179) state that the nuptial blessing by the priest is obligatory; c. 14 and 112 relate to marriage, but do not come from Benedict Levita. Isaak of Langres, *Capitulare* (ca. 860–80), in *MGH Cap. episc.* 2, pp. 161–241, is a compilation devoted to rulings from Benedict Levita; chapters III, IV, and V deal exclusively with marriage, as does chapter XI, c. 2, 13, 14, 19, 28. Of these V, 6 (= Ben. Lev., lib. III. c. 179) and XI, 29 (= Ben. Lev., lib. III. c. 389) make the priestly blessing compulsory.

The *Pseudo-Isidorian Forgeries* deal with three areas of concern regarding marriage. First, the prevention of unlawful unions. This is nothing new—we have seen it before in all the canonical legislation of the Carolingian period. But it remains crucial. For the clerical authors the prevention of sinful unions is their prime concern.

The second area of concern, and this *is* new, relates to a detailed prescribed procedure for contracting a lawful marriage. Although most of the elements—parental consent, public rites, betrothal, bridal gift, handing over of the bride to her husband—are secular customs, they have been "Christianized." They are ascribed to fathers of the Church and to popes, and are set in a Christian moral context. Those embarking on matrimony must fast and practice chastity. If one marries in the correct way, one will please God. The priestly role in marriage becomes important. The blessing becomes obligatory, and must be according to the book, the sacramentary. This, however, is the ideal; it describes how these reformers would like things to be. What happened in practice is clear from the brief parenthesis in the version of the *Pseudo-Evaristus* decretal just mentioned.[86] Despite the elaborate procedure for concluding a lawful Christian marriage, including the priest's blessing, described as obligatory, what really counts in the end are only two entirely secular elements: the couple's consent and the public betrothal with both families' approval.

A third area of concern surfaces in the *Pseudo-Isidorian Forgeries*: the reward of healthy descendants or the penalty of handicapped offspring. Those who are deaf to stern admonitions are hit in a vital spot: the health of their children.

THE legal rules framed by princes and bishops in the Carolingian period establish the following rules for marriage: a man may not marry a kinswoman by blood or marriage, a nun, an unfree woman, or the betrothed or the wife of someone else. Divorce is forbidden except on grounds of adultery, and then remarriage is forbidden. These are the basic principles adhered to throughout the whole period. As the reforms continued, though, other factors played a part in the regulatory process. For instance, there was an increasing degree of moralization about the nature and meaning of marriage, to which the rules then attached greater value. Priestly blessing of the nuptials was made compulsory, as were such secular customs as public betrothal, the bridal gift, and the formal handing over of the bride. Rules were laid down for how a marriage should be performed according to

86. See above, p. 33.

the book. But when it was a matter of deciding whether a marriage was or was not lawful, it was back to the basic principle: if a marriage is not unlawful, then it is lawful.

Apart from this evolution in content there also was a "technical" development. When we compare the standard of rulings on marriage at the start of the Carolingian reforms with that in the middle of the ninth century, it is apparent that in the meantime the reformers had acquired a collection of the "correct" rules and a "correct" sacramentary containing a nuptial blessing. Using those rules they had created an easy-to-use thematic compendium of canonical rulings, the *Collectio Dacheriana.* And, finally, those rulings that were considered essential but could not be found anywhere were fabricated in the *Pseudo-Isidorian Forgeries.*

The authors who wrote at the time of Lothar's matrimonial case stand at the end of all these developments. Not only have ideas on marriage changed, but the whole regulatory apparatus available to them had evolved over the previous hundred years. There is a world of difference between the uncertainty of Bishop Magingoz in the third quarter of the eighth century, perplexed by the contradictory rules on marriage in the Church fathers, and the self-confidence of Hincmar of Reims a century later, who could mobilize a whole army of authorities in support of his opinions. And where those written authorities were lacking, the Pseudo-Isidorian forgers had assisted the righteous cause by fabricating them.[87]

We have looked at the canonical weapons with which the actors in Lothar's matrimonial drama fought each other. The knives have been sharpened: the play can begin. Or almost. First we must check out the chorus that provides the commentary to Lothar's drama.

---

87. One of the most important authors involved in Lothar's case, Hincmar of Reims, was the first user of the *Pseudo-Isidorian Forgeries* to quote the false decretals literally, see Fuhrmann, *Einfluß* 1: pp. 211–15.

I.2

A Cause Célèbre

The Divorce Case in the Sources

The drama of Lothar's divorce was played out at the very highest political level, and many people stood to gain or lose by it. It gave rise to fierce emotions, strong opinions, allegations, and rumors that we find reflected in a variety of sources.[1] Narrative accounts of the case were written; letters were sent, and in some cases read out in public; it was discussed at gatherings of religious and secular magnates. The decisions or agreements that emerged from those discussions were often recorded in writing. Formal documents such as treaty texts and charters were issued. And Hincmar, from 845 until 882 the learned archbishop of Reims, devoted a bulky treatise to the matter.

Most of these sources depict Lothar as a black sheep. As they see it, he was besotted by his mistress Waldrada and behaved like an irresponsible lecher. Lothar acquired a bad name, and a thousand years after his death, historians still had little good to say of him. Robert Parisot, for instance, maintained that "for a man as weak and vacillating by nature as this prince to display such persistence and stubbornness it was not enough for him to have loved Waldrada passionately, she herself must have had a passion for rule and made her lover march to her drum."[2] Carlrichard Brühl summarizes the caricature of Lothar found in many histories as follows: "Lothar is a weakling wallowing in lasciviousness, entirely enslaved to Waldrada, and

---

1. Hincmar of Reims describes the situation as "rumor running rampant" in *De divortio*, p. 130: "Vulgante fama," as does John, abbot of St. Arnulf of Metz, in *Ex Translatione Sanctae Glodesindis* c. 28, p. 506, edition in n. 1: "Fama . . . vulgatur."
2. Parisot, *Royaume*, p. 144.

his whole life and being are focused solely on pushing through his immoral marriage. And in doing so he destroys his kingdom."[3] In assessing the value of the sources we shall always have to consider who the writers were and what the nature of their involvement was in Lothar's divorce case. In the noncontemporary sources there is less direct involvement, but the legend making increases: Lothar's notoriety has spread through time and space, and not without some distortion of the original information.

Narrative Sources

The way this "rumor" spread can be seen, first, in narrative sources. Here we are interested mainly in a number of annals and chronicles. In both of these, events were recorded year by year in chronological order. The principal difference between the two types of sources was when each was written. Annals were written up, in principle at least, at the end of each year. Chronicles were written all at once, as a single historical account, often well after the events described. As a result, there are marked differences in the writers' perspectives on those events. The information recorded can also vary considerably in length from one work to another. Sometimes we have only brief marginal notes in tables for calculating time; sometimes we have detailed accounts. In the years between 741 and 829 the chancery of the Carolingian kings even developed a kind of semiofficial historiography, the so-called Royal Frankish Annals, with the major events of each year being recorded under the direction of the head of the chancery, the archchaplain.[4] The annals and chronicles discussed here have one major point in common: they do not speak favorably of Lothar. More than that, most of them dismiss him in highly negative terms.

The most detailed account is to be found in the so-called *Annales Bertiniani*, which take their name from the place where the oldest complete manuscript was found: the Abbey of St.-Bertin in northwest France. They are the continuation in the West Frankish kingdom of the Royal Frankish Annals, which stop in 829 in the turmoil of the wars between Louis the Pious and his sons. One copy of these annals, however, contains later material (830–35) added somewhere in the West Frankish realm by an anonymous scribe from the chancery of Louis the Pious. In 835 archchaplain Prudentius, later bishop of Troyes, took over the work. When, after the death of Louis the Pious (840), his widow, Judith, went to join her son, Charles the Bald, she took with her in her retinue what remained of the staff and possessions of

3. Brühl, "Hincmariana," p. 57.
4. WL 2: pp. 245–55. McCormick, *Annales*, pp. 11–17.

Louis' palatine chapel. Among these were archchaplain Prudentius and his copy of the Royal Frankish Annals. At the court of Charles the Bald the annals were continued as his semioffical historiography. In a letter to Archbishop Heigil of Sens, Hincmar of Reims calls them "the annals of the deeds of our kings."[5] It is this same Hincmar, archbishop of Reims (845–82) and the most important cleric in the West Frankish realm, who continues the annals after Prudentius's death in 861. When Hincmar takes over the character of the annals changes. They become much more detailed, including a great deal of information garnered from letters and official decisions. Hincmar is at the heart of political affairs, one of the best-informed people of his time. He also sets a very personal stamp on the annals, which center more and more on himself. As their editor, Léon Levillain, remarks, from being "the deeds of our kings" (*Gesta regum nostrorum*) the *Annales Bertiniani* become "the deeds of Hincmar" (*Gesta Hincmari*).[6] Although they are undoubtedly partisan, vain, and spiteful, they are also exceptionally informative.[7] Both Prudentius and Hincmar were extremely hostile toward Lothar, which can partially be explained by their allegiance to their lord, King Charles the Bald, rival of Lothar, but in Hincmar's case a malicious, personal tone can be discovered as well.

The manuscript transmission of their East Frankish counterpart, the *Annales Fuldenses*, once thought to have been written in Fulda, is extremely obscure—and the debate on the authorship certainly has done nothing to clarify matters.[8] In any case the annals are linked to the East Frankish court since their writers probably have to be sought in the circle of the East Frankish court chaplains. For the years 840–63 the *Annales Fuldenses* can probably be regarded as contemporary records, written in Mainz on the authority of the East Frankish archchaplain Grimald, the brother of one of Lothar's most important followers, Theutgaud, archbishop of Trier, which might explain why Lothar's marital problems are totally absent in these annals up to 863. After that the transmission for the years 863–69 becomes

---

5. *Ep. Hinc.*, p. 196: "Annali gestorum nostrorum regum." Hincmar says that Charles had lent him a book with this title, which he had returned to Charles in Heigil's presence. See the English translation of *Annales Bertiniani*—Nelson, *Annals of St-Bertin*, pp. 9–11, 91.

6. *Annales Bertiniani*, ed. Levillain, pp. XIV–XV.

7. Ibid.

8. The authors are unknown, though some names have been very confidently mentioned in the literature. Anyone wishing to make the attempt should read the literature on the subject by Kurze (the editor) and Hellmann. The easiest to follow is Löwe's account, in WL 6: pp. 671–87. He regards a new edition as essential, given the debatable nature of Kurze's edition. A similar opinion is in the English translation of *Annales Fuldenses*: Reuter, *Annals of Fulda*, pp. 1–9.

very complicated, since some of the manuscripts give markedly differing versions, with some more and some less unfavorable to Lothar. In any case this section was later revised, with some passages interpolated or omitted. The annals were revised and continued only in 870, under the direction of Liutbert, archbishop of Mainz, the archchaplain and archchancellor of King Louis the German, who in 869 had just conquered half of Lothar's realm, disregarding Lothar's immediate heirs, his son and brother, which could explain the change of tone that they take, becoming unfavorable toward Lothar.[9]

The *Annales Xantenses* were not, as was once thought, written in Xanten. For the period up to 861 the original text was probably written by Gerward, court librarian to Louis the Pious. The work was probably reedited in Cologne between 870 and 876 and the record brought up to 873 by a staunch supporter of King Louis the German, who is thus unfavorable to all the other kings, including Lothar.[10] The dating throughout is one year in arrears.

The *Annales Laubacenses* and the *Annales Lobienses* take their names from the monastery of Lobbes, situated in Lothar's realm, where they were thought to have been written. In the case of the *Annales Laubacenses* this is not impossible, though it cannot be proved. The *Annales Lobienses* were probably written in Liège around 870. Both consist of markedly similar notes that are found nowhere else. These notes are short and have a neutral tone toward Lothar.[11]

The Chronicle of Regino of Prüm was completed in 908 by Regino, former abbot of Prüm monastery. Regino worked on his chronicle over a number of years in St Martin's monastery at Trier, where he became abbot after being driven out of Prüm. Regino gives detailed information about the time of Lothar II. Evidently he had done his homework, for he refers to all manner of written sources (including a codex of letters and council decisions that was still in Trier around 1600[12]) as well as to oral traditions gleaned from older people (*seniores*).[13] He regards Lothar's reign, with hindsight, as an utter failure.

---

9. WL 6: pp. 671–87.

10. According to Löwe, "Studien," Gerward's entries for the years 852–61 were summarized and a new historical account written for 863–73. The only extant manuscript of these annals is to be found among other historiographic works in a twelfth-century codex originating in Egmond.

11. Both annals exist only in a single manuscript. For a description of the works which surround these annals, see Kurze, "Annales Laubacenses," Kurze, "Annales Lobienses," and Boschen, *Annales,* pp. 98–103.

12. A copy of part of this is in Rome, Biblioteca Vallicelliana ms. I 76.

13. Werner, "Zur Arbeitsweise," pp. 97–100; Löwe, "Regino."

Ado, bishop of Vienne (860–75), wrote a concise chronicle of the world that runs to 870 and was probably written soon after that date.[14] For six years, from 863 to 869, Ado had been a bishop in the kingdom of Lothar II. He would certainly have been well informed about the divorce case, but he does not say a great deal about it, though he does reveal himself as a declared opponent of Lothar's attempt to gain a divorce. However, he did not write his work until after 870, that is, after Lothar's death and under his new lord, Lothar's enemy Charles the Bald, who had just taken over half of Lothar's kingdom.

The *Liber Pontificalis*, produced at the papal court, contains the official biographies of the bishops of Rome from St. Peter to the end of the ninth century.[15] There are three popes who are important to our story. The first is Benedict III (855–58). Here the information is rather dry and factual,[16] as is the first part of the biography of his successor, Nicholas I (858–67), one of the main players in Lothar's case. The author of the second part, from 860 on, is better informed. He shows evidence of having been present at important events and works material from the papal archives into his account.[17] As he aims at glorifying Lothar's opponent, Pope Nicholas, he describes Lothar in the darkest manner possible. The biography of Adrian II (867–72), rather surprisingly, leaves out Lothar's divorce altogether, although Adrian certainly was involved, although, in hindsight, in a not very flattering way.

We can conclude from all this that there are only two or three narrative sources that give accounts of Lothar's divorce case without the benefit of knowing how this case ended: the *Annales Bertiniani* and the *Liber Pontificalis*. The brief entries in the *Annales Laubacenses* may also be contemporary. In the *Annales Fuldenses* and in the *Annales Xantenses* those sections that do mention Lothar's divorce were written after 869, that is, after Lothar's death. Thus, all the major authors were either contemporaries hostile to Lothar, like Prudentius and Hincmar, or they already knew how Lothar's case ended when they wrote their accounts, which strongly influenced the

---

14. WL 5: pp. 623–24.

15. From the mid-seventh century on the accounts are contemporaneous; usually they were written shortly after the death of the pontiff in question, but sometimes they were begun during the subject's lifetime. The writers probably worked in the papal treasury; Davis, *Book of Pontiffs*, pp. XXXVII–XXXVIII, and Davis, *Lives of the Eighth-Century Popes*, pp. IX–X.

16. *Liber pontificalis*, ed. Duchesne vol. 2, pp. V–VI, Davis, *Lives of the Ninth-Century Popes*, pp. 161–62.

17. Duchesne, the editor of the *Liber Pontificalis*, ed. Duchesne 2: pp. VI–VII, regarded the papal librarian Anastasius as the author of this part of the work. Davis, *Lives of the Ninth-Century Popes*, pp. 189–90, and Bougard, "Anastase," convincingly attribute this and the subsequent biography of Pope Adrian II to John the Deacon.

way they described the events.[18] This is clearly a case of "winners' history," describing Lothar the loser.

Letters

There is one type of source that demonstrates particularly well how rumors were spread, and that is letters. A number of people took a hand in Lothar's divorce case by sending out letters. And of course the writers all had their own interests, which partly determine the information they provide. Quite apart from the content of the letters, the correspondence itself usually had a markedly conversational character and much attention was always devoted to its form and style. Sometimes whoever brought the letter was additionally charged with reading it out, describing its contents or commenting on it. Letters were often public, in the sense that they were meant to be read aloud in the presence of an audience.[19] In short, letters were admirably suited for use as propaganda.

That we are reasonably well informed about Lothar's divorce case is partly due to the fact that two prolific letter writers involved themselves in it, Pope Nicholas I and Hincmar of Reims. Both revealed themselves as opponents of Lothar, at first rather cautiously, but later on in more and more malicious and insulting tones. Pope Nicholas especially showed himself a tireless correspondent. Of some fifty letters, written by various interested parties, that form a very important collection of sources for our story, Nicholas is either the sender or the addressee of most of them.[20] Obviously

18. In addition we have three late tenth-century monastic histories and an Italian history: Folcuin's *Gesta Abbatum Lobiensium* from Lobbes; the account of the refounding of the monastery of Lure, the *Vita Sancti Deicoli*, probably written by the monk Theoderic of Trier; an account of the translation of St. Glodesinde written by John, abbot of St. Arnulf of Metz: *Ex translatione S. Glodesindis*, see pp. 235–36. The relevant passage from the *translatio* is published by Waitz in a note to the universal chronicle of Metz, in *MGH SS* 24: pp. 506–7; for the attribution to John of St. Arnulf, see WH 1: p. 179. All three provide information on local events in Lothar's time. See Dierkens, "Production," pp. 251–57, and Thomas, "Mönch," pp. 50–52. The *Libellus de imperatoria potestate in urbe Roma* is a short antipapal work written, probably in Spoleto, around the first decade of the tenth century, according to WL 4: pp. 425–26. Its editor, Zucchetti, *Libellus*, p. LXVII, gives a somewhat later date. The anonymous author sides with Emperor Louis II and against Pope Nicholas I.

19. Cf. Constable, *Letters*, and Fransen, *Décrétales*.

20. Editions in *MGH Epp. Karol. aevi* 4 and in *MGH Conc.* 4: pp. 43–45, 123–26, 132–33, Hincmar's letters in *MGH Epp. Karol. aevi* 6, one letter from Gunthar published by Fuhrmann, "Original," and one from Anastasius in *MGH Epp. Karol. aevi* 5. The letter from Archbishops Gunthar of Cologne and Theutgaud of Trier has survived because it was included by Hincmar in the *AB* aº 864, pp. 107–10, and also, in a slightly different, shorter form, in some versions of the *AF* aº 863, pp. 60–61. According to Nelson, *Annals of St-Bertin*, pp. 114–16, n. 10, and the editor Levillain, p. 108, n. 1, Hincmar changed the text.

Pope Nicholas did not write these letters in his own hand. He often even left it to Anastasius, the later papal librarian, to draft, dictate, and correct them, at least from 863 on. This same Anastasius also served as a supplier of information that could be used to justify Nicholas's monarchistic ambitions.[21] Just how great Nicholas's aspirations as pope were we shall see in act 5, but much of Nicholas's resentment toward Lothar seems to stem from the fact that Lothar and his bishops did not accede to these ambitions.[22]

We know of many letters because they were included in other sources, such as annals, but collections of letters were also made. The compiler might reuse the letters he drafted in whole or in part. Some collections were kept and added to after the death of the compiler, especially when they concerned important issues and authorities whose pronouncements could later be used as arguments. Letter collections of the bishops of Rome, in particular, who had a relatively well-equipped chancery, have withstood the ravages of time.[23] It is not really surprising, then, that we have a large number of Pope Nicholas's letters. This does not mean, however, that everyone in his own time shared his view of events, though the fact that his view is comparatively well documented might—wrongly—tend to give that impression. For we have only a fraction of the total correspondence on the issue of Lothar's marriage, as is clear from the fact that many of the surviving letters are replies to others that have been lost.

Fortunately, we have other sources for the vicissitudes of Lothar's divorce case, among them a letter collection that includes nonpapal correspondence. This collection, which tells us something of Lothar's point of view, contains letters from Lothar himself and his bishops and was almost certainly compiled by Bishop Adventius of Metz (858–75). Adventius not only compiled it, he also composed many of the letters under his own name and, it is safe to assume, in the name of other bishops and of Lothar himself.[24]

Council Rulings

As we have seen, church councils in the ninth century also dealt with actual cases, one of which was the matter of Lothar's marriage. Several times

21. Ertl, "Diktatoren," pp. 83, 105–6. See also Fuhrmann, *Einfluß* 2: pp. 247–72.

22. See below, pp. 153–54, 159–62.

23. Constable, *Letters*; Fransen, *Décrétales*; for the tradition of letter collections, see Garrison, "'Send More Socks.'"

24. *Epistolae ad divortium Lotharii pertinentes*, and one letter published separately in *MGH Conc.* 4: pp. 43–45. All these letters have been preserved in the Codex Vallicelliana I 76; an analysis of this codex is in Staubach, *Herrscherbild*, pp. 154–74, 278–284B. For Adventius, see also Gaillard, "Évêque."

councils were convened to discuss and pronounce judgment on the case. So far as we can make out, these were fairly small assemblies.[25] The first four councils were held in Lothar's territory, and most if not all of the participants were bishops from his own realm. It is therefore not surprising that the conclusions they reached were highly agreeable to Lothar. But a dismal fate awaited these rulings. The texts of the first two Councils of Aachen (in January and February 860) are known to us only because Hincmar included them in his treatise *De divortio Lotharii,* and there he demolishes their findings. Moreover, he quotes only fragments of the rulings of the second Aachen council, while of the first council he actually gives two versions, the first much vaguer than the second. The three texts have the character of minutes, with the councils' proceedings and conclusions summarized in separate points, and with no agreement between the different points.[26]

In the case of the third Council of Aachen, on 29 April 862, fate has been kinder to us and left us two undamaged records of this council that agree in content, though not word for word.[27] Of the fourth council, held in Metz in June 863, no texts have survived. Most of what we know about it comes from narrative sources such as the *Annales Bertiniani,* the *Annales Fuldenses,* and the *Liber Pontificalis.*[28] Two further councils on Lothar's case may have been held in his realm, but we know next to nothing about them. We have an undated letter from a number of Lotharingian bishops inviting their

25. The first (January 860) and third (April 862) Councils of Aachen are concerned with Lothar's case, the second (February 860) also with a number of other cases: c. 16–19 relate to Lothar, c. 1–15 are missing, but at least one other topic was the divorce of Engeltrude and Boso; see *De divortio,* pp. 121–22, 231. The Council of Metz also considered the case of Engeltrude and Boso; see *Ep. Nic.,* no. 18, pp. 284–86, and no. 53, pp. 346–47. Adventius of Metz says that decisions were also taken on monastic reform: *Cartulaire de Gorze,* p. 107.

26. Edition in *De divortio,* pp. 115–16, 119–22.

27. The Trier codex containing the letters of Adventius and Lothar (codex Vallicelliana, I 76) also contains a report of this council. In another manuscript (Vaticana Palatina, Lat. ms. 576) written in Reims at the end of the ninth century we even find four consecutive texts relating to the issue of Lothar's marriage. The first of these consists of a statement by Lothar in which he sets out his case before the assembled bishops of his realm and asks them for a judgment. The second contains the bishops' decision. The third is a treatise on Lothar's case by some unnamed bishops, whose opinion is diametrically opposed to the council's decisions. Lastly, the fourth text contains a collection of arguments for and against divorce, consisting mainly of biblical quotations. The writer is anonymous and there are no direct references to Lothar's case. Edition of all texts is in *MGH. Conc.* 4: pp. 68–85, labeled consecutively A, B, C, D, and E. See also Staubach, *Herrscherbild,* pp. 181–87.

28. *AF,* a° 863, p. 57; *AB,* a° 863, p. 98; *Liber pontificalis* 2, p. 160, see also *MGH Conc.* 4: pp. 134–38.

West Frankish colleagues to such a council.[29] In addition, in the *Annales Bertiniani* Hincmar briefly speaks of a Lotharingian council in 866, but his account is somewhat tendentious and cannot be verified.[30]

The two other important councils concerning Lothar's marriage took place outside his borders and show the other side of the case. Held in 863 and 869, they were presided over by Pope Nicholas I in 863 and by Pope Adrian II in 869. The conclusions of the 863 Council of Rome, in which Nicholas condemns Lothar and his supporters, were publicized by the pope in letters, of which four addressed copies have been preserved. These letters were intended to be read aloud and then passed on.[31] The council of 869, presided over by Pope Adrian II, was held in Rome or Monte Cassino. Lothar's case was only one of the matters discussed here.[32]

Treaty Texts

As we have already said, King Lothar's attempts to obtain a divorce constituted a political issue of the first order. It was fought out at the highest political level, notably by Lothar's kinsmen. Chief among these were the kings of the other realms of the empire: Lothar's brothers Charles, king of Provence, and Emperor Louis II, king of Italy, and his uncles Louis the German, king of East Francia, and Charles the Bald, king of West Francia. On several occasions some or all of them concluded agreements regarding Lothar's case, sometimes with Lothar himself, sometimes against him.[33] No one king could make good his threats without the support of powerful followers. Consequently, virtually all these meetings were attended also by

29. *Ep. Lot.* no. 13, pp. 228–30, and *MGH Conc.* 4: pp. 198–200. Hartmann, *Synoden*, p. 285, and Staubach, *Herrscherbild*, p. 201, date these to 865, unlike the older literature, which gives 867.

30. *AB*, aᵒ 866, pp. 132–33. The fragment published by Hampe of a council text or letter about an unspecified divorce case probably does not relate—contrary to Hampe's opinion—to Lothar's case, and neither do several later forgeries. See Heidecker, *Kerk*, p. 52, n. 44.

31. *Ep. Nic.*, pp. 284–87: no. 18 to Ado of Vienne, no. 19 to Hincmar of Reims and Wenilo of Rouen, no. 20 to the bishops of the realm of Louis the German, no. 20 to all the bishops of Gaul, Germania, and Italy. The letter to Hincmar was copied in the *AB* aᵒ 863, pp. 99–103, that to Louis the German's bishops in the *AF*, aᵒ 863 pp. 58–60; edition also in *MGH Conc.* 4: pp. 147–58.

32. *MGH Conc.* 4: pp. 363–79. For this text's significance for the reception of Pseudo-Isidore, see Fuhrmann, *Einfluß* 2: pp. 273–77. Hartmann, *Synoden*, p. 297, is noncommittal.

33. Treaties between Lothar II, Louis the German, and Charles the Bald were concluded at Coblenz (860), in *MGH Cap.* 2: pp. 152–58, 297–301, and Savonnières (862), in *MGH Cap.* 2: pp. 159–65. Treaties between Charles the Bald and Louis the German at Tusey (865), in *MGH Cap.* 2: pp. 165–67, and Metz (867 or 868), in *MGH Cap.* 2: pp. 167–68.

a whole troop of the high aristocracy: bishops, abbots, and the lay nobility. They, ultimately, had to support the agreements. The texts of the treaties usually consisted of a statement by each king followed by a summary, divided into chapters, of terms agreed to by all those present. Such agreements often used the texts of previous treaties between Carolingian kings; for instance, most of the chapters of the treaty concluded at Coblenz in 860 between Louis the German, Charles the Bald, and Lothar II recapitulate the Treaty of Meerssen (851) between Lothar I, Louis the German, and Charles the Bald.[34] Most of these treaties were clearly public in nature. Their terms were read out and circulated. The Treaty of Metz between Louis the German and Charles the Bald (867 or 868), however, is an exception. This was a secret pact in which the two kings divided their nephews' kingdoms between them, even though said nephews were still in the prime of life.

Charters

To push through his divorce Lothar needed to win the support of powerful people. One way of doing this was by making gifts to them or to religious institutions, such as monasteries, in which they had an interest. Often we have documentary records of such gifts. In addition, powerful individuals who happened to support Lothar could ask all manner of favors of him, such as a gift or an office for one of their own followers. The royal charters that record the granting of such favors then record the identity of the person who interceded with the king on behalf of one of his connections. They are referred to as "*intervenientes*."[35] Finally, there is one document in which Lothar makes it absolutely clear whom he regards as his wife and his son. In formal phrases King Lothar refers to Waldrada as "our most beloved wife" and their little son Hugo as "our son."[36]

Lothar's divorce case thus offered opportunities for significant material gain. His supporters could be rewarded, but those who opposed him could lose their property, as we can see from the case of Gorze Abbey, founded in the eighth century, which changed hands several times between 855 and 869 in the ups and downs of Lothar's marital fortunes.[37]

---

34. Coblenz (860), in *MGH Cap.* 2: pp. 155–57, Second Treaty of Meerssen (851), in *MGH Cap.* 2: pp. 72–74.

35. Edition in *D Lot.II.*

36. *D Lot.II* no. 19 (18 May 863), p. 415: "amantissimae coniugis nostrae Waldradae et filii nostri Ugonis."

37. Founded by Bishop Chrodegang of Metz (742–66), Gorze Abbey was among the most important monastic houses in the Carolingian empire. The dispute about the abbey

Hincmar of Reims' Treatise *De divortio Lotharii*

Occasionally we are lucky enough to have firsthand information that has survived the calamities of many centuries. One such instance is a manuscript from Reims that was written in 860 when the battle over Lothar's divorce was at its height. The manuscript contains a lengthy treatise on the legal and moral aspects of the divorce, set down by one of the main players, Hincmar, archbishop of Reims (845–82). The manuscript consists of a codex of 124 parchment folios and seems to have been Hincmar's own working copy.[38] He used it as a personal reference book and regularly supplemented it with new passages when he received new information that he thought useful. Only the beginning of the codex is damaged: the first four folios have been cut out.[39]

The original text of the codex consists of three parts, written with some intervals between them. The first two parts constituted a treatise that may have had no title, although we cannot be sure of this since the first four folios of the manuscript have been lost. Only later, in the first modern edition, was it given the title *De divortio Lotharii regis et Theutbergae reginae* (On the divorce of King Lothar and Queen Theutberga).[40] Hincmar wrote the work not for himself but at the request of other people. After Lothar and Theutberga had been divorced at two synods in Aachen in January and February 860 some bishops and great nobles from Lothar's kingdom asked Hincmar and a few other bishops for advice on certain aspects of the case, since they disagreed with the decisions of the Aachen synods.[41] They sent Hincmar the rulings of the first Synod of Aachen and a list of eight questions. Hincmar responded with a lengthy treatise of twenty-three questions (having subdivided the original eight) and as many answers (*interrogationes* and *responsiones*), in which he made clear that he was against the divorce. The questions and answers relating to the council text, together with a foreword (the *praefatio*, like many other prefaces written after the main

---

and its involvement with Lothar's divorce case is apparent in the documents recording gifts to Gorze, which have been collected and copied in a cartulary. Edition: *Cartulaire de l'abbaye de Gorze*.

38. In this I follow the editor, Letha Böhringer.

39. Bibliothèque Nationale de France, Paris, ms. lat. 2866, originally in the possession of the Abbey of St.-Rémi in Reims. I have used Böhringer's edition of *De divortio*. Her introduction and commentary to this edition are of real value for the understanding of Hincmar's treatise and differ greatly from what Devisse, *Hincmar Archevêque*, who had also studied the manuscript, says of it in his biography of Hincmar.

40. *Opuscula et epistolae Hincmari Remensis archiepiscopi*, ed. J. Cordesius, Paris, 1615, pp. 283–493; see: *De divortio*, ed. Böhringer, p. 34.

41. *De divortio*, p. 112.

text) and a conclusion, make up the original text of the first part of *De divortio*. Six months after the first list the same individuals sent Hincmar a second list of seven questions, the answers to which form the second part of *De divortio*. Later, but still in 860, the codex acquired a third part, a treatise on another divorce case that Hincmar had already discussed to some extent earlier in *De divortio*, that of Boso and his wife, Engeltrude, entitled *De uxore Bosonis*.[42]

By birth a member of the Frankish aristocracy, Hincmar entered the monastery of Saint-Denis at a very early age (probably around 810/13). There he became a pupil of Abbot Hilduin, archchaplain to Louis the Pious, and through Hilduin he gained access from 822 to the royal court and to politics. After Hilduin sided with Louis' sons in their rebellion against their father in 830 the king banished both him and Hincmar to the monastery of Corvey. Later Hincmar regained Louis' favor and returned to Saint-Denis. Thereafter he remained a loyal supporter of Louis the Pious and, after Louis' death, of Charles the Bald, who appointed him archbishop of Reims in 845.[43] Reims was one of the most important West Frankish bishoprics; indeed, it was one of the most important church provinces in the whole Frankish empire. Hincmar thus became a prominent figure on the Frankish political stage, a role he would play with relish and energy until his death in 882. With his succession to Reims, however, he had inherited a skeleton in the closet—his predecessor, Bishop Ebo. Ebo had been dismissed in 835 for opposing Louis the Pious; in 840/41, after Louis' death, he was able to return for a short time but was then permanently removed from his episcopal throne. Questions about the legality of Ebo's dismissal—and thus also of Hincmar's succession—would dog Hincmar for years to come.

The first part of *De divortio* must have been written between March and May 860.[44] It is a fair copy made after a corrected dictation. Toward the end it seems to have been a rush job, with three scribes working simultaneously on the last quire. Probably a copy of this part was presented at the meeting of the Frankish kings, nobles, and bishops at Coblenz in early June 860. In the preamble to his foreword, written in letter form, Hincmar addresses himself to "the glorious lords kings and reverend fellow bishops and all

42. Edited in *Ep. Hinc.*, pp. 81–87.

43. For biographical details see Rudolf Schieffer, "Hinkmar," and Devisse, *Hincmar Archevêque*, pp. 1089–97.

44. After February 860, the second Synod of Aachen, and six months before 22 October 860, the Synod of Tusey at which part 2 of *De divortio* was cited, which in turn was written six months after receipt of the questions for part 1.

those gathered in the bosom of the Catholic Church."[45] Hincmar also protected the anonymity of those who had commissioned him, who were after all acting against their lord, Lothar.[46] Several copies must have been in circulation. Hincmar certainly assumed that Bishop Gunthar of Cologne could consult one, for he refers to it in a letter to Gunthar.[47]

By his own account Hincmar received the set of seven questions to which he responded in part 2 six months after the first series.[48] Since this part of *De divortio* was cited at the Synod of Tusey (which began on 22 October 860), it must have been written in September/October 860. During the summer of 860 Hincmar appears to have changed his attitude toward Lothar (we shall see why later), which results in a different tone in the second part.

―――――――――

LOTHAR's bad reputation is already apparent in most of our sources. The narrative sources, certainly, almost all speak of him in negative terms. They were either produced by opponents of his who were directly involved in the case, or written only after his death when it was clear that things had turned out badly for him. The letters, the council texts, and Hincmar's treatise *De divortio* were written at the height of the battle over Lothar's marriages. Almost without exception their authors are partisan, either for Lothar or against him. But far more source material survives from Lothar's opponents than from himself and his supporters. In fact, the voice of Lothar and his followers can be heard almost exclusively in letters and council records in two fortuitously preserved manuscripts.[49] Elsewhere something of it survives, but "reworked" by other authors, in *De divortio*, in the *Annales Bertiniani*, and in the *Annales Fuldenses*. Genuinely neutral observers with a detached view of the case hardly exist, with the possible exception of the brief records in the *Annales Laubacenses* and *Lobienses* and some parts of the *Annales Fuldenses*. Thus, most of the members of the chorus that provides the commentary to Lothar's drama are often singing in the wrong key. And now, with this warning in mind, it is time for the drama to begin.

45. *De divortio*, p. 107: "Dominis regibus gloriosis et venerandis consacerdotibus nostris ac cunctis in sinu catholicae ecclesiae collocates."
46. Ibid, p. 112.
47. In *Ep. Hinc.*, p. 87; see *De divortio*, ed. Böhringer, pp. 25–26. So when Hincmar wrote this in October–November 860, in connection with the Synod of Tusey, he had already put part 1 (question 22) and part 2 (question 28) of *De divortio* in the public domain.
48. *De divortio*, p. 235.
49. Letters and council rulings in Rome, Biblioteca Vallicelliana ms. I 76, originally from Trier, and Biblioteca Vaticana Palatina lat. ms. 576, originally from Reims. See below, pp. 42–43. If these two manuscripts had not survived, we would have had no firsthand documentation from Lothar's side.

II A MARITAL DRAMA IN SIX ACTS

Act I

Lothar Ascends the Throne and Marries Theutberga, 855–857

Two of our main players appear on the political stage in 855. The old Emperor Lothar I is gravely ill; sensing his end approaching, he summons his magnates and in their presence divides his realm among his sons. The eldest, Louis II, receives the kingdom of Italy and the imperial title; Lothar II, about eighteen years old, is given the northern part of the Middle Kingdom, later named Lotharingia after him; and the young Charles, still a child too young to rule, gets the kingdom of Provence.[1]

In the same year Lothar marries Theutberga, the sister of Hucbert, counselor to Lothar I and one of the most powerful nobles at the court of the young Lothar II.[2] Theutberga looks like a good match; the marriage links him to a distinguished and powerful family. But alas! "King Lothar," so Regino of Prüm writes in his chronicle fifty years later, "entered into matrimony with Queen Theutberga and from that sprang much calamity, not only for himself but also for his whole kingdom, as will appear from what follows."[3] Lothar's marriage to Theutberga has been forced on him by Hucbert; at least, so Lothar will later claim. Had he not married her, he would

---

1. *AB* aº 855, p. 71, Regino aº 855, p. 77, *AF* aº 855, p. 46, *Annales Lobienses* aº 855, p. 232. In 841 we have the first mention of Lothar II as the small son of Lothar I: *AF* aº 841, p. 32. The *AB* record in 853, p. 67, that he has been guilty of adultery; he must thus have been at least fifteen years old in that year. In 855, according to a letter by Adventius van Metz, he was still "*adolescentulus*," *Ep. Lot.* no. 5, p. 215. In 869 the *Annales Laubacenses* still call him a "*iuvenis*," young man (the word *iuvenis* could be used even of a man of thirty), *Annales Laubacenses* aº 868, p. 15 (incorrect dating). Based on some of this, Parisot, *Royaume*, pp. 78–79, dates his birth to 837–39.

2. *Annales Lobienses* aº 855, p. 232.

3. Regino aº 856 (Regino's dating is a year out), p. 77: "Lotharius rex Thietbirgam reginam sibi in matrimonium iunxit, ex qua coniunctione maxima ruina non illi solum, sed etiam omni regno eius accedit, sicut in subsequentibus luce clarius apparebit."

have risked losing his kingdom; Hucbert had told him so in terms that could not be misunderstood.[4]

Young as he is, Lothar does not go to his wedding a virgin. While still living at home with his father he had a lover called Waldrada. At the time of his marriage he probably already has children by her; however that may be, she will give him four children, one son and three daughters. For the moment this mistress of his, our third main player, is waiting in the wings; she will make her voice heard later.[5]

At two crucial moments in this act, Lothar's accession and his marriage to Theutberga, we see powerful political forces in action. Both reveal something of the balance of power between a king and his great nobles. Lothar's marriage to Theutberga could significantly affect this balance, creating as it did a powerful political alliance.

The Accession: The Political Power of the King and Nobles

Before we begin, we must first explain who these great nobles were, these "magnates" referred to in the sources as *proceres, optimates,* or *principes regni.* They were members of a group of leading families within the aristocracy, some two to three hundred of them in the Carolingian realm north of the Alps, who were extremely rich. They occupied important positions at court and it was from their ranks that the holders of important offices, such as counts, bishops, and lay abbots, were recruited.[6] The Carolingian kings

4. A fragmentary text by Adventius van Metz, which can be dated to 863, from his letter collection, published in *Ep. Lot.* no. 5, p. 215. For this text, see below pp. 110–12.

5. Werner, "Nachkommen," genealogy on unbound paper folded into the back cover of the volume. Hugo, the son of Lothar and Waldrada, is mentioned in a document of 863: *D Lot.I,* no. 19, p. 415. But he is also listed, together with two of his sisters (Bertha and Ermengarde), in the *Liber Memorialis* of Remiremont. Schmid, "Karolingischer Königseintrag," pp. 100–123, dates this record to December 861. Gaillard, *D'une réforme,* pp. 46–47 n. 36, doubts the possibility of this exact date. Lastly, a passage in Hincmar's *De divortio,* written in the spring of 860, very probably refers to him: *De divortio,* p. 226. In 879 Hugo became politically active when the death of Louis the Stammerer created a power vacuum in the West Frankish realm, *AB* aº 879, p. 239. In 880, at the latest, Bertha married Theutbald, *AB* aº 880, p. 242: probably in 879 or 880, since in 880 Hugo made his first attempt to seize power with Theutbald as a major ally. She was probably born between 857 and 861. Ermengarde never married, but entered a convent. Of her birth we know only that it was before 861. The third sister, Gisela, was to be married off to the converted Norseman Godfrid in 882 or 883, Regino aº 882, p. 120, *AF* aº 883, p. 100; she must therefore have been born between 862 and 866.

6. Dhondt, *Frühe Mittelalter,* pp. 36–37, 53–55. In 1939 Gerd Tellenbach drew up a list of 111 individuals from forty-two families active during Charlemagne's reign whom he could identify. This has been systematically evaluated in Schmid, "Programmatisches," esp. pp. 119–22. Dhondt names roughly two to three hundred families. For the noble families in the Caro-

were dependent on them to gain and exercise power, but conversely the great nobles were also dependent on the kings.

The Nobles' Role in the Succession

Two principles governed the succession of the Frankish kings, hereditary succession and election, with the balance between the two depending on the actual situation at the time.[7] In addition to these two principles there was a further element to confirm a king in his position: anointing. The first principle was based on the hereditary succession of all eligible male offspring of the royal house, in this case the Carolingians. "Eligible" meant that they were physically fit and were not cloistered monks. Although the sons of the previous king were the preferred candidates to succeed their father, other male members of the Carolingian house could also lay claim to the realm of their deceased kinsman. (See genealogy of the Carolingians in appendix 2.)

Second, there was elective succession, with the great nobles of a kingdom choosing their king. This gave them the opportunity to exercise their influence, but their choice of candidates was limited. Often the old king appointed his successor or successors, whom the nobles were then expected to confirm. Whether they still did so after the king's death was another matter, but usually they abided by the old king's wishes. In the mid-ninth century the choice was still confined to members of the Carolingian family. The first non-Carolingian to be elected king was Boso of Vienne in 879 (but he had an extremely ambitious Carolingian wife, Ermengarde).[8] After the death of Charles the Fat in 888 this example was followed by numerous others. "The territories did not wait for their natural lord, but each decided to beget a king out of its own body," Regino says expressively.[9] For Regino

---

lingian empire under Charlemagne and their origins, see Werner, "Bedeutende Adelsfamilien," esp. pp. 121–33, Nelson, "Kingship and Royal Government," and Airlie, "Aristocracy."

7. Dhondt, "Élection," translated into German as "Königswahl und Thronerbrecht" in *Königswahl*, ed. Hlawitschka, pp. 144–89; Tellenbach, "Grundlagen." Both differ from Schlesinger, "Karlingische Königswahlen," who sees a gradual development of the principle of elective monarchy, first in the West Frankish realm and then in the East Frankish.

8. *AB* a° 879, p. 239; Regino a° 879, p. 114. Hincmar sees the ambition of Boso's wife, Ermengarde, daughter of the late king Louis II of Italy, as the main driving force behind his coronation. Also interesting is the cautious way in which Boso begins his first charter: "Ego Boso, Dei gratia id quod sum" (I Boso, by the grace of God, that what I am), followed immediately by the pretensions of his consort, "necnon et dilecta conjux mea Hirmingardi proles imperialis" (and my dear wife Ermengarde, imperial child), *D Provence* no. 16 (25 July 879), p. 31. Only in subsequent charters does he style himself king, e.g., *D Provence* no. 17 (8 November 879), p. 32.

9. *AF* a° 888, pp. 116–17; Regino a° 888, pp. 129–30: "Non naturalem dominum prestolantur, sed unumquodque de suis visceribus regem sibi creari disponit." Here it should be noted that some of them had a Carolingian mother or grandmother.

the natural lord is the lord by birth, thus from the royal, Carolingian, house.

The succession in the West Frankish kingdom following the death of Louis the Stammerer in 879 provides a striking illustration of the different principles. Louis the Stammerer had two sons, Louis and Carloman, both still young. The elder, Louis, was just sixteen and was appointed by his father as his successor. However, a section of the West Frankish nobility decided to divide the kingdom between the two sons, or rather between the two groups of nobles who would determine the boys' policies. But a third group of West Frankish nobles invited Louis the Stammerer's cousin, Louis the Younger of East Francia, to assume the throne. He made an attempt to secure the West Frankish realm, but allowed himself to be bought off with part of it, much to the fury of his wife who, according to Hincmar, scolded him roundly on his return, telling him that if she had accompanied him he would have had the whole kingdom.[10] Louis the Younger made no further attempts on West Francia, because at this time his brother Carloman was lying gravely ill, and he had designs on that inheritance also. Even more ambitious than Louis' wife was Ermengarde, who in that same year was trying to win the West Frankish realm for her husband, Boso. And finally there was yet a fifth, less fortunate Carolingian claimant: Hugo, the son of Lothar II and Waldrada.[11]

We find the same principles at work in the accession of Lothar II. The old Emperor Lothar summoned the great men of his realm and in their presence divided his territories between the two sons who were still with him, Lothar and Charles. The eldest son, Louis II, had already been given his share, Italy.[12] However, the magnates were evidently apprehensive about young Lothar's uncle, Louis the German. They went to Louis with young Lothar to ask Louis' approval of Lothar's accession, explaining that it was their wish that he should reign over them. And Louis did in fact agree.[13] This was in line with the arrangements for the succession worked out by Charlemagne and Louis the Pious, in which they had specified that the uncles were obliged to give their consent if "the people" wanted just one of their brothers' sons to succeed his father.[14]

---

10. *AB* a° 879, p. 238: "Audiens autem hoc uxor illius, satis moleste tulit, dicens quia si illa cum eo venisset, totum istud regnum haberet."

11. *AB* a° 879, pp. 236–39.

12. *AB* a° 855, p. 71; Regino a° 855, p. 77.

13. *AF* a° 855, p. 46.

14. The *Divisio Regnorum* (806) of Charlemagne c. 5, in *MGH Cap.* 1: p. 128; the *Ordinatio Imperii* (817) of Louis the Pious c. 14, in *MGH Cap.* 1: pp. 272–73.

This episode clearly shows how important the support of the great nobles was; and an even clearer demonstration followed a year later, when the three brothers met at Orbe, in the center of their kingdoms, to discuss the division of their inheritance. Both Louis and Lothar were dissatisfied with their share. First, Louis complained to his uncles that he had received too little, since Italy had been a gift from his grandfather Louis the Pious and therefore came from a previous division of territory.[15] Now he demanded a share in this new inheritance. He and Lothar quarreled so violently about this that they came close to drawing weapons on each other. Lothar then tried to deprive his young brother Charles of his inheritance by having him tonsured as a monk. And again it was the same magnates who physically pulled Charles away from Lothar and gave him his share of the inheritance as their father, Lothar, had arranged.[16] That it was actually the magnates who apportioned the inheritance is again apparent after young Charles, who had long suffered from epilepsy, died in 863. Both his brothers tried to win the support of as many of the region's leading figures as possible, but again it was the magnates who carried out the negotiations on the eventual division of the territory.[17]

Young Lothar's accession was confirmed by a Christian ritual: anointing. In 856 "the magnates of the late Lothar resolved to make his son Lothar king of Francia by holy unction."[18] The Carolingians had given religious legitimacy to their takeover of power from the previous dynasty, the Merovingians, by having themselves anointed king by their bishops or, if at all possible, by the bishop of Rome. The anointing ceremony gave the king a sacred, semiclerical status: he became the Anointed of God. Anointing seems to have been carried out particularly when the succession had not gone smoothly. Evidently an extra religious legitimation was invoked to strengthen the king's position. Here we have to distinguish between the anointing of kings and of emperors. Carolingians who became emperor were all anointed, some even prior to the beginning of their imperial reign. The office of emperor had universal Christian pretensions, and being anointed by the bishop of Rome was part of this. At first most nonimperial anointings were of the early Carolingians who had displaced the Merovingians. Later the rite was performed in the West Frankish kingdom when Charles the Bald and his son Charles the Younger were seeking to

15. *AB* a° 856, p. 72.
16. *AB* a° 856, p. 73.
17. *AB* a° 863, p. 96.
18. *AB* a° 856, p. 72: "Proceres quondam Hlotharii filium eius Hlotharium regem Franciae etiam sacra unctione constituunt."

establish their power in Aquitaine (848 and 855) and Lotharingia (869), and on the difficult accessions of Louis the Stammerer and his two young sons. We have just referred to an anointing in the Middle Kingdom, that of Lothar II. No instances of East Frankish kings being anointed are known, with the exception of the contested king Zwentibold (895).[19] In subsequent changes of dynasty almost all non-Carolingian kings would have themselves anointed.[20]

The Interdependence of King and Nobles

Even after a king's accession the great nobles continued to play a prominent part in his political activities. From their ranks came the counselors who had direct access to the king. At formal gatherings of the court the king met with them and together they reached decisions on the governance of the realm. This was evidently a process of lobbying and of give and take, depending on the balance of power at the time.[21] The king depended on his magnates for military support and the running of his kingdom, rewarding them with lucrative offices and fiefs. And these rewards enabled them in their turn to bind large numbers of followers to themselves.

The support of his nobles was vital if a king was to keep his kingdom. When another Carolingian laid claim to his brother's or nephew's realm, he would try to detach his kinsman's followers from him by making them promises. And on occasion a group of magnates became so dissatisfied with their own king that they would invite the king of another territory to assume power.[22] If the latter thought he had sufficient support among the disaffected nobles or those who simply thought they had more to gain under the new lord, then he would risk an attempt. These tactics are clearly visible in Louis the German's invasion of the kingdom of Charles the Bald

19. For the list of anointed Carolingian kings, see Brühl, "Fränkischer Krönungsbrauch," pp. 321–26, partially corrected by Nelson, "Inauguration Rituals," pp. 56–65.

20. Brühl, "Fränkischer Krönungsbrauch," pp. 321–26.

21. An account of this process for the reign of Charles the Bald (based mainly on Hincmar's *De ordine palatii*) in Nelson, *Charles the Bald*, pp. 45–50, and Nelson, "Legislation and Consensus," pp. 100–111.

22. Examples of this are the repeated invitations by Aquitanian nobles to Louis the German and his son (*AB* aº 854, pp. 68–69; *AF* aº 854, p. 44), the invitation by nobles of the West Frankish realm to Louis the German (*AB* aº 856 and 858, pp. 72, 78–79; *AF* aº 858, pp. 49–51), and later to Louis the Younger (*AB* aº 879, pp. 235–39). The many rebellions centering around one or another of the sons of Louis the German can also be seen as a similar phenomenon, cf. Goldberg, *Struggle for Empire*, pp. 263–86. In every case discontented nobles aligned themselves with a Carolingian and rebelled against their own king. See Tellenbach, "Grundlagen," pp. 216–20.

(858)[23] and in Charles the Bald's maneuvers against Charles of Provence (861).[24] In a conflict between two kings the outcome usually depended on who had managed to attract the greatest number of supporters. Many nobles remained on the sidelines, eventually joining the side they expected to win. This is already apparent in the struggle for the succession following the death of Louis the Pious, when Lothar had the most followers at first. He made many promises and people thought that, as the future victor, he had the most to distribute. Some, however, decided to wait and see. Then the tide turned, Lothar was forced to retreat, and his supporters, having lost faith in him, left him in droves. Even lavish material rewards could not bind them to him. Lothar even distributed some heirlooms left him by his grandfather Charlemagne among his followers, but in vain.[25] In choosing sides the magnates were governed not simply by greed but also by fear of ending up on the losing side. The *Annales Bertiniani* say that Louis and Charles "persuaded or subjected everyone in their territories, some by force, some by threats, some by giving them offices and fiefs, and some by agreeing to their conditions."[26] For if one joined the losing side one could be punished by the eventual victor with loss of fiefs or in a few cases even with death.[27] A similar thing happened in 858 at the confrontation between the armies of Charles the Bald and Louis the German at Brienne. Charles and his followers saw that Louis' supporters were in the majority, because a large number of the West Frankish nobles had gone over to him. Charles then wisely decided to retreat, whereupon most of his own troops also deserted.[28]

A king who lost the support of his nobles was in danger of losing his kingdom. This is apparent from a letter from Lothar's bishops to those of Charles the Bald. In it they expressed their support for their king, Lothar, and guaranteed that he had the backing of his followers. Charles was not to gamble on expelling Lothar from his realm, they warned, in the false belief that Lothar's people (that is, his nobles) had abandoned him. They maintained that this was a wicked lie, put out by faithless people with evil intentions.[29]

23. *AB* a° 858, pp. 78–79; *AF* a° 858, pp. 49–51.
24. *AB* a° 861, p. 87.
25. *AB* a° 842, p. 41.
26. *AB* a° 841, pp. 36–37: "Hludowicus autem et Karolus, alter ultra, alter citra Rhenum, partim vi, partim minis, partim honoribus, partim quibusdam condicionibus omnes partium suarum sibi vel subdunt vel conciliant."
27. Tellenbach, "Grundlagen," pp. 263–64.
28. *AB* a° 858, p. 79, *AF* a° 858, pp. 50–51.
29. *Ep. Lot.* no. 13 (according to Staubach, *Herrscherbild*, pp. 201–8, it dates from the first half of 865), p. 229.

Further evidence of the importance of the great nobles comes from the treaties between the kings. A number of these treaties concern the division of the Carolingian empire and relations between the royal brothers, cousins, and nephews. The meeting at Orbe between Lothar I's sons is recorded only in the *Annales Bertiniani*, but treaty texts from other meetings have survived. It was the great nobles, the king's loyal followers, who negotiated the text. Following the negotiations, the text itself, consisting mainly of statements by the kings, was drawn up by a group of their closest advisers. In the case of the Treaty of Coblenz (862) we know their names; there were forty-six of them.[30] These statements were read out by the kings to a wider circle of counselors. The Treaty of Savonnières tells us that all together, for the three kings, there were two hundred counselors. They could refuse to accept the statements as framed, and at Savonnières they did just that.[31] Lastly, the final, agreed-on statements were read out to the "people" (*populus*), by which—as usual—is meant the nobles.[32] We also know the number of counselors involved in an earlier Treaty of Coblenz (842): forty per king, giving a total of 120 counselors for the three kings who negotiated the text.[33] The Treaty of Metz (867/68) specified that the partition of the realms of Louis II and Lothar II should be done with the agreement of all their loyal followers.[34]

The king was dependent on his nobles, but the converse also applied. A king rewarded his loyal followers with offices and fiefs. The nobles would therefore seek to position themselves as close to the king as possible in order to acquire influence, offices, and riches. And in principle the king could also deprive them of those offices and fiefs—as is clear from the cases when nobles lost the king's favor and with it their offices and much of their possessions. A king could use the offices and fiefs taken from nobles who had fallen out of favor to bind a new group of powerful nobles to him.[35] And one of the most obvious ways of forming an alliance with a powerful noble family was by marriage.

---

30. *MGH Cap.* 2: p. 154; see also Schneider, *Brüdergemeine*, p. 33. For some of the attendants, see pp. 135–38.

31. *MGH Cap.* 2: p. 165; see also *AB* aº 862, pp. 94–95, and Schneider, *Brüdergemeine*, pp. 40–42. For this meeting, see below, pp. 103–4, 146.

32. Werner, "Bedeutende Adelsfamilien," pp. 83–84; Schneider, *Brüdergemeine*, p. 42.

33. Schneider, *Brüdergemeine*, p. 42.

34. *MGH Cap.* 2: p. 168.

35. Tellenbach, "Großfränkische Adel," pp. 69–70; Wollasch, "Adlige Familie," pp. 172–75; Schmid, "Struktur," pp. 20–21. We shall come upon many examples of this in the course of Lothar's case; see esp. act 4, pp. 101–2, 142–47, but also the change in the balance of power and its personal consequences in act 2, pp. 69–72.

Lothar's Marriage to Theutberga: Marriage as an Alliance between Noble Families

Theutberga was the sister of Hucbert, one of the most important nobles in the kingdom and abbot of several abbeys. The marriage between Lothar and Theutberga was advantageous to both parties.

Hucbert was the son of Count Boso, a faithful follower of Lothar I who traveled to Italy in his retinue.[36] After the death of old Boso his son of the same name inherited the family's Italian possessions. We find him as Count Boso in the service of Louis II.[37] Hucbert himself, as a married cleric, was abbot of Saint-Maurice d'Agaune and duke of the so-called Duchy of Transjura, the area of Switzerland between the Jura and the Alps. He features as intercessor and counselor in a number of charters of Lothar I and Lothar II.[38] This means that people had sought Hucbert's aid in gaining a favor from the king, which was then recorded in a charter.

This was a family whose members were rich in property and offices, and by judicious marriages they had formed a string of alliances with other powerful families. (See appendix 2 for a genealogy of the Bosonids.) Boso, the brother of Hucbert and Theutberga, was married to Engeltrude, daughter of Count Matfrid, another influential counselor of Lothar I.[39] Matfrid's son, also called Matfrid, was one of the most important of Lothar II's nobles. We find him among the magnates listed in the Treaty of Coblenz (860) and he is named as intercessor in several charters.[40] That

---

36. Modern historians have bestowed the name Bosonids on his descendants and relatives by marriage. Virtually all the names by which noble families of the Carolingian period are known were devised by later historians. See Bouchard, "Bosonids," and Depreux, *Prosopographie*, p. 147. In 826 old Boso exchanged possessions in Beek (Netherlands) for others in Italy; see Leupen, "Karolingische villa Beek," pp. 378–88, and Leupen, "Nogmaals Beek"; Tellenbach, "Großfränkische Adel," pp. 62–63.

37. His son Boso is mentioned in *I placiti del regnum Italiae* no. 78, p. 283 (a° 874). See, for him, Hlawitschka, *Franken*, pp. 158–62. For his divorce, see inter alia: *Ep. Hinc.*, pp. 81–87, *De divortio*, pp. 231–32, 244–46, and below, pp. 77 and 97. For his inheritance: *Ep. Joh. VIII*, pp. 102–3, and 115.

38. *D Lot.I* no. 96, p. 234 (7 May 846); *D Lot.II*, nos. 1 and 2 (26 October 855 and 9 November 855), pp. 384–85. Regino a° 859 (incorrect dating), p. 78. Hucbert was then already an abbot, as earlier documents show, including of Saint-Maurice, as witness a letter from Pope Benedict III (855–58), *Ep. Ben.*, pp. 612–13. He had also, according to the same letter, attempted to get his hands on the monastery of Luxeuil. In 862 Charles the Bald granted Hucbert the abbey of Saint-Martin at Tours, *AB* a° 862, p. 88. In 862–63 he forcibly made himself master of that of Lobbes, in Lothar's kingdom; Folcuin, *Gesta Abbatum Lobiensium*, p. 60; Dierkens, *Abbayes*, pp. 109–11.

39. For Matfrid, Count of Orléans, and his family, see Depreux, "Comte Matfrid," and Depreux, *Prosopographie*, pp. 329–31.

40. *D Lot.II* no. 5 (28 June 856), pp. 389–90; no. 11 (18 June 859), pp. 399–400; no. 31 (20 January 867), pp. 435–36.

Hucbert and Matfrid were allies is apparent in 846 when they combined to intercede with Lothar I.[41] A sister of Hucbert and Theutberga was married to Count Bivin, brother to a former high official at the court of Louis the Pious, the *hostiarius* (a dignitary at court responsible for receiving people) Richard, who, like Boso, had followed Lothar I to Italy.[42] Further evidence that Bivin and his wife came from prominent families is the fact that in 869 their daughter, Richildis, became the second wife of Charles the Bald.[43] In 856 Bivin was appointed lay abbot of Gorze by Lothar II.[44]

There is an interesting parallel to Lothar's accession and marriage in the first marriage of Charles the Bald. In 842, amid the conflict about the division of the territories of his father, Louis the Pious, Charles married Ermentrude, the niece of a certain Adalhard. Adalhard had been a favorite of Louis the Pious, who had given him the post of seneschal, the official responsible for running the royal household, organizing its supplies, and supervising the staff. This office enabled him to bestow favors and state property on many people, and he thus acquired a large number of followers. In his *History of the Sons of Louis the Pious*, Nithard takes the view that it was to gain the support of this influential man that Charles married his niece.[45]

The marriage policy of this powerful family followed a distinct trend. In almost every generation one of its members established a marriage tie with the Carolingian house. Count Beggo, a first cousin of Adalhard's father, Leuthard, was married to a daughter of Louis the Pious, Alpais. Beggo was one of Louis' main supporters during the early years of his reign. The fathers of Beggo and Leuthard were brothers. Leuthard's parents were Gerard I, Count of Paris, and Rotrude, who probably was a granddaughter of Charles Martel. A generation after the union of Ermentrude and Charles the Bald, their son, Louis the Stammerer, would again take a bride from the same family: Adelaide, daughter of another Adalhard, also Count of Paris,

41. See previous note, 40.

42. He is mentioned, together with his brother Richard and Gerard of Vienne, in *D Lot.I* no. 68, pp. 181–82; charter confirmed by Lothar II: *D Lot.II* no. 23, pp. 420–21. Tellenbach, "Großfränkische Adel," pp. 62–63, Depreux, *Prosopographie*, pp. 363–65.

43. *AB* a° 869 and 870, pp. 167, 169, for the marriage of Bivin's daughter, Richildis, to Charles the Bald.

44. *Cartulaire de Gorze* no. 55 (July 856) p. 98, no. 56 (856) p. 99, no. 57 (857) p. 101, no. 58 (857) pp. 102–3, no. 60 (863) p. 108. The first document to mention Bivin dates from July 856. His predecessor, Bishop Drogo of Metz, who like previous occupants of the episcopal throne of Metz also ran the affairs of the Abbey of Gorze, had died on 8 December 855; see Oexle, "Karolinger," pp. 281–82, 351–53.

45. Nithard, *Historia filiorum Ludowici* IV, 6, p. 142. Nelson, *Charles the Bald*, pp. 127–30. For Adalhard: Depreux, *Prosopographie*, pp. 80–82.

the grandson of Beggo and Alpais.[46] (See appendix 2 for a genealogy of the descendants of Gerard, Count of Paris, and of Beggo).

We find a similar pattern of marriages in the family of Hucbert and Bivin. Theutberga's marriage to Lothar (855) was, as far as we can tell, the first time they supplied a wife for a Carolingian king, in which case we can regard the marriage of Theutberga's niece Richildis to Charles the Bald in 869 as the second success for the family's marriage policy. Subsequently two other members of the family each married the daughter of a Carolingian king. Hucbert's son, Theutbald, married Bertha, a daughter of Lothar II (before 880),[47] but it was Boso of Vienne, Bivin's son, who carried off the greatest prize by marrying Ermengarde, daughter of Louis II of Italy (876).[48]

These marriage alliances clearly had a dynamic of their own. The kings looked to gain powerful allies, but those allies themselves gained in importance through the marriage connection because, temporarily at least, they were closer to the center of power, the king. If they made good use of that position, they became attractive prospects for a future marriage alliance.

In 855 and 856 Hucbert was at the peak of his power. By marrying his sister to Lothar he had gained for himself an influential position close to the king. As counselor he could influence the king's decisions and reward his own people, such as his brother-in-law Bivin, thus binding an important group of people to him. In 858, when Lothar first attempted to repudiate Theutberga, this group was still strong enough to force him to take her back.[49] Even in 860 Hucbert and Theutberga still had supporters at court who protested against her removal.[50]

The marriage policy of the leading families among the great nobles admirably demonstrates the interdependence of these families and the Carolingian kings. The kings sought support from powerful families related to them by marriage, who in turn derived power and possessions from the

46. Louis and Adelaide thus had a common great-great-great-grandfather (the father of Beggo and Gerard I of Paris, probably also called Beggo). Moreover, another great-great-grandfather of Adelaide was also the grandfather of Louis (Louis the Pious). For the reasoning on these family relationships, see Levillain, "Girart," esp. pp. 226–27. On the other hand, Louis, *Girart*, pp. 1–27, and Werner, "Nachkommen," pp. 429–41, regard Stefanus, Leuthard, and Beggo as brothers, all three being sons of Gerard I. This would make the relationship even closer and give Louis and Adelhaide two great-great-grandfathers in common. For Adalhard's ancestors in general, see Louis, *Girart*; for Beggo, see Depreux, *Prosopographie*, pp. 120–22.

47. *AB* a° 880, p. 242.

48. *AB* a° 876, p. 201; Regino a° 877, p. 113; *AF* a° 878, p. 91.

49. *AB* a° 858, p. 78, see below, pp. 64, 67.

50. Hincmar, *De divortio*, p. 122.

relationship, consolidated or even expanded their position, and so remained attractive as partners in future unions.[51]

The alliance between Lothar and Hucbert seems to have been advantageous to both parties. Lothar was able to establish himself on the throne with the support of Hucbert's followers, and Hucbert gained more influence. Nobody asked the future couple how they felt about each other, but political marriages were really nothing unusual. And yet, as far as we can ascertain, the feelings of both partners were to have a decisive effect on the course of Lothar's story.

---

51. Among them were not only the families of Boso and Adalhard but also, for instance, the Etichonids; see below, pp. 59–61.

Act II

An Unsuccessful Attempt
at Divorce, 857–859

*In 857 Lothar repudiates Theutberga.[1] He gives a very powerful reason for
doing so: the most appalling rumors have been circulating about her.[2] Says Hincmar:
"Even the women gossip about it at their looms."[3] Before the marriage, so it is said,
Hucbert forced his sister to sleep with him and committed sodomy with her. On top of
that, according to the wildest and most bizarre of the rumors, Theutberga supposedly
aborted the fruit of that incestuous relationship.[4] Because of the nature of the accusations Theutberga's reputation is so gravely besmirched that unless they can be proved to
be false it is impossible for her to continue as wife and queen. Hucbert takes the ending
of the marriage as a declaration of war. He embarks on a long guerrilla campaign
against Lothar that continues until Hucbert's death in battle in 864.[5]*

*According to secular, but Christianized, legal procedure, to prove her innocence
Theutberga must undergo an ordeal by hot water. She or a substitute—and Theutberga has a substitute available—must plunge her hand into a cauldron of boiling*

1. *AB* a° 857, p. 74.

2. A text of the first Council of Aachen (January 860) is in the second version, later incorporated by Hincmar in *De divortio* and preserved only in this work, *De divortio*, p. 119,
c. 1, and the text of the second Council of Aachen (February 860), also preserved via *De
divortio*, pp. 121–22, c. 16.

3. Hincmar refers to this matter in January 860, when he asks Adventius of Metz
whether the case brought against Theutberga in 860 is based on the same rumors as the
previous one in 857–58, *De divortio*, p. 130: "Etiam feminae in textrinis suis revolvunt."

4. The events are recounted in a petition by leading nobles of Lothar's realm to
Hincmar of Reims, drawn up in February or March 860. This petition too is known only
from Hincmar, *De divortio*, p. 114. For the accusations in the other sources see below,
p. 68.

5. *Annales Laubacenses* and *Lobienses* a° 858, p. 15, p. 232; Regino a° 866 (incorrect
dating), p. 91; *AX* a° 866, p. 32.

water and if the hand is then found to be "uncooked," as the source puts it, that is taken as a divine verdict that she is innocent. The substitute takes the test, and the outcome is good.[6] *For the time being Lothar has no alternative but to take her back, "under pressure from his people. But he does not admit her to his bed and treats her as a prisoner."*[7]

Over the years Lothar tried to maintain good relations with his uncles Charles and Louis. On his accession he had already allied himself with Louis the German.[8] Now he also makes a treaty with Charles the Bald, which in turn leads to one between Louis the German and Louis of Italy.[9] Toward the end of 858, however, events start to move rapidly. Louis the German attempts to conquer the whole realm of his brother Charles—an attempt that narrowly fails. After initial successes Louis is forced to retreat to his own kingdom; with him go most of the nobles who defected to him from Charles.[10]

The marriage of Lothar and Theutberga had lasted less than two years. And severing the marriage bond also meant breaking the alliance between Lothar and Theutberga's family. Just as the marriage had been a matter of great political importance, so also was the divorce. This was no divorce by mutual consent. Lothar broke with Theutberga unilaterally, and obviously he had to justify his action to the great men of his realm. He accused Theutberga of the most appalling things and consequently she had to defend herself according to the law of the day.

Lothar had his reasons for divorcing Theutberga. He hated her, at least so some sources claim.[11] In addition, according to the same sources, he still loved his boyhood mistress, Waldrada,[12] who—in contrast to the childless Theutberga—had given him several children.[13] That Theutberga had produced no children does not necessarily mean that she was barren. They had been married for less than two years when Lothar made his first attempt

6. *De divortio*, p. 114. Brief reports of the ordeal in the texts of the first Council of Aachen, January 860 (second version), and the second Council of Aachen, February 860, both preserved only in later additions to Hincmar's *De divortio*, p. 120, c. 2, and p. 122, c. 16.

7. *AB* aº 858, p. 78: "Lotharius rex, cogentibus suis, uxorem quam abiecerat recipit, nec tamen ad thorum admittit, sed custodiae tradit." "His people" here probably means the great nobles at Lothar's court.

8. See above, p. 54.

9. *AB* aº 857, p. 74. The text of the oaths taken by Charles and Lothar is in *MGH Cap.* 2: pp. 293–95. They swear to support one another and confirm the provisions of earlier treaties between the brothers Charles the Bald, Lothar I, and Louis the German.

10. *AB* aº 858–859, pp. 78–80; *AF* aº 858–859, pp. 51–53. An account of the events is in Nelson, *Charles the Bald*, pp. 169–89.

11. *AB* aº 860, p. 82; Regino aº 864, p. 80.

12. Regino aº 864, p. 80; *AB* aº 862, p. 93.

13. For these children, see above, act 1, n. 5.

at divorce. Theutberga had had little time to prove her fertility and, given Lothar's aversion to her, little opportunity.[14] The decisive reason for breaking the marriage alliance probably lay in the changed balance of power. Lothar evidently considered—though perhaps rather prematurely—that the time was ripe to evict Hucbert and his kin from their position of power with the support of other people.

The First Attempt at Divorce

Divorce was an option available to the Frankish nobility. A major reason for it was the wife's adultery. If this was proved, it was not unknown for a man to kill his wife.[15] It was not possible, though, for a man to repudiate his wife for no good reason, let alone kill her. At the very least, he had to reckon with the vengeance of her family.[16] In addition the wife could bring her case before the comital or royal courts, where she could clear herself of the charge by undergoing trial by ordeal.[17] Lothar first tried to gain a divorce by a "secular" procedure, in that it was laymen who pronounced judgment. But this does not mean that there was no clerical involvement in trial by ordeal. When deciding whether to hold an ordeal priests were consulted. The priesthood supported the procedure; without a priest, the whole ritual of the ordeal was impossible, for the whole thing was carried out in a Christian, religious context.[18] What was the procedure followed by Lothar in this case, and why had these accusations been made?

14. Some modern historians give Theutberga's barrenness as the principal reason for the divorce, among them Bauer, "Rechtliche Implikationen," pp. 44–45. However, the first reference to her childlessness dates only from 866; see below, p. 151.

15. See, e.g., *De divortio*, pp. 144–45, *Ep. Nic.*, pp. 674, 677 (for these texts, see below, pp. 80, 164); Rouche, "Mariages," pp. 841–43; Kottje, "Eherechtliche Bestimmungen," p. 217.

16. An example of his in-laws' reaction to a man who sought to be rid of his wife is the case of Count Stephan of Auvergne, who had to flee from his father-in-law, Count Raymond, when he sought to divorce Raymond's daughter. See for this Hincmar's letter, discussed below, pp. 97–98, and Nelson, *Charles the Bald*, pp. 196–98.

17. Trial by ordeal features in the Germanic law codes of the Visigoths, Burgundians, Langobards, Franks, and Frisians. For records of it, see Nottarp, *Gottesurteilstudien*, pp. 50–59, and Ganshof, "Preuve," pp. 78–79, Bartlett, *Trial*, pp. 4–12; in the *Lex Salica* and the *Lex Ribuaria* the hot water test is used for unfree persons, for "*antrustiones*," as a subsidiary procedure for a "foreigner" who cannot find enough oath-helpers and when there are no witnesses or when someone is accused of giving false evidence: see *Pactus Legis Salicae* 14.2, 16.5, 53, 56, 73, 81, 112, 132, pp. 64–65, 74, 200–203, 210–14, 242–46, 251, 262, 267; *Lex Ribuaria* 35 (31).5, p. 87. For trial by ordeal in general, see Bartlett, *Trial*, Brown, "Society," and, for a concise description and clear opinion, Van Caenegem, "Reflexions."

18. Hincmar defends the procedure of trial by ordeal in *De divortio*, pp. 146–76, although he opposes the punishment prescribed by secular law for adulterous wives should they be found guilty, pp. 144–45.

Trial by Ordeal

The text of a petition sent to Hincmar by some magnates from Lothar's realm includes an account of the ordeal procedure by which Lothar
sought to rid himself of Theutberga. First, Theutberga was formally accused. Then an attempt was made to decide the case by producing witnesses or oath-helpers, men who supported the claims of one or the other
party by swearing an oath on their behalf, but this failed.[19] After that a
trial by ordeal was held, specifically an ordeal by hot water. Theutberga
did not undergo it herself, but left this extremely painful business to a
surrogate.[20] She had to pick an object out of a cauldron of boiling water.
What this object was the text does not say, but other similar cases used
one or more stones, a twig, or a ring. The latter would be tied to a string
and lowered some way into the water. The accused or his/her surrogate
then had to remove the object from the cauldron. The usual procedure
was that the injured hand would then be bandaged and sealed. Three or
four days later the bandages were removed and the hand examined.[21] In
Theutberga's case the hand was adjudged "uncooked" and she was therefore found not guilty.[22] "Uncooked" probably meant that the hand was
healing normally and the flesh had not mortified. Other accounts of trials
by ordeal relate that after an ordeal by boiling water those responsible
looked to see whether "the hand was swollen and whether blood or pus
was coming from it."[23]

Who decided on a trial by ordeal, and who determined the result? The
magnates' text says this: "The substitute for that woman underwent the ordeal of the boiling water according to the judgment of the lay nobility and
after consultation with the bishops and with the agreement of the king
himself."[24] When Hincmar describes the case he says that it took place "by
the advice of the lay nobility, with the agreement of the bishops and by royal
decree" and that Theutberga was reinstated "with the agreement of the lay

---

19. *De divortio*, p. 114.
20. Ibid.
21. For the course of events in an ordeal by boiling water, see Nottarp, *Gottesurteilstudien*, pp. 87–88, 249–50, 255–59.
22. *De divortio*, p. 114.
23. Nottarp, *Gottesurteilstudien*, pp. 87–88, the account of a case that happened in
France around 1090, "inflatans admodum et excoriatam sanieque iam carne putri effluen-
tem," and an Anglo-Saxon ritual (ninth/tenth century, in many respects strongly resem-
bling Frankish examples) in *Gesetze der Angelsachsen* 1: p. 407, *Iudicium Dei* II, c. 5–6; see
also Nottarp, *Gottesurteilstudien*, pp. 249–50.
24. *De divortio*, p. 114: "Iudicio laicorum nobilium et consultu episcoporum atque ipsius
regis consensu vicarius eiusdem feminae ad iudicium aquae ferventis exiit."

nobility and the reconciliation and blessing of the bishops."[25] Three parties were thus involved in the decision: the lay nobility resolved on a trial by ordeal, after consulting the bishops, and then they asked the king's consent. Then the trial itself took place. The text of the Lotharingian magnates tells us little of how the ordeal itself was carried out. It must, however, have been done with episcopal help. Extant descriptions of trials by ordeal reveal a ceremony directed by a priest. Numerous blessings, prayers, and instructions on procedure survive, which had to be spoken by a priest during the ceremony. The cauldron was placed in the atrium of the church. The priest blessed the spot and the cauldron using holy water, and then a mass was celebrated. The accused made his or her confession before God and the priests, doing penance and receiving communion, then swearing an oath on the gospels and on relics. The priest prayed to God for justice, and then exorcised the water in the cauldron and sprinkled the hand of the accused with holy water before it was plunged into the boiling water.[26]

Who determined the outcome? Who declared the burns healed? The text does not say precisely, but the same three parties who had decided on the ordeal were involved. The lay nobles had affirmed their assent and the bishops had reconciled the parties and pronounced a blessing. After that—not in Hincmar's version, but in that of the list of questions submitted to him—the verdict was confirmed by royal decree.[27] The lay nobles are invariably mentioned first in the decision process, but it is very clear that the bishops played a vital role when for want of witnesses a trial by ordeal was decided on.

In Theutberga's case an effort was made to secure the agreement of those involved, both in the decision to hold a trial by ordeal and in the eventual verdict. The judgment had to be accepted, or at least not contested, by all. Here it was decided that Theutberga's surrogate had survived the ordeal "uncooked," and Theutberga was therefore declared innocent. The majority of Lothar's nobles accepted this, and so he was obliged to take her back.

The Reason for the Accusation

Lothar had gambled high, and he had lost. Obviously he had personal and political motives for divorcing Theutberga, but why these outrageous

---

25. Ibid., p. 160: "Per consilium laicorum nobilium, consensu episcoporum ac decreto regio . . . non solum consensu nobilium laicorum . . . cum reconciliatione et benedictione episcoporum."

26. See the offices, blessings, and prayers in the *Formulae*, solely for ordeals by boiling water, pp. 647–48, 650–51, 658, 662, 670, 677–78, 679–80, 682–84, 688–89, 703–4. The earliest is probably to be found in the eighth-century *Sacramentarium Gellonense*, CCSL 159: pp. 484–85.

27. *De divortio*, pp. 114, 160.

accusations? The charge against Theutberga was no trivial matter: incest with her brother, and that in an unnatural manner "as men do with men."[28] It was not just a wife being accused here; the name of a whole family was being dragged through the mud. Moreover, the gravity of the charge justified Lothar's actions: a woman so besmirched was not fit to be a wife. Their marriage should never have taken place. Lothar may also have had in mind that Old Testament abominations such as incest and sodomy (Leviticus 18 and 20, Deuteronomy 27) constituted an absolute bar to marriage. This would mean that his marriage to Theutberga was invalid, which, as some church rulings also stated, left open to him the possibility of remarrying.[29]

The charges of incest and "unnatural," "male homosexual" sex may seem highly implausible in conjunction with the third charge, abortion. The text of the Lotharingian magnates, as given in Hincmar, states that Hucbert committed with his sister Theutberga the offence of "male congress between the thighs, as men are used to do with men" and that Theutberga then became pregnant and aborted the fetus.[30] Evidently, even in the ninth century pregnancy as a consequence of sexual congress "between the thighs" seemed unlikely to most people. Indeed, in his response to this list of questions Hincmar consigns this particular charge to the realms of fantasy as preposterous.[31] But did Lothar really bring all these charges? The accusation of incest, certainly,[32] and probably also that of unnatural sex,[33] but resultant pregnancy and abortion? It was in the interests of those who compiled the list of questions to make the accusation seem ridiculous and suggest that Lothar had simply made the whole thing up in order to obtain a divorce from Theutberga. But we can certainly not rule out the possibility that the accusation of incest was true and that Hucbert had indeed sexually abused his sister Theutberga. Hucbert, as is clear from other sources, was well known as a violent, aggressive, and sexually debauched individual.[34]

28. For the exact accusations in the various texts see below, n. 30, 32, and 33.

29. For the canon law arguments on this, see pp. 84–85, 105–7.

30. *De divortio*, p. 114: "Masculino concubitu inter femora, sicut solent masculi in masculos turpitudinem operari."

31. See below, p. 82.

32. The Aachen council of 862 and the episcopal letter of 861 spoke of the charge of incest, as we have seen; in *MGH Conc.* 4: p. 72, c. 3, p. 76; *Ep. Lot.* no. 2, p. 211.

33. The Aachen council of February 860 (quoted via Hincmar) accused them of incest and unnatural fornication: *De divortio*, p. 121, whereas Prudentius's *AB*, a° 860, p. 82, speaks of incest and sodomy.

34. A letter from Pope Benedict III (855–58) summarizes a long list of complaints against Hucbert, including some of a sexual nature: *Ep. Ben.*, pp. 612–13. Although the list does contain some stereotypes (see Felten, *Laienäbte*, pp. 15–32), it provides clear indications of Hucbert's reputation. Regino of Prüm and the *Annales Xantenses* take a more or less negative view of him: Regino a° 866, p. 91; *AX* a° 866, p. 23. Folcuin, *Gesta Abbatum*

Ermengarde's Family: The Marriage Alliance
Continued in the Children

Lothar's accusations against Theutberga led to open war with Hucbert. Not only did he lose a powerful ally, he also gained a powerful enemy. True, he deprived Hucbert of all his fiefs and offices, but it is indicative of Hucbert's power that Lothar was unable to oust him from his lands in Burgundy. Eventually he would go so far as to cede this territory to his brother Louis II,[35] who in turn gave it as a fief to his cousin, Conrad, who finally succeeded in disposing of Hucbert in 864.[36] Lothar could permit himself such a mighty enemy only if he could rely on support from other people. And of course the fall of a powerful counselor and his followers provided many others with a unique opportunity for promotion. Offices and fiefs became vacant, and Lothar could use these to reward his new followers. One way in which Lothar found support was by appealing to a family connection created by a previous marriage, that of his father, Lothar I, and his mother, Ermengarde. The alliance thus forged between their two families continued into the next generation. Lothar appealed to his kinsmen on his mother's side, of whom Hincmar specifically names Liutfrid, Lothar's uncle.[37]

Liutfrid's sister Ermengarde was Lothar's mother. By marrying her Lothar I had allied himself with the family of his closest adviser, Hugo, Count of Tours, the father of Ermengarde and Liutfrid. The family held numerous properties in Alsace. They were descended from Eticho, who was Duke of Alsace in the late seventh century, which is why they are known to historians as the Etichonids. Eticho's descendants held the positions of duke and count in Alsace and had interests in many religious houses, including some of their own founding (see genealogy of the Etichonids in appendix 2).[38]

Lobiensium, is the most outspoken, p. 60: "Hucberto Deo et sanctis odibili" (Hucbert, hated by God and the saints). Hincmar too takes a far from favorable view of him in the *AB* a° 862, p. 88. He is also the main advocate of having Hucbert brought before the court for his crimes against Theutberga and denying him asylum in the territory of another king: *De divortio*, p. 187.

35. *AB* a° 859, p. 82.

36. *Annales Laubacenses* and *Lobienses* a° 858, p. 15, p. 232; Regino a° 866 (incorrect dating), p. 91; *AX* a° 866, p. 23; *AB* a° 864, p. 116; Andreas of Bergamo, *Historia* c. 9, pp. 226–27.

37. *AB* a° 862, pp. 93–94.

38. Members of this family founded the monasteries of Hohenburg, Murbach, Honau, and Erstein and exercised great influence over them. They also had links with the abbeys of Weissenburg and Remiremont. Liutfrid, and his son Hugo after him, were lay abbots of Moutier-Grandval (Münster-Granfelden). Immunity for this abbey was granted them by Lothar I and confirmed by Lothar II: *D Lot.I* no. 105, p. 250, no. 106, pp. 251–53, and *D*

This alliance brought Hugo and his kinsmen yet more influence, possessions, and wealth. Hugo, now Count of Tours, together with Matfrid,
Count of Orléans, for a long time played a leading role during the reign of
Louis the Pious. The bond between Matfrid and Hugo was further
strengthened by Hugo's marriage to Matfrid's sister Ava.³⁹ Both had thrown
in their lot with Hugo's son-in-law, Lothar I, and remained loyal to him
through good times and bad. Together they traveled in Lothar's retinue to
Italy, where they acquired lands and offices and where they eventually died
in a epidemic in 836/37.⁴⁰ Hugo also established connections by marriage
with two other great families. His daughter Adelaide married Conrad,
brother of Judith, second wife of Emperor Louis the Pious, and his daughter Bertha married Gerard, Count of Paris, who as Count of Vienne would
later become the most important man in the realm of his young nephew,
the underage Charles of Provence.⁴¹

On the death of Hugo, grandfather of Lothar II, his son Liutfrid succeeded to his father's offices and fiefs in Italy. When Louis the Pious died
in 840, however, Hugo's son-in-law Lothar I demanded his share of Louis'
territories north of the Alps and received the central portion of the Carolingian empire. The center of Lothar's power shifted from Italy to the
Rhineland, and Liutfrid too returned north. He left behind the elder of
his two sons, also called Liutfrid, in his Italian possessions and took the
younger, Hugo, north with him. In 849 we find the elder Liutfrid as lay abbot of Moutier-Grandval.⁴² Meanwhile, in 844 Lothar I had sent his eldest
son, Louis II, to Italy to rule there as king.⁴³ There was thus a migration
between territories, from north to south and back again, with a kinsman,

---

Lot.II no. 28, pp. 430–31. The family's importance is evident from the numerous mentions
in Bruckner, *Regesta Alsatiae*, nos. 103, 110, 112–14, 122–24, 127, 130, 133, 134, 137, 147,
280; see also Vollmer, "Etichonen"; Wilsdorf, "Etichonides," and Wilsdorf, "Monasterium"; Borgolte, "Geschichte der Grafengewalt," pp. 4–35, Depreux, *Prosopographie*, pp.
262–64.

    39. For Matfrid, see Depreux, "Comte Matfrid"; for his marriage ties with Hugo, pp.
360–62.

    40. Hlawitschka, *Franken*, pp. 54–55; Depreux, "Comte Matfrid," pp. 368–69.

    41. Gerard's status is evident from the charters of Charles of Provence: *D Provence*, no.
1 (10 October 856), pp. 1–3, no. 5 (855–60), pp. 10–12, and no. 9 (22 December 862), pp.
18–20; see also Hincmar's letter to Gerard (October 861), in which he assured him—and
not the youthful Charles—that he had nothing to do with a possible attempt by Charles
the Bald to seize the realm of Charles of Provence: *Ep. Hinc.* no. 142, p. 115. In addition, we
know of an embassy by Gerard to Pope Nicholas I from a letter from Nicholas to Ado of
Vienne: *Ep. Nic.* pp. 312–14. Gerard of Vienne was a brother of Adalhard, seneschal to
Louis the Pious; see Werner, "Nachkommen," pp. 429–432, and the biography by Louis,
Girart, pp. 1–118.

    42. Hlawitschka, "Franken," pp. 221–26.

    43. *AB* a° 844, pp. 45–46.

often a son, always being left in one of the realms. But Liutfrid's position close to the center of power, the court of his brother-in-law Lothar I, was undermined by the marriage of the new ruler, Lothar II, to Theutberga: another counselor, Hucbert, was now closer to the king. The new alliance with the king's brother-in-law, Hucbert, pushed that with the old ally, his uncle Liutfrid, into the background.[44]

Lothar could therefore count on Liutfrid's support in ridding himself of Theutberga.[45] The second person whom Hincmar names as his support and refuge is a certain Walther.[46] On numerous occasions this trusted counselor of Lothar would carry out difficult missions and lobby on his lord's behalf. But we have no clear information on his family connections.[47]

But what had changed in the previous two years to make Lothar think that he could now dispense with Hucbert? First, he had to some extent established himself as king. Had he perhaps listened to advice from people who wanted to bring Hucbert down? There were signs that Hucbert's network of marriage alliances was beginning to fall apart. His brother Boso's marriage to Engeltrude, daughter of Count Matfrid, was on the rocks. Engeltrude found herself a new lover, Wanger, left her husband, and ran away with him. This too would end in a notorious divorce case, with which many people concerned themselves—often the same people as in Lothar's case.[48]

44. There are other instances in which new marriage alliances lead to conflict with allies from previous such alliances. The kinsmen of Hildegard, mother of Louis the Pious, lost their positions to kinsmen of his new wife, Judith, especially to her brothers, Conrad and Rudolf. Schmid, "Struktur," pp. 39–40, Hellmann, *Heiraten*, pp. 90–93. Nelson, *Charles the Bald*, pp. 176–79, is highly critical of the way in which the rivalry between these family groups is often described as a kind of factional strife. She strongly emphasizes the personal nature of these struggles for power. But even when it is a matter of individuals fighting for power, the rival connections on which they called to achieve power and influence were ties of kinship created by marriage.

45. For Liutfrid's activities as an envoy in Lothar's divorce case, see *Ep. Lot.* no. 1, pp. 209–10; *AB* a° 865, p. 117.

46. *AB* a° 862, pp. 93–94.

47. Walther went to Rome as ambassador in 860 and 866. There he has the title "comes"; *Ep. Nic.* p. 327, also *Ep. Hadr.* p. 697. His activities as a lobbyist are evident from a letter from Adventius of Metz to Theutgaud of Trier, *Ep. Lot.* no. 4, p. 215. In *D Lot.II* no. 6 (12 November 856), p. 391, he intercedes. Regarding Walther's ties of kinship, we might think—very cautiously—of some kinship with Waldrada. The first part of their names is the same, and variations on elements of names were common within kinship groups; though it is true that "Walt-" is a common element in names. So far as is known, none of our sources mentions any relationship between them.

48. This marriage must have effectively ended around 857, as witness a letter from Pope Nicholas in *AB* a° 863, p. 102, which says that she already has been separated from Boso for seven years. Hincmar's letter to Gunthar of Cologne (autumn 860) says that she had then been apart from Boso for three years, in *Ep. Hinc.*, p. 83. In practice, the case of Engeltrude and Boso has much in common with Lothar's. There are family connections— Boso is Theutberga's brother and Engeltrude is Lothar's second cousin—and religious

And finally, in the shifts in power Hucbert's brother-in-law Bivin would lose the Abbey of Gorze.[49]

At any event Hucbert had been driven from court, but Lothar had not yet succeeded in having his divorce from Theutberga publicly acknowledged, even though they no longer lived together as man and wife. As soon as he thought the time was right, he would try again.

---

authorities often discuss or pronounce upon both cases at the same time, as do Pope Nicholas in the above-mentioned letter and Hincmar of Reims in *De divortio*, see below, p. 97. See also Bougard, "En marge."

49. The last record of Bivin as abbot of Gorze is in 857. In 858 he is no longer mentioned, *Cartulaire de Gorze*, pp. 102–6. In 863 it appears that he was deprived of the abbacy by Lothar II at the request of the new bishop of Metz, Adventius (858–75), *Cartulaire de Gorze*, p. 108.

Act III

A Second Attempt at Divorce and the Involvement of Hincmar of Reims, 859–860

Louis the German's invasion of the kingdom of his brother Charles the Bald is followed in late 858 and 859 by a period of violent upheaval. New coalitions are formed, defectors have their property confiscated, kinsmen are on a war footing with one another. Everywhere discord and disunity prevail. The religious leaders, and especially the bishops, engage in feverish activity in an effort to calm the crisis. This is evident from, among other things, the comparatively large number of councils held in 859 and 860, at which the restoration of peace is the main item on the agenda.[1] In 859 they even hold two general councils, attended by dozens of bishops from the realms of Charles the Bald, Lothar II, and Charles of Provence. The bishops do not shrink from condemning those who break the peace, even when they are kings.[2] In the course of the year 860 peace returns: in June 860 the bishops' efforts are crowned with success when a treaty between the three kings, Charles the Bald, Louis the German, and Lothar II, is concluded at Coblenz.[3] One figure who plays a prominent part in this process is Hincmar, archbishop of Reims. It is Hincmar who, after the defection of Wenilo, arch-

---

1. See the list of councils in Hartmann, *Synoden*, pp. 245–59, 494; and the editions in *MGH Conc.* 3: pp. 253–89.

2. Especially the Council of Metz (28 May to 4 April 859), with an associated episcopal embassy to Louis the German, and the Council of Savonnières (14 June 859), attended by at least forty bishops and three abbots, *MGH Conc.* 3: pp. 437–44, 447–89. A letter in which the West Frankish and Lotharingian bishops invited the bishops from the realm of Louis the German to a joint council at Troyes must be dated to this time (probably spring 859), *MGH Conc.* 4: pp. 434–35; Staubach, *Herrscherbild*, pp. 168–72. For the history of the years 858–60, see Halphen, *Charlemagne*, pp. 307–25.

3. *MGH Cap.* 2: pp. 152–58; *AB* a° 860, p. 83; *AF* a° 860, pp. 54–55. Charles of Provence and Louis II of Italy are included in this treaty. Penndorf, *Problem*, p. 51, sees Lothar, not the bishops, as the force behind the Treaty of Coblenz. He was certainly closely involved in this peace initiative, but the bishops played a key role in the entire process.

bishop of Sens to Louis the German, gathers the remaining West Frankish bishops in resistance to Louis and it is also Hincmar who gains the support of the Lotharingian and Provençal episcopate. The subsequent embassy of these bishops to Louis the German is led by Hincmar, whose position reaches its apogee at the treaty of Coblenz, when he is the first to sign this treaty at the head of the entire Frankish episcopate.[4]

Meanwhile Lothar tries for a second time to divorce Theutberga, on this occasion by appealing to his bishops. On 9 January 860 four bishops and two abbots, specifically Archbishops Gunthar of Cologne[5] and Theutgaud of Trier,[6] Bishops Franco of Liège[7] and Adventius of Metz[8] and Abbots Heigil of Prüm[9] and Odelingus of Inden, together with a few other, unnamed, trusted supporters of Lothar, gather at the court in Aachen.[10] Theutberga too appears before this company. She declares, so the bishops will write in their report on the council, that she is unworthy to continue as a married woman. "Before God and his angels," she bares her heart and confesses to them "every secret relating to the rumor that had arisen." The "rumor"—as will become apparent—concerns her sexual relations with her brother. True, the "inner wound" that she "confesses" to God and the bishops was not dealt her of her own volition but

---

4. Nelson, *Charles the Bald*, pp. 180–93; Halphen, *Charlemagne*, pp. 311–25.

5. Gunthar, archbishop of Cologne (850–70), scion of a noble Frankish family and probably the fifth successive bishop of Cologne from that family; kinsman of Hilduin, archchaplain to Charles the Bald, and of Hilduin, the former abbot of St.-Denis, archchaplain to Louis the Pious and teacher of Hincmar of Reims; brother (or uncle) of Hilduin, bishop-elect of Cambrai (in 862) and Cologne (in 869) where he had exercised secular rule since as early as 866. Weinfurter and Engels, *Series Episcoporum* V, Germania I, pp. 131–37; *AB* a° 862, 866, pp. 107, 111, 126; *AX* a° 871, p. 29; Regino a° 869, pp. 98–100; letter from Gunthar, Theutgaud, and Harduic to Hincmar of Reims, in *MGH Conc.* 4: p. 133.

6. Theutgaud, archbishop of Trier (847–68), scion of a noble family with possessions and offices in the Moselle-Saar region, succeeded his uncle Hetti (814–47); brother of Grimald, abbot of St. Gall, archchancellor to Louis the German (856–58 and 860–70); related to Waldo, abbot of St. Gall, Reichenau, and St.-Denis, and thus also to the Carolingians; see Geuenich, "Beobachtungen," pp. 565–68. For Hetti, see Depreux, *Prosopographie*, pp. 244–46; for Grimald, Depreux, *Prosopographie*, pp. 221–22.

7. Franco, bishop of Liège (854/58–901): Carolingian, pupil and kinsman of Drogo, bishop of Metz. See Weinfurter, *Series Episcoporum* V, Germania I, pp. 59–60; according to Sedulius Scotus, he is a "*Karolide*," quoted in Weinfurter, pp. 59–60; see also Werner, "Nachkommen," separate genealogy.

8. Adventius, bishop of Metz (858–75), brought up in Metz by his "foster-father" Bishop Drogo (823–55), a son of Charlemagne; he also had ties of friendship with Charles the Bald; see *Ep. Lot.* no. 9, pp. 222–23.

9. Heigil (Egilo), abbot of Prüm (853–60); from his youth a friend and correspondent of Lupus, abbot of Ferrières; resigned as abbot of Prüm in 860; subsequently appointed abbot of Flavigny by Charles the Bald and later archbishop of Sens (865–71; Regino a° 853, p. 76, a° 860 p. 78; *Ex Translatione et Miraculis S. Reginae*, pp. 449–51; *D Charles le Chauve* 2: p. 325; *Ep. Nic.* to Heigil, pp. 644–46; Lupus of Ferrières, *Correspondence* 1: pp. 130, 136, 150–52, 224–28; 2: pp. 6, 22, 68).

10. *De divortio*, p. 120.

under duress, but it is in any event so terrible that she no longer feels herself worthy to share a royal or a marital bed or to marry anyone at all.[11] *The bishops and abbots allow her, as she supposedly requested, to enter a convent.*[12]

The small gathering in Aachen is clearly intended as preparation for a larger council. King Lothar's divorce case is regarded as so sensitive and so important that the bishops attending want their decision supported by others of their rank. Bishops from other realms are invited to a second council. One of the most important invitees is Hincmar, archbishop of Reims, and it is Adventius, bishop of Metz, who personally delivers the invitation to him. Hincmar receives Adventius hospitably but does not appear at the council, which is held in mid-February 860, giving all manner of excuses.[13] *Seven bishops do attend, though, from three kingdoms, those of Charles the Bald, Lothar II, and Charles of Provence, along with a large number of laymen who are again not named.*[14] *These bishops are no strangers to one another, of course; they have met before at councils in previous years.*[15] *At this council Theutberga hands over a document written at her request in which, filled with a sense of guilt, she confesses "before God and his holy angels and before the reverend bishops and the noble laymen" the shameful acts committed by Hucbert.*[16] *Those present are overcome with revulsion and pain. But then they turn to Lothar and ask him if he has perhaps put pressure on her to make a false confession. Not at all, says Lothar, he has known of this for years. But he kept silent, even after the result of the trial by ordeal, to hide the shame. But now that the evil rumor has spread far and wide, hiding it is no longer possible and the matter has to be laid before the bishops for judgment.*[17] *Theutberga too is repeatedly ques-*

---

11. For the confession of her "inner wound," see *De divortio* (second version of council text) c. 4, p. 120, and c. 3, p. 120; for her unworthiness to share a marital bed, see *De divortio* (first version), c. 6, p. 115; for the royal and marital bed, *De divortio* (second version), c. 4, p. 120.

12. *De divortio* (first version), c. 3, p. 115; (second version) c. 5 and 7, p. 120.

13. *De divortio*, pp. 130–32. Lothar and his bishops were evidently busy mustering support for their case. Another important person they tried to win to their cause was Louis, abbot of Saint-Denis and archchancellor to Charles the Bald, a first cousin of Lothar's father. Certainly it is no coincidence that on 26 January 860 the monastery of St.-Denis received a gift from Lothar. *D Lot.II.* no. 13, pp. 402–4, to St.-Denis at the request of abbot Louis.

14. *De divortio*, p. 121. Also present was Hatto, bishop of Verdun (847–70), a former oblate of St.-Germain in Auxerre, who was granted a dispensation for his consecration by the Synod of Savonnières (859); see *MGH Conc.* 3: p. 460; according to Duchesne, *Fastes* 3: p. 74, he was in charge of the abbey of Echternach, 856–64.

15. Compare the lists of participants at the two Aachen meetings with those of the councils of Metz and Savonnières (859), in *MGH Conc.* 3: pp. 438 and 462–63. Aachen, January 860, in *De divortio*, p. 120; February 860, in *De divortio*, p. 121.

16. *De divortio*, p. 121: "Deo et sanctis angelis eius ac venerabilibus episcopis sive nobilibus laicis."

17. *De divortio*, c. 16, pp. 121–22.

tioned, but continues to "persist steadfastly in her confession."[18] And after a thorough investigation the bishops decide to impose a public penance on her and send her to a convent.[19]

Lothar is now divorced from Theutberga. The matter has been resolved, or so it appears. But Hincmar of Reims seems deliberately to have contrived to stay clear of the whole affair and many, or at least some, people are not happy with the decision.[20] A number of dissatisfied individuals from Lothar's kingdom—we do not know their names, but they include laymen as well as bishops—approach bishops from other parts of the empire with a request, in the form of a list of questions, that they should evaluate the correctness of the procedure followed and the verdict pronounced.[21] One of those approached is Hincmar of Reims, who in a lengthy treatise severely criticizes the legal procedure employed. Six months later Hincmar receives a second list of questions from the same dissatisfied magnates; his answers to these questions make up the second part of his treatise.[22]

Having failed in his attempt to rid himself of Theutberga by "secular" proceedings, Lothar then tried to divorce her using an "ecclesiastical" procedure. Here a third power comes into play, alongside those of the king and the secular nobility: that of the bishops. Ignoring the outcome of the trial by ordeal, Lothar sought an episcopal decision. But would canon law allow Lothar to divorce Theutberga? And could he then remarry—for he had not the slightest intention of remaining single—and could he marry Waldrada?

One bishop in particular takes a leading role here: Hincmar, archbishop of Reims. Indeed, the lion's share of what we know of these events comes from Hincmar's treatise *De divortio*; but Hincmar is one of the members of our chorus, commenting on our cause célèbre, which means that we have to

18. *De divortio*, p. 122: "Immobilis in sua confessione perduravit."

19. *De divortio*, c. 19, p. 122. In a letter to Pope Nicholas I, probably from 861, Lothar's bishops state that they have imposed a penance on Theutberga, after she had made a public confession: *Ep. Lot.* no. 1, p. 211; see also *AB* a° 860, p. 82.

20. Who these dissatisfied individuals were cannot be precisely determined. In any case, Theutberga's most important kinsmen were deprived of their offices at that time, and the dissatisfied ones included bishops. One might think of Bishop Arnulf of Toul who is, as an important dignitary from the Lotharingian heartland, remarkably absent from Lothar's political dealings, or Harduic of Besançon, absent from all the Aachen councils. Note also that Heigil, abbot of Prüm, went over to Charles the Bald during this year, see above, n. 9.

21. *De divortio*, p. 112; on p. 114, the list of questions in the Lotharingian magnates' petition refers to Hincmar in the third person; very probably it was sent to a number of people.

22. See below, pp. 85–86.

treat him with a measure of caution.[23] He describes events from his own perspective, and we have few ways of checking on him. This, however, also provides us with a unique opportunity. By examining Hincmar's enormous work closely, and placing it in its political and scholarly context, we can in several instances observe how Hincmar, one of the most important politicians and scholars of his time, changed his arguments to fit his political position and how he adapted his sources to fit his arguments.

Here we shall consider three questions with regard to *De divortio*. First, the legal status of marriage: What, in Hincmar's eyes, constituted a lawful marriage? Under what conditions could one marry, divorce, and remarry? And how did Hincmar apply his general rules to Lothar's case? Second, the competence of the bishops: Why and on what conditions are bishops authorized to concern themselves with marriage in general, and Lothar's marriage in particular? Third, the political context: Where Lothar's case was concerned, Hincmar was not a politically neutral outsider. He had links with a number of Frankish aristocrats, including his king and overlord Charles the Bald. To what extent was Hincmar influenced by his political position in expounding his rules and in their practical application?

The Legal Status of Marriage

As we have said, *De divortio* consisted of Hincmar's answers to a series of questions. Some of these were general in nature, whereas others related specifically to aspects of Lothar's divorce case. Two questions had nothing at all to do with Lothar but concerned a different matrimonial case, that of Boso and Engeltrude.[24] In his answers, after a few introductory remarks,

---

23. Hincmar's treatise is our most important source for the two Aachen meetings mentioned above.

24. In the first three questions and answers he describes the sequence of events and parries certain below-the-belt personal attacks (of which more later). Answers 4, 5, and 23 contain general theory on marriage. Answers 6–13 and 18–22 deal much more specifically with the cases concerned, namely those of King Lothar and (in answer 22) of Boso. Answers 6–9 deal with the validity of the trial by ordeal, 10–11 with the procedure followed in Aachen, 12 with the charges of incest, sodomy, and abortion (this chapter contains an exceptional number of lengthy marginal additions, again of a general nature), 13 and 18–21 with Lothar's penance, divorce, and remarriage, 14 with oaths in general, 15–17 with sorcery, 22 with Boso's marriage, while 23 is again general in nature, about divorce on grounds of a vow of chastity. Incidentally, the text of question and answer 22 and 23 in the *capitulatio* (*De divortio*, p. 105) does not accord with their actual content—probably due to an error in copying. The entire second part of *De divortio* is explicitly casuistic, dealing mainly with competence to pronounce judgment and procedural matters. Only answer 4 refers to Lothar's marriage and answer 5 to that of Boso.

Hincmar begins with general expositions on a number of topics, including marriage, which he then applies to the *casus Lotharius*.

General Rules

The core of Hincmar's general theoretical discussion of marriage answered a composite question (answers 4 and 5) formulated as follows:

> If the offence becomes known after the marriage is contracted, how should the marriage take place, what matrimonial law should apply and how and on what grounds may they divorce? And after their divorce may the man or the woman aspire to marry again and is the judgment the same for both, whichever of them had sinned in this marriage?[25]

In short, under what conditions is one permitted to marry, divorce, and remarry?

In answer to the question of what constitutes a lawful marriage Hincmar quotes the familiar Decretal of Pseudo-Evaristus, which sets out in detail how a lawful marriage should be concluded. In doing so, however, he also adopts the decretal's internal inconsistency. A proper marriage involved the following elements: the betrothal by parents and kinsmen, the bridal gift, the blessing by the priest, the handing over of the bride by attendants, and finally a few nights spent chastely in prayer. All these elements are regarded as obligatory. At the end, however, everything is thrown wide open by requiring as compulsory elements only "of their own will" (*voluntas propria*) and "lawful vows" (*vota legitima*).[26]

Hincmar then spells out what is *not* a lawful marriage: unions with those betrothed to others, with abducted women, with unfree persons.[27] Regarding the ban on marriage with unfree women he quotes the famous decretal of Pope Leo to Bishop Rusticus of Narbonne, in which the pope lays down that a union with someone who is not free cannot be a marriage. The condition of being unfree constitutes an impediment to a valid marriage.

---

25. *De divortio*, p. 132: "Si de commisso post initum coniugium reputatur, qualiter debeat iniri coniugium qualisque lex habeatur coniugii et qualiter vel pro quibus rebus valeat separari, et si post disiunctionem utrum vir aut femina ad aliam debeat copulam adspirare vel si pari iudicio quiscumque eorum in coniugio peccans debeat iudicari." Question 5 reiterates the second part of question 4, from "qualiter vel pro quibus rebus." Here we find Hincmar splitting into two what was originally the second question ("*secundo capitulo*") put to him.

26. Ibid., p. 133, via an earlier dossier (cf. Böhringer, "Eherechtliche Traktat," p. 39), taken from: *Ps.-Isid.*, pp. 87–88. For the text, see p. 32 above. Hincmar made an error in copying: "petita legibus detur" in Pseudo-Evaristus becomes "petita legibus dotetur" in Hincmar (both in his dossier and in *De divortio*), which does not make any sense.

27. *De divortio*, pp. 133–34.

Moreover, any such union with an unfree woman, once ended, is no impediment to a subsequent marriage. The unfree woman can be manumitted and can then lawfully be married or she can be repudiated, when the man is at liberty to make a lawful marriage with a free woman.[28] In principle, there is no ban on second marriages.[29] Hincmar concludes this whole string of quotations with the remark that "in this manner marriages are concluded and lascivious relationships entered into."[30]

In answer to the question under what circumstances divorce is compulsory or permissible, Hincmar states that a couple may part in order to lead a life of chastity, "for the love of perpetual continence."[31] Their marriage is then terminated on grounds of "service to God." However, only the sexual relationship is ended. The bond between the partners themselves—in Hincmar's words, "the bond forged according to God"—is not.[32] He also explains that separation in order to live a life of chastity is permitted only if both partners desire it. By their marriage man and woman have become one flesh, and so it is not possible for one half of the union to embark on a life of abstinence while the other is left behind in the world.[33]

A second reason for divorce is adultery. Divorce on the grounds of adultery is permitted, both to husband and wife.[34] Divorce because of the infertility of either partner, however, is not. After all, Hincmar says, the fact that one is incapable of sexual congress, and thus of producing children, does not breach the bond of marital fidelity. Here Hincmar follows Augustine in quoting as an example the marriage of Joseph and Mary.[35] At the same time he answers the question whether men and women should be judged equally before the law. His answer is: yes, they should.[36] But it would be wrong to conclude from this that Hincmar was affirming the fundamental equality of men and women.[37] Quite apart from the question

28. Ibid., p. 134, Leo the Great to Rusticus of Narbonne, in Leo the Great, *Epistolae*, col. 1204; for this decretal, see above, p. 26. Hincmar makes one change to Leo's text: "cuiuslibet locus clericus" becomes "quis"; "some cleric" giving his daughter in marriage becomes a neutral "someone."

29. *De divortio*, pp. 134–35.

30. Ibid., p. 135: "Ecce quibus modis sociantur coniugia vel contubernia usurpantur."

31. *De divortio*, in answer 5, pp. 135, 140. See also the *Capitulatio ad resp. 11*, p. 102, with a slightly different text; also briefly on pp. 126, 129, 173–74, and finally at length on pp. 232–34.

32. *De divortio*, p. 126: "Propter servitutem Dei."

33. Ibid., p. 233, also pp. 129 and 173.

34. Ibid., pp. 136–37.

35. Ibid., pp. 135 and 142.

36. Ibid., pp. 136 and 143.

37. On the basis of passages like this Jane Bishop has sought to turn ninth-century bishops such as Hincmar into proto-feminists of sorts asserting the fundamental equality of men and women. Bishop, "Bishops," esp. pp. 77–84. See also McNamara and Wemple,

of just how, given the social context, people in the ninth century could have visualized such equality of the sexes, Hincmar almost immediately comes out with a different view. For he states that men should be judged not simply in the same way as women, but even more strictly. Women are, after all, the "weaker sex" and "weak vessels." Men are the "heads" and "governors" of women.[38]

Here Hincmar is attempting to restrain his hearers—men of the nobility—from ill-treating their wives, repudiating them, or simply having them murdered, on charges of adultery or for any other reason. His argument follows a line set out in Saint Paul's letter to the Ephesians, which states that a man must love his wife as his own body, because the man is to the woman as the head to the body, as Christ to the Church. Implicit in this love are the privileged position of the man and the subjection of the woman.[39] This image of the man as the head and the wife as the body is taken to considerable lengths. The man must love his wife as his own body and give the same care to both. If any part of his body is affected by cancer or decay, he must—after consulting a doctor—cure it or cut it away. Hincmar pursues this train of thought still further. If the man finds his spouse to be sinful, he must, because he loves her, correct her, and if that does not help he must repudiate her, again on the advice of the "qualified physician," the bishop, who can prescribe penance. This use of medical imagery in describing penance is not an isolated instance; it can also be found, for instance, in the Benedictine Rule.[40] Hincmar's approach to the matter of love (called by him *dilectio*) of a husband for his wife resembles here that of a Benedictine abbot for his monks. He approaches the subject with a frame of mind that is strongly influenced by his monastic background. Loving your own body means correcting and controlling it, and the same goes for a man loving his wife.

A number of the arguments adduced by Hincmar—you may not kill your slave girl, so neither may you kill your wife, or you must not covet your neighbor's wife, nor his slave, nor his cow, his sheep, his ass, or his other possessions (this from Exodus 20:17), where he finds it necessary to insist on the *essential difference* between them—point to a social context in which the

---

"Marriage," p. 103. For an analysis of the issues regarding equality of the sexes, see Heene, *Legacy*, pp. 191–266, esp. pp. 209–45; 261–66, Goetz, "Frauenbild," pp. 30–41; Demyttenaere, "Vrouw," pp. 236–61; Demyttenaere, "God" pp. 210–34.

38. *De divortio*, p. 143: "Capita et rectores sunt mulierum, fragilioris scilicet sexus et vasis infirmioris." This from a much-quoted verse: 1 Peter 3:7.

39. *De divortio*, p. 144, quoting Ephesians. 5:23–28.

40. *De divortio*, p. 144. For Hincmar's medical imagery, see Morrison, "Unum," esp. pp. 618–21, and also the reference to the *Regula Benedicti*, ed. De Vogüé, 2: p. 550–53, c. 28, with which Hincmar, as a former monk, must certainly have been familiar.

question of fundamental equality of the sexes simply does not arise. Hincmar takes pains to persuade his audience that they must love their wives and that they are not allowed to kill them. This can indeed be seen as an attempt to protect from excessive violence a group whose social status is potentially fragile, but not as a plea for sexual equality.

The third group of divorces mentioned by Hincmar are those that have occurred "for no lawful reason." These, it goes without saying, are forbidden.[41] Hincmar concludes by remarking that there are also numerous legal regulations concerning incest, which he will not address here[42] but will return to later.[43]

After a divorce on the grounds of adultery neither partner is permitted to remarry while the other is still living. Hincmar states that this applies to both the guilty and the innocent party and to both wife and husband.[44] Finally, remarriage following a divorce "for no lawful reason" is of course forbidden, given that such a divorce is itself forbidden.[45]

In sum, then, when asked what Hincmar considers to be a lawful marriage, we can give three different answers. That there can be three different answers to the same question may seem surprising, but it is entirely understandable once we analyze how Hincmar used his sources.[46] First there is the maximum option: a marriage with all the trappings, entered into in accordance with a whole series of customs such as betrothal, bridal gift, public nuptials, solemnization by a priest, and obligatory chastity once the marriage has taken place—all in accordance with the *Pseudo-Isidorian Forgeries*. Second, the scaled-down version of this, again following Pseudo-Isidore: a marriage entered into "voluntarily" and with "lawful vows" is also valid. Third, the minimum requirement: certain unions are specifically forbidden, namely the familiar list—marriages to those betrothed to other people, to abducted women, to unfree persons, and to relations. Divorce is permitted on grounds of adultery, and the rules apply equally to husband and wife. Partners are also allowed to separate in order to enter the cloister, but only by mutual agreement. In neither case is remarriage permitted during the lifetime of the partner. For this set of rules Hincmar relies on the *Collectio Dacheriana*.

41. *De divortio*, p. 137: "sine causa" and "nulla praecedente causa."
42. Ibid.
43. Ibid., pp. 194–96.
44. Ibid., pp. 136–37.
45. Ibid., p. 137.
46. For an analysis of the way Hincmar composed his treatise and his use of sources, see Heidecker, *Kerk*, pp. 100–108, 225–30; Heidecker, "Gathering."

The Arguments Applied: The Lothar Case

After his general discussion of marriage Hincmar turns to the specific questions put to him about Lothar's case. He starts by discussing the legal procedure by which Lothar had been divorced from Theutberga. Then he explains the conditions under which Lothar could be divorced from Theutberga and then be permitted to remarry, even to marry Waldrada.[47]

In these chapters Hincmar first argues for the validity of the trial by ordeal that had cleared Theutberga of the charges against her some years before.[48] Then he rejects the procedure followed at the two councils of Aachen: no plaintiff and no witnesses had been present; Theutberga acted both as a sort of plaintiff and as defendant, and that was not permitted.[49] Theutberga's secret testimony and written confession did not by themselves constitute sufficient grounds for the bishops to pronounce a public judgment.[50] The person supposed to have actually committed the crimes, namely Hucbert, was not even summoned to the hearing.[51] For the marriage of Lothar and Theutberga to be dissolved without proper reason being shown is impermissible.[52] Hincmar regards the charge of sodomy and consequent abortion as false,[53] because pregnancy as a result of sexual activity without coitus seems to him impossible: "It is unheard of in the world, nor under this heaven can it be read in the scripture of truth, that without coitus the womb of a woman receives seed and conceives and that a woman with a closed womb and unbreached maidenhead gives birth as a virgin to a live child or a miscarriage, save only the holy and blessed Virgin Mary."[54] In his view, Theutberga had been pressured into admitting the charges.[55]

Hincmar then addresses the question whether, should the charges against her be true, Theutberga could be or must be divorced from Lothar. His answer is: Yes. If Theutberga were guilty of incest, sodomy, and abortion, committed before her marriage to Lothar, this would render her unfit

47. See below, p. 85, n. 70.
48. *De divortio*, answers 6–9, pp. 146–67.
49. Ibid., answer 10, pp. 168–74.
50. Ibid., answer 11, pp. 174–76. Right at the beginning, in answer 1, Hincmar had said that Theutberga's secret confession should not have been made public, ibid., pp. 117–19.
51. Ibid., answer 12, pp. 184–85.
52. Ibid., p. 176, and in the *capitulatio* to question 11, p. 102.
53. Hincmar equates the charges of unnatural sexual relations, said by his informants to have been laid against Theutberga, with sodomy, ibid., pp. 179–82.
54. Ibid., p. 182: "A seculo enim non est auditum nec de sub isto caelo in scriptura veritatis est lectum, ut vulva femine sine coitu semen susceperit atque conceperit et clauso utero et inaperta vulva seu integra carne vivum vel abortivum peperit, excepta sola singulariter beata et benedicta virgine Maria."
55. Ibid., p. 184.

for any conjugal union. Here Hincmar refers primarily to laws from the Old Testament books of Leviticus and Deuteronomy, which punish "abominable" sins, such as incest and sodomy, with death.[56] In doing so he has to resolve a problem arising from his Old Testament quotations. Hincmar states, following Augustine, that the death penalty from the "old law" (the Old Testament) was changed in "the Church" to the sentence of excommunication.[57] People who have committed grave sexual offenses such as incest, sodomy, other "irrational fornication," or abortion are banned from normal Christian social life till they have mended their ways and done penance for their sins. The consequence of this is that they are forbidden to marry. Hincmar concludes that if Theutberga were convicted of abortion, sodomy, and incest by the correct procedure she would then be ineligible to marry anyone at all.[58] But he had just maintained that the procedure followed was *not* correct.

Another question put to Hincmar was whether Lothar ought to do penance because he had supposedly committed adultery with a concubine after he had heard the charges against Theutberga and been forbidden to have carnal relations with her.[59] Here too Hincmar's answer is in the affirmative, that Lothar must do penance for adultery. Theutberga had been joined to him as his lawful wife, and since this marriage had not been lawfully dissolved any carnal intercourse with someone else constituted adultery, for which he must do penance.[60] Hincmar's argument runs as follows: Theutberga was Lothar's lawful wife. She had been "lawfully betrothed to him, provided with a bridal gift and honored with a public wedding." Here Hincmar deploys a number of elements from the decretals of Pope Leo and Pseudo-Evaristus that featured so prominently in his general discussion. He has formulated a set of three prerequisites for lawful marriage that he will use again and again. All three are essentially secular actions: betrothal, bridal gift, and wedding.[61] Here Hincmar uses this trio specifically to prove that Lothar and Theutberga had been lawfully married; thus, it was not his

---

56. Ibid., pp. 177–81.
57. Ibid., p. 194.
58. Ibid., pp. 194–96.
59. Ibid., p. 196.
60. Ibid.
61. Ibid., p. 197: "Legaliter desponsatam, dotatam et publicis nuptiis honoratam" See also ibid., p. 205 (referring to a marriage in the diocese of one of Hincmar's suffragans): "Post desponsationem et dotis titulum ac nuptiarum celebritatem"; p. 222, with a reference to Leo's decretal: "Post desponsationem legitime dotari et publicis honestari nuptiis."; p. 231 (on the marriage of Boso and Engeltrude): "Legaliter desponsata, legitime dotata, publicis nuptiis honestata." For the decretals of Pseudo-Evaristus and Leo referred to here, see above, pp. 26, 32.

purpose here to establish formal conditions for marriage in general. The most important element in concluding a marriage is probably the betrothal: a number of remarks made in passing by Hincmar put the betrothed and the married woman on a par with each other,[62] and his replacement of the term "emancipation" in Pope Leo's decretal by "betrothal" also points in this direction.[63] Hincmar then states that, so long as it had not been proved that their marriage should not have taken place or that one of them had died, this was indeed adultery. And for adultery one had to do penance.[64]

Toward the end of the first part of *De divortio* Hincmar answers the question of whether Lothar is allowed to take a new wife. Hincmar says that if the charges against Theutberga are untrue she can obviously be reunited with her husband.[65] Should she be found guilty, then Lothar can remarry.[66] First, though, he must do penance for adultery with his concubine. In this case remarriage is permitted, yes, but no more than that: it is tolerated.[67] Lothar can even marry his "concubine," with whom he had previously committed adultery.[68] The reasoning is that remarriage is possible when the marriage has been dissolved by the death of one of the partners, and this could be death either of the body or of the soul. An incestuous woman is equated to one dead in soul. A further striking point is that the union of Lothar and Theutberga is here branded as incest, even though they are not related either by blood or marriage:

> This is clearly shown by the testimonies of the Scriptures and the pronouncements of the saints, that he may marry, should he so wish, a concubine with whom he is said to have committed adultery, naturally on condition that his lawful wedded wife either was found innocent, but dead in body, or that she was found dead in soul by reason of it being legally proved that this relationship with her must be adjudged incest and no marriage even in name.[69]

---

62. *De divortio*, p. 134: "'Joseph, son of David, do not fear to accept Mary as your wife,' i.e., your betrothed" ("'Joseph, fili David, noli timere accipere Mariam conjugem tuam,' id est desponsatam") (Matthew 1:20). The last three words are Hincmar's addition, but accord with a tradition that goes back to Augustine (for this passage in Augustine see Philip Reynolds, *Marriage*, p. 326). There then follow the *canones* on "sponsae"; also *De divortio*, p. 183; the distinction is between the periods prior to the betrothal and after the union with her husband.

63. Something similar also appears in c. 12 of the Council of Mainz (852). See above, pp. 26–27.

64. *De divortio*, pp. 197–203.

65. Ibid., chapter 18, pp. 217–18.

66. Ibid., answer 18, pp. 218–19, in the *capitulatio*, p. 104.

67. Ibid., answer 20, pp. 219–20 and 104.

68. Ibid., answer 21, pp. 220–26; summarized in the *capitulatio*, pp. 104–5.

69. Ibid., p. 223: "His scripturarum testimoniis atque sanctorum dictis manifestatur, quomodo concubinam, cum qua adulterasse dicitur, si voluerit, in coniugium sibi sociare

This argument is in line with that found in Leviticus, where it was stated that the mandatory penalty for anyone guilty of incest and sodomy was death. Hincmar, however, had equated this punishment (following Augustine) with excommunication, although the status of the convicted individual was still clearly that of a dead person. In that case remarriage with a concubine is permitted. Although this can be tolerated, it is certainly not honorable. At most, it is allowed because it signifies a transition from a bad situation, that of living with a concubine, to a better one, the elevating of that concubine to a wife.[70] Hincmar does stress that Theutberga must first have been found guilty by a correct legal procedure, "according to a lawful judgment by illustrious men and a priestly decision,"[71] and that Lothar must first have done penance.[72] Should he not do so, he could be terribly punished in his descendants. Hincmar confronts him with the fate of King David, who lost a son born of a similar relationship.[73]

The second series of questions in *De divortio*, which Hincmar received six months later, has little to do with the marriage as such. Only one question relates directly to the marriage of Lothar and Theutberga: If Lothar cannot marry another woman, nor keep his present concubine, is Theutberga obliged to return to him whether she wants to or not?[74] Some months have passed since Hincmar responded to the first series of questions, and he clearly assumes that the charges against Theutberga have not been substantiated. Thus, when mentioning adultery as a reason for divorce, he does not consider the possibility of Theutberga's adultery, but only the adultery of Lothar. By now Lothar has become the sole guilty party. He recapitulates what, in his view, are the possible grounds for divorce in this case: namely adultery—by which he means Lothar's adultery with his concubine—and a vow of sexual abstinence. Adultery could lead to a total divorce; in abstinence the conjugal bond between the partners continued to exist. Hincmar says that after a divorce due to adultery the partners should be reconciled with each other, but that this must not be forced upon them.[75]

---

praevaleat, videlicet si aut uxor legaliter accepta et innoxia erga illum inventa mortua fuerit corpore vel si inventa fuerit anima adeo mortua, ut ipsius cum ea copula incestus et nullo coniugii nomine deputandus legaliter comprobetur."

70. Ibid., pp. 221–22, referring to Leo's decretal regarding the (unfree) concubine. Devisse, *Hincmar Archevêque* 1: p. 409, reaches—with no reasoning that can be substantiated—the opposite conclusion, namely that according to Hincmar's ruling Lothar could *not* marry Waldrada.

71. *De divortio*, pp. 224–25: "legali virorum inlustrium iudicio et sacerdotali decreto."

72. Ibid., p. 226.

73. Ibid.

74. Ibid., part 2, question 4, p. 242.

75. Ibid., part 2, answer 4, pp. 242–44.

Hincmar no longer mentions the possibility of remarriage. In Hincmar's view only two courses are now open to Lothar: lifelong abstinence or reconciliation with Theutberga.

———————

To sum up: Hincmar applies different rules for a lawful marriage in different places. First, there is the maximum option, marriage with all the trappings. He puts great emphasis on the blessing of the new couple. (From this, among other things, he will derive the authority of priests to intervene in divorce cases.) But such a marriage, in line with the Pseudo-Evaristus decretal, is an ideal to be aimed at; moreover, as we have seen, it is self-contradictory. When Hincmar wants to check whether a marriage is lawful, he looks to see whether a betrothal has taken place, a bridal gift been provided, and a wedding held. In such cases he says nothing of a nuptial blessing. The key element here is the betrothal. Hincmar also makes clear what marriages are not lawful: the familiar proscribed unions with unfree persons, with relations, with abducted women, and with those betrothed to others. To these Hincmar adds one further category: marriage to anyone contaminated by incest, sodomy, or abortion is also forbidden.[76]

Hincmar's rules on divorce are familiar. Divorce is permitted after adultery and, by mutual consent, in the event of a vow of chastity. And Hincmar is emphatic that these rules apply to both men and women. In both cases remarriage is forbidden while the partner is still alive. But when the partner is dead—either in body or in soul—it is possible to remarry.

The Powers of the Bishops

In *De divortio* Hincmar sets out how a marriage should be made and broken according to religious rules, by religious authorities. Here we must think in the first place of the bishops. And this obviously raises the issue of the relationship between religious and secular laws and between religious and secular authorities. Marriage, after all, was also the concern of secular law and secular judges. The problem became even more acute when the marriage in question was that of the secular authority par excellence, the king himself.

What is Hincmar's position on the question of why and under what conditions bishops can concern themselves with marriages in general, and with King Lothar's marriage in particular?

———————

76. Lifelong penance for abortion can also be found in, for instance, c. 21 of the Council of Mainz (847), in *MGH Conc.* 3: pp. 171–72.

Hincmar addresses the general issue of jurisdiction in two ways. First, in the legal approach, he explains the relationship between secular and religious laws as they relate to matrimonial cases in general, and describes the functions of secular and religious judges in such cases. Second, he argues for priestly involvement on the grounds of the priest's liturgical function. And in the particular case of King Lothar's marriage a further problem arises: the relationship between the king and the bishops.

The Relationship between Religious and Secular Laws

At first glance, in some parts of *De divortio* Hincmar appears to be saying that it is for secular judges to judge their peers: married laymen must rule on marriages. It is the duty of the secular judges to ascertain the true facts of what happened and then pronounce a just judgment. Only then, when the accused has been found guilty, may the bishops set a penance.[77] To illustrate this Hincmar quotes the example of the Diet and General Synod of Attigny (822), where a case between a noble couple, Northilde and Agimbert, was judged by laymen. Emperor Louis the Pious decided to refer the case to the bishops. They, however, referred it back to the married laymen, who were more familiar with cases of this kind.[78] "The bishops' discretion pleased the nobles," says Hincmar, "because judgment over their wives was not taken from them and there was no infringement of the secular laws by the episcopal order."[79] But these are ideal cases, showing how things ought to be. If all goes well, if there is no conflict between the two laws and their courts, if they both come to the same decision, then naturally there is no problem. But what happens when the secular court makes a decision that the religious judges disagree with? Of course secular laws must be obeyed, Hincmar says repeatedly,[80] but they must be in accordance with "*christianitas*."[81] There is a hierarchical difference between the two types of law. There are higher laws than the secular ones, namely what Hincmar terms "the divine and apostolic laws," by which he evidently means Christian rules drawn from the Bible, council rulings, papal decretals, and patristic writings. To illustrate the hierarchical relationship between secular and religious rules Hincmar uses the image of God as the Judge who on the Day of Judgment

77. *De divortio*, pp. 123, 139, 141. From this, Daudet, *Études*, pp. 94–122, wrongly concludes that Hincmar gives precedence to the secular court over the religious, where proceedings before the secular court have commenced.

78. *De divortio*, pp. 141–42.

79. Ibid., p. 142: "Nobilibus autem laicis sacerdotalis discretio placuit, quia de suis coniugibus eis non tollebatur iudicium nec a sacerdotali ordine inferebatur legibus civilibus praeiudicium."

80. Ibid., pp. 137, 141, 176.

81. Ibid., pp. 145, 146, 183, 228.

pronounces judgment on mortal men. "And then," Hincmar writes, "you will not be judged according to the laws of the Romans, the Franks, or the Burgundians, but according to the divine and apostolic laws."[82] What it comes down to is this: secular laws have to be tested against divine and apostolic laws. And this is why Hincmar fulminates against men who, pleading secular law, put their wives to death for adultery. In his view these secular laws are contrary to divine and apostolic law and therefore are not to be applied in such cases.[83]

The bishop has to answer to God on the Day of Judgment for the behavior of the flock entrusted to him. That means that he must keep a close eye on the beliefs and morals of his sheep.[84] In principle this supervision could extend to almost any area, depending on how broadly matters of faith and morality were defined. One important way of punishing those who offended against rules of faith and morality was penance. By imposing penance a bishop cleansed the offender of his sins.[85] At the same time the bishop controlled the behavior of the offender, who was forbidden to perform certain acts so long as he was in a state of penance. In serious cases a bishop could banish someone from normal society as a public penitent. And once the penance was completed it was also the bishop's task to receive him back into the community.[86]

The Liturgical Role of the Priest and the Powers of the King

Another argument Hincmar advances to support the view that a priest must be involved in matrimonial issues relates to the priest's liturgical role as intermediary between God and mankind. Hincmar links the priest's blessing of a marriage with the authority to judge it. Marriage was instituted by God in Paradise through the blessing he gave to Adam and his wife in the words "increase and multiply" (Genesis 1:28). This blessing has, so says Hincmar, been continued down to the present day by "the vicars of Christ and the successors of the apostles," that is, the bishops, who bestow it on the pious faithful. Therefore, those who have been joined together by the episcopal office (*ministerium sacerdotale*) cannot be parted without the knowledge of the bishop.[87] Hincmar concludes that "we have given the laws, which decree that married people must be divorced because of the love of

82. Ibid., p. 145: "Sciant se in die iudicii nec Romanis nec Salicis nec Gundobadis, sed divinis et apostolicis legibus iudicandos."
83. Ibid.
84. Ibid., pp. 111, 171.
85. Ibid., pp. 197–203 and pp. 250–51 on penance.
86. Ibid., p. 198.
87. Ibid., pp. 138–39. On the institution of the law of marriage by God in Paradise, see also pp. 229–30, and on the priestly blessing derived from it, see p. 236; briefly, without lengthy argumentation: pp. 136 and 137.

God or the admission of sin, and this must be with the knowledge of the priest, since from him they received the blessing to enter the state of matrimony." In short, the priest blessed the marriage, and so it cannot be dissolved without his cooperation.[88] Hincmar claimed an authoritative text as the basis for this statement, but contrary to his customary procedure he did not actually name his source: "Further, an authority states that lawfully contracted marriages that are dissolved in whatsoever manner may not be severed without the knowledge of the priest and without lawful judgment."[89] This "authority" serves as the main support to the claim for priestly involvement in divorce, so it is of extraordinary importance to Hincmar. Alas, he did not manage to find the quote, which proved to be nonexistent. In other sources we have seen that the blessing of the bride or of the couple is intended to ensure the birth of numerous and healthy offspring. With Hincmar, however, this blessing acquires a totally different purpose: it serves as a legal argument to support the bishop's authority.

It goes without saying that these general rules also apply to Lothar's case. But this case is special, because it concerns a king, someone who by virtue of his position is himself a judge. The function of a Christian king closely resembles that of a bishop, and it is the duty of a Christian king to correct the behavior of his subjects. He has received this authority from God, and must answer for it to God on the Day of Judgment. The rite for the anointing of kings is modeled on that for bishops.[90] Here there is clearly a possible conflict between the powers of the bishop and those of the king. Can the bishop sit in judgment on the king? And, if so, why and how?

For all the similarities, there are also differences between king and bishop, which Hincmar sets out clearly. There is a hierarchical difference between the two because of the bishop's greater responsibility. The bishop's authority is superior because his responsibility is greater, because at the Day of Judgment he has to answer to God for the spiritual welfare of his entire flock, including the king.[91]

88. Ibid., p. 140: "Haec ideo dicta sint, cur leges posuimus, ut coniugati sive amore Dei sive admissione peccati cum sacerdotali conscientia separentur, unde benedictionem ineundi acceperunt coniugium."

89. Ibid., p. 136: "Deinde auctoritas sequitur ut, quocumque modo legitime inita coniugia separentur, non sine sacerdotali conscientia et absque legali iudicio debeant separari." This accords with the rulings of the Councils of Rome of 826 and 853, but Hincmar does not confine himself to separations on grounds of vows of chastity but extends priestly authority to all divorces. See above, p. 24. He is a strong adherent of extreme views on the application of the *conscientia episcopi.*

90. *De divortio*, pp. 110, 188, 189. See also Congar, *Ecclésiologie*, pp. 292–303; Morrison, *Two Kingdoms*, pp. 263–64; Nelson, "Kingship, Law."

91. *De divortio*, pp. 111, 247.

As part of his responsibility for spiritual well-being a bishop imposes penance, even on a king.[92] It is a bishop's duty to judge and correct the sins of his flock, even when the sinner is a king—or, more than that, *precisely* when the sinner is a king. A king acts as an exemplar. His misconduct can lead others into bad ways. If he is contaminated by sin there is a considerable danger of the contagion spreading to his subjects. Hincmar says that it is vital for a king to correct himself. Then he is a good king, and as the fount of law he stands above the law. If he does not do so, then he is subject to the law and must be corrected to prevent further contamination.[93]

This at once raises the issue of procedure, for exactly how should one judge a king? Hincmar has a strong preference for having important matters judged by a general council, for in his view general councils have the greatest authority and are the best sources of justice. He applies the passage in the Bible where Christ says to the apostles "where two or three are gathered together in my name, there am I in the midst of them" (Matthew 18:20) to general episcopal councils.[94] When bishops assembled in council reach a judgment unanimously and in accordance with the canons of previous councils and the decretals of the popes, then it is not only the assembled bishops that do so but all their predecessors with them. They are then assembled in God's name and in His presence.[95] And for this reason, according to Hincmar, Lothar's case must be judged at a general council attended by the bishops of all the Carolingian kingdoms. More precisely, it was a matter that concerned the whole Carolingian empire, for Hincmar still regarded that as a single unit "according to God's will gathered into one hand" by the ancestors of the present Frankish kings. This unit still existed, despite the subsequent partitions. It was still one realm, which was at the same time one Church, ruled by "one government, as though by one man and one ruler."[96] And within this unit, at once realm and Church, supreme power lay with the general episcopal councils. It was for them to rule on Lothar's case, because it was a matter that affected everyone. After all, it concerned the marriage of a king and a queen, and if this case was not resolved correctly the spiritual welfare of everyone in the entire realm would be in peril. If they "did not continue

92. Ibid., pp. 201–3, 247, 248–49; see also De Jong, "Power."
93. *De divortio*, pp. 246–58, and the conclusion, pp. 258–61.
94. Ibid., p. 240. For the authority of the bishops as a body, see ibid., pp. 239–41.
95. Congar, *Ecclésiologie*, pp. 133–35, 170–71; Sieben, "Konzilien."
96. *De divortio*, p. 187: "Sicut unus homo et unus rector in uno regimine esse debent, dividi nullatenus debent."

steadfastly in the true faith and good works in the unity of the Christian church," they would all be lost.[97]

This idea of the whole Carolingian empire and the Church as one unit, for which the bishops assembled in council bore supreme responsibility, was nothing new. We find it clearly expressed at several councils from the years 858–60 in which Hincmar played a leading role. And the bishops were able to make good their pretensions, at least for a time. They succeeded in bringing about a reconciliation between the various Carolingian kings, who after Louis the German's incursion into the realm of Charles the Bald had been for some years in a state of cold war with each other.[98] One notable point, however, is that Hincmar now proposed that the general council to rule on the case of Lothar's marriage should be held in consultation with the bishop of Rome. After all, he said, "the Church of Rome is the mother of all churches."[99]

———————

HINCMAR has a very clear conception of the bishops' competence to judge in matrimonial cases. His principal arguments are, first, legal: a bishop's authority is greater than that of a secular judge, because his responsibility is greater. He is, after all, answerable to God for the spiritual welfare of his flock. A bishop must correct that flock's errors of belief and morality by imposing penance on them. And if his sheep do not obey, he must banish them from the flock. Second, the priests have a monopoly on the liturgical function. Because marriage was instituted by God, says Hincmar, it must be blessed by a priest; and because a priestly blessing cannot be undone by a layman, this means that the marriage cannot be ended without a priestly judgment.

---

97. Ibid., pp. 107–8: "Qui fide recta et bonis operibus in unitate sanctae ecclesiae non permanserit." Also, pp. 124–25, 130, 236–42, see also the quotation in the introduction, p. 5 above, *De divortio*, p. 236.

98. See Council of Quierzy (858), in *MGH Conc.* 3: pp. 408–27, esp. pp. 424–27; Metz (859), in ibid., pp. 438–44, esp. p. 438, opening speech of the assembled bishops; ibid., p. 442: c. 9, to Louis the German; ibid., p. 444: Louis the German's answer to the envoys of this council. A letter from Lothar's and Charles's bishops to those of Louis the German, in *MGH Conc.* 4, p. 44. Council of Savonnières (859), in *MGH Conc.* 3: pp. 458–88, esp. pp. 458–59, c. 2, and Charles the Bald's *libellus proclamationis* for this council, *MGH Conc.* 3, p. 465, c. 3; Council of Tusey (860), in *MGH Conc.* 4, pp. 123–24, esp. the synodal letter, pp. 223–24. See also Leupen, *Bisschoppen*, p. 18, and Leupen, "Ecclesia."

99. *De divortio*, p. 107: "Sancta Romana ecclesia ut omnium ecclesiarum mater et magistra." The recommendation to consult the bishop of Rome in this matter already appears in Hincmar's letter to Adventius of January/February 860, which he included in *De divortio*, p. 132.

This far-reaching competence to judge is not restricted to judging the ordinary members of the flock, but also extends to anointed rulers of a sacral character, who have received their power from God. For their spiritual welfare too the bishops are responsible, and their conduct too the bishops must correct by means of penance. Cases involving kings are far weightier, even, than those of the common sheep. For a king's wrongful behavior can plunge the whole empire, all of Christendom—which Hincmar regarded as a single entity—into ruin. Therefore, such cases had to be judged by the highest power in that Christendom, in that empire: a general episcopal council, at which the bishops, in accordance with the canons of their predecessors, unanimously, with God in their midst, restored the proper order of things.

Hincmar's Rules in Their Political Context

In *De divortio* Hincmar set out the rules for marriage, divorce, and remarriage and explained where the authority to judge such matters lay. In expounding these rules and in their practical application, however, how far was Hincmar influenced by his political position? We shall compare Hincmar's opinions on matrimonial cases in different political situations. How did his reactions in Lothar's divorce case change with changing political circumstances relating to that case? Did his reactions in other marital cases differ from those in Lothar's case, and to what extent did he trim his rules and his intervention to the political context?

Hincmar and Lothar's Divorce

Hincmar's involvement in the case began on 25 January 860. On that day he received two important visitors: the bishop of Laon, also called Hincmar and, not coincidentally, his nephew, and the bishop of Metz, Adventius. They had come to discuss with him a highly sensitive, secret matter concerning Lothar and Theutberga.[100] Adventius obviously told Hincmar about the first assembly of bishops held in Aachen in January 860 and probably gave Hincmar a report of this council to read.[101] At this meeting Theutberga had appeared before the assembled bishops. She asked permission to enter a convent, because she was not fit for marriage, but refused to explain the true nature of the events that made her unfit to be a wife:

---

100. Ibid., p. 130.

101. Hincmar included the text of this council (first version) in *De divortio*, pp. 115–16. He says that in their discussion Adventius did not tell him the secret matter mentioned in this report, ibid., p. 130.

"I acknowledge," she said, "and I know of myself, that I am not worthy to continue in marital union. And on this I now give you the testimony of Bishop Gunthar here present, to whom I have confessed it; he knows that I am not worthy." And then she suddenly turned to the bishop and said imploringly: "I ask you," she said, "bishop, that in the way you know best you make your brothers understand that it is as I have testified of myself."[102]

With this she relinquished the floor to her confessor Gunthar, the principal church dignitary in Lothar's realm.[103] Gunthar then related to those present the sins Theutberga had confided to him in her confession.[104] But those who, like Hincmar, read the reports of this council still did not know what those sins were; they were not specified in either of the two versions of the report.[105]

It seems that Hincmar was feeling ill during his conversation with Adventius.[106] Indeed, he was quite often plagued by gout and chronic stomach trouble.[107] A note he sent to Adventius the day after their conversation shows that he was far from happy with what he had said at the time. Evidently Hincmar had told Adventius that the matter could best be dealt with at a general council, at which Hincmar himself or representatives of the West Frankish episcopate should be present. In his note he now tried to avoid becoming involved in this sensitive matter that Adventius had come to discuss with him. Hincmar offered his apologies, but he was not well and would first have to study this complicated case thoroughly and then consult with his suffragans, all of which would take time.... [108] Something had obviously dawned on Hincmar. Surely this secret matter that Adventius had mentioned to Hincmar couldn't refer to the old charges against Theutberga, of which the trial by ordeal had cleared her two years

102. Ibid., p. 115, c. 6: "'Recognosco,' inquit, 'et de me ipsa scio, quia non sum digna in coniugali copula permanere. Et inde vobis testem adhibeo praesentem episcopum Guntharium, cui ego confessa fui; ipse enim novit, quia ego non sum digna.' Quae etiam mox se vertens ad ipsum episcopum implorando aiebat: 'Rogo,' inquit, 'episcope, ut istos tuos confratres, sicut melius scis, intellegere facias, quia ita est, sicuti de me testimonium perhibui.'"

103. Regino regarded Gunthar as the orchestrator of these religious divorce proceedings, a° 864, pp. 80–81. It is certainly clear from the council reports that Gunthar played the lead role. He was the first bishop to speak and also the first to pronounce the verdict. *De divortio*, p. 115, c. 6, 8; p. 120, c. 4.

104. Ibid., p. 116, c. 8.

105. Ibid., pp. 115–16 (first version), pp. 119–20 (second version).

106. Ibid., p. 130.

107. For Hincmar's health, see Devisse, *Hincmar Archevêque* 2: pp. 1104–5; Schrörs, *Hinkmar*, pp. 470–71.

108. *De divortio*, pp. 130–32; there then follow Hincmar's excuses for his and his representatives' absence from this general synod.

before? There was no need to make a mystery of that, everyone knew about it.[109]

Hincmar's initial reaction to the report of the first Aachen council incriminating Theutberga had evidently been sympathetic, though later, when writing *De divortio*, he wanted little more to do with the matter. Probably he had even promised his support for a general council to rule on Lothar's case. Soon after, though, he realized what a hornet's nest he was getting into and tried to wriggle out of the business. There was every reason to take a sympathetic stance, given the political situation at the time. Relations between Charles the Bald and Lothar were good: both of them were opposed to Louis the German, and relations between the bishops of their two realms were excellent. They met each other frequently at councils and sent joint embassies to Louis the German. The presence of two West Frankish bishops, Hildegar of Meaux and Wenilo of Rouen, at the second Aachen council fits with this political climate. Hincmar too was on good terms with Lothar. In his response he did his best not to cause him offense and was lavish in his excuses and pretexts for not attending the second Aachen council.[110]

Hincmar advised Adventius to have the case decided by a general council in which the bishop of Rome, the pope, should also be involved. The calling of this general council was entirely in line with what we have seen of Hincmar's views. He had a broad theological argument for consulting the pope: Rome was the mother of all churches.[111] But Hincmar also reminded Adventius of a very practical consideration, one that went to the heart of the problem of the conflicting powers of bishop and king. Adventius should proceed with extreme caution if he approached the bishop of Rome in Lothar's case. He should weigh carefully what he said, for if at all possible he must avoid offending his lord.[112] It was easy enough to claim authority, but these bishops also had other loyalties that were important to them. They had an obligation of loyalty to their king, their lord, their "senior," by whom they had been appointed and whose realm they had a duty to protect. At councils Hincmar and his fellow bishops might well claim the authority to judge kings, but when doing so was politically inopportune they were still likely to hesitate—as we see here.

Despite this, Hincmar did become involved with the case again some months later when he received the aforementioned list of questions from

---

109. Ibid., p. 130.
110. Ibid., p. 131.
111. See above, p. 91.
112. *De divortio*, pp. 1, 32.

dissatisfied Lotharingian bishops and laymen. He could not ignore this, for two reasons. First, the story had been put about that Hincmar had endorsed the decisions of the second Aachen council by sending as his representatives his fellow bishops Hildegar of Meaux and Wenilo of Rouen. Furthermore, he supposedly had given his verbal approval to the way the Lotharingian bishops were handling the affair and later confirmed it in writing in a letter to Adventius of Metz.[113] In the third chapter of *De divortio* Hincmar denies both allegations, and as proof he includes copies of his two letters to Adventius.[114] A second thorny issue was the procedure followed. Theutberga had been convicted on the basis of a published written admission of guilt. This was the same procedure that had been used to condemn and remove Hincmar's predecessor, Bishop Ebo of Reims. In their question to Hincmar the Lotharingian notables explicitly and provocatively make this connection: "Is it permissible, just as with the secret confession of the former Bishop Ebo, to judge the arguments of this secret case using the confession of the aforesaid woman?"[115] This put Hincmar in a difficult position, for if he simply rejected this procedure he would at the same time jeopardize the legality of his succession to the episcopal see of Reims. He thus had to explain that the dismissal of a bishop and the repudiation of a wife were two essentially different things that required quite different procedures.[116] This meant that Hincmar could no longer stand aloof. He had to take sides, and he sided against Lothar's divorce plans as put forward at Aachen.

In the first part of *De divortio* Hincmar opposes the condemnation of Theutberga and refers the case to a general council. To a certain extent he agrees with the arguments of the Lotharingian bishops, saying that, should the charges be proved, Lothar would indeed have to divorce Theutberga, and could then marry Waldrada. However, Theutberga's guilt was not proved. Six months later, when Hincmar wrote the second part of *De divortio*, his tone changed. In the first place, not everyone in Lothar's realm was happy with his response. Some of Lothar's supporters evidently countered by maintaining that bishops had no right to judge a king—and certainly the bishops of another king could not do so. Their reaction is expressed in *De divortio* as follows: "A king is subject to nobody's laws and judgments save to those of God, who appointed him as king in the realm

113. Ibid. , pp. 114, 129.
114. Ibid., question and answer 3, pp. 129–32.
115. Ibid., p. 125: "Quoniam ad instar secretae confessionis quondam Ebonis episcopi de argumentis huius cause latentis ex confessione praefatae femine debeat iudicari." Also p. 114.
116. Ibid., question and answer 2, pp. 125–29.

which his father bequeathed to him. . . . What he does and how he rules comes about by divine ordinance, as it is written: 'The king's heart is in the hand of the Lord; he turneth it whithersoever he will' " (Proverbs 21:1).[117] This is a clear statement justifying royal authority, in this case that of Lothar. We cannot, however, treat it as a verbatim record of what Lothar's supporters actually said. We have it thirdhand, via two intermediaries who were anything but well disposed to Lothar's marriage policy. It was recorded by Hincmar, and he had it from the opponents of Lothar's divorce who had sent him the second list of questions. It was very much in their interest to render the pronouncements of Lothar's supporters in an exaggerated form and so provoke a vigorous counterreaction from Hincmar. Certainly Lothar's supporters would have defended their king, and very likely they had recourse to the above biblical quotation, but it is questionable whether they put it quite so bluntly.[118]

In any event, Hincmar reacted as though he had been stung by a hornet: "This is not the voice of a true Christian but of a blasphemer filled with a devilish spirit."[119] A king is indeed not subject to the law, Hincmar says, if he rules faultlessly and if he corrects himself, his own thoughts and actions, in a proper way. But if he does not do this and sins, he comes under the law and must be corrected by the bishops.[120]

Moreover, the relationship between Charles the Bald and Lothar started to change dramatically toward the end of the year 860. Lothar distrusted Charles and had made an alliance with Louis the German.[121] Hincmar's outburst against Lothar and his bishops fitted the changed political situation. He no longer proceeded from the hypothetical possibility that Theutberga was guilty. His basic assumption now was that Lothar was guilty, and specifically of adultery.[122] On top of this, Hincmar now devoted part of his treatise to the subject of the bad king who must be judged for his sins by the bishops.[123]

---

117. *De divortio*, p. 246: "Cor regis in manu Dei, quocumque voluerit, vertet illud" (Proverbs 21:1).

118. Anton, "Synoden," p. 101, and Anton, *Fürstenspiegel*, pp. 357–62, goes too far when, based mainly on this passage, he attributes to the Lotharingian bishops a "theocratic" ideology demanding absolute, God-willed powers for the king. He calls Lothar's supporters "Hofabsolutisten" (court absolutists). Kern, *Gottesgnadentum*, pp. 204, 358–59, does see the distortion of this passage in Hincmar, but draws no implications from it as to the content of these utterances, which he describes as "Hoftheorie" (court theory). For writings on royal powers by Lothar's bishops, see below, pp. 128–30.

119. *De divortio*, p. 247: "Haec vox non est catholici Christiani, sed nimium blasphemi et spiritu diabolico pleni."

120. See above pp. 89–91.

121. *AB* a° 860, pp. 83–84, without mentioning a reason for this.

122. See above, p. 85.

123. *De divortio*, pp. 146–58, see above pp. 90–91.

Hincmar in Other Matrimonial Cases

How consistent was Hincmar in dealing with matrimonial cases? To find out, I will compare his actions in Lothar's case with those in some other matrimonial cases. We have already encountered the failed marriage of Boso and Engeltrude earlier in *De divortio*. In October or November 860 Hincmar wrote a further treatise on this in letter form, entitled *De uxore Bosonis*, using very largely the same arguments as he had with regard to Lothar in *De divortio*. His verdict is that the case should be referred back to the archbishop in whose province it had first been dealt with, the archbishop of Milan. Boso and Engeltrude were within his area of responsibility and under his jurisdiction. Other bishops, in this case those of Lotharingia, should not meddle in it.[124]

A second case concerns the efforts to gain a divorce by Count Stephan of Auvergne (late 860). In this case Hincmar sent an opinion on canon law to some fellow bishops who had to decide the case at an episcopal council. Again he had his own political interests. Here it was a matter of making peace between two important family groups in the West Frankish realm, one of which included kinsmen of his own.[125] Count Stephan sought to have his marriage annulled because prior to that marriage he had supposedly had sexual relations with a kinswoman of his later wife. Although he had subsequently married his wife, he had not—at least, so he maintained—had sexual intercourse with her. Here Hincmar cites many of the same authorities he had already used in *De divortio*, but in this case he comes to a different conclusion. On the one hand, he interprets Pope Leo's decretal to Rusticus as meaning that without sexual intercourse there is no marriage.[126] On the other hand, he fails to quote Augustine's statement that the conjugal bond is not broken if physical intercourse is impossible—a quotation that he does use in *De divortio*.[127] He also quotes a canon that allows divorce on grounds of the husband's impotence and permits the wife to remarry.[128]

---

124. *De divortio*, part 1, question and answer 22, pp. 226–32, part 2, question and answer 5, pp. 244–46, and *De uxore Bosonis*, *Ep. Hincmar*, pp. 81–87.

125. Nelson, *Charles the Bald*, pp. 196–98.

126. *Ep. Hinc.*, pp. 87–107, on pp. 95–97. He uses the same quotations on dissolution of marriages for adultery and on remarriage as in *De divortio*, pp. 194–96. For the interpretation of Leo's decretal, see Gaudemet, "Indissolubilité et consommation"; Fransen, "Lettre d'Hincmar"; here the sexual completion of marriage, the consummation of a marriage as a condition of its validity, appears for the first time in the Church's rules. This passage from Hincmar was included in the Decretum of Gratian and would later become *the* authority in such cases.

127. Augustine, *Contra Iulianum*, quoted in *De divortio*, p. 135.

128. *De nuptiis Stephanii*, in *Ep. Hinc.*, p. 97: Hincmar refers here to the Synod of Estinnes. This canon is not to be found there, but it is in Benedictus Levita, Lib. II c. 55 and 91. Its content tallies with c. 17 of the Edict of Verberie (756); see above, p. 29, and ch. 1.1 n. 22.

This runs counter to the rules quoted in *De divortio* prohibiting divorce on grounds of the infertility of either partner.[129] In Stephan's case Hincmar suggested that the marriage should be dissolved and a settlement acceptable to both parties be made between the two kinship groups involved.[130]

An interesting parallel is a case that confronted Bishop Paulinus of Reggia some years later. This too concerned a man's refusal to marry his betrothed, the reason given being his fornication with a kinswoman of said betrothed, in this case her mother. Because his prospective mother-in-law was already dead it was no longer possible to bring testimony to prove this fornication. Paulinus had his suspicions, however, and sought advice from Pope John VIII (872–82). John's advice was to reach a judgment by oath-taking, if the person concerned was suitable, or otherwise by trial by ordeal. In the meantime the marriage must not take place and the husband-to-be must remain chaste.[131] In this case the man who wanted to break his marriage contract was not immediately believed, and an attempt was made to discover the true facts. The procedure suggested by Pope John in this case is thus diametrically opposed to Hincmar's advice regarding the marriage of Stephan of Auvergne.

All these matrimonial cases involved members of the high aristocracy. But there is one other example, and one which, like Lothar's, was played out at the kingly level: the divorce and remarriage of Charles the Bald's eldest son, Louis the Stammerer. Against his father's wishes Louis had married Ansgarde, by whom he had had two sons. His father compelled him to put this wife aside and marry another woman, Adelaide.[132] When Louis was crowned king by Pope John VIII in 878 he wanted this second wife to be crowned a queen, but Pope John refused.[133] Hincmar was certainly aware of Louis' divorce of Ansgarde, which was contrary to current canon law, but in the *Annales Bertiniani* he says not a word about it. Nor did Louis' divorce and remarriage prevent Hincmar from anointing and crowning him king with his own hands.[134] After Louis' death, however, Hincmar had changed his political allegiance and sided with his two young sons by his first, divorced wife Ansgarde. Abbot Goslin then reproached him for having made no effort to prevent the divorce of their mother.[135] The back-

---

129. *De divortio*, p. 142, quoting Augustine, *De bono coniugali* XV (17), in *CSEL* 41, pp. 209–10.

130. Nelson, *Charles the Bald*, pp. 196–98.

131. *Ep. Joh. VIII*, p. 331. The editor classifies this letter under the "Epistolae dubiae."

132. Regino a° 878, p. 114; for Louis' marriage see below, pp. 102, 114–15.

133. *AB* a° 878, p. 227.

134. *AB* a° 877, p. 219.

135. The only surviving record of this is in Flodoard's registers, Flodoard, *Historia Remensis Ecclesiae* III, c. 19, p. 261.

ground to this complaint is probably that after the death of Louis the Stammerer Goslin had supported another candidate's claim to the West Frankish throne, namely Louis the Younger of East Francia. Evidently Goslin is reproaching Hincmar for inconsistency. Either Louis' first marriage was lawful and the sons born of it were legitimate, in which case Hincmar should have protested against its dissolution, or the marriage was unlawful, in which case the sons were bastards and as such could have no claim to the throne.[136]

HINCMAR's stance regarding Lothar's divorce case hardened more and more as events progressed. Originally he tried to distance himself from it to some extent. Only when clearly drawn into it by other people, through rumors of his approval and a list of questions addressed to him personally, did he become involved. And then he stood very much on his dignity and claimed far-reaching powers for the bishops. As the case progressed he reacted more and more strongly to any questioning of these powers. This hardening in his attitude paralleled the growing hostility between Charles the Bald and Lothar II.

The divorce cases of Stephan and Louis the Stammerer clearly demonstrate how far Hincmar was governed by the political situation in formulating his rules and in his intervention. Since in Stephan's case it was necessary to make peace between two hostile family groups, Hincmar trimmed the Church's rules to fit the case in question. He selected the rules that suited him, left out what did not suit him, and his interpretation, certainly of Pope Leo's decretal, was decidedly innovative. One cannot always escape the impression that perhaps the same authorities could just as well have been used to reach a different verdict, if the interests of those concerned had been different. In the case of Louis the Stammerer Hincmar clearly avoided any involvement in the matter and did not venture to oppose his lord, King Charles the Bald, let alone make any attempt to have a general council convened to have this grave matter—which, after all, concerned the marriage of a future king—decided by the bishops. When, years later, the sons of the dissolved marriage succeeded their father as kings, Hincmar simply acted as if the divorce had never taken place.

136. For this affair, see Brühl, "Hincmariana"; Hlawitschka, *Lotharingien*, pp. 224–40, and Werner, "Nachkommen," pp. 437–41.

Act IV
Lothar's Allies and His Marriage to Waldrada, 860–862

The Treaty of Coblenz brings peace between the three kings, but this political situation, seemingly so harmonious and so favorable to Lothar, is not to last. Quite soon after the treaty, still in the final months of 860, Lothar—who still does not entirely trust Charles the Bald—concludes an alliance with Louis the German. Theutberga leaves Lothar's kingdom and joins her brother Hucbert in the kingdom of Charles the Bald.[1] She retracts her confession. She and her family refuse to accept the verdict of Lothar's bishops and ask Pope Nicholas I (858–67) to review their judgment.[2] Thereupon Lothar's bishops also approach the pope. Two of them travel to Rome to obtain papal approval for Lothar's divorce. They want to refute the "malicious lies" spread about Lothar by his enemies.[3]

1. *AB* a° 860, pp. 83–84, is our only source for this episode. The reason for Lothar's fear is not mentioned, but the fact that his enemy Hucbert was to be found shortly afterward in Charles the Bald's kingdom, where he was joined by his sister, might have caused him concern. It seemed that enemies of his were gathering there, unhampered by Charles. Lothar's suspicion later appeared to be well founded in view of Charles' aggressive policy toward him and his brothers in the following year, which may have been already apparent to some well-informed people.

2. No letters from Theutberga and her family have survived. We know of their existence through letters from Nicholas: *Ep. Nic.* no. 3, to the bishops at the Council of Metz (23 November 863), p. 269, no. 11, "Commonitorium" (863), p. 277, no. 16, to Hucbert (May 863), p. 282.

3. The embassy of Theutgard of Trier and Hatto of Verdun is announced in a letter from Lothar's bishops, *Ep. Lot.* no. 2 (autumn 860–61), pp. 210–12; p. 211, "Argumento falsitatis." At the same time there is an embassy by Counts Liutfrid and Walther, who, according to Hincmar, were two of the chief advocates of Lothar's divorce; see *AB* a° 862, pp. 93–94, p. 71, above. This, together with the mission of Theutgaud and Hatto, is announced in a letter from Lothar, *Ep. Lot.* no. 1, pp. 209–10, which is phrased in very general terms and does not even mention the divorce.

Quarrels break out within the royal families, with far-reaching consequences for the political balance of power. In 861 Louis' eldest son, Carloman, rebels against his father. Carloman's relations by marriage lose their fiefs, both in Louis' and in Lothar's realms, and seek refuge with Charles the Bald. They are followed by many prominent nobles who three years earlier had left Charles' kingdom after supporting the failed invasion by Louis the German. Most of their fiefs are returned to them.[4] The body of powerful nobles in Charles the Bald's kingdom is now considerably larger, and this stimulates his expansionist urge. In late 861 he makes an unsuccessful attempt to acquire the territory of the young, epileptic Charles of Provence. By doing so he breaks the Treaty of Coblenz.[5] Lothar and Louis the German send ambassadors to Pope Nicholas I with a letter asking him to rebuke Charles the Bald, who is threatening the peace.[6]

In the spring of 862 events take a different turn. Louis the German and Carloman settle their differences,[7] while Charles the Bald quarrels with his daughter Judith and his sons Louis the Stammerer and Charles. All three of them contract marriages without informing their father. Judith is the first to do so. At this time she already has five years of marriage behind her and has outlived two husbands. After the death of her first husband, Aethelwulf of Wessex, she married his·son Aethelbald. When Aethelbald too died in 860 the twice-widowed but still youthful Judith returned to the Continent, where Charles the Bald shut her up in a convent. Probably he intended to look for another politically suitable husband for her. Be that as it may, Judith decides, with the approval of her brother Louis the Stammerer, to have herself "abducted" by Count Baldwin of Flanders.[8] Charles the Bald is furious. He has Baldwin, Judith, and all who aided them excommunicated by his bishops at a council.[9] Judith and Baldwin flee to Lothar's kingdom, where he gives refuge to his cousin and her

---

4. It is likely that the reprisals against Carloman's in-laws are a result of his rebellion (in which they may even have taken part). For some speculations on the reasons for these purges, see *Annals of Fulda*, trans. Reuter, p. 48 n. 7. Goldberg, *Struggle*, pp. 263–69, is outspoken in explaining the purges as a consequence of Carloman's rebellion. The two sources they mention do indeed link the two events, but not in the same order: *AB* a° 861, p. 85 (where Hincmar's redaction begins) and *AF* a° 861, p. 55 (probably written in 863).

5. *AB* a° 861, p. 87. See also *Ep. Hinc.* no. 42, p. 115, to Gerard of Vienne, in which Hincmar assures him that he has nothing to do with any possible takeover of the realm of Charles of Provence by Charles the Bald.

6. *Ep. Lot.* no. 3, pp. 212–14. The letter was probably drawn up at a meeting between Lothar and Louis and their close advisers at Remiremont in December 861, Schmid, "Königseintrag," pp. 113–23 (in contrast to the edition). According to this letter (p. 213), Charles' incursion took place at the instigation of exiled incorrigible traitors who were accepted by Charles as his loyal followers.

7. *AF* a° 862, p. 55; *AB* a° 862, p. 90.

8. *AB* a° 862, pp. 87–88.

9. Ibid., p. 88. Hincmar clearly had a hand in this, for he announces the sentence in letters, *Ep. Hinc.* no. 148, p. 118, to Bishop Theoderic of Cambrai; no. 155, p. 120, to Rorik the newly converted Norseman; and no. 156, p. 120, to Bishop Hunger of Utrecht. In these letters he says that no one is to give shelter to the excommunicates.

husband.[10] Charles the Bald, already at odds with Judith and Louis over the abduction, now also falls out with his second son, Charles, when he too marries without informing him. Finally, Louis strikes the crowning blow: soon after, at the beginning of Lent 862, he too marries against his father's wishes.[11]

Both Judith and Baldwin and young Charles appeal to the Holy See to resolve the issue of their marriages; Baldwin even travels to Rome to speak to Pope Nicholas in person.[12] The Pope thus finds the list of issues in which his intervention is sought growing longer. The divorce of Lothar and Theutberga and the military aggression of Charles the Bald are certainly not the least important items on the list. But Nicholas takes his time. Not until 23 November 862 does he eventually send out letters announcing an embassy that is to settle both these questions.[13]

Lothar does not wait for Nicholas's reply. He wants to marry Waldrada and have her proclaimed queen. To achieve this he takes the route mapped out for him by his bishops. On 29 April 862, a week after Easter, nearly all the bishops in his kingdom gather in Aachen for that purpose: Gunthar of Cologne, Theutgaud of Trier, Adventius of Metz, Hatto of Verdun, Arnulf of Toul,[14] Franco of Liège, and probably also Hunger of Utrecht[15] and Rathold of Strasbourg.[16] This assembly of eight bishops decides how to proceed in the matter of Lothar's marriage.[17] Lothar declares to the

10. Charles the Bald reproaches Lothar for this in his statement at the meeting at Savonnières (November 862) c. 5, in *MGH Cap.* 2: pp. 160–61; also in *AB* a° 862, p. 95.

11. *AB* a° 862, pp. 90–91.

12. *Ep. Nic.* no. 7, pp. 272–74, to Charles the Bald on the case of Baldwin and Judith; no. 8 to Queen Ermentrude for her to mediate in that case; no. 9, pp. 274–75, on the case of Charles the Younger. *Ep. Nic.* no. 12, pp. 278–79 (863), concerns the reconciliation of Charles the Bald with his sons Charles and Louis.

13. *Ep. Nic.* nos. 3–6, pp. 268–72, to the bishops summoned to a council at Metz, to Lothar, to Louis II, and to Charles the Bald regarding the case of Lothar; nos. 7–9 regarding Baldwin and Charles the Younger; see preceding n. 12.

14. Arnulf bishop of Toul (848/59–871).

15. Hunger, bishop of Utrecht (854–66), probably already a priest in Utrecht in 838, was elected bishop in 854 when the first-choice candidate declined the post. In 858 he had to leave Utrecht because of constant Norse attacks and Lothar gave him the monastery of Odiliënberg, close to Aachen, as his seat; Weinfurter and Engels, *Series Episcoporum* 5, Germania 1, pp. 178–79; *Oorkondenboek Utrecht* 1: no. 63, p. 71; *D LD* no. 68 (18 May 854), pp. 95–96; *D Lot.II* no. 7 (2 January 858), pp. 392–94.

16. Rathold, bishop of Strasbourg (840–after 873), already bishop-elect in 840, suffragan of the archbishop of Mainz, received from Louis the German a confirmation of a grant of immunity to the church of Strasbourg issued by Louis the Pious; see Duchesne, *Fastes* 3: pp. 173–74; *D LD* no. 75 (30 March 856), pp. 109–10.

17. Gunthar, Theutgaud, Adventius, Hatto, and Franco had also attended the earlier Aachen synods at which Theutberga's divorce was pronounced. Arnulf of Toul, Hunger of Utrecht, and Rathold of Strasbourg were new; Bishop Theoderic of Cambrai did not attend; he died not long after (July–August 862). Also absent was Harduic, archbishop of Besançon (847–ca. 870). Harduic nonetheless was politically active, jointly with Gunthar and Theutgaud; see *MGH Conc.* 4: pp. 124–26, 133, and *Ep. Hinc.* no. 164, pp. 141–42. In 869 Lothar made a gift to the church of Besançon at Harduic's request, *D Lot.II* no. 33 (22 January 869), pp. 438–40.

gathering that he would have kept Theutberga had she been found fit to share his mar-
riage bed and not been tainted by a pernicious incestuous defilement.[18] However, he
definitely needs a partner "to quench the fire of his youthfulness," and so he desires to
marry for the good of his body and his soul, for it is better to marry than to live in
lechery.[19] The bishops confirm yet again that the divorce from Theutberga is correct,[20]
but they also have something to say about Lothar's behavior. In their view he has sinned
by entering into an illicit relationship with a concubine, for which he should have
done penance. But since he already completed a penance for this—at least, so Bishop
Theutgaud of Trier claims[21]—they argue that they cannot forbid the king to take a
wife and beget children.[22]

Some time later they also maintain—and going by the available texts this is some-
thing new—that he was already legally bound to Waldrada even before he married
Theutberga.[23]

In any case, Lothar marries Waldrada and presents her as his queen. She makes a
public appearance with a retinue, after which she is received as queen in the royal hall
to loud acclamation and is crowned.[24] At around this time Charles the Bald is recon-
ciled with his son Louis when the latter returns to him and asks his forgiveness.[25]

Finally, at the instigation of Louis the German efforts are made to bring about a
reconciliation between Charles the Bald and Lothar. At first Charles is extremely
hostile to Lothar and refuses to so much as speak to him.[26] But on 3 November 862
Charles the Bald, Louis the German, and Lothar II, each of them attended by his
great magnates, meet at Savonnières. Charles the Bald and his advisers hand Lothar
a written statement in which they accuse him on three counts.[27] Each of the three

18. Council of Aachen (862) (1st version, text A), c. 3, in *MGH Conc.* 4: p. 72.

19. Ibid., pp. 72–73: "iuvenilis aetatis ardorem," *Contestatio Hlotharii* (text B), p. 75.

20. Council of Aachen (1st version, text A), c. 10, in *MGH Conc.* 4: p. 74 (2nd version, text C), p. 76.

21. Council of Aachen (1st version, text A), c. 3, in *MGH Conc.* 4: p. 73 (2nd version, text C), p. 76.

22. Council of Aachen (1st version, text A), c. 10, in *MGH Conc.* 4: p. 74 (2nd version, text C), pp. 77–78.

23. We find this set down in a letter, only part of which has survived, from Adventius of Metz written after the Council of Metz (June 863): *Ep. Lot.* no. 5, pp. 215–17; for a discussion of this text, see below, pp. 111–12. However, a letter from Nicholas from early 863 tells us that Lothar had already put forward this argument: *Ep. Nic.* no. 11, p. 277.

24. *AB* a° 862, pp. 93–94; Regino a° 864, p. 82 (incorrect dating). For arguments regarding a precise date, see summary in Staubach, *Herrscherbild*, pp. 447–50, n. 212; cf. Buc, *Dangers*, pp. 66–67.

25. *AB* a° 862, p. 92. This, too, like the marriage to Waldrada, is recorded between two events that can be dated to 15 August and 17 September.

26. For the preparations for this meeting, see Prinz, "Unbekanntes Aktenstück," and for the edition of the letter of the first embassy led by Altfrid of Hildesheim, ibid., pp. 262–63.

27. *AB* a° 862, p. 94. The written statement contains ten capitula in *MGH Cap.* 2: pp. 159–63.

relates to a marriage. First, Lothar is harboring the runaway adulteress Engeltrude, his cousin.[28] He had also given asylum to the excommunicated Baldwin and Judith, also his cousin.[29] And lastly, in the matter of his own marriage he is ignoring the advice of Charles' bishops and of Pope Nicholas.[30] Only if Lothar promises to mend his ways are Charles and his bishops prepared to accept him into their company.[31] And Lothar does indeed promise amendment, in a declaration drawn up by his advisers.[32] The statements are then read out to the select group of the three kings' closest advisers. In them Lothar, Louis, and Charles solemnly promise to love one another as true brothers, uncles, and nephews. But afterward Charles still tries to pillory Lothar in public by having the text containing his accusations read out to all the assembled nobles of the three kingdoms. This meets with resistance from his uncle Conrad, who is also related to the other kings.[33] For the moment Charles gives in, but later he ensures that everyone is aware of his grievances against Lothar.[34]

The conflict surrounding Lothar's marriage was spreading. Both parties looked for and found allies—Theutberga and her family to right the wrong done to them, Lothar to make Waldrada his queen. Most of the bishops in Lothar's realm rallied to his side. They took up their canonical weapons and justified his actions by appealing to the rules of the Church.

Lothar also had the support of kinsmen, not only from his own kingdom, such as his uncle Liutfrid and his uncle by marriage Conrad, but from the other kingdoms as well. His brothers, Louis and Charles—the latter in the person of his guardian, their common uncle by marriage Gerard of Vienne—were on his side but had little power outside their own territories. In these years it was his uncle Louis the German who proved his most important ally. The ties of kinship, though, can cut two ways. They can lead to solidarity and alliance, but also to rivalry and enmity, as is very apparent in the behavior of Lothar's uncle Charles the Bald.

Both parties also appealed to the bishop of Rome, the pope, but more on this in act 5. Here I will focus on the bishops and kinsmen of Lothar who took his side. Four topics need to be considered. First, again, the question of what canonical weapons the bishops used and how they wielded them in

---

28. *MGH Cap.* 2: c. 4, p. 160; also *AB* a° 862, p. 95. Lothar's maternal grandmother, Ava, is Engeltrude's aunt (her father's sister); see genealogy of the Bosonids in appendix 2. Lothar calls Engeltrude his *"propinqua"* (relative), *De divortio*, p. 244; the explanation given there, n. 5, is incorrect.

29. *MGH Cap.* 2: c. 5, pp. 160–161; also *AB* a° 862, p. 95.

30. *MGH Cap.* 2: c. 6, p. 161; also *AB* a° 862, p. 95.

31. *MGH Cap.* 2: c. 9, p. 162; also *AB* a° 862, p. 95.

32. *MGH Cap.* 2: pp. 164–65, esp. c. 2; *AB* a° 862, p. 94.

33. *MGH Cap.* 2: p. 165; the *adnuntiationes*: ibid., pp. 159–65; *AB* a° 862, pp. 94–95.

34. *MGH Cap.* 2: p. 165; *AB* a° 862, p. 95.

dealing with the issue of Lothar's marriage. Second, the source from which the bishops derived the authority to concern themselves with the marriage of their king. Third, the extent to which the bishops' action was determined by the political context of Lothar's kingdom, the "Lotharingian realm." And the final topic brings us to the heart of this political context: What part did ties of kinship play in the exercise of political power and what solidarities, or rivalries, did they create?

The Legal Status of Marriage: The Arguments of Lothar's Bishops

According to his bishops, Lothar's marriage to Waldrada was lawful and that to Theutberga was not. In their opinion Lothar could divorce Theutberga in order to remarry. The question is why they took this position and to what extent their views were in accordance with canonical tradition. The sources allow us to follow the reasoning of Lothar's bishops at the 862 Council of Aachen in fair detail. But quite soon afterward it becomes apparent that the bishops were developing a very different line of argument from the one they had employed at Aachen.

The Arguments at the Aachen Council of 862

In 862 Lothar's bishops cited a number of traditional rules. In principle a man may not repudiate his wife, nor may a woman leave her husband.[35] An incestuous relationship between man and woman can in no sense be called a marriage; anyone persisting in such a relationship must be excommunicated.[36] A man may repudiate his wife on grounds of adultery. A woman may leave her husband if he abandons the Christian faith, commits adultery, or abuses her sexually.[37] A woman who has left her husband for these reasons may in principle not remarry. The rules for men, however, are not the same as those for women. Thus, a woman who leaves her husband because of his adultery is not allowed to remarry; a man who repudiates his wife because of her adultery may do so.[38]

---

35. Council of Aachen (862) c. 8, in *MGH Conc.* 4: pp. 73–74 and 76–77. The argument consists mainly of quotations. A key quote is Ambrosiaster, *Commentarius in epistulas*, 1 Cor. 7:11, pp. 74–75. See ch. 1 n. 9.

36. Council of Aachen (862) (1st version, text A), in *MGH Conc.* 4: pp. 73–74; (2nd version, text C), in *MGH Conc.* 4: pp. 76–77.

37. Council of Aachen (862) (1st version, text A) c. 8, in *MGH Conc.* 4: pp. 73–74; (2nd version, text C), in *MGH Conc.* 4: pp. 76–77.

38. Council of Aachen (862) (1st version text A), in *MGH Conc.* 4: pp. 73–74.

That none of this was relevant to Lothar's case does not seem to have bothered the bishops greatly. With constant references to Ambrosiaster they interpreted the rules in line with their conclusion. They equated incest—and the incestuous relationship of Hucbert and Theutberga— with extramarital sex, with adultery.[39] As far as they were concerned, Lothar could repudiate Theutberga and marry someone else. They re- garded the union of Theutberga and Lothar, following on the aforesaid incestuous relationship, also as a forbidden incestuous union (*incestuosum coniugium*), which was prohibited by the authoritative canonical rules.[40] It could not be called a marriage.[41] The precise meaning of the canons was pushed aside by the supposition that incest irrevocably tainted both those involved. Anyone besmirched by an incestuous relationship was accursed, following the Old Testament law: "Cursed be he that lieth with his sister" (Deuteronomy 27:22). According to Holy Writ he was to be shunned and it was forbidden even to share food with him. To be joined in matrimony with such a person was not allowed. At first sight the rule would seem to apply not to Theutberga but to Hucbert, but the bishops saw it dif- ferently. Theutberga had publicly admitted that she had been contaminated by an incestuous relationship with her brother. Thus she was no longer fit to be a wife, and so her marriage to Lothar was not a genuine marriage.[42] Consequently, not only could Lothar marry again, it was even advisable for him to do so to avoid the danger of a new illicit relationship.[43]

The views of the bishops and those of Hincmar of Reims are remarkably similar in content: Lothar may remarry if it is proved that Theutberga has been sexually abused by her brother. The difference is that, according to Lothar's bishops, Theutberga's confession had furnished the necessary proof, while according to Hincmar it had not. On another point too the bishops' views were diametrically opposed to those of Hincmar. The bish- ops quoted Ambrosiaster at length and approvingly, and Ambrosiaster forbids a woman who has left her husband on grounds of adultery to re- marry, but permits a man to do so. Hincmar, by contrast, following Je- rome and Augustine, adhered to the tradition that forbade both partners to remarry after a divorce on grounds of adultery.[44] Hincmar was aware of

---

39. Council of Aachen (862) (1st version text A), c. 9–10, in *MGH Conc.* 4: p. 74.
40. Ibid.
41. Council of Aachen (862) (2nd version, text C), p. 76.
42. Ibid.: "Maledictus, qui dormierit cum sorore sua, filia patris vel matris sue."
43. Council of Aachen (862) (1st version, text A) c. 10, in *MGH Conc.* 4: p. 74; (2nd ver- sion, text C), pp. 77–78.
44. We have already encountered these conflicting traditions, for instance in Magin- goz. See above, pp. 11–14.

both traditions. He was familiar with the Ambrosiaster commentary, but did not use the passages that conflicted with his own views.[45]

Certain clerics, however—we do not know which ones—apparently held a quite different opinion, which they set down in writing together with their reasoning. This was added to version 2 of the records of the Aachen council.[46] The authors focused their criticism on three points in the reasoning that had declared Lothar's marriage to Theutberga invalid, and consequently concluded that the marriage was valid. In doing so they put forward ideas on marriage and divorce that on a few points also differ completely from those aired by Hincmar in *De divortio*.

The first point of difference concerns the remarriage of a husband after repudiating his wife for adultery.[47] In their view this was not permitted.[48] We hear a new note, too, regarding the verdict of Lothar's bishops on the legality of his marriage to Theutberga. The bishops had ruled that there could be no question of this being a lawful union, because prior to her marriage Theutberga had no longer been a virgin but had been "corrupted," and corrupted by her own brother.[49] To this the writers say that the wife, if she had been faithful to her husband during her marriage, could not be condemned for old sins committed before her marriage:

Whatever may have happened before she married, if after marrying she remained faithful to her husband by being mindful of chastity, then the earlier corruption does not detract from the later chastity. Even had she been a whore or a wanton, even had she previously been exposed to many

45. See Heidecker, *Kerk*, p. 107.
46. Council of Aachen (862) (text D), in *MGH Conc.* 4: pp. 78–86. That it was a response to the written text of the council appears on p. 84, n. 65, also p. 68. We do not know who the authors are, except that, judging from their writings, they are learned scholars. There was certainly opposition to Lothar's divorce plans within his realm, as became clear on both occasions when he tried to divorce Theutberga. Someone such as Theutberga, with her family relations and connections, must always have retained some support. Among Lothar's bishops one might identify Arnulf of Toul as an opponent; see above, act 3 n. 20. This anonymous text, however, seems to be something different. It offers some very clear lines of argument that are so completely different from all the previous texts on Lothar's divorce—including the ones opposing it—and so clear that if they had been voiced before they would probably have sunk the arguments of Lothar's bishops. As a matter of fact some of these arguments are so familiar to later thinking that one would suspect the authenticity of this text, if it were not in a ninth-century manuscript. These authors have not, like others in Lothar's case, just browsed through Augustine's works, mining them for authoritative quotations, but seem really to have read and understood Augustine. This all points toward political outsiders with a thorough knowledge, who reacted to the previous text with a brilliant exposé.
47. Council of Aachen (862) (text D), in *MGH Conc.* 4: p. 78.
48. Ibid., p. 84.
49. Ibid., p. 84: "*corrupta.*"

"corruptors," if she has maintained the marital bond intact then the purity of her later life has washed away the stains of her previous life.[50]

The "holy purity of marriage" (*sanctimonia coniugali*), so the authors maintain, washes away the corruption of one's past life, as also happens with baptism and the vow of continence with which, as a monk or otherwise, one dedicates oneself in a particular way to the service of God.[51] The authors attribute a healing effect to marriage, and in that sense one could call their view of marriage "sacramental." This healing effect is bound up with "chastity" within the marriage. Such chastity clearly refers here to relations between husband and wife in which lust plays no part. If sexual contact does take place, then it does so either with the aim of producing children or as a consequence of the duty of each partner always to prevent the other from lapsing into adultery.[52]

The sins that had besmirched the woman prior to her marriage could not contaminate her husband if they lived chastely together:

> And if, as people say, she did then incur that stain, what has that to do with her husband, if he lived chastely with her? How can the besmirching of the wife besmirch her husband when after her marriage she has lived chastely with him? The husband who is linked to such a person need not fear that he will be accursed, because Solomon says: "He that keeps an adulterous wife is foolish." Given that she maintained her chastity after he married her, her old transgressions shall not be counted against her, since turning to good she has cleansed herself, just as a faithful person is one no longer faithless, and a humble person one no longer proud, and a holy person is one no longer tainted, so is a chaste woman one no longer unclean and so also by the sanctity of abstinence the filth of adultery is not to be counted against the pure marriage.[53]

50. Ibid.: "Quicquid ante fuerit, priusquam nupserit, si fidem, postquam nupsit, marito castitatem tenendo servaverit, antiqua corruptela posteriori castitati non preiudicat. Licet enim fuerit meretrix, licet prostituta, licet multis corruptoribus exposita, si nuptiale incontaminatum foedus servaverit, prioris vitae maculas posterior munditia diluit. Dicit enim apostolus: 'Et hec quidem fuistis, sed abluti estis, sed sanctificati estis, sed iustificati estis.' (1 Corinthians 6:11)."

51. Council of Aachen (862) (text D), in *MGH Conc.* 4: pp. 84–85.

52. This is in line with Augustine's ideas on chastity (*castitas*) and continence (*continentia*) within marriage: *De bono coniugali* X(11), XI(12–13), XXII(27), ed. Combes, pp. 48–55, 84–87. Here, however, the evident healing effect of marriage and the comparison with baptism give marriage a character that, to my knowledge, is nowhere else so clearly described in this period.

53. Council of Aachen (862) (text D), in *MGH Conc.* 4: p. 85: "Denique si quemadmodum fertur, illa pollutionem incidit, quid ad virum pertinet, si cum ea caste vixit? Aut quomodo coniugis pollutio coniugem polluere potest si caste, postquam nupta est, vixit

These dissenting clerics also came up with a very practical argument. It is far from unknown, they say, for the partners to have had sexual relationships prior to their marriage. If everyone who had engaged in fornication before their marriage was to be allowed to divorce because of it things would get entirely out of hand, for this was a very common situation. "Let us be silent as to the women, but a man who comes to his bride as a virgin is a rare, or rather a nonexistent, being."[54]

A third and last point on which these authors take a divergent view is when they claim that the rulings prohibiting an incestuous union are not applicable to Lothar and Theutberga. Canon law does indeed forbid incestuous unions, but does not apply here since there is no question of this being a marriage between blood relations.[55]

In the manuscript this treatise is immediately followed by a letter from an anonymous priest to an anonymous bishop, which peters out in a large stain in the middle of a sentence on the last page of the codex. Sadly, then, we do not know the author's ultimate answer to the question, which is clearly a reaction to the previous texts, of whether it is permissible to dissolve a lawfully contracted marriage on the grounds of a previous relationship with a kinswoman.[56]

To sum up, the argument put forward by the Lotharingian bishops at the 862 Aachen council was very much the same as Hincmar's in *De divortio*. It was permissible for Lothar to divorce and remarry because of Theutberga's incest committed before their marriage. In this case remarriage was even advisable, to avoid lapsing again into fornication. Where Hincmar's views and those of his Lotharingian colleagues differ is that the latter maintained that a man who had repudiated his adulterous wife could then remarry, while according to Hincmar he could not. On this last point his views coincided with those of the unknown authors who opposed the decisions of this Aachen council in their treatise. The remaining views on marriage to be found in this treatise are quite different in tenor from

---

cum coniuge? Nec timendum ne maledicto sit maritus cum tali iunctus propter illud, quod Salomon dixit: 'Qui tenet adulteram stultus est' [Proverbs 18:22, *Vetus Latina* version], quoniam postquam ei nupsit castitatem servavit, non enim antiqua reputanda sunt delicta, si melior conversatio iam purgavit illa, sicut enim fidelis iam non est infidelis, et sicut humilis iam non est superbus, et sicut sanctus iam non est immundus, sic castus iam non est impurus, sic quoque coniugium continentiae sanctitate mundum adulterii sordibus non est addictum."

54. Ibid., pp. 85–86: "Ut de mulieribus taceamus, rarus aut nullus est vir, qui cum uxore virgo conveniat."

55. Ibid, pp. 84–85.

56. Council of Aachen (862) (text E), in *MGH Conc.* 4: pp. 86–89.

those of both the Aachen council and Hincmar.[57] The dissident writers rejected the view of incest as a contagion that could also infect third parties. The most striking difference, though, is that they came up with a "sacramental" concept of marriage. Marriage cleanses people of their old sins, as though it were a penance. By living a proper, chaste married life, sins committed prior to the marriage are washed away. In any case, in their view the canons relating to incest did not apply here because there was no question of any incest, that is, no blood relationship between Lothar and Theutberga.

The Argument after the Aachen Council: The Valid Marriage of Lothar and Waldrada

After the Aachen council of April 862 Lothar's bishops changed their argument regarding his divorce from Theutberga and his marriage to Waldrada. This is clear from two letters they wrote, one from Adventius of Metz, the other from Gunthar of Cologne and Theutgaud of Trier.[58] The clever fencing with canonical rules is over; now a quite different line of argument emerges, one that gives us a glimpse into a quite different reality, namely the social rules and customs that actually prevailed, with or without the canonical rules. The focus now is on marriage as it actually was among the Frankish nobility, and these rules and customs were probably what really counted.

True, the accusations against Theutberga were repeated in these letters, as was the assertion that partly because of them she could not continue as queen. But the most important argument advanced now is that Lothar's marriage to Theutberga was in fact his *second* marriage.[59] Waldrada was the lawful wife, because she had been bound to Lothar before he married Theutberga. What, then, in the eyes of Lothar's bishops, made the marriage of Lothar and Waldrada valid? And why, according to them, could Waldrada certainly not be described as a concubine?

---

57. For a comparison of the use of sources of the Aachen council by the dissenting priests and Hincmar, see Heidecker, *Kerk*, pp. 134–37, 331–32.

58. Part of a treatise or letter by Adventius of Metz written after the Council of Metz (June 863), edition in *Ep. Lot.* no. 5, pp. 215–17. A letter from Gunthar of Cologne and Theutgaud of Trier to Pope Nicholas I, in *AB* aº 864, c. 7, p. 110. The version of this letter in the *AF* aº 863, pp. 60–61, does not contain this last c. 7 on Waldrada. It is possible that Hincmar distorted this c. 7 in his *Annales Bertiniani*, for instance, by omitting words. The text could have been clearer, more convincing, and more detailed.

59. Adventius of Metz, in *Ep. Lot.*, no. 5, pp. 215–17. A letter from Pope Nicholas I written early in 863 already mentions that Lothar had put forward this argument: *Ep. Nic.* no. 11, p. 277.

A few preliminary remarks are appropriate here. By now it should be evident that no clear and established body of religious rules on marriage had yet taken shape. This was even more the case with secular rules. There were no strictly formulated, generally valid, and systematically applied laws regarding marriage. Indeed, the nature of early medieval secular law is such that one has to wonder whether any such laws existed at all.[60] What did exist, though, were ways in which marriages were usually contracted and ways in which they could not be. When we examine these two letters it is clear that the authors' intention was not to establish the conditions with which in their view a marriage must comply, but to indicate features that would prove that *this* marriage, the marriage of Lothar and Waldrada, was valid. The features they referred to were the status as free persons of both partners, the consent of their relatives, public betrothal, bridal gift, and conjugal fidelity and love.

Adventius of Metz describes an event that should constitute sufficient proof that Waldrada was Lothar's wife. He states that Waldrada was joined to Lothar by his father, Emperor Lothar I. "This did not take place off in a corner, for," says Adventius, "truth has no corners."[61] It happened during a public ceremony, in the presence of bishops and great nobles as witnesses. Some of these, for instance Lothar's uncle Liutfrid and his tutors, stated as much, says Adventius, adding—for safety's sake—that he himself had not been present because at the time he was not yet a bishop.[62] At this ceremony the union of Waldrada and Lothar was confirmed by formal agreement on the bridal gift: a hundred homesteads, no less. These were given to Lothar by his father, to be passed on to Waldrada later, for young Lothar was underage and could not yet dispose of his property himself.[63] The ceremony had all the hallmarks of a betrothal: a public ritual with witnesses, the consent of the family, the settling of the bridal gift. Its status was further enhanced by its being conducted by Emperor Lothar I. The phrasing of this text is highly "imperial," with a strong emphasis on the imperial function and terms such as *consules* for

---

60. For a discussion of this, see, to name just a few, Nehlsen, "Zur Aktualität"; Schott, "Stand"; McKitterick, *Carolingians and the Written Word*, pp. 23–75; and three collective volumes: *Giustizia*; *Gewohnheitsrecht*, ed. Dilcher; *Leges*, ed. Dilcher and Distler.

61. *Ep. Lot.* no. 5, p. 215: "Quod non in angulo patratum fuit, quia veritas non habet angulos," and p. 216. Cf. the *Codex Theodosianus*, ed. Krueger, p. 93, Lib. III, tit. I, "De contrahendo emptione," no. 2.2, relating to openness in buying and selling, which forbids such transactions "*in exquisitis cuniculis*" (in hidden corners).

62. *Ep. Lot.* no. 5, pp. 215–16.

63. Ibid., p. 215.

judges and *senatores* for the magnates.[64] A final significant point legiti-
mizing the union with Waldrada is her descent; Adventius states emphati-
cally that she is of noble birth.[65]

In an open letter to Pope Nicholas, Bishops Gunthar of Cologne and
Theutgaud of Trier strongly object to the use of the term "concubine" for
Waldrada. At the time she was a free virgin (*ingenua virgo*) and thus certainly
no concubine. Moreover, the marriage was entered into with the consent of
the parents and the two of them live in fidelity, affection, and conjugal love.
Although there is indeed a reference to "laws," it is so vague that it is hard to
discern what laws are being referred to:

> The divine and canon law clearly demonstrates and the estimable secular
> laws also show that it is permitted to no one to give a free virgin to a man as
> concubine; and certainly not when that girl never wished to assent to an un-
> lawful union. And because she was joined to her husband with the parents'
> consent, with fidelity, affection, and conjugal love, she must certainly be re-
> garded as a wife and not as a concubine.[66]

The arguments with which the bishops sought to underpin Waldrada's position as wife are her social status as a free woman, parental consent to the
union, public betrothal, and the fact that fidelity and conjugal love existed
between her and Lothar.

The first important element in the bishops' reasoning, to be found in
both texts, is Waldrada's status. She is a free woman.[67] That both partners

---

64. Ibid., pp. 215–16. Incidentally, the beginning of this treatise, preceding the passages
on the action of Lothar I, is not in the manuscript. The copyist says that he "has omitted
the excessively long digression on the authority of kings and priests" (omissum exordium
longissimum de regum et sacerdotum auctoritate) (ibid., p. 215). This probably included
the argument for imperial powers.

65. Ibid., pp. 215–16.

66. Letter from Gunthar of Cologne and Theutgaud of Trier to Pope Nicholas I, in *AB*
aº 864, c. 7, p. 110: "Lex divina et canonica apertissime probat, etiam et venerandae seculi
leges adstipulantur, quod nulli licet ingenuam virginem alicui viro tradere in concubina-
tum, maxime si illa puella numquam inlicite adsentire copulae voluit; et quia suo viro
parentum consensu, fide, affectu ac dilectione coniugali sociata est, uxor profecto, non
concubina, habenda sit." The written Frankish law that comes closest, but certainly does
not fit the case exactly, is *Lex Salica* 13.8: *Pactus Legis Salicae*, pp. 60–61; see also *Lex Salica*
D-text 14.7, p. 54: and E-text 15.4, p. 55. However, Roman law also regards a concubine as
unfree; see above, pp. 26–27. In general, references to *leges* that prove impossible to find in
the written *leges barbarorum* occur more often than not. Moreover, as we have seen, it is
also possible that Hincmar has distorted this text. The canonical law is probably the
much-quoted decretal of Leo to Rusticus (see above, pp. 26–27).

67. See preceding note. It is also apparent from a letter from Nicholas that people have
testified that Waldrada is a free woman. *Ep. Nic.* no. 53, to Louis the German (31 October
867), p. 351. Schmid, "Königseintrag," pp. 128–34, argues on the basis of data on names

should be free was an absolute prerequisite for a valid marriage.[68] In strict technical terms this was only a problem if the partner was the unfree property of someone else. Otherwise one could manumit her (or him, but usually it was a woman), if necessary after first purchasing her, before making her one's wife. In Waldrada's case, however, the issue is different, since she was certainly not unfree; it was the label "concubine" applied to her by her opponents that sparked the reaction.

The next point raised by Gunthar and Theutgaud is parental consent.[69] They do not say whether this means the bride's parents or the bridegroom's, but it goes without saying that the consent of the bride's father (or, if he was no longer alive, of the close male relative whose ward she was) was essential.[70] Approval could also be asked of other relatives, however, though usually the father's view seems to carry most weight. Hincmar of Reims tells of a girl who was married with her father's consent, but against the express wishes of her mother. The wedding went ahead—evidently the father's will was law—but the marriage was not a success. Here, though, Hincmar slips in a few words, saying that although the father's will might well be law, usually people listened to the mother as well.[71] Marriage seems to have been a matter for groups of family members, in which many relatives could express their opinions.[72] In most cases, however, the view of the

---

derived from *libri memoriales* that Waldrada came from a noble family, but not from the highest aristocracy. Brunner, *Oppositionelle Gruppen*, pp. 138–39, conversely, does place her in the high nobility, and specifically in what he terms the "old" nobility. However, Brunner's conclusions are mainly based on a highly speculative use of name correspondences.

68. Prohibitions in the *Lex Salica*: *Pactus Legis Salicae*, 13.7–13.9, pp. 61–62, and *Lex Salica*, D-text: 14.6–14.7, 14.10, E-text 14.3–14.4, 14.7, pp. 54–55; in the other Germanic law codes, see Drew, "Notes," pp. 64–65; "Family in Frankish Law," p. 9; "Family in Visigothic Law," p. 7; "Law of the Family," p. 21. On prohibitions in capitularia and council texts, see above pp. 17–23. Pohl-Resl, "Quod me legibus," pp. 206–7, has shown that exceptions to these were still possible.

69. Letter from Gunthar of Cologne and Theutgaud of Trier to Pope Nicholas I, in AB a° 864, c. 7, p. 110. See above, n. 58.

70. Such consent was required by various Germanic law codes; see Drew, "Notes," pp. 59–64; "Germanic Family," pp. 7–11; "Family in Frankish Law," pp. 4–5; "Family in Visigothic Law," pp. 5–7; "Law," pp. 18–19. For the role of the bride's father, see Heidrich, "Besitz," pp. 134–35. Kottje, "Eherechtliche Bestimmungen," p. 217, is mistaken in stating flatly that a girl could marry even without her parents' consent. The laws he quotes are penalties applied in very specific cases, with the effect of banishing a girl from her family group. For a woman to marry without the consent of her kinsfolk was permitted only in a few very precisely defined exceptional circumstances. Obligatory parental consent also appears in the Pseudo-Evaristus decretal, see above, p. 32, and the second *capitulare* of Bishop Gerbald of Liège, c. 4, in *MGH Cap. episc.* 1: p. 27.

71. *De divortio*, p. 205.

72. In the *Formulae* the consent of the relatives is required in the *Formulae Salicae Lindenbrogianae*, in *MGH Formulae*, p. 271; the *Collectio Sangallensis*, *MGH Formulae*, pp. 406–7;

bride's father was decisive. He had to give his consent. The marriage of Judith and Baldwin was invalid precisely because it lacked the consent of the bride's father, Charles the Bald. This, though, was something that could always be put right. A good year after her abduction Charles did in fact give his daughter Judith permission to, as Hincmar puts it, "lawfully bind herself to Baldwin in marriage."[73]

In addition, the consent of the bridegroom's father was also often required. Certainly that was the case when the bridegroom-to-be was underage, as were the young Lothar at the ceremony described by Adventius and Charles the Bald's son Charles the Younger. Not for nothing does Hincmar stress that when Charles married he was not yet fifteen, the age of majority according to Frankish custom.[74] Subsequently nothing more is heard of the wife of Charles the Younger. Eighteen months after his marriage Charles himself would be mortally wounded during a playful brawl with his comrades.[75] Paternal consent was also required, though, for Louis the Stammerer, who was of age. For precisely this reason—the lack of paternal consent—the two sons of this first marriage were branded as bastards and thus barred from the succession by Boso of Vienne. Regino of Prüm describes this as follows:

> Louis the Stammerer, when still impelled by the flush of his youth, had joined himself in marriage to a noble girl, Ansgard by name, who gave him two sons. . . . But because he took her without the knowledge and consent of his father, he was later forbidden by that same father to keep her and she was parted from him forever by making him swear an oath under duress.[76] . . .

---

three *Formulae* that have survived unbound (actually specific decrees), *MGH Formulae*, pp. 538–539, 539, 540. In the *Passio Maxellendis* the mother plays a part, see c. 4, 5, and 7. She tries to persuade her daughter and is involved in the decision-making process within the family. In the *Vita Rictrudis* some of the bride's relatives appear to protest: Hucbald of Saint-Amand, *Vita Rictrudis*, p. 299. A ruling of a council in the mid-eighth century forbids a man to marry off his stepdaughter against the wishes of the stepdaughter, her mother, and her kinsmen: *Decretum Compendiense* (757) c. 6, in *MGH Cap.* 1, p. 38; see above, p. 18, n. 22. For her marriage to Baldwin, Judith had the consent of her brother Louis the Stammerer.

73. *AB* a° 863, p. 104: "Balduino . . . legaliter coniugio sociari." The mediators we know of are Pope Nicholas I and Judith's mother, Ermentrude. *Ep. Nic.* nos. 7 and 8, pp. 272–75; Nicholas writes to Charles about Baldwin, *Ep. Nic.*, p. 273.

74. *AB* a° 862, pp. 90–91. Pope Nicholas, who was asked to mediate in this conflict, writes in a letter to Charles the Bald that the young Charles had married without paternal consent, *Ep. Nic.* no. 9, p. 275.

75. *AB* a° 864, p. 105, a° 866, p. 130.

76. See above, pp. 98 and 102. Regino a° 878, p. 114: "Habuit autem [Louis the Stammerer] cum adhuc iuvenilis aetatis flore polleret, quandam nobilem puellam nomine Ansgard sibi coniugii foedere copulatam, ex qua duos liberos suscepit. . . . Sed quia hanc sine genitoris conscientia et voluntatis consensu suis amplexibus sociaverat, ab ipso patre

Boso considered Louis' young sons as of no account and regarded them as bastards, because their mother had been scorned and repudiated at Charles' command.[77]

Evidently Louis the Stammerer had been married to his wife Ansgard for some years before repudiating her in order to marry Adelaide.[78] Some years later Louis the German would also refuse consent for the betrothal of his son Louis the Younger.[79] And young Louis' marriage did not take place.

What other arguments were advanced to support the validity of Lothar's marriage to Waldrada? Adventius describes the solemn ceremony in which they were betrothed to each other. In some ways this resembles the procedure we find in two saints' lives, written around 900, which describe the course of events "according to custom" in the making of a marriage.[80] The *Vita Rictrudis* says that Rictrude was "according to the customs betrothed to her husband, provided with a bridal gift, and accepted by him in marital community of life."[81] In the *Passio Maxellendis* the father of Maxellendis and her future husband agreed to the union. Then, on a prearranged day, in public, in the presence of kinsfolk and neighbors, according to custom, she was formally betrothed and her right to the bridal gift confirmed. These promises were binding. The wedding, when the bride was handed over to the bridegroom, would take place later.[82] This strongly resembles the public ceremony at which, in the presence of witnesses, Lothar was bound to Waldrada after the bridal gift was specified. The wedding would take place later, but the promises were binding.

In ninth-century Frankish society the betrothal was the most important element in the making of a marriage.[83] Both families publicly gave their

---

postmodum est ei interdicta et interposito iurisiurandi sacramento ab eius consortio in perpetuum separata."

77. Regino a° 879, p. 114: "pro nihilo ducens adulescentes filios Ludowici et velut degeneres despiciens, eo quod iussu Caroli eorum genetrix spreta atque repudiata fuerit."

78. For the problem of how long this first marriage lasted, see Brühl, "Hincmariana"; Hlawitschka, *Lotharingien*, pp. 224–40; and Werner, "Nachkommen," pp. 437–41.

79. *AB* a° 865, pp. 123–24. Immediately before, Charles the Bald had dismissed Adalard from all his offices.

80. Hucbald of Saint-Amand, *Vita Rictrudis* (dated 907), p. 299: "Iuxta morem desponsatur." *Passio Maxellendis* (according to Scherf, *Ontstaansgeschiedenis*, pp. 27–65, written at Cambrai between the mid-ninth century and 995), c. 5: "Ad desponsandum secundum morem."

81. Hucbald of Saint-Amand, *Vita Rictrudis*, p. 299: "Dignus plane vir, qui maritus existeret dignae Rictrudis a quo iuxta morem desponsatur, dotatur, atque in contubernium matronale . . . assumitur."

82. *Passio Maxellendis*, c. 4, 5, 8.

83. The great importance of betrothal is apparent from Hincmar (see above, pp. 83–84) and from a ruling by a Frankish council of 852: Council of Mainz (852), c. 12, in *MGH*

consent and the business side of the matter, the bridal gift, was agreed on. In fact it was now impossible for either party to back out of the agreement except by paying a hefty fine.[84]

According to Adventius, Emperor Lothar I had decided on lands to be given to Waldrada as her bridal gift (*dos*) "so that the union should be seen to be proper and manifest."[85] On the one hand, the bridal gift was the business side of the union, in which the bridegroom or his father gave land or other property to the bride. After her husband's death these were at her disposal and she in turn would leave them to their joint offspring. The bridal gift was publicly announced at the betrothal ceremony and might be put in writing, then or later, in a charter of dotation. The moment when the property actually changed hands could vary, either there and then at the betrothal or later, sometimes at the wedding.[86] The bridal gift was one of a series of gifts exchanged by the families of the bride and bridegroom; each necessitated a gift in return, thus weaving a web of mutual ties. The exact nature, form, and timing of the gifts were subject to some variation according to time and place. In general, we can regard the bridal gift as a present from the bridegroom to the bride in exchange for her fertility— the children she would give him—and at the same time as a means of providing her with economic security, so that after his death she would not be left destitute.[87]

Conc. 3: p. 249 (see above, pp. 26–27). In his encyclopaedic work *De Universo* Hrabanus Maurus collected a wealth of knowledge on marriage, for which he relied heavily on the *Etymologiae* of Isidore of Seville. He used this selectively, however, omitting some passages and adding others, leaving out entries on marriage and adding some on betrothal; see, in detail, Heidecker, *Kerk*, p. 145 n. 92.

84. Drew, "Notes," pp. 59–63; "Germanic Family," p. 8; "Family in Frankish Law," p. 5; "Family in Visigothic Law," pp. 7–8.

85. Adventius, in *Ep. Lot.* no. 5, p. 215: "Et ut haec copula iusta esse patesceret."

86. Examples of charters of dotation are in *MGH Formulae: Formulae Andecavenses* no. 34, p. 16, *Formulae Marculfi* Lib. II, nos. 15–16, pp. 85–86, *Formulae Turonenses*, no. 14, pp. 142–43, *Cartae Senonicae*, no. 25, p. 196, *Formulae Salicae Lindenbrogianae*, no. 7, pp. 271–72, *Formulae Augienses B*, no. 25, pp. 358–59, *Collectio Sangallensis*, no. 18, pp. 406–7, *Formulae extravagantes* 1: nos. 9–12, pp. 538–41; provision of a bridal gift, with and without a written charter, in the *Lex Ribuaria*, 41.1–41.2, p. 95; see also Drew, "Germanic Family," p. 8; "Family in Frankish Law," p. 5; "Family in Visigothic Law," pp. 5–6; Kottje, "Eherechtliche Bestimmungen," pp. 214–15; Lauranson-Rosaz, "Douaire"; Le Jan-Hennebicque, "Aux origines"; De Bruin, "Levende schakel," pp. 79–89; Heidrich, "Besitz," pp. 125–27; Pohl-Resl, "Quod me legibus"; Pohl-Resl, "Vorsorge"; Stafford, "Mutation."

87. Demyttenaere, "Wat weet men," p. 29, De Bruin, "Levende schakel," pp. 89–98; for a contrary view, see Lauranson-Rosaz, "Douaire," Le Jan-Hennebicque, "Aux origines," and Hughes, "From Brideprice" (her account of Lothar's case [pp. 274–75] is incorrect). Much of the literature on the bridal gift is confused, partly due to differences in terminology. In the ninth century there was quite a wide variation in customs; the principal com-

Apart from its business element, on occasion the bridal gift could evidently also serve as proof of the legal validity of a marriage.[88] A marriage that had come about in an irregular way without a betrothal, by abduction for instance, could always be put right later by obtaining parental consent and giving a bridal gift.[89] The charter of dotation was the prime written evidence of the union, even when it was drawn up later.[90] Adventius refers to the giving of Waldrada's bridal gift as proof, but without mentioning a charter. Here the means of proof lay in the evidence of those present. Now it may be no coincidence that we have only two extant charters of dotation from the Carolingian kings: from Louis II (5 October 860) and from Charles the Fat, youngest son of Louis the German (1 August 861).[91] Although we know of earlier bridal gifts given to consorts of Carolingian kings, these are the first and only royal charters of dotation from the ninth century.[92] Louis II's charter for his *"sponsa"* (betrothed) Angilberga was actually antedated to 851.[93] But this does not mean that the whole document is a forgery. The bridal gift may well have been made in 851 and the written record of the transaction set down nine years later, when Louis and Angilberga had been married for years and had children. But is it pure chance that precisely these two documents have survived, or did two Carolingian kings, soon after Lothar's matrimonial case became an issue at the

mon factor was that a gift was transferred from the bridegroom's side to that of the bride, and that at a certain time the bride gained control over that gift.

88. Hincmar expressly mentions this several times; see above, pp. 78–83. Mikat, *Dotierte Ehe, rechte Ehe,* even regards the "dos" as *the* vital element that makes a lawful marriage.

89. Drew, "Notes," pp. 61–63; "Germanic Family," p. 8; "Family in Visigothic Law," p. 5; De Bruin, "Levende schakel," pp. 86–87. See also Council of Meaux-Paris (845–46) c. 64, in *MGH Conc.* 3: p. 115, where this procedure is forbidden and punished by public penance and obligatory lifelong abstention, though the latter could be commuted to the payment of a fine. In principle, though, the union was not dissolved; thus also Ben. Lev., Lib. III, c. 395.

90. Some forms for charters of dotation, influenced by Roman law, make such a charter obligatory: *Formulae Marculfi,* Lib. II, no. 14, in *MGH Formulae,* p. 85; *Formulae Turonenses,* nos. 14 and 15, in *MGH Formulae,* pp. 142–43; a loose formulary from the Fleury area, first half of the ninth century, p. 539. By contrast, in the *Formulae Salicae Lindenbrogianae* no. 7, *MGH Formulae,* pp. 271–72: "Per hanc cartolam, libellum dotis, sive per fistucam atque per andelangum"; thus, the choice of "a charter or a twig and a glove."

91. *D Lud.II* no. 30, pp. 125–27, and *D LD* no. 108, pp. 155–56. The property given by Louis the German to his son Charles was intended to serve as a bridal gift. These possessions later passed to the abbey of Andlau, founded by Charles' wife, Richardis. The date is 1 August 861 or 862, with 861 more likely, since in *AB* aᵒ 862, p. 93, Charles' marriage is recorded before the late summer campaign of 862.

92. Lothar I's bridal gift to Ermengarde surfaces when she later uses it to found Erstein monastery. *D Lot.I* no. 106, pp. 251–53. See also Le Jan, "Douaires," pp. 72–73, 77–78.

93. *D Lud.II,* pp. 126–27; Von Pölnitz-Kehr, "Angilberga."

highest level, seek to reinforce the validity of their marriages by providing documentary proof?

One final argument validating the marriage is used only by Gunthar and Theutgaud: the fidelity, affection, and love that exist between the couple. Here they were pleading the actual state of an existing marriage.[94] Fidelity (*fides*) also features in a number of clerical writings on marriage,[95] yet fidelity of this kind need not come from a purely clerical context. For instance, "*fidissimae*," most faithful, is one of the terms used by Einhard for his wife, Emma, in his correspondence. After her death Einhard writes a number of letters to his friend Lupus of Ferrières in which he voices his sorrow and despair following the death of his wife. He tells how much he misses her, especially in the doing of his many daily tasks. Lupus tries to comfort him. Another term for Emma is "*carissime*" (dearest) and the word Einhard uses to describe his feelings for Emma is "*amor.*"[96]

The conjugal love Gunthar and Theutgaud insist on probably also refers to the children of Lothar and Waldrada; they, after all, are the living proof of it.[97] In their view this, among other factors, legitimated the marriage of Lothar and Waldrada. That a genuine marriage existed was plain for all to see.

The arguments adduced by Lothar's bishops in these two texts refer exclusively to secular marriage customs. No priest was involved in any way, except probably as one of the anonymous witnesses. Not only does the reasoning in these two texts differ from that in texts from previous years, so also does the tradition on which that reasoning is based. In the arguments from the years 860–62 all the authors appealed primarily to religious tradition, with numerous quotations from the Bible, canons, and patristic works.

94. Letter from Gunthar of Cologne and Theutgaud of Trier to Pope Nicholas I, in *AB* aº 864, c. 7, p. 110.

95. For example, Jonas of Orléans, *De institutione laicali* Lib. II., c. 4, col. 174–77. Most famous is Augustine's trio: "Fides, proles, sacramentum."

96. Lupus, *Correspondance* 1: pp. 12, 14, 16, 20, 22, 30. Rouche, "Early Middle Ages," pp. 479–80, is mistaken in saying that in the early middle ages the word "*amor*" never appears in a positive sense as love. In fact it does, for example in the correspondence of Einhard and Lupus, *Correspondance* 1: pp. 24, 28, 34. For Pope Nicholas I, too, love, in this case "*affectus*," was a factor that argued for the validity of a marriage; see his letter of mediation to Charles the Bald in the affair of Judith and Baldwin, pp. 157–58 below. The word *affectus*, like *consensus*, is often used in Roman law as a condition for a valid marriage; see below, p. 156.

97. See also *De divortio*, p. 206, as the result of episcopal "marriage counseling": "Et fugato odio diabolico coniugalis amor inter coniuges integratus nunc usque cum debito amore perseverat atque coniugati subole numerosa congaudent" (And after the devilish hatred had been driven out and conjugal love restored between the couple, he continued in conjugal love and the couple rejoiced in numerous descendants).

After 862 writers still referred to these religious authorities, it is true, but apart from a few biblical passages they did not quote them.[98]

THE text of the third Synod of Aachen still spoke of the concubine—and this must mean Waldrada, though they avoided using her name—with whom Lothar lived following his divorce from Theutberga. After this synod, in Lothar's party there was no longer any question of Waldrada being a concubine; on the contrary, every effort was made to show that Waldrada's marriage to Lothar was a lawful marriage and not concubinage. Even so, the reaction of Gunthar and Theutgaud to the use of the term "concubine" for Waldrada was unusually strong, as we have seen. This raises the question of what lies behind the change in the use of this term, and what the description "concubine" might mean at this time.

Most modern historians have tried to solve the problem by making Waldrada a so-called *Friedelfrau*. Alongside the so-called *Muntehe* there supposedly existed among the Franks also a so-called *Friedelehe*. However, this *Friedelehe* is an invention of modern historians, which deserves to be discarded.

The theory on marriage in the early middle ages that still predominates today ascribes to "Germanic" society a set of clearly distinct and well-defined types of marriage. According to this theory the two most important types of "Germanic" marriage were the so-called *Muntehe* (sometimes also called *Sippenvertragsehe*) and the so-called *Friedelehe*.[99] This dualism in marriage types is largely due to the theory about marriage put forward by Herbert Meyer in the 1920s and '30s.[100] Meyer stated that the ancient Germans had two equal types of marriage. The first was the *Muntehe*,

---

98. Adventius, *Ep. Lot.* no. 5, p. 216: Exodus 20:14; Psalms 72:27; Ephesians 5:5; 1 Corinthians 6:9–10; Luke 16:18 (N.B. he does *not* quote Matthew 5:32 or 19:9, with the clause "except it be for fornication"; here the editor is in error); Romans 12:18; letter from Gunthar of Cologne and Theutgaud of Trier to Pope Nicholas I, in *AB* a° 864, p. 110, c. 7. Probably they were referring to the decretal of Leo to Rusticus.

99. Among many others, Bitel, *Women*, pp. 179–81; Le Jan, *Famille*, pp. 262, 271–77; Kottje, "Eherechtliche Bestimmungen," pp. 213–19; Mikat, *Dotierte Ehe*, pp. 49–56; Goetz, "Frauenbild," p. 15; Rouche, "Early Midde Ages," pp. 174–76; Rouche, "Mariages," pp. 845–46; Wemple, *Women* (with a different definition), pp. 12–14, 34–35, 56, 79, 83, 90. More careful is Ogris, "Friedelehe," who is critical, but nonetheless in favor of maintaining something like a *Friedelehe*. Objections have been voiced, often only in a detail or in a passing comment, by Nelson, *Annals of St.-Bertin*, p. 116, n. 12; Joch, "Karl Martell," pp. 150–51; Philip Reynolds, *Marriage*, pp. 71–72, 108; Ebel, "Sog. Friedelehe" and *Konkubinat* (on Icelandic texts only).

100. Meyer, "Friedelehe."

characterized by betrothal, parental agreement, and bride price, in which the protection of and the legal responsibility for the wife (*Munt*) were transferred from the woman's kin to her husband. The second was the *Friedelehe*, a valid marriage, between partners of equal social status, concluded by consent of both partners—as Meyer puts it, "*zu Lust und Liebe,*" (out of sexual desire and love)—without a parental agreement. In this *Friedelehe* the wife remained part of her father's family and did not become her husband's responsibility, nor was she entitled to his protection. The public acts required for the *Friedelehe* were the public procession of the bride to the groom's house and the so-called *Morgengabe*, a gift from the husband to his wife made on the morning after the wedding night. Meyer based his ideas on the theories of Johann Jakob Bachofen (1815–87) about primitive Germanic society; he posited the existence of a matriarchate, from which developed a type of law that Bachofen called *Mutterrecht*. Bachofen's theories have long since been rejected, but Meyer still held them to be true and he considered the *Friedelehe* to be the marital type sprung from the so-called *Mutterrecht*, the *Muntehe* the type sprung from the so-called *Vaterrecht*, the law that, in Bachofen's and Meyer's view, emanated from the patriarchate that succeeded the matriarchate. According to Meyer the *Friedelehe* was the ancient Germanic form of marriage from which everything that was beautiful and decent in marriage originated.[101]

Meyer's theory was almost immediately criticized by Rudolf Hübner, who branded it a bold hypothesis that was lacking any consistency.[102] Nonetheless, Hübner's criticism attracted little attention and Meyer's theory became generally accepted. After 1945 some of its rough edges were smoothed out. The links between the *Mutterrecht* and the "Urgermanentum" ("original" Germanic society that supposedly had existed) disappeared. The theory that the consensus between both partners as a constitutive element of marriage had originated in the *Friedelehe* was dropped by most historians, since it was obviously also part of Roman law. The remaining characteristic features of the *Friedelehe* were that both partners were of equal social status, that the agreement of the families was not required, and that the woman was legally not subject to her husband but to her own kin group.

However, can we verify this theory? Is there anything in our early medieval sources that proves the existence of this *Friedelehe*? The most impor-

---

101. Ibid., esp. pp. 212–14, 241, about consensus as the "common Germanic basis" of the "Friedelehe," pp. 242, 280, about the woman belonging to her father's "Sippe" and the "Mutterrecht," finally the valuation on p. 283.

102. Hübner, *Grundzüge*, pp. 619–20, 622–23, 641–43.

tant text by far that is quoted as proof for this is a ruling in the *Lex Salica*, the law of the Salian Franks. The *Lex Salica* is a very important text indeed, with eighty-four extant manuscripts dating from the eighth, ninth, and tenth centuries, most of them from the ninth. It was widely copied in the early middle ages. Because of its manuscript tradition it is also a complicated text.[103] The text as the twentieth-century editor prints it is a reconstruction, the text as he thought it had once been. It reads in the version he thought to be the oldest as follows: "If someone with a free girl out of free will, both agreeing, (secretly) has committed fornication, (and this is proven) which they call *firilasia* on the *mallberg*, then he is due 1,800 denarii, which is 45 solidi."[104] If we look at "firilasia," the word that is supposedly referring to the word *Friedelehe*, we notice that this exact word does not appear in any manuscript. Two manuscripts give it in different versions: "firilayso" and "fredolasio,"[105] three others in even stranger versions: "Fribasina," "Frilafina," "Fribafina."[106] One wonders whether these copyists had a clue what they were writing down. This does not seem to refer to a widely known type of marriage called *Friedelehe*. None of the other seventy-eight manuscripts have words that show any resemblance to "firilasia."

Does this text refer to any kind of marriage? I think it does not. What it does mean becomes clear when we look at the preceding laws, which are arranged according to a well-established order. This series of laws deals with similar offenses, starting with the most severe one, demanding the heaviest fine, and ending with the least serious one with the lowest fine: from taking away someone's wife, to committing fornication by force with a free, unmarried girl, to fornication with a free unmarried girl, which in our case is not by force but with her consent.[107] Obviously this does not

---

103. Six major versions are distinguished by the editor, each consisting of a group of manuscripts from the eighth to the tenth century. The so-called A-text, probably written in the early sixth century and extant in four mss. (from the end of the eighth and the ninth century), is considered to be the oldest. The best analysis of the manuscript tradition is McKitterick, *Carolingians and the Written Word*, pp. 40–60. The most recent editions are *Lex Salica* and *Pactus Legis Salicae*.

104. *Pactus Legis Salicae*, XV. 3, pp. 70–71: "Si quis cum ingenua puella spontanea voluntate ambis convenientibus (occulte) moechati fuerint (cui adprobatum fuerit), mallobergo firilasia sunt, MDCCC denarii qui facint solidos XLV culpabils iudicetur." There were sometimes added words in the vernacular with the mention of *malbergo* (meaning, in court, "*mallus*"). The word "*occulte*" (secretly) in parentheses raises a question. Authors referring to this text as evidence for *Friedelehe* generally leave it out (if they quote the text at all). It is obvious that fornication in secret is not the same as a marriage, let alone a generally recognized type of marriage. Looking at the manuscript evidence it appears that only two out of eighty-four mss. (albeit in the A-text) do *not* use "*occulte*."

105. *Pactus Legis Salicae*, MSS A2 and C6.

106. *Lex Salica* XV. 3, pp. 56–57, MSS D7, 8 and 9.

107. *Pactus Legis Salicae*, XV. 3, pp. 70–71.

refer to some kind of "Germanic marriage" but to an offense, secret fornication of a man with a free girl. The fact that she did consent lessened the offense, however. If not, this would have been the more serious offense of rape, which was dealt with by the preceding law.

Regarding another text, from the *Lex Baiwariorum*, which is sometimes adduced as evidence for the *Friedelehe*, it is difficult to understand how this could ever have been seen as referring to a marriage: "If someone fornicates with a free woman, with her consent, but does not want to marry her . . ."[108]

The next text quoted as evidence for the existence of the *Friedelehe* is the passage in Einhard's *Vita Karoli* about Charlemagne's daughters. They supposedly had chosen the *Friedelehe* type of marriage. However, the text simply says that "Charlemagne did not give his daughters into marriage, but kept them with him in his house till his death, because he could not bear to live without them."[109] We do know that his daughters had partners and children, but there is nothing that proves that the relations of Charlemagne's daughters were *Friedelehen*, concluded without the agreement of their father. Somehow I find it hard to imagine that anyone would have dared enter into a sexually based relationship with one of Charlemagne's daughters without asking her father's permission. Einhard's main point is that Charlemagne's daughters stayed in their father's house. Getting married would normally have meant leaving his home. The unusual feature of these relationships was apparently that they were uxorilocal: the men moved in with their women, while for the Franks the opposite was usual. A man "led his wife into marriage" (*uxorem duxit*) or "took her with him" (*uxorem sibi sociavit*). Anyway, the case of Charlemagne's daughters seems to have been a special one, in view of who their father was. I have not been able to find any evidence of *Friedelehen* that meet the mentioned criteria, in Frankish early medieval sources.[110]

Meyer found another important collection of evidence for his theory in Old Scandinavian sources. In these mainly eleventh- to thirteenth-century Old Icelandic sources, the old Germanic society would have been reflected, since Icelandic society as depicted in these sources would show great similarities with the "original" Germanic societies on the Continent.

108. *Lex Baiwariorum*, VIII. 8, p. 357: "Si quis cum libera per consensum ipsius fornicaverit et nolet eam in coniugium sociare." Ibid., VIII, 17, p. 316, is not about *Friedelehe* either, but about breaking a promise to marry.

109. Einhard, *Vita Karoli*, c. 19, p. 25: "Omnes secum usque ad obitum suum in domo sua retinuit, dicens se earum contubernio carere non posse."

110. That the marriage of William the Conqueror's parents, which is sometimes also called a *Friedelehe* by modern historians, cannot be considered as such, has convincingly been shown by Philip Reynolds, *Marriage*, pp. 110–12.

In these Icelandic sources a *frilla*, the partner of a free man, is mentioned. According to Meyer, these were women joined in *Friedelehe* with their husbands. However, Else Ebel has recently reviewed these same Old Icelandic sources and has reached the conclusion that in the Old Icelandic sagas and in Icelandic law there is no sign of this so-called *Friedelehe*. According to her, Meyer has taken his examples out of context. The women named *frilla* are either women of a lower social status or wives of priests (because even if these sources are meant to reflect a pure Germanic society they date nonetheless from after the eleventh-century Gregorian reform). Furthermore, the word *frilla* could be used as an insult for a woman living in a dishonorable relationship.[111]

In conclusion, Meyer's theory on the *Friedelehe* is overdue for the dustbin. It is a theory without any foundation in the sources. He concocted the term, based on far-fetched and long-since rejected nineteenth-century theories, and it has been haunting historiography ever since, leading students and scholars who are trying to get a grasp on early medieval marriage into confusion.

We should not view marriage in early medieval society as being regulated by strictly formulated and always valid laws. Reading through the sources one often gets the impression that the confusion is not so much about, for example, who does what to whom, but about the names used for this, either in medieval sources or by modern historians. Here a strict legalistic approach unnecessarily complicates things. It seems more useful to investigate, for example, what "concubine" meant in actual cases.

In the texts from 860 to mid-862 Lothar's bishops argue mainly from canon law. They speak of a wife, Theutberga, to whom Lothar had been formally married and who had publicly functioned as his wife, but whom he now wished to repudiate. Then there was also another woman, Waldrada, with whom Lothar was living and who was in practical terms his wife. This woman the authors had to call a concubine. They could not call her a wife, even if Lothar had previously been lawfully married to her, without creating major problems with the canonical rules, for Lothar would then be a bigamist.[112] What is clear is that they tried to promote Waldrada to wife as quickly as possible.

From mid-862 on, though, they maintained that Waldrada was certainly not to be regarded as a concubine. But what is meant by a "concubine"? When the sources brand a man's female partner a "concubine" they may

111. Ebel, *Konkubinat*, and "Sog. Friedelehe."

112. This is precisely what happens when they change their arguments in 862; see below, p. 153.

mean any one of a number of things, because there is no such thing as one specific type of relationship denoted by the term "concubinage." It is very clear, however, that the "concubine" ranks below the "lawful wife" in status.[113] "Concubine" can refer to a whole range of different relationships between a man and a woman, relationships entered into for different purposes and fulfilling different functions. First, there was the union between one free and one unfree partner. The unfree wife of a free man is labeled a concubine by the Church fathers, in line with a current meaning of the word in Roman law.[114] Then there were many permanent relationships between free individuals that were not marriages. As Jonas of Orléans writes in his *De Institutione laicali*:

> There are people who from lasciviousness or desire for worldly honor, instead of waiting for the time when they are worthy of that worldly honor, wallow in the mire of lasciviousness and prior to their marriage corrupt themselves in various ways and lose their virginity, which they ought to preserve until the time when they shall receive their lawful wife. And thus they deprive themselves of the blessing that God gave to the first human couple, and which in the Church is now bestowed on those who marry by the priestly office according to canonical authority and the customs of the Roman Church. And because of this there prevails the pernicious practice that only very seldom are bride and bridegroom blessed, according to the established liturgical order, by the celebration of a mass.[115]

This concubinage was a not uncommon premarital stable relationship between free persons. Evidently this was a relationship that had not been sealed by a public ceremony, as a betrothal or a marriage was, but which was not dishonorable or devoid of legal and practical consequences.

113. It would be desirable to investigate a large number of references to "concubines" and "wives"; what follows is based on a limited number of references.

114. Brundage, "Concubinage," pp. 2–3; Gaudemet, "Legs," pp. 147–48, 156–57; Pope Leo I made a sharp distinction between concubine/slave and wife/free woman; see above, p. 26.

115. Jonas of Orléans, *De institutione laicali* Lib. II. c. 2, col. 170–71: "Quidam laicorum amore libidinis superati, quidam vero ambiendi honoris terreni cupiditate ducti, imo praestolandi tempus quo honores mundi nancisci valeant, interim in coeno luxuriae se volutantes, antequam ad copulam connubii accedant, diversissimis modis se corrumpunt et virginale decus, quod usque ad tempus legitimae uxoris accipiendae conservare debuerant, amittunt, nec non et benedictione, qua Deus copulae primorum hominum benedixit, et ea quae nunc in Ecclesia per sacerdotum ministeria secundum canonicam auctoritatem, et sanctae Romanae Ecclesiae morem nupturis exhibetur, se privant. Unde etenim damnanda consuetudo inolevit, ut perraro sponsus et sponsa in missarum celebratione, secundum praemissum ordinem, benedicantur."

Moreover, on occasion the relationship was entered into out of worldly ambition. The children of such relationships were able to inherit from their parents.[116] The dividing line between concubinage and a "lawful" marriage could be flexible. A concubine could later advance to being a wife. Naturally there were also other kinds of nonmarital relationships between free people, with other ends in view. For instance, there was the concubine of a man who had been married and already had sufficient heirs; his relationship with his concubine could be primarily one of affection or of sex. The term could also refer to a second wife. Some authors were unwilling to describe a second wife as a lawful wife while the first wife was still living. Finally, the word "concubine" could also be used simply as a term of abuse, to disqualify a relationship or the children born from it.

The use of the term "concubine" for Waldrada refers to several of these situations. Waldrada had had a premarital relationship with Lothar when the latter was still living with his father. Possibly it was even intended that they should marry each other, as Lothar and Liutfrid maintained. After the first attempt to divorce Theutberga, Lothar and Waldrada had lived together as man and wife, though without the divorce having been definitively settled for all those concerned.[117] Waldrada was therefore Lothar's number-two wife. In addition, the label of concubine acted as a term of abuse that smacked unpleasantly of servitude.

We often find this kind of relationship among the Carolingian kings. Concubinage in the sense of a premarital steady relationship with a free woman was a common phenomenon among the young sons of Carolingian kings. One might imagine that fathers did not necessarily insist on a public betrothal ceremony with a bridal gift when a king's son chose their daughter as partner, with all the attractive prospects of influence, riches, and royal descendants that this held out. Some of these relationships with

---

116. Jonas of Orléans, *De institutione laicali* Lib. II. c. 2, col. 171. For the definition of such children, see also Hrabanus, *De Universo*, col. 188 (= Isidore, *Etymologiae* IX, V, 19); see Winterer, "Stellung," on inheritance by natural children in Langobardic law. Among the Franks, natural children could evidently sometimes inherit. For instance, Engeltrude's son from her second relationship, with Wanger, after she had left her first husband, Boso, inherited some of her possessions, against the protests of Pope John VIII, who demanded the legacy for the daughters of Engeltrude's first marriage, who were probably still living in Italy. Letters from John to Louis the Younger, Liutbert, bishop of Mainz, and Engeltrude's brother Matfrid, *Ep. Joh. VIII* (878), pp. 102–3, 114–15. Engeltrude had evidently divided her estate between, among others, her son Godfrid, her brother Matfrid, and King Louis the Younger.

117. See the remarks in the letter by Lothar's bishops, *Ep. Lot.* no. 2, p. 211. Pope Nicholas's judgment was still awaited.

concubines were later upgraded to "lawful marriage" when the prince had become a king. This was the case, for example, with the marriages of Louis the Pious and Ermengarde and of Louis II and Angilberga.[118] Sometimes, though, such a concubinage was terminated when the prince found someone more attractive (politically, in most cases) as a marriage partner. After the death of his first wife the king could again take a concubine, whom he could later marry as his second wife. Charles the Bald took Richildis as his concubine as soon as he learned of the death of his first wife, Ermentrude, and married her a few months later with due ceremony, after a formal betrothal and bridal gift. For some years he had been hoping for a new son to succeed him, as the special coronation ceremony for Ermentrude three years earlier had shown. Their four sons who had reached adulthood had all suffered a tragic fate. Charles the Bald's relations with his eldest son, Louis the Stammerer, had always been disastrous, since they disliked each other and Charles did not consider him a fit successor. His heir apparent, also named Charles, had been killed in a brawl, while the two youngest boys, Carloman and the sickly Lothar, had been destined for careers in the church. After the death of his brothers Charles and Lothar, Carloman considered himself a possible successor to the throne but was hampered by the fact that meanwhile he had been ordained, something that Charles the Bald and many others were not willing to overlook. Nonetheless, he made several bids for power, gaining a large amount of support. His last rebellion proved fatal to his hopes, since Charles finally had his son's eyes put out. Ermentrude died in 869 after bearing Charles more than a dozen children; the rest were girls, or sons who did not reach adulthood. As soon as Charles heard that Ermentrude was dead and buried he sent Boso to fetch his sister Richildis and took her to his bed. Richildis would give him one child after another until Charles' death, but all the sons died in childhood.[119] Sometimes, when a king was more advanced in years, he would have concubines, often of lower social standing, with whom he would spend what remained of his life; Charlemagne and Lothar I are instances of this.[120] In practical terms there was probably little differ-

---

118. Konecny, *Frauen*, pp. 73, 118–21; for various types of relationships that could be described as concubinage, see also Stafford, *Queens*, pp. 62–71.

119. *AB* a° 869 and 870, pp. 167, 169. For Ermentrude's coronation ceremony, see above, p. 28.

120. Konecny, *Frauen*, pp. 65–71. See the charter of Lothar I in which he frees his concubine Doda, *D Lot.I* no. 113 (19 April 851), pp. 262–63; in *D Lot.I* no. 138 (9 July 855), p. 309, she appears as intercessor. She and Lothar I had a son with the markedly Carolingian name of Carloman; however, he was not included in the succession, *AB* a° 853, p. 67.

ence between the position of some of these concubines, provided they were of noble birth, and that of lawful wives. In many cases the children of a concubinage that did not progress to a lawful marriage also had the right of succession. Often, however, the succession depended mainly on the political situation at the time. There is ample evidence for sons of women who had at some time been labeled concubines and who still became king. An important factor in the disputes about the succession of the sons of "concubines" is that during the reign of Louis the Pious religious concepts of marriage had gained greater influence. Louis had had his sons lawfully married and had decreed in his *Ordinatio Imperii* that sons of concubines could not succeed their father as king. He himself married again after the death of his first wife and, so far as we know, during his marriages he had no concubines.[121] In this he differed from his forebears, Mayor of the Palace Pippin II, Charles Martel, and Charlemagne, who were clearly not monogamous.[122] Henceforth the Christian norm of indissoluble, monogamous marriage would be used as a political weapon, for instance to stigmatize sons as not being born of a lawful marriage and thus exclude them from the succession.[123]

Lothar's bishops rejected the pejorative use of the term concubine: Waldrada was Lothar's wife, not his concubine. Their relationship had all the hallmarks of a marriage: they were both free, the parents had approved their union, there had been a public betrothal with a bridal gift, and they lived together in fidelity and love. By the time the bishops wrote this Waldrada had already been crowned queen, and as the new queen she had been publicly acclaimed by the people.[124] In Lothar's charters she is described as his beloved wife[125] and their names, together with that of their little son Hugo, were perpetuated in the *liber memorialis* of Reichenau monastery,

---

In 861 Doda was in the retinue of Lothar II at Remiremont, Schmid, "Königseintrag," pp. 103–4.

121. *Ordinatio Imperii* c. 15, in *MGH Cap.* 1: p. 273; Konecny, *Frauen*, pp. 86–97, and Konecny, "Eherecht."

122. Konecny, *Frauen*, pp. 45–57, 65–71. Mayor of the Palace Pippin II was succeeded by sons from various concurrent marriages; Joch, "Karl Martell." For Charlemagne, see Rudolf Schieffer, "Karl Martell," pp. 310–14, Jarnut, "Bruderkampf," pp. 167–70, and the letter from Pope Stephen III, *Ep. karol. aevi* 1: p. 561.

123. Konecny, *Frauen*, pp. 86–156; Stafford, *Queens*, pp. 62–71. For the succession of the sons of Louis the Stammerer, see Brühl, "Hincmariana," pp. 60–77; Hlawitschka, *Lotharingien*, pp. 221–40; Werner, "Nachkommen," pp. 437–41; and above, pp. 98, 114–15.

124. *AB* a° 862, pp. 93–94; Regino a° 864 (incorrect dating, immediately after a quotation from the Council of Aachen [862]), p. 82.

125. *D Lot.II.*, no. 19 (18 May 863), p. 415: "Amantissimae conjugis nostrae Waldradae et filii nostri Ugonis."

where the monks were to pray for the souls of the three of them until the end of time.[126]

The Powers of the Bishops

During these years, Lothar followed the line laid down for him by his bishops in the matter of his marriage. What arguments did these bishops use to justify their actions in the marital affairs of Lothar, their king? Two themes are central to their reasoning: the function of the king, and that of the bishops in relation to their king.[127]

The texts originating from Lothar's circle stress the unique position of the king. He is appointed by God, through hereditary succession. The king, who derives his power from God, is Christ's viceroy on earth. If he performs his task correctly, after his death he will be rewarded by Christ.[128] The king's power is justified by stating that it is the will of God that he should wield that power. Repeatedly cited in this context are Proverbs 21:1, "The king's heart is in the hand of the Lord; he turneth it whithersoever he will," and Paul's epistle to the Romans 13:1, "There is no power but of God."[129]

We should not interpret this reference to the king's divine authorization as meaning that Lothar is here declaring that he can therefore do whatever he wants.[130] Neither in the council texts nor in the letters of Lothar and his

126. *Verbrüderungsbuch Reichenau*, Facsimile p. 8A: "Hlotharius rex, Waldrada, Hug."

127. We find these arguments in the records of the Aachen council of 862 and in letters from the bishops and from Lothar himself. Lothar's letters and his written statement at the 862 Aachen council were very probably composed by bishops, the letters almost certainly by Adventius of Metz, for all of them appear in Adventius's letter collection. Stylistic comparison with Adventius's letters reveals striking similarities: see Staubach, *Herrschersbild*, pp. 154–74, 181–87, 278–84B. Lothar's statement at the Aachen council is thoroughly clerical in its approach, peremptorily insisting on episcopal involvement in the case. That is not to say, of course, that Lothar took no part in the framing of the letters and statement.

128. *Ep. Lot.* no. 7, p. 218; *Ep. Lot.* no. 17, p. 236; Council of Aachen, 29 April 862 (1st version, text A) c. 1, in *MGH Conc.* 4: p. 72.

129. *Ep. Lot.* no. 7, p. 218: "Non est potestas nisi a Deo" (Romans 13:1); also *Ep. Lot.* no. 14, p. 232: "Non est potestas nisi ab ipso." In the report of the Aachen council of 862 and in the letter from Lothar's bishops and those of Charles the Bald to the bishops of Louis the German, in *MGH Conc.* 4, p. 45, Proverbs 21:1 is used. As we already commented (pp. 95–96 above) Proverbs 21:1 was probably also used as a counter to Hincmar's *De divortio*.

130. Anton, "Synoden," pp. 92–118, 124, and Anton, *Fürstenspiegel*, pp. 357–62, describes the Lotharingian bishops as representatives of a specifically Lotharingian political ideology that emphasizes the divine legitimation of kingly rule. He even speaks of "Hofabsolutisten" (court absolutists). This Lotharingian ideology would contrast with a "westfränkisch-kirchliches Gesellschaftsmodell" (western Frankish ecclesiastical model of society), according to which the king had to answer to God for his actions but had been consecrated and must be corrected by his bishops. Anton's theories on these two

supporters is there any suggestion of Lothar demanding powers as a God-appointed king. Above all, we must not see this too much in black and white. The letters particularly, which put most stress on the king being divinely appointed, are those of a king fighting for political survival.[131] In the years after 862 Lothar's political situation became increasingly perilous. People were threatening to depose him and deprive him of his kingdom, and he defended himself against this threat. Consequently, the reasoning was not "I am a king appointed by God and so I can do as I like," but rather "I am a king appointed by God and so you are not allowed to depose me."

The same texts, though, also assign a significant role to the bishops. Lothar's statement to the Aachen council almost overwhelmed his bishops with important functions:

> You are appointed as mediators between God and men. To you is entrusted the care of our souls. You provide the medicines for the wounds, which are our sins. You have the power to bind and to loose and you are our teachers and guides. . . . The royal power has to acknowledge the supreme authority of the episcopal dignity, by which both orders of the Church's faithful are, after all, ruled and governed by God's authority.[132]

But Lothar also demanded something of his bishops. They were responsible for his spiritual welfare, and therefore they had to cure him of his sins. They had to advise him, cleanse him of his sins by imposing penance on him, and, finally, prevent him from sinning again.[133] On the one hand he was obliged to follow their advice, but on the other much of the responsibility also rested on the bishops' shoulders. They must not give advice that could not be followed; Lothar made that very clear. He was young

---

conflicting models and the conclusions he draws from them regarding a regional Lotharingian sense of solidarity seem to me incorrect. I shall reserve my arguments on this matter for another work.

131. In letters from Lothar to Pope Nicholas, reacting to the papal letter in which Nicholas dismissed the archbishops of Cologne and Trier and threatened to depose Lothar as well, *Ep. Lot.* no. 7, p. 218; on false accusations against Lothar made to Nicholas: *Ep. Lot.* no. 14, p. 232; in the letter from the bishops of Lothar and Charles the Bald to those of Louis the German (in *MGH Conc.* 4: p. 45) the biblical quotation (Proverbs 21:1) is used less as a justification of royal power than as an elegant form of appeal to King Louis to act correctly, that is, in this case to allow his bishops to attend a synod; in the Aachen council report (in *MGH Conc.* 4: p. 72), this quotation is used to describe the king's proper behavior, achieved through episcopal correction.

132. Council of Aachen (862), *Contestatio Hlotharii*, in *MGH Conc.* 4: p. 74. The same argument in a letter from Lothar's bishops to their colleagues in the realm of Charles the Bald, *Ep. Lot.* no. 13, p. 229.

133. Council of Aachen (862), *Contestatio Hlotharii*, in *MGH Conc.* 4, p. 74; (1st version, text A) c. 1–3, p. 72; (2nd version, text C), p. 76; see also the letter from Lothar's bishops to their colleagues in the realm of Charles the Bald, *Ep. Lot.* no. 13, p. 229.

and needed a wife "to quench the fire of his youthfulness." He was not allowed to keep a concubine, nor to take back his former wife, and in view of his upbringing lifelong abstention was not a viable option for him. They must therefore find a solution that was right for his body and his soul.[134] This was all the more necessary because, as king, his conduct was inextricably bound up with the fate of his kingdom, his people, and the Church, which it was his duty to protect. If the path the bishops set out for him was not the right one, they too would have failed in the execution of their appointed task.

These ideas of the far-reaching powers of the episcopacy, with their reference to the bishops' power as holders of the keys, their authority to bind and to loose everything on earth, their duty to care for each individual soul and to cure sins, including those of the king, are familiar concepts. They are in line with what we have already seen in the writings of Hincmar of Reims and in the reports of the great Frankish councils of 858–60. This is not surprising, given that both Hincmar and the majority of Lothar's bishops were present at those councils.[135]

Lothar's Bishops in Their Political Context

We have seen that during these years most—though certainly not all—of Lothar's bishops supported their king in his attempt to divorce in order to remarry. What were their motives for doing so, and why did they call on the above-mentioned arguments on the legal status of marriage? The first thing that strikes one about their reasoning on this point is the radical change it underwent in the course of 862. How can we explain this? On the one hand, we must look for their motives in the obligations they owed as bishops to their king, which were political as well as religious in nature. On the other hand, the bishops did not act solely out of an altruistic sense of duty. They also had something to gain. And both motivations are closely interwoven with the exercise of political power in the Carolingian empire.

The Legal Status of Marriage in Its Political Context: The Change of Argument

In the summer or autumn of 862 Lothar's bishops came up with new arguments to support their contention that Lothar's marriage to Theutberga was invalid and that to Waldrada valid. In doing so they no longer argued

---

134. Council of Aachen (862) (1st version, text A) c. 3, in *MGH Conc.* 4: pp. 72–73: "Iuvenilis aetatis ardorem ferre non posse"; *Contestatio Hlotharii, MGH Conc.* 4: p. 75.

135. See above, act 3, n. 15.

purely from canon law, but drew mainly on secular laws and customs. Since these are still the same bishops as before, we have to wonder why they opted for a new and different justification in the second half of 862. I will try, cautiously, to work out some possible reasons.

One possibility is that this change in argument is connected with the changed situation regarding the proof of Theutberga's guilt. The entire canonical proceedings stood or fell with Theutberga's confession. This was indeed available to the bishops, even set down on paper and publicly attested to, but Theutberga herself had escaped from the convent to which she had been sent. Now she was everywhere proclaiming that her confession had been extorted under duress and that she was innocent. Her protests were supported by her family and by Charles the Bald and had already reached the ears of Pope Nicholas I. The evidence on which the divorce had been based was in danger of falling apart, and so new arguments were needed. It was now claimed that Lothar's marriage to Waldrada was valid because it had been contracted before he married Theutberga. The marriage to Theutberga was a second marriage, which had moreover been forced on Lothar, and was therefore invalid. The argument now shifted to the legality of the original marriage, that of Lothar and Waldrada.

Another possibility is that the union with Waldrada had already been regarded as a valid marriage prior to this, but that there is no record of this in sources dating from before 862. In that case, Lothar would already have had a steady relationship with Waldrada before his accession, one that was not entered into without formality and that had at least social implications. Waldrada was the partner of the crown prince. Whether there ever really was a solemn public betrothal and bridal gift in the presence of great nobles and bishops, as described by Adventius, is doubtful. Adventius covers himself by saying that he himself was not there.[136] It seems more likely that, if any such formality took place, it did so "in a corner," consisting perhaps simply of the consent of Lothar senior.

Be that as it may, the relationship was terminated by Lothar's marriage to Theutberga, which—this much at least is clear—was the result of political opportunism and not of conjugal passion. The ending of a relationship entered into in youth was nothing uncommon among Carolingian rulers. The same went for the discarding of one wife in order to marry another, as Charlemagne and even Louis the Stammerer did, though such actions were very much dependent on the political balance of power. What Lothar did was not particularly strange in itself, but he did it in a different way and under different political circumstances. We shall look more closely at those

136. Adventius, in *Ep. Lot.* no. 5, p. 216.

circumstances later. The way in which he tried to free himself of his wife Theutberga in 860–62 was by means of canon law proceedings. This does not mean that he did not in fact, just like his forefathers, already have another wife who acted as such in the sight of all: Waldrada. With the passage of time their union was seen as a continuous relationship in which Waldrada was for years, apart from one interval of eighteen months, the woman at Lothar's side and the mother of his children.

The Obligations of the Bishops

As we have seen, it was the bishops' religious duty to care for the spiritual well-being of their king. They had to point out to him his moral failings, correct his behavior, and cleanse him of his sins. Because the well-being of the king was bound up with that of his kingdom, this meant that they were also responsible for that kingdom. But that was not all, for in a very real way the bishops were part of the kingdom's government. We find bishops playing every possible role: as ambassadors and letter writers for their king, as part of the royal retinue publicly attesting their support, on occasion as political intriguers. They were part of the political establishment that controlled what went on in the Carolingian empire. They were among those followers of a king who had been given an office by him or by his predecessor and carried out its functions for him. They had sworn to be faithful to him and had a duty to advise and assist him in maintaining his kingdom. The loyalty they owed to the hereditary monarch is apparent from statements by Lothar himself and by his bishops.[137]

In practice the two functions of the bishops—religious, with the concern for spiritual welfare, which included sacral means such as penance, and political, with loyalty to the king and support for his power—clearly overlapped. This is splendidly illustrated by two letters from Adventius of Metz, copies of which he kept in his letter collection. Writing to Theutgaud of Trier, he begins with the cryptic words, "We humbly beseech you, by God and for God's sake, that no other mortal man may see this letter, but that ravenous Vulcan may devour it after you have read it."[138] In plain language, burn this letter as soon as you've read it! This letter, like one to

137. Letter from Gunthar of Cologne and Theutgaud of Trier to the other bishops of their realm, *AB* a° 864, pp. 107–8; Council of Aachen, 29 April 862, *Contestatio Lotharii*, in *MGH Conc.* 4: p. 75; letter from Lothar's bishops to their colleagues in the realm of Charles the Bald, *Ep. Lot.* no. 13, p. 229.

138. Adventius to Theutgaud, *Ep. Lot.* no. 4, p. 214: "Praesentes apices per Deum et propter Deum humiliter precamur, ut nullus alius mortalium videat, sed Vulcanus edax perspectos consumat." For the dating of these letters, see Staubach, *Herrscherbild*, pp. 188–92, which convincingly dates them, in contrast to the edition, to shortly before 2 February 863. See also Buc, *Danger*, pp. 64–66.

Hatto of Verdun, is a secret missive to a colleague. Adventius impresses on them that they must reveal the contents of the letter to no one except Lothar, their lord.[139] They must make sure that Lothar listens to them and is not seduced into any rash action.[140] For the situation is now critical. Adventius has learned from two sources, namely from the realms of Charles the Bald and Louis the German, that Lothar is in danger of being excommunicated by Pope Nicholas if he does not end his relationship with Waldrada. Adventius now suggests that Lothar should come to Flörching (near Thionville) two days before the feast of the Purification (2 February). There he should be cleansed of his sins by three selected, trusted bishops by begging forgiveness in their presence, sighing and in tears, and promising to mend his ways. Then he should be accepted back by the bishops, signifying that he has done penance and is absolved of his sins. After this he should swear an oath regarding his lawful marriage, which should be repeated by his selected trusted followers. "After that," says Adventius, "he can, without imperiling his soul or risking the diminution of the realm given him by God, celebrate the feast of the Purification in the church of St. Arnulf in Metz. If he does not do this, he will irrevocably plunge himself and us, who are loyal to him for the sake of God and of the world, into ruin." [141] The bishops thus expunge their king's sins in secret, so that he cannot be accused. They use their sacral powers to save the soul and the kingdom of their king, and thus also themselves; and all while citing the loyalty they owe him and their episcopal duty of the cure of souls. Theutgaud had already done the same thing when, during Lent 862, he had absolved Lothar "according to divine counsel and his own" of the sin he had committed by taking a concubine. Then Lothar, cleansed of sin, could appear before the Council of Aachen a week after Easter and with a clean slate ask for a new marriage.[142] The extent to which they used penance as an instrument is clear when we look at the last, equally cryptic sentence of Adventius's letter to Theutgaud: "After all, it seems to us better

---

139. *Ep. Lot.* no. 4 (see preceding note) and no. 15, p. 233: "Hi ergo apices sub sigillo confessionis mittuntur, ita videlicet, ut propter Deum vobis sit, ne ullus mortalium praeter vos et nostrum seniorem, si volueritis, ullatenus videat."

140. *Ep. Lot.* no. 4, pp. 214–15.

141. *Ep. Lot.* no. 15, pp. 232–33, on p. 233: "Sicque ... absque omni periculo animae suae et a Deo sibi concessi regni minoratione ecclesiam sancti Arnulphi liber ac securus in Purificatione sanctae Mariae, eandem sanctam festivitatem celebraturus introeat. Alioquin se ipsum et nos omnes qui illi secundum Deum et secundum saeculum fideles sumus, ad inrecuperabilem perditionem, ut veri simile cernitur, perducet."

142. Council of Aachen (862) (1st version, text A) c. 3, in *MGH Conc.* 4: p. 73: "Iuxta divinum atque suum consilium." See above, p. 103. For penance by the king, see De Jong, "Power."

to feign a sickness than for the exhausted stomach to reject the remedy prepared by God."[143] In other words, it is better to do penance, even if one has not committed that particular sin. Even if Lothar has committed no sin by marrying Waldrada, it is better that he should now do penance. Here the use of the sacral remedy is purely tactical.

What the Bishops Stood to Gain

Obviously, the bishops had every reason to show loyalty to their king. He could reward them with gifts to their church, favors to family and friends, and influence on his decisions, in much the same way as he rewarded his lay supporters. Conversely, he could also make things difficult for them if they opposed him. This worked well so long as Lothar was able to hold on to his kingdom. The vicissitudes of some lay abbacies clearly demonstrate the workings of this reward principle and how all this was interwoven with the matter of Lothar's divorce.

On his accession Lothar had had to distribute offices among his followers. Of these the family of his brother-in-law Hucbert, in particular, received a very generous share. Hucbert himself evidently had a taste for abbeys; he was lay abbot of St.-Maurice and later tried to get his hands on Luxeuil and Lobbes as well,[144] while his brother-in-law Bivin became lay abbot of Gorze. A number of these acquisitions were at the expense of bishops who had previously administered those monasteries. Hucbert displaced Aimonius, bishop of Sion, from his post as abbot of St.-Maurice.[145] At this time Gorze monastery was run by Drogo, bishop of Metz. It had been founded by Bishop Chrodegang of Metz and still maintained close links with the bishops of Metz, some of whom were even buried there.[146] After Drogo's death in 855 Gorze passed to Bivin. Following his first attempt at divorce Lothar stripped Hucbert and Bivin of their possessions.[147] Lothar had some difficulty in asserting his authority in St.-Maurice, but Bivin vanished from Gorze, whereupon Lothar gave it to Adventius, the new bishop of Metz. Adventius "restored the status quo" and brought the monastery back under Church control, citing his episcopal authority as vicar of Christ.[148] In this he also was very much in accord with one of the major points raised at the great councils of 858–59: the struggle against lay abbots

---

143. *Ep. Lot.* no. 4, p. 215: "Aptius enim nobis cernitur simulari infirmitas, quam ut praeparatam a Deo medicinam languens stomachus reiciat."
144. See above, pp. 59–61.
145. Dupraz, "Capitulaire," pp. 257–60.
146. Oexle, "Karolinger," pp. 281–82, 351–53.
147. See above, pp. 71–72.
148. *Cartulaire de Gorze* no. 60, pp. 106–7.

and the attempt to restore Church property to the control of the religious authorities, in this case the bishops.[149]

LOTHAR's bishops supported their king because it was their religious duty to do so: as bishops, as supreme guardians of faith and morals, indeed of the whole Church, for which they were answerable to God. This support for their king could pay dividends, also in purely material terms, as is apparent from Adventius's struggle against lay abbacy. Here we see that not only do the political interests coincide, so also do the arguments. Both in his support for the king and in his combating of lay abbacy Adventius invoked the bishop's religious function as vicar of God. In addition, the bishops owed a duty of loyalty and support to their king as his followers. They did a great deal of the political handiwork. And in doing so they also employed their sacral tools, as in the penitential cleansing of Lothar.

Alliances and Family Ties

The high religious authorities, and especially the bishops, were major players on the political stage of the Carolingian empire. But here too the political situation was to a considerable extent determined by relationships— both hostile and amicable—between kinsmen. As an illustration, consider the following event, which I have already mentioned and which clearly demonstrates the importance of family ties in the political setup: the Treaty of Coblenz of July 860.

Those who concluded this treaty invoked a moral code that required that brothers, nephews, and uncles should be united in solidarity.[150] Here there was a direct connection with the occasion for the treaty: a conflict between two close kin, the brothers Charles the Bald and Louis the German, in which their nephew Lothar II was closely involved. The three of them did not

---

149. Council of Quierzy (858) c. 7, in *MGH Conc.* 3: pp. 413–17: resistance to the alienation of Church property, in which the bishops invoked their status as "vicarius Dei"; c. 8–10, pp. 417–19: ban on giving monasteries to laymen. At the councils of Valence (855) c. 8, Macon (855) c. 1–2, and in a hard-to-place council text from this period, c. 1–2, in *MGH Conc.* 3: 358, 375–76, 489, we also find rulings that seek to keep religious property out of the hands of laymen. As early as the Council of Yütz (844) c. 3, in *MGH Conc.* 3: p. 32, there was resistance to lay control of monasteries. Here, though, there was as yet no recourse to the argument that the bishop as "vicarius Dei" was responsible for supervising the monasteries. Certainly, however, there was a struggle against lay abbacy in Lotharingia also; on this point too there is no distinction between a Lotharingian and a West Frankish ideology, contrary to the views of Anton, "Synoden," pp. 100–101.

150. Coblenz (860) c. 2–3, in *MGH Cap.* 2: 157.

conclude the treaty by themselves, however. The three kings each had a large retinue, which not only supported them and negotiated the terms on their behalf but when all was settled also signed their names to the treaty. It turns out that a great many of the most prominent lay supporters were linked to the Carolingians by ties of blood or marriage. The treaty was signed by forty-six magnates: thirty-three laymen and thirteen prelates (see genealogy no. 5 in appendix 2). Among them we find the following individuals:[151]

> Conrad[152] and Rudolf,[153] brothers-in-law of Louis the Pious and Louis the German, maternal uncles of Charles the Bald and maternal uncles by marriage of Louis II, Lothar II, and Charles of Provence. They were accompanied by their sons Conrad,[154] Hugo,[155] and Rudolf,[156] first cousins of all the aforementioned kings.
>
> Adalhard, maternal uncle of Ermentrude, wife of Charles the Bald[157]

151. *MGH Cap.* 2, 154. For the participants and their family relationships, see genealogy no. 5 in appendix 2.

152. Conrad, son of Welf, see Fleckenstein, "Herkunft," pp. 119–26, and Depreux, *Prosopographie*, pp. 156–57. Throughout this period he held possessions in Alemannia (see Borgolte, *Grafen Alemanniens*, pp. 165–70); he was count in Argengau and Alpgau in 839/49–56, but as late as 861 he exchanged properties there, according to *D LD* no. 103 (1 April 861), p. 149.

153. Rudolf, son of Welf: abbot of St.-Riquier, Le Mans (†866), a highly influential figure in the realm of Charles the Bald. He intercedes as "avunculus" of Charles the Bald in *D Charles le Chauve* no. 111 (26 February 849), 1: pp. 293–97; no. 183 (29 February 856) on behalf of his abbey of St. Riquier, 1: pp. 485–88; no. 256 (15 July 863), 2: p. 80; no. 265 (23 April 864), 2: pp. 97–99. *AB* a° 866; according to the annals of Murbach (ed. Lendi), he died a° 864 (the record of the death of a whole group of "*principes regni*" in 864 is in each case one or two years too early). Depreux, *Prosopographie*, p. 358.

154. Conrad, son of Conrad and Adelaide; Count of Auxerre, *D Charles le Chauve* no. 261 (2 December 863), 2: p. 91 on properties in Auxerre that he had received from Charles and used as "*dos*" for his wife Waldrada; no. 268 (860–64) 2: pp. 103–7; no. 412 (17 July 876), 2: pp. 421–23. In 864 he held fiefs from Louis II of Italy in the Alpine region, where he killed Hucbert; Andreas of Bergamo, *Historia* c. 9, pp. 226–27, Regino a° 866, p. 91, *AX* a° 866, p. 23, *AB* a° 864, p. 82.

155. Hugo, son of Conrad and Adelaide. Between 853 and 859 abbot of St.-Germain of Auxerre, see *D Charles le Chauve* no. 156 (10 June 853), 1: pp. 411–13, nos. 214–15 (11 September 859), 1: pp. 540–44, on p. 544 described as "Propinquus noster." Under Lothar II he held secular authority for a time over the bishopric of Cologne (864–66), see *AB* a° 864, 866, pp. 111, 126; *AX* a° 866, pp. 23–24; under Charles the Bald from 866, he was Count of Anjou and Tours and abbot of St.-Martin in Tours, and later guardian of Louis the Stammerer, see *AB* a° 866, p. 132; also *D Charles le Chauve* no. 307 (27 December 867), 2: pp. 179–81, no. 319 (30 January 869), 2: pp. 201–2, no. 396 (date uncertain), 2: pp. 377–80, nos. 437–38 (12 July 877), 2: pp. 477–82.

156. Rudolf, son of Rudolf, abbot of St.-Riquier.

157. Adalhard, former seneschal of Louis the Pious; see Depreux, *Prosopographie*, pp. 80–82. Originally he was based in the realm of Charles the Bald. He appears as intermediary in *D Charles le Chauve* no. 20 (23 February 843), 1: pp. 413–16; he may also be the intercessor "illuster vir Adalardus comes" in no. 157 (2 February 853), 1: pp. 413–16. See Werner,

Arnust,[158] father-in-law of Louis the German's son Carloman and related to Adalhard. Also present were their common kinsman Berengar[159] and Adalhard's kinsman Sigeard.[160]

Liutfrid, maternal uncle of Louis II, Lothar II, and Charles of Provence[161]

Erchanger (Erkingar), later the father-in-law of Charles the Fat[162]

Giselbert, son-in-law of Lothar I and brother-in-law of Lothar II[163]

Leutulf, later the father-in-law of Louis the Younger[164]

"Untersuchungen" (1958), pp. 274–75, and (1959), pp. 155–56. As against this Nelson, *Annals of Saint-Bertin*, p. 67 n. 1, states that Adalhard moved to the Middle Kingdom as early as 844. He could possibly be the *"fidelis"* and *"illuster comes"* Adalhard mentioned in a few charters of Lothar I from 852–53: *D Lot.I* nos. 124, 126, 128, pp. 282–85, 287–88, 289–90; later certainly in the Middle Kingdom. From 858 to 861 he was an intercessor in charters of Lothar II, see *D Lot.II* nos. 5 (28 June 858) and 14 (13 September 860), pp. 390, 405, but he was exiled by Lothar at the instigation of Louis the German. Then in 861 Charles the Bald appointed him to supervise his son Louis the Stammerer and to combat the Norsemen, see *AF* a⁰ 849, p. 38, *AB* a⁰ 861, pp. 85, 87; in *D Charles le Chauve* no. 258 (29 October 863), 2: pp. 84–85, he appears as a witness; probably he is also the intercessor Adalhard, count and abbot of St.-Quentin in *D Charles le Chauve* no. 251 (12 January 863), 2: pp. 73–76. In 865 he and his family lost the fiefs they held from Charles the Bald and at the same time his daughter's betrothal to Louis the Younger was broken off by Louis the German, *AB* a⁰ 865, pp. 123–25.

158. Arnust (or Ernst), the most important nobleman in the realm of Louis the German, lost his fiefs in 861, *AF* a⁰ 861, p. 55, where he is hailed as "Summatem inter omnes optimates suos." Mentioned in *D LD* no. 7 (832), p. 9; no. 40 (847), p. 62; no. 72 (855), p. 102; †865 *AF* a⁰ 865, p. 63.

159. Berengar, son of Count Gebhard; brother of Count Uto and Abbot Waldo, "*nepotes*" of Arnust, "*propinqui*" of Adalhard; in 861 he lost the fiefs he held from Louis the German, *AB* a⁰ 861, p. 85, *AF* a⁰ 861, p. 55; he then received fiefs from Charles the Bald, which he lost in 865, *AB* a⁰ 865, pp. 123–25. He is a witness in two charters of Charles the Bald: *D Charles le Chauve* nos. 258–59 (29 October 863 and 4 November 863), 2: pp. 83, 89; in 866 he had to surrender the fiefs he had again received from Louis the German and joined Louis the Younger in rebellion, *AF* a⁰ 866.

160. Sigeard, count, with Arnust, Uto, Berengar, and Waldo, was dismissed from his offices by Louis the German in 861; "*propinquus*" of Adalhard, see *AB* a⁰ 861, p. 85, *AF* a⁰ 861, p. 55; mentioned as Count of the Scheidgouw, *D LD* no. 94 (858), p. 136.

161. Liutfrid, son of Hugo, Count of Tours; brother of Lothar I's wife, Ermengarde, and Conrad's wife, Adelaide; †866, see Annals of Murbach (ed. in Lendi), † a⁰ 864. For Liutfrid, see above, pp. 87–90.

162. Erkingar (Erchanger), count in Alemannia and Alsace (†864/66), see *AB* a⁰ 862, p. 93; clashes with Lothar I (from 854) and Lothar II, *D Lot.I* no. 69 (843), pp. 183–84, no. 133 (854), pp. 296–98, Borgolte, "Geschichte der Grafengewalt," pp. 28–35, Borgolte, *Geschichte der Grafschaften*, p. 124; according to Borgolte, *Grafen Alemanniens*, pp. 105–9, he is not identical with, but a kinsman of, Erchanger, Count of the Breisgau. According to the annals of Murbach, he died a⁰ 864 (ed. in Lendi).

163. Giselbert, count in the Maasgouw; see Nithard, *Historia* III, c. 3, p. 90: a "Gislebertus comes Mansuariorum" on the side of Lothar I after the battle of Fontenoy (841). In 846 he abducted a daughter of Lothar I, but was subsequently reconciled with him in 848, *AF* a⁰ 846, p. 36, a⁰ 848, pp. 37–38.

164. Leutulf, count or duke of Saxony (†865), *AX* a⁰ 866, p. 23; according to the Annals of Murbach † a⁰ 864 (ed. in Lendi); *D LD* no. 52, pp. 71–72, *D LJ* no. 3, p. 336.

Everard, brother-in-law of Charles the Bald[165]

Matfrid, a cousin of Lothar II; his paternal aunt Ava was Lothar's maternal grandmother.[166]

Boso, brother of Theutberga, Lothar's former brother-in-law[167]

Atto, here listed among the laymen, may have been a kinsman of Lothar.[168]

Franco, bishop of Liège, was a Carolingian by birth; he had also been brought up by Drogo, bishop of Metz (823–55) and son of Charlemagne.[169]

If we look more closely at this range of relationships, it is apparent that the bonds of kinship could be ambivalent. Not only could they—obviously—create solidarity between individuals, they could also be a source of rivalry. And this brings us to the real issue: the role of kinship ties in the forging of alliances.

Charleses, Louises, and Lothars: Solidarity and Rivalry between Brothers, Uncles, and Nephews on Their Fathers' Side

It is, of course, no accident that the Carolingian kings all had the same names. Children were named after relations. For a child to be given a name not previously used in the family was extremely unusual. Consequently, the names Charles, Louis, and Lothar (and also Carloman, Pippin, and Drogo) were reserved for the Carolingian family.[170] Usually names were

---

165. Everard, Margrave of Friuli (†865), husband of Gisela, daughter of Louis the Pious and Judith; *AX* a° 866, p. 23; according to the annals of Murbach, he died in 864; see the edition in Lendi at a° 864. In 858, he was ambassador of Louis II to Louis the German, *AF* a° 858, p. 48.

166. Matfrid, son of Matfrid, Count of Orléans; brother of Engeltrude, the former wife of Boso (brother of Theutberga and Hucbert). The elder Matfrid's sister Ava was married to Hugo of Tours. Thus, Matfrid and Liutfrid are cousins; Lothar II, Conrad, and Hugo are second cousins of Matfrid; see Depreux, "Comte Matfrid," pp. 360–67.

167. Boso, son of Boso, brother of Hucbert and Theutberga and of Bivin's wife; *De divortio*, p. 244, also mentions his presence.

168. In 869 a Count Atto, a kinsman of Lothar II (*"consanguineus noster"*), had possessions in the bishopric of Besançon, see *D Lot.II* no. 33 (22 January 869), pp. 438–40. However, the name Atto/Hatto was very common.

169. Franco, bishop of Liège (854/58–901), Carolingian, pupil and kinsman of Drogo, bishop of Metz. See above, p. 74.

170. "Louis" and "Lothar" are actually names from the Merovingian royal house, appropriated by the Carolingians together with the kingship. Charlemagne named his sons Louis and Lothar after his father, Pippin, had taken over the kingship from the Merovingians. Something similar happened when Boso of Vienne, in 879 the first non-Carolingian to be proclaimed king, named his son Louis (after his maternal grandfather, Louis II of Italy). And in the final step up the ladder this Louis, known as the Blind, called his infant son Charles Constantine. After becoming king, Hugo of Arles, the son of Lothar II's daughter

chosen from both the father's and the mother's side. In this respect the Carolingians, as the royal family, were rather a special case: they chose the names of their intended successors from among their ancestors in the strict male line. Their names marked people out as members of a kinship group, with rights to the offices and possessions of that group.[171] Here too the Carolingian royal house was a special case. Although a not inconsiderable proportion of those offices and possessions could also be passed down through the female line, this certainly did not apply to the kingship. Belonging to the same kinship group brought with it, as we have said, both solidarities and rivalries, as will become very apparent from the behavior of Lothar's closest relatives on his father's side. The conflicts between Lothar and his brothers and uncles provide a textbook example of this dual effect.

That there should be solidarity among kinsmen is a principle often stressed in the sources, and this applied also to the Carolingian kings. Kinsmen shared the same blood, and should therefore love and help one another. The royal brothers, nephews, and uncles were bound to one another. They were, as they sometimes put it, "Our bone and our flesh" (Genesis 29:14).[172] Such solidarity, rooted in affection, between people of the same blood, bound by what is termed *consanguinitas*, was an important social norm.[173] To break the ties of affection and blood-kinship was regarded as a serious breach of social standards. When Charles the Bald tried to seize the kingdom of his nephew Charles of Provence, Louis the German and Lothar II reproached him for breaking the bonds of brotherly friendship

---

Bertha, called his son after his great-grandfather Lothar. Le Jan, *Famille*, pp. 201–6, argues that the names Pippin, Louis, Lothar, Charles, and Carloman were used only for sons intended to succeed to the throne. This does seem to have been the preference, but it was far from an absolute rule. A son of Charlemagne's daughter Rotrude was also called Louis (abbot of St.-Denis, †867), while the son of Lothar I and Doda was called Carloman. Two longawaited heirs of Charles the Bald, who however died young, were called Pippin and Drogo. See Werner, "Nachkommen," genealogy in supplement.

171. Werner, "Liens"; Bouchard, "Family Structure" and "Bosonids" (both articles are reworked as chapters in Bouchard, *Those of My Blood*, pp. 59–97) argues for the dominance of patrilineal descent.

172. In the capitularia of Savonnières (862), Charles the Bald about Lothar: c. 10, in *MGH Cap.* 2: p. 162, and Tusey (865), Charles the Bald, and Louis the German about Lothar: c. 6, in *MGH Cap.* 2: p. 165, "Os nostrum et caro nostra est." The reference in this edition, Genesis 2:23, is incorrect; it relates to the creation of Eve, while Genesis 29:14 concerns the bond between Laban and his nephew Jacob. For this quotation, see also the letter from Pope Nicholas to Louis the German, *Ep. Nic.* no. 49, p. 333.

173. Schneider, *Brüdergemeine*, pp. 80–84, 111–12, 119–22, 171, Genzmer, "Germanische Sippe," and Kroeschell, "Sippe," for the kinship group as a legal entity. In a legal sense, though, it is in the first place usually restricted to close relatives. See Murray, *Germanic Kinship*, for the kinship group among the Franks in the *Lex Salica*.

and blood-kinship.[174] Regino of Prüm leveled the same criticism at Louis the German when he invaded the realm of his brother Charles the Bald.[175]

Love between brothers, uncles, and nephews is frequently mentioned in the texts of the treaties made between the Carolingian kings. In these treaties they promised to behave toward each other as true brothers, nephews, and uncles.[176] At their meetings this fraternal friendship was sometimes ostentatiously displayed. The texts then show the brothers together, united in true harmony and amity.[177]

Sadly, these almost idyllic scenes did not accord with hard political reality. Relations between the Carolingian brothers, uncles, and nephews were often dominated not by love for each other but by mutual envy, jealousy, and mistrust. The main cause of this was the common rights of those in the kinship group to positions and possessions. All the Carolingians claimed rights to the inheritance of the entire Carolingian empire, so far as they were in a position to do so. They fought fiercely over it. When he divided up his realm in 806 Charlemagne forbade his sons—even then—to kill or maim his grandsons, their nephews, to put out their eyes, or to make them monks against their will without due process of law.[178] Evidently he expected no better of his brood. The succession to Louis the Pious was marked by violent strife among his sons, who bitterly contested their father's legacy among themselves. Not one of the agreements they concluded with each other was regarded as final. Time and again, whenever a favorable opportunity appeared, they tried to annex the realms of their brothers, and later of their nephews. We have already seen the attempts of Louis the German to seize the kingdom of Charles the Bald in 858, and of Charles the Bald to supplant Charles of Provence in 861.[179]

The policy pursued by Lothar's uncles with regard to their nephew— here we are briefly running ahead of the events—can also be explained by this. Lothar certainly took it that way. He saw the treaty concluded by Charles and Louis in 865 as a direct attempt to deprive him of his king-

---

174. *Ep. Lot.*, no. 3, p. 213 (Lothar and Louis the German to Nicholas I).

175. Regino a° 866 (incorrect dating), p. 90.

176. Coblenz (860), Louis c. 2–3, in *MGH Cap.* 2: p. 157; Savonnières (862), Charles c. 10, in *MGH Cap.* 2: p. 162; Louis c. 2, in *MGH Cap.* 2: p. 163; Charles c. 2, in *MGH Cap.* 2: p. 164; Lothar c. 2, p. 164, repeats the foregoing.

177. Schneider, *Brüdergemeine*, pp. 113–14; Halphen, *Charlemagne*, pp. 270–71, 286, 301–32.

178. *Divisio Regnorum* (806) c. 18, in *MGH Cap.* 1: pp. 129–30.

179. See above, pp. 64–101.

dom.[180] For the same reason he reacted to a discussion between Louis and Charles in 867 by immediately switching his alliance.[181]

That neither uncle had the slightest scruple about depriving his nephew of his kingdom is apparent from the text of a secret agreement between Louis and Charles in which they divided up the realms of their two nephews even though the latter were still very much alive, young, and in good health. The text of the oath sworn by Charles and Louis ends like this:

> And if it pleases God to give us some part of our nephews' realms, so that we receive and divide it, according as we or our joint loyal supporters, appointed by mutual agreement, find fitting and just, then I promise truly to help and support the other in the agreement, holding, preserving, and defense of this division, both of that which we already have and of what God will yet give us of the aforementioned realms. And this I shall do without guile, without deceit, and without theft of the divided property, as a proper brother owes to his true brother. And so that he may help me in this in the same way.[182]

This shows very clearly how flexible the social rules were in practice. By invoking the familial bond between brothers the nephews are dispensed with; and still it is thought necessary to emphasize that neither party shall steal from or deceive the other. It is already taken for granted that they will keep only the first part of the oath—the acquisition of the loot—and not the second—not to rob or cheat each other.

The sons of Lothar I also squabbled at first over their inheritance. At their first meeting after their father's death the brothers Lothar and Louis quarreled so violently that they drew weapons on each other. Then Lothar tried to rob little Charles of his portion by having him made a monk. Both times it was the attendant nobles who calmed things down.[183] After this initial confrontation, relations between the three brothers were

180. See below, p. 150. *AB* aº 865, p. 117, after the meeting between Charles and Louis and their embassy to him: "Hlotharius vero putans, quod sibi regnum subripere et inter se vellent dividere."

181. *AB* aº 867, p. 136.

182. *MGH Cap.* 2: p. 168: "Et si Deus nobis amplius adhuc de regnis nepotum nostrorum donaverit et in acquirendo ac in dividendo sicuti plus aequaliter aut nos aut nostri communes fideles invenerint quos communi consensu elegerimus et in ipsa divisione consentiendo et in habendo et in conservando atque defendendo tam istud quod habemus quam et quod nobis de praefatis regnis Dominus concesserit absque dolositate aut deceptione vel superabreptione illi sincerus auxiliator et cooperator ero sicut frater vero fratri per rectum esse debet; in hoc ut ipse similiter erga me conservet." For this treaty, see below, p. 173; see also Calmette, *Diplomatie*, appendix 3, pp. 195–200, which gives the date as the end of June 868. Parisot, *Royaume*, pp. 296–99, puts it in 867.

183. See above, p. 55; *AB* aº 856, p. 73.

generally good. When necessary, Louis and Lothar supported each other.[184] And when young Charles died in 863 they divided his realm between them.[185]

Lothar's uncle Charles the Bald emerged more and more as Lothar's most powerful rival. He disapproved of Lothar's behavior in his divorce case and had cast covetous eyes on the realms of his nephews Lothar and Charles of Provence. And Lothar's harboring of Charles' runaway daughter Judith and her husband Baldwin, Count of Flanders, just added fuel to the fire. During the years 860–64 Lothar's relations with his other paternal uncle, Louis the German, were good. After that the relationship between the three kings would become ever more clearly one of shifting alliances, with two of them joining forces against the third.

In the Carolingian family it was not only uncles and nephews who were at odds with one another. Conflicts between sons and fathers were also a regular occurrence. Some of these, certainly, had to do with proposed divisions of the inheritance. Often, too, a king's son would rebel in an attempt to make himself independent of his father and establish his own rule in part of the territory. Sometimes these rebellions of sons were connected with their marriage plans, where the purpose of the marriage was to bind a powerful kinship group to them. Examples of this are the conflicts between Charles the Bald and his sons Charles the Younger and Louis the Stammerer and between Louis the German and his son Louis the Younger. Ever since Carloman's revolt against Louis the German in 861, a kind of crown-prince disease seemed to have been endemic. Almost every year saw an attempted rebellion by one or another of the sons of Charles the Bald or Louis the German.[186]

Solidarity, even love, between brothers, uncles, and nephews was the official social norm. In reality, though, the fact that each had a claim on a common inheritance led to a huge rivalry between them.[187] In fact, among the Carolingian brothers, uncles, and nephews we find more instances of rivalry than of solidarity, so that even public declarations of mutual support often relate to an alliance directed against another brother, uncle, or nephew.

184. See esp. Louis II's interventions on behalf of Lothar II, in acts 5 and 6, and Lothar's military support for Louis in 866/67, Regino a° 866, pp. 93–94.

185. *AB* a° 863, p. 96.

186. See the cases mentioned above, pp. 102–3, also *AB* and *AF*, almost annually from 861 on.

187. The conflicts over inheritance among the Saxon nobility in the tenth/eleventh centuries are described by Leyser, "German Aristocracy," pp. 36–38.

Family Ties and Compromises between Common and Conflicting Interests: The Political Expertise of Uncle Conrad

It was not only among close relatives on the father's side that the bonds of kinship were ambivalent. So too were other family ties, especially in the matter of alliances. This was due to the highly ambivalent effect of marriage in creating alliances.[188] Through marriage one acquired immediate allies and also, in the longer term, a larger kinship group. And the link between two families that was forged by a marriage continued in the children of that marriage. They would be able to find potential allies among relatives by marriage of their parents' generation (their uncles and aunts) who, with their children (cousins), had now become blood relations. Moreover, these people's relatives by marriage (uncles and aunts and cousins by marriage) also became potential allies. And thus the group of possible allies expanded. The other side of this coin was that at the same time one's potential allies came to include more people whose interests might conflict with one's own. This could lead to a fragmentation of the kinship group, when within the group as a whole factions would form to promote common interests that conflicted with those of other family members. These interest groups could be of short duration, as short as the community of their members' interests. Afterward it was possible to form new factions with other family members who had other shared interests. For this reason it was always necessary to take into account the common and conflicting interests of one's family members. The political game was to a great extent a matter of finding a compromise between the two.

When we look at the situation regarding political power, we see that among the people who support each other there are many who are related by blood or marriage. Uncles, nephews, brothers-in-law, and fathers-in-law help one another, intervene on one another's behalf, and provide one another with offices and property. We have already seen this system of mutual support in action with Hucbert and Liutfrid. Even so eminent a Church dignitary as Archbishop Gunthar of Cologne was accused of enriching his relatives with the possessions of the bishopric of Cologne.[189]

Sometimes we find the various family members acting in concert, or suffering collective misfortune, as did the kinsmen of Arnust and Adalhard, all of whom lost their fiefs. But this was not always the case. We must not think of the families of the Frankish aristocracy as great clans whose members always pursued a common policy. In the ninth century great families

---

188. On the ambivalence of marriage, see Demyttenaere, "Wat weet men," pp. 27–29.
189. *AX* a° 865, p. 22.

whose members always act in concert, as though they were a political party, do not exist. In this respect the names given to these families (most of which are not contemporary) are somewhat misleading.[190] When the various members of a family had common interests, or no conflicting interests, then we can see them acting together. We always have to look at the field in which this family group acts as a unit. If it is something relatively noncontroversial, such as praying for one another's souls and those of their forebears, the group may be very extensive. In such a case it will cover three, four, or very occasionally five generations of kinsmen.[191] That a group of relatives prayed together is not to say, however, that the same people automatically supported one another when it came to politics.

People might very well have interests that differed from those of their kinsmen, and often this led to kinsmen finding themselves in different camps. The fact that in the Frankish aristocracy a great many people were related—after all, they were constantly marrying each other— exacerbated this situation. If a conflict arose between two people and one had family ties with both of them, sometimes one had to make a choice. On the other hand, the fact that one *could* choose had its advantages. One could swing the balance to the winner's side and claim a reward for doing so. Or one could try to use one's influence on both parties to calm the conflict.

The family of Conrad, son of Welf (whose descendants are known to historiography as Welfs), provides the most complicated example of a noble family linked to the Carolingians (see the genealogy on the Welfs in appendix 2). They had a variety of family ties with all the Carolingian kings.[192] This large number of connections gave them an exceptional position. In general we can say that the political game of the Frankish aristocracy centered on two elements that mutually reinforced each other: influence and possession. Influence led to acquiring possessions, and wealth acquired through possessions led to influence. Besides this, influence could also be based on political knowledge.

---

190. For this problem, see Nelson, *Charles the Bald*, pp. 174–79, Leyser, "German Aristocracy" and *Rule*, Bouchard, "Family Structure," Toubert, "Carolingian Moment," pp. 390–96, and Le Jan, *Famille*, pp. 59–153, 225–62.

191. Schmid, "Problematik," p. 20, and Schmid, "Struktur," p. 8. See the genealogies in appendix 2. In any event, after five generations families made new marriage alliances with each other. There are various possible explanations for this. It could mean that they then no longer regarded each other as kinsmen. Or it could be that a further marriage after five generations was a conscious attempt to limit the number of potential conflicting interests within the kinship group. On marrying within the family and incest legislation, see Le Jan, *Famille*, pp. 305–27, De Jong, "Unsolved Riddle" and "Limits."

192. See genealogy of the Welfs in appendix 2.

When we consider the first element, possessions, it is noticeable that the Welfs had possessions in almost all the kingdoms. In order to observe the pattern of acquiring and losing possessions in the political game, we can distinguish several types of possessions, according to the period of time they were in the hands of a family. This period of time seems to have been an important criterion, sometimes even more important than whether these possessions were held as fiefs or as allodial property (usually defined as property owned outright, with no strings attached). So the Welfs held on to a group of possessions in southern Germany that the family had acquired earlier, and which they retained even when other possessions were lost in the political upheavals. Part of this complex of south German properties was originally a royal possession, acquired after the marriage of Judith to Louis the Pious.[193] Possessions more recently acquired were more easily lost than those that had been in the family for some time, whether these were allodial properties or fiefs. It probably was very unusual to expropriate old family possessions along with the fiefs of former favorites fallen into disfavor. In any case, at a meeting of the kings and their followers in 859 there was talk only of an attempt to restore fiefs (*honores*) to supporters who had defected.[194] The Treaty of Coblenz in 860 made a clear distinction between different types of possessions: on the one hand allodial property that had been inherited or received from the previous king; on the other, allodial property received from the present king and fiefs. The king could negotiate on the second group if his disloyal supporters returned to him. The first group had to be returned to them if they promised to keep the peace:

> And their allods which they inherited or acquired and what they received as a gift from our lord father, with the exception of what comes from a gift by myself, I shall give them. . . . But regarding the allods which they received from me, and also the fiefs for those who return to me, I shall act as I wish, in the way that in consultation with him [my brother] I find best.[195]

193. Fleckenstein, "Herkunft," pp. 119–26; Rösener, "Strukturformen," pp. 142–45; Borgolte, *Grafen Alemanniens*, pp. 165–70, 290–91. Welf, possibly one of Conrad's sons but certainly a kinsman, remained there, but Conrad himself also held possessions and the office of count there. One of their most important possessions, the Schussengau, was still part of the Carolingian *fiscus* in 816: see Rösener, "Strukturformen," p. 143, n. 63.

194. *AF* aᵒ 859, p. 53. In the case of Arnust's family too the distinction is made between offices that they lose and their own property that they keep, *AF* aᵒ 861, p. 55.

195. Coblenz (860), in *MGH Cap.* 2: p. 158: "Et illorum alodes de hereditate et de conquisitu et quod de donatione nostri senioris habuerunt excepto illo, quod de mea donatione venit, illis concedo. . . . Sed et de illis alodibus, quos de mea donatione habuerunt, et etiam de honoribus, sicut cum illo melius considerabo, illis qui ad me se retornabunt, voluntarie faciam."

When distinguishing between properties the most important criterion is not their status as fief or allod but who gave them. He who gave something could, if the recipient did not fulfill his obligations, take it back again. But for possessions of longer standing, those inherited from members of one's own family or given by the father of the present lord, this was not the case.

Because the Welfs had ties of kinship with all the Carolingian kings and possessions in all the kingdoms of the empire, they also had a great deal to lose in the conflicts between the kings. Sometimes they had to take sides, as in 858 when Louis the German invaded the realm of Charles the Bald. Conrad's sons, Hugo and Conrad, initially supported Louis, who looked the likely winner, but then changed sides and went over to Charles. This cost them the fiefs they held from Louis the German, but yielded profits in the West Frankish realm.[196]

Sometimes the policy of Conrad and his family was aimed at reconciling the Carolingian kings. Often they had more to lose than to gain in the wars between those kings. Thus, at the gathering at Savonnières in 862 we find Conrad speaking out plainly against Charles the Bald's statement violently attacking Lothar. Conrad protested when Charles read out this statement at a meeting of a select group of counselors, and on his advice the majority decided that the statement should not be read out in public. Conrad attended this gathering as an adviser to Lothar and Louis and was in a powerful position. That this was not the first time he had held such a position and known how to make use of it is apparent from Hincmar's irritation at this incident. He describes Conrad's reaction to Charles' statement as follows: "Mainly on the recommendation of their adviser Conrad, who as usual relied on arrogant, worthless, and empty knowledge, which profited neither himself nor most of the others, they were unwilling that what Charles reproached Lothar for should be made public."[197] Hincmar and Conrad already knew each other from previous encounters, and evidently Conrad was in the habit of putting forward arguments that did not please Hincmar. Conrad's position at the highest level is attested to by his presence among the thirty-three lay negotiators at Coblenz in 860. In the list of signatories he is named first among the laymen, with Hincmar heading the list of

---

196. *AF* a° 858, p. 51. Nelson, *Charles the Bald*, pp. 178–79, puts the defection of Hugo and Conrad the Younger in 853 and not in 858, unlike Reuter in *Annals of Fulda*, trans. Reuter, p. 43 n. 18.

197. *AB* a° 862, pp. 94–95: "Usi consilio praecipue Hludowicus et Hlotharius Chuonradi sui consiliarii, Karoli autem avunculi, qui superciliosa, sed frivola et nec sibi adeo nec pluribus proficua, more sueto, scientia nitebatur, ne innotescerentur populo causae, quas Karolus Hlothario reputabat, penitus reiecerunt." Also *MGH Cap.* 2: p. 165.

prelates.[198] Conrad not only had a wealth of family connections, he also knew how to use them, for a tie of blood or marriage also made it easy to approach someone. All manner of information could be gleaned in an informal conversation. One could try to find out how someone would react in a conflict situation, what his interests were, what was acceptable to him and what was not.[199] Someone with many family connections in different kingdoms could thus gain a considerable insight into the political situation, into the way other great nobles could be expected to behave. Such a person would be a most desirable counselor, an important lobbyist in negotiations. Evidently Conrad fitted this description, and his insight into the political balance of power was the "worthless" knowledge that so annoyed Hincmar.

But Conrad and his family did not confine their political activities to reasoned discussion and the formation of alliances. That pleasant image can be discarded straightaway. Sometimes they settled disputes by brute force. Conrad's sons came to blows with Hucbert mainly in the Alpine region, where both sides had important possessions. In the end it was Conrad's sons who slew Hucbert in battle, and it was Conrad the Younger who subsequently held the duchy of Transjura, which was initially given him in fee by their cousin Louis II.[200]

Ties of kinship, whether by blood or marriage, were a source of potential allies. One could count on political support from various family members, providing there were no serious conflicting interests. And family connections were not the only way of finding allies. Ties of friendship and vassalage were another possibility.[201] Another element that could create a powerful bond was proximity, living together, for instance growing up in the same house with someone or in someone's care.[202] These various kinds of ties could reinforce one another, making the relationship between two individuals still closer. For instance, a sister of Lothar II had a son called Wicpert. When his parents died, young Wicpert was brought up by Lothar II, and later Wicpert in turn raised Lothar's young son Hugo after his father's death.[203]

---

198. *MGH Cap.* 2: p. 154.

199. Althoff, *Verwandte*, pp. 81–82.

200. See below, p. 150.

201. Althoff, *Verwandte*, gives a clear account of the efficacy of these three ties. See earlier work on these and other bonds, which created solidarity and led to group formation, in Dhondt, "Groepsvorming" (revised version of "Solidarités").

202. Adventius of Metz and Franco of Liège were both brought up by Drogo of Metz in his house; this gave them good connections with Drogo's kinsmen, for instance, with Lothar II and Charles the Bald. It probably also created a bond between the two of them.

203. Hlawitschka, "Kaiser," pp. 368–70. Wicpert is also in Lothar's retinue in Remiremont (861), Schmid, "Königseintrag," p. 114. But Hugo would later prove singularly ungrateful: Regino a° 883, pp. 120–21.

Making political alliances was to a great extent a matter of reaching a compromise between the common and conflicting interests of various family members. If one had a great many powerful kinsmen and managed to maintain and make good use of those connections there was the prospect of a significant political career. Their family connections with all the Carolingian kings provided Conrad and his descendants with important positions. Ultimately their policies would prove highly successful. They would achieve so much power and become so close to the kings that in 888 Conrad the Younger's son Rudolf could be proclaimed king of Burgundy.

Lothar relied for political support both on the bishops of his realm and on a network of kinship alliances. His bishops supported him in several ways. They provided the grounds for his divorce and his remarriage, using all kinds of arguments, even conflicting ones, depending on the specific political situation of that moment. As the political situation changed, so too did the arguments. Their support for him was based on a double loyalty. First, they had a religious duty to care for their king and uphold the kingdom and, second, they were loyal to him as his followers. As such they did a good deal of the political handiwork, for which their king greatly rewarded them. Another important element of support for Lothar lay in his network of kinship ties. These ties, however, were double edged. They could be highly beneficial, but they also could be a source of rivalry, for example, over inheritances and important positions. The success of the political game depended largely on the ability to play the right relations at the right moment in the right way.

Act V

Pope Nicholas Intervenes and Theutberga Is Reinstated, 863–867

Now that all parties have asked him to intervene, it is Pope Nicholas's turn. He sends envoys across the Alps to convene a council at Metz, at which the case can be judged by bishops from all the kingdoms.[1] The council takes place in June 863, but the papal ambassadors are joined only by bishops from Lothar's realm. Consequently, the decisions of the council, presided over by the two most important bishops of that realm, Gunthar of Cologne and Theutgaud of Trier, are favorable to Lothar.[2]

Gunthar and Theutgaud travel to Rome in person to present the council's rulings to Pope Nicholas for approval.[3] They gain access to Nicholas through the intercession of Emperor Louis II. Nicholas totally disagrees with the rulings. He has Gunthar and Theutgaud condemned at a synod. He then sends a letter to all the bishops of Christian Europe in which he inveighs in the strongest terms against Lothar and the council rulings.[4] They are invalid, he says. They are the rulings of a heretical council that looks favorably on adultery and must therefore be "termed a bordello."[5] Gunthar and Theutgaud, as those most responsible, are deprived of their sees and forbidden to carry

---

1. Letters introducing this mission: *Ep. Nic.* nos. 3–6, 10–11, 16.

2. No record of this council has survived; we know of it from *AF* aº 863, p. 57, *AB* aº 863, p. 98, and the *Liber pontificalis*, p. 160, translated in Davis, *Lives of the Ninth-Century Popes*, pp. 227–28, see *MGH Conc.* 4: pp. 134–38.

3. *AB* aº 863, p.98; *AF* aº 863, p. 57.

4. The letter has survived in copies sent to various addressees: *Ep. Nic.* nos. 18 (to Ado of Vienne) and 21 (to the bishops in Gaul, Germania, and Italy) of 30 October 863, a copy addressed to Hincmar of Reims and Wenilo of Rouen in *AB* aº 863, pp. 99–103, and a copy (to the bishops of Louis the German) in one group of manuscripts of *AF* aº 863, pp. 58–60.

5. The most recent edition of this council is in *MGH Conc.* 4, p. 152: "prostibulum appellari."

out any further priestly functions.[6] *He says that because of his conduct Lothar can no longer be regarded as king.*[7] *And with these words he provides arguments for any dissident who might wish to evict Lothar from his throne.*

Naturally, those concerned do not take this lying down. Gunthar and Theutgaud complain to Emperor Louis II. The emperor feels that his honor has been impugned. How dare the pope, and one elected with his support at that, treat the bishops he had introduced so ungraciously! Livid with rage, so Hincmar writes, he takes his army and marches on Rome.[8] *Emperor Louis intends to take Nicholas prisoner, but the latter flees from his palace and takes refuge in St. Peter's, where he devotes himself to fasting and praying. After this—and for many people "after this" means "because of this"— Louis falls seriously ill and has to abandon his attempt. In the end Louis' wife, the Empress Angilberga, brings about a reconciliation between her husband and the pope.*[9]

In these years the first of the major players vanish from the scene. The young, epileptic King Charles of Provence succumbs to his disease in 863.[10] *Since he leaves no descendants his realm is divided between his brothers Louis and Lothar. Hucbert too meets his end. In 864 he is killed in a fight with Conrad's sons.*[11]

In February 865 Charles the Bald and Louis the German meet and advise their nephew Lothar to mend his ways, for his own sake and that of his kingdom.[12] *Lothar understands the political significance of this "advice" very well: his uncles are taking advantage of the situation to threaten his kingdom. Lothar now finds himself cornered. Previously he was always able to combine with one of his uncles against the other, but now that his ally of the last few years, Louis the German, is making common cause with Charles the Bald, he has to change tactics. Through his brother, Emperor Louis II, he makes contact with Pope Nicholas, who sends Arsenius, bishop of Orte, to mediate between the kings.*[13]

Lothar sees that he has no option but to take Theutberga back. Since her escape from the convent Theutberga has been living in the realm of Charles the Bald; now, with every mark of honor and accompanied by two West Frankish bishops, she is escorted to

6. *AB* a⁰ 863, p. 100, the covering letter of the council canons; council c. 2, in *MGH Conc.* 4, pp. 152–53; *AF* a⁰ 863, p. 57.

7. Covering letter to canons, in *AB* a⁰ 863, p. 99.

8. *AB* a⁰ 864, pp. 105–6. For Pope Nicholas's election with the support of Louis II, see *AB* a⁰ 858, p. 78.

9. *AB* a⁰ 864, pp. 106–7. The early tenth-century *Libellus de imperatoria potestate*, pp. 200–204, gives a different version of these events. For a discussion of the two versions, see below, pp. 165–66.

10. *AB* a⁰ 863, p. 96.

11. Regino a⁰ 866 (incorrect dating), p. 91; *AX* a⁰ 866, p. 23; *AB* a⁰ 864, p. 116; Andreas of Bergamo, *Historia*, c. 9, pp. 226–27.

12. The treaty in *MGH Cap.* 2: pp. 165–67; mentioned in *AB* a⁰ 865, pp. 116–17: *AF* a⁰ 864, pp. 62–63, describe only the treaty between Louis and Charles and give the date of the meeting as September 864.

13. *AB* a⁰ 865, pp. 117, 118; *AF* a⁰ 865, p. 63.

Lothar by the papal ambassador. On 3 August 865, in a solemn public ceremony attended by many secular and clerical magnates and a great crowd of people, Lothar reinstates his "ex" as his queen and his wife.[14]

Waldrada has to leave Lothar. She is ordered to accompany the papal ambassador to Rome, and indeed she sets out on the journey.[15] But she never reaches Pope Nicholas in Rome. At a given moment—exactly when is unknown—Waldrada refuses to go any further and returns to Lothar's realm; not to Lothar, true, but to some place where it is easy for them to meet.[16]

Lothar has been forced to yield to the combined might of his two uncles and Pope Nicholas, but he does not give up. He has lost this battle, but the war is not over yet. In this same year, 865, he concludes an alliance with Charles the Bald.[17] Together they appeal to the pope for the marriage of Lothar and Theutberga to be dissolved.[18] Theutberga herself also requests a divorce: she is barren, the marriage to Waldrada took place before her own, and she wants to enter a convent. She wishes to go to Rome herself to put her case to Nicholas—all this to the astonishment of the pope.[19] Suddenly the same parties who had asked him to oppose the divorce have now joined Lothar in arguing for it. But the pope gives not an inch; he holds to his decisions. Theutberga must stay with Lothar instead of coming to Rome. Nicholas fulminates against Lothar who, he assumes, has pressured Theutberga into requesting the divorce.[20] And, because she did not come to Rome to ask his forgiveness, he excommunicates Waldrada.[21]

Pope Nicholas had been drawn into the affair by all those concerned. After some consultation he pronounced in favor of the validity of Lothar's marriage to Theutberga. Nicholas had no direct interest in the case. What mattered to him was realizing the papal claim to be the supreme authority, able to judge other bishops and secular rulers. And he backed up his words with deeds: he condemned King Lothar and Archbishops Gunthar and Theutgaud.

It is one thing to formulate claims to power, however; making them effective is quite another. Yet at first Nicholas was largely successful in this

---

14. *AB* a° 865, pp. 119–21; *AF* a° 865, pp. 63–64 (in one ms. group only; the other two ms. groups do not mention it).

15. *AB* a° 865, p. 122; *AF* a° 865, p. 64 (see above, n. 14). *Ep. Nic.* no. 42, pp. 315–16.

16. *Ep. Nic.* no. 42, p. 315 and no. 47, p. 326; *AF* a° 867, p. 66. Possibly she stayed at the royal estate at Ham, where the church belonged to Lobbes monastery, as Folcuin, *Gesta Abbatum Lobiensium* c. 13, p. 61, says.

17. *AB* a° 865, p. 121.

18. *AB* a° 866, pp. 128 and 129–30.

19. As is apparent from Nicholas's answers to Theutberga and Charles, *Ep. Nic.*, no. 45 (to Theutberga), pp. 319–20; no. 48 (to Charles the Bald), pp. 329–32.

20. *Ep. Nic.* nos. 45 (to Theutberga), pp. 319–22; 46 (to Lothar), pp. 322–25; and 48 (to Charles the Bald), pp. 329–32, all of 24/25 January 867.

21. *Ep. Nic.* no. 42, pp. 315–16.

too. He deprived Gunthar and Theutgaud of their episcopal offices and forced Lothar to take Theutberga back. And this was in large measure due to the political situation at the time.

Pope Nicholas and the Legal Status of Marriage

What Pope Nicholas understood by a lawful marriage can be deduced from his letters. However, it is important not to lump together all his letters on marriage. They fall into three groups, according to their subject and thus also as regards their reasoning. The majority of them relate to the specific case of Lothar and Theutberga. In a handful of letters he also sets out general rules for marriage and divorce. Finally, he also passes judgment in a few other matrimonial cases. These three groups of letters and arguments invite comparison, a comparison that may help us understand how Nicholas selected his arguments in Lothar's case.

The Validity of Lothar's Marriage

In a letter to his envoys prior to the Council of Metz Nicholas instructed them to find out whether there really was a lawful marriage between Lothar and Waldrada. In doing so they were to apply the following criteria:

> You must first carry out a careful investigation and if you find that this king has taken to wife the aforementioned Waldrada after the arranging of the bridal gift, in the presence of witnesses, according to the law and the customary ritual for celebrating nuptials, and that this same Waldrada was openly and manifestly united with him in matrimony, then you must investigate why Lothar subsequently repudiated her and married the daughter of Boso. . . . If however it should be in no way proved that Waldrada was a lawful wife, nor that she was joined to our son Lothar in a wedding celebrated according to custom, namely by blessing by a priest, then you should suggest to him that he should not make much trouble and reconcile himself with his lawful wife.[22]

Here the criteria for a lawful marriage are the bridal gift, the witnesses, the wedding ceremony, and the public nature of the marriage—all secular

22. *Ep. Nic.* no. 11, a so-called *Commonitorium*, p. 277: "Ubi primum diligenti investigatione inquirite et si eundem gloriosum regem praedictam Waldradam praemissis dotibus coram testibus secundum legem et ritum, quo nuptiae celebrari solent, per omnia inveneretis accepisse, et publica manifestatione eadem Waldrada in matrimonium ipsius admissa est, restat, ut perscrutemini, cur illa repudiata sit vel filia Bosonis admissa. . . . Si vero minime probatum fuerit Waldradam uxorem fuisse legitimam neque nuptiis secundum morem celebratis per benedictionem scilicet sacerdotis filio nostro Hlothario extitisse coniunctam, suggerite illi, ut non moleste ferat legitimam . . . reconciliari uxorem."

customs—with the addition of the priestly blessing of the union. If this had taken place then one could speak of a lawful marriage—although Nicholas was not saying that these were the only criteria. If it could be shown that these criteria had been met—and Nicholas evidently had his doubts about that—then Lothar was still not out of the woods. In that case, after all, he was twice married. That he had married Theutberga out of fear or under coercion was no excuse. By this second marriage he set worldly gain above the welfare of his soul, and for that he must be condemned.[23] "But," Nicholas writes, "if it cannot be proved that Waldrada was a lawful wife, then you must advise Lothar not to make trouble for himself and to be reconciled with his lawful wife, at least if she proves to be innocent."[24]

But Lothar did not opt for this solution. He stood by his marriage to Waldrada. In the autumn of 862 he had gone so far as to marry her and have her crowned in a public ceremony, without waiting for Nicholas's verdict on his matrimonial case. This last point in particular piqued Nicholas.[25] The relationship between them would never be the same again. In 863 Nicholas condemned Lothar for an offense that will not surprise anyone who has read his letter to his ambassadors: fornication with two women.[26] In any event Lothar had two wives, and that was one too many. For Nicholas the verdict was self-evident: he gave no further explanation, nor did he refer to Church law. He did not even discuss the arguments from secular or canon law put forward by Lothar's bishops, which infuriated Gunthar and Theutgaud.[27]

Two years later, in 865, through his envoy Arsenius, Nicholas forced Lothar publicly to acknowledge the validity of his marriage to Theutberga. According to Nicholas, Lothar and Theutberga were indissolubly bound to each other. But Lothar was not to be so easily caught. A few months later he tried a different tack, concluding an agreement with both Charles the Bald and Theutberga. This time Theutberga herself asked Nicholas for a divorce, putting forward three arguments. She began by stating that the

23. *Ep. Nic.* no. 11, p. 277.
24. Ibid.: "Si vero minime probatum fuerit Waldradam uxorem fuisse legitimam . . . suggerite illi, ut non moleste ferat legitimam sibi, si ipsa innocens apparuerit reconciliari uxorem."
25. Letter to the bishops of Gaul and Germania, assembled in Metz (early 863), *Ep. Nic.* no. 10, pp. 275–76.
26. Nicholas's letter in *AB* a° 863, p. 99.
27. See below, pp. 161–62. See also Kottje, "Päpstlicher Autoritätsanspruch," who concludes from this that Nicholas's conduct in Lothar's matrimonial case was determined by the issue of competence. I would not go so far. The Church's rules on morality are certainly one issue here, but a very simple and obvious one, concerning fornication and bigamy, which required no further canon law exposition. For a critical evaluation of Kottje's contrasting of "authority" and "right," see Goetz, "Auctoritas," pp. 39–40.

marriage of Lothar and Waldrada was lawful. Nicholas immediately brushed this aside. The possible marriage of Lothar and Waldrada was none of her business. Nicholas himself knew the ins and outs of it far better, and he had definitively decided that Lothar would never, ever, be permitted to marry Waldrada, not even if Theutberga should die. Case closed.[28] Theutberga's second reason for requesting a divorce was her barrenness—the first time this argument is advanced in plain terms. But this too made no impression on Nicholas. According to him, that Theutberga had no children had nothing to do with barrenness; it was Lothar's fault.[29] Finally, Theutberga also asked for a divorce in order to lead a celibate life. But that too was forbidden. It was permitted only if both partners embarked on a life of celibacy.[30]

Nicholas put great emphasis on the fact that husband and wife must remain together, and literally in each other's company. For this reason he forbade Theutberga to come to Rome. If she left Lothar's proximity it would not be she who sat at Lothar's side as his wife; that place would be taken by Waldrada. And then people would think of Waldrada as his wife.[31] Evidently, whoever sat beside the king was regarded as his wife.

In the case of Waldrada and Theutberga we have an exceptional situation, for even after 865 Waldrada proves to have all the political power proper to a queen, even though Theutberga had the official title. If someone wanted a favor from Lothar, it could be gained through Waldrada. Supposedly she even had a hand in the appointment of bishops. Her influence is apparent in the mention of her as intercessor in a charter for a daughter of Louis the German. Nicholas protested violently against the fact that Theutberga—in his eyes the rightful wife and queen—could only look on while an excommunicated adulteress, Waldrada, carried out the functions that belonged to Theutberga.[32]

General Rules on Marriage

All the foregoing arguments and rulings on marriage relate to this one case. But Nicholas also produced general texts that included among other things regulations on marriage. The most detailed of these is a long letter

---

28. *Ep. Nic.* no. 45, to Theutberga (24 January 867), p. 320. The same arguments are used in the letter written at the same time to Lothar, *Ep. Nic.* no. 46, p. 323.

29. *Ep. Nic.* no. 45, to Theutberga (24 January 867), p. 320. Also no. 46, to Lothar (24 January 867), p. 324. In this letter to Lothar Nicholas also quotes the ban on divorce (save on grounds of adultery) from Jerome, *Commentarius in Matheum* III, 19: 9, p. 167.

30. *Ep. Nic.* no. 45, to Theutberga (24 January 867), pp. 321–22. Also no. 46, to Lothar (24 January 867), p. 324.

31. *Ep. Nic.* no. 45, to Theutberga, p. 320.

32. *Ep. Nic.* no. 50, p. 334, on episcopal appointments, and no. 51, to Louis the German, p. 337; *D Lot.II.* no. 34, p. 441, for Waldrada as intercessor.

he wrote in 866 to Boris, the newly converted khan of the Bulgars (who had been solicited by both Roman and Greek missionaries), in which he gave a great deal of advice on all kinds of subjects. In one section he explains at length how a marriage should properly be contracted:

> I shall describe the custom, such as you say the Greeks have for nuptials, in which I shall shun discursiveness of style and apply myself to a concise account of the usages regarding these unions which the holy Church of Rome has received and observes to this day. Our people, both men and women, do not wear a band of gold or silver or other metal on their heads when they enter into the bonds of matrimony. After the betrothal, which is the binding promise of the future nuptials and is celebrated with the consent of those who enter into it and those under whose authority they are, after the betrothed man shall have betrothed himself to his betrothed by means of a pledge, namely by placing a ring on her index finger as a pledge and by handing over to her the mutually agreed-on bridal gift with a document recording that agreement, they shall both, in the presence of guests invited by both sides, shortly after or at a suitable time—since this must not take place before the lawfully appointed time—be led to the nuptial ceremony. And firstly, in the church of the Lord, with the gifts which they must offer to God, they are led by the priest's hand to their places and only then do they receive the blessing and the heavenly veil, according to the example with which God placed the first people in Paradise and blessed them with the words "Go forth and multiply" and so on. But it is also written of Tobias, that before he came to his wife he offered up a prayer to the Lord with her. He or she does not receive the veil, however, who is marrying for the second time. After this, on leaving the church they wear crowns on their heads, which are always kept in the church for this special purpose. And when the nuptials are celebrated in this way they will henceforth lead an indivisible life as appointed by God. These are the laws of nuptials; these are they, with other solemn nuptial agreements which I cannot at present recall. We do not consider it a sin, however, if not all these things are done in marrying, as the Greeks, by your account, assure you; especially when some people are so oppressed by poverty of goods that no help at all is offered to them to prepare for this. And in this case according to the laws only the agreement is required of those whose union it is. If this agreement (*consensus*) is the one thing lacking in the marriage, that renders all other festivities, even including coïtus, worthless, as the great Church father John Chrysostom testifies: "The will makes the marriage, not the coïtus."[33]

33. *Ep. Nic. ad Bulgaros* c. 3, pp. 569–70: "Consuetudinem, quam Graecos in nuptialibus contuberniis habere dicitis, commemorare prolixitatem stili vitantes carptim morem, quem sancta Romana suscepit antiquitus et hactenus in huiusmodi coniunctionibus tenet ecclesia, vobis monstrare studebimus. Nostrates siquidem tam mares quam feminae, non ligaturam auream vel argenteam aut ex quolibet metallo compositam, quando nuptialia foedera contrahunt, in capitibus deferunt, sed post sponsalia quae futurarum sunt nuptiarum promissa

A great deal of what Nicholas says is already familiar to us, since it was also mentioned in the Pseudo-Isidorian decretals: the consent of the parents or guardians, betrothal with a bridal gift, which is also set down in writing, and with witnesses, then offerings to the church, priestly blessing, and continence on the wedding night (the reference to Tobias). Some of these elements clearly derive from Roman law. The most striking feature is what Nicholas defines as the one absolutely obligatory element: the agreement of the prospective partners. This too comes from Roman law, though here Nicholas cites a Church father as authority.[34] Immediately preceding this passage in his letter, when discussing impediments to marriage, Nicholas refers in so many words to rulings from Roman law.[35] These forbid marriage to relatives and those who have become relatives through adoption. In the same letter he also forbade polygamy and the repudiation of a wife other than for adultery.[36] He did allow marriage to a widow, with a reference to St. Paul.[37]

In two other letters also, one to Archbishop Charles of Mainz and the other to Archbishop Harduic of Besançon, Nicholas gave his judgment on marriages between relatives by blood or marriage. This he forbade, refer-

---

foedera quaeque consensu eorum, qui haec contrahunt, et eorum in quorum potestate sunt celebrantur, et postquam arrhis sponsam sibi sponsus per digitum fidei a se anulo insignitum desponderit dotemque utrique placitam sponsus ei cum scripto pactum hoc continente coram invitatis ab utraque parte tradiderit, aut mox aut apto tempore ne videlicet ante tempus lege diffinitum tale quid fieri praesumatur, ambo ad nuptialia foedera perducuntur. Et primum quidem in ecclesia Domini cum oblationibus, quas offerre debent Deo, per sacerdotis manum statuuntur sicque demum benedictionem et velamen caeleste suscipiunt, ad exemplum videlicet, quod Dominus primos homines in paradiso collocans benedixit eis dicens: 'Crescite et multiplicamini' et cetera. Siquidem et Thobias antequam coniugem convenisset, oratione cum ea Dominum orasse discribitur. Verumtamen velamen illud non suscipit qui ad secundas nuptias migrat. Post haec autem de ecclesia egressi coronas in capitibus gestant, quae semper in ecclesia ipsa sunt solitae reservari. Et ita festis nuptialibus celebratis ad ducendam individuam vitam Domino disponente de cetero diriguntur. Haec sunt iura nuptiarum, haec sunt praeter alia, quae nunc ad memoriam non occurrunt, pacta coniugiorum sollemnia. Peccatum autem esse, si haec cuncta in nuptiali foedere non interveniant, non dicimus, quemadmodum Graecos vos astruere dicitis, praesertim cum tanta soleat artare quosdam rerum inopia, ut ad haec praeparanda nullum his suffragetur auxilium. Ac per hoc sufficiat secundum leges solus eorum consensus, de quorum coniunctionibus agitur. Qui consensus si solus in nuptiis forte defuerit, cetera omnia etiam cum ipso coitu celebrata frustrantur, Iohanne Chrysostomo magno doctore testante, qui ait: 'Matrimonium non facit coitus, sed voluntas.'"

34. *Corpus Iuris Civilis* I: *Digesta* 35.1.15, p. 540, and 50.17.30, p. 921: "Nuptias enim non concubitus sed consensus facit," pp. 540, 921. And in a slightly different wording: *Digesta* 24.1.32.13: "Non enim coitus matrimonium facit sed maritalis affectio." According to Gaudemet, "Legs," pp. 150–51, this quotation is not from John Chrysostom but from an anonymous sermon: *Opus imperfectum in Matthaeum,* homilia 32. See also Laiou, "Consensus."

35. *Ep. Nic. ad Bulgaros* c. 2, p. 569; there then follows *Corpus Iuris Civilis* I: *Institutiones* 1.10.1–2, ed. Behrends, pp. 14–15.

36. *Ep. Nic. ad Bulgaros* c. 51, p. 586, c. 96, p. 597.

37. *Ep. Nic. ad Bulgaros* c. 3, p. 570, referring to 1 Corinthians 7:8–9 and 7:39.

ring to well-known canons. In discussing the possibility of ever marrying someone else after such a relationship, on one point he made conflicting pronouncements. In his letter to Harduic he rejected remarriage by people divorced by reason of incest or kinship by marriage during the lifetime of the former partner. In the letter to Charles of Mainz, however, he allowed remarriage after penance to those who had had sexual contact with two persons who were siblings—that is, each was a brother or sister of the other, or with other relatives by blood or marriage, as listed in Holy Scripture.[38]

Finally, there is a letter from Nicholas to Bishop Ado of Vienne, which probably relates to Lothar's case although his name does not appear in it. Ado had asked Nicholas if someone who, without a ruling by a general council, had repudiated his lawful wife, to whom he had been lawfully betrothed, could marry someone else or take a concubine in her place. Nicholas's answer, naturally, was No![39] A second question was whether someone—again Ado names no names—could repudiate his wife if between her betrothal and bridal gift and her first sexual intercourse with her husband she had been deflowered, without the latter being aware of it. And could he do so even if some time had passed since then, and could he then marry someone else as though the first woman had been no genuine wife, or alternatively take a concubine? Here too the answer is no. "And we do not permit that those who are united in lawful matrimony and who for some time have been one body shall divorce."[40] Nicholas here seems to be pronouncing against a divorce and a second marriage that bear a remarkable resemblance to those of Lothar. There is one important difference, however. In Lothar's case Theutberga's incest had been a factor from the beginning. Not a word is said of it here.

Nicholas in Other Matrimonial Cases

We have already seen that Nicholas was involved in at least three other matrimonial cases, namely those of the three children of Charles the Bald: Judith, Louis, and Charles. Each of them asked him to mediate in the conflict with their father that had arisen when all three of them married without his consent. Nicholas did indeed succeed in gaining Charles the Bald's consent

---

38. *Ep. Nic.* no. 123, to Harduic of Besançon (early 865), pp. 641–42. Nicholas to Charles, archbishop of Mainz (858–63), in *Ep. Nic.* ("spuriae"), pp. 675–76 and 677. There is a question mark over this letter to Charles; the editor places it among the "spuriae et dubiae," but according to Hartmann, *Konzil von Worms*, p. 56, it is genuine.

39. *Ep. Nic.* no. 106, to Ado of Vienne (late 861/early 862) c. 1, p. 618.

40. *Ep. Nic.* no. 106, c. 2, p. 619: "Nec hoc consentimus, ut hi qui legitimo nuptiarum foedere coniunguntur et unum corpus per aliquod temporis spatium efficiuntur, divortium faciant."

to Judith's marriage to Baldwin of Flanders, though probably we should not underestimate the role played in this by Judith's mother, Ermentrude.[41] Nicholas asked Charles to settle the matter amicably, stressing that Baldwin certainly loved Judith and that Judith had given her consent.[42] Of the marriage of Charles the Younger he said that this should indeed not have taken place without his father's consent, but he was reluctant to declare it invalid on those grounds. Unless there were other reasons that ruled out a marriage between these two, he was not willing to grant them a divorce.[43]

IN his most important theoretical pronouncements on marriage Nicholas states that one element is absolutely crucial to the validity of a marriage: the agreement of the partners. This follows a tradition of Roman law with which he was familiar. When he deals with actual cases, however, this agreement is barely mentioned. When he wants to check whether a marriage is lawful he looks for overt characteristics of marriage, secular characteristics, but also the priestly blessing. He seems to prefer not to dissolve marriages, even where elements such as paternal consent are lacking. Only prohibited relationships—and here we should probably think of marriages to relatives, nuns, and other men's wives—must be dissolved. His views on divorce on grounds of infertility or entry into a monastery were those current at the time, as were the authorities he quoted to support them. Here, Nicholas's opinions and quotations strongly resemble those of, for example, Hincmar of Reims, though they are not the only ones existing in this period. However, the influence of Nicholas's pronouncements in Lothar's case extends beyond this one case. They eventually ended up divorced from the context in which they were made, in the *Corpus Iuris Canonici*, the official collection of canon law of the Roman Catholic Church.[44]

---

41. *Ep. Nic.* no. 8, to Ermentrude, pp. 274–75.

42. *Ep. Nic.* no. 7, p. 273. "*Affectio*" of the man for his wife as an indicator of marriage is also found in Roman law, see above, n. 34, and *Codex* 5.17.11, in *Corpus Iuris Civilis*, p. 213 (and *Nov.* 22.3, in *Corpus Iuris Civilis*, p. 149).

43. *Ep. Nic.* no. 9, p. 275.

44. In the *Corpus Iuris Canonici 1: Decretum Gratiani*: the *Commonitorium* to Rathold and John, *Ep. Nic.* no. 11, in Causa 31, quaestio 2, c. 4, col. 1114; letter to Lothar, *Ep. Nic.* no. 46, in Causa 11, quaestio 3, c. 3, col. 642–43; letter to Charles the Bald, *Ep. Nic.* no. 48, in Causa 27, quaestio 2, c. 26, col. 1020; letter on the dismissal of Gunthar and Theutgaud and the quashing of the Metz council rulings, *Ep. Nic.* nos. 18–21, in Causa 11, quaestio 3, c. 10, col. 645–46, and Causa 2, quaestio 1, c. 21, col. 449; two fragments of letters to Lothar (*Ep. Nic.* no. 22), in Causa 24, quaestio 3, c. 19, col. 996, and Causa 11, quaestio 3, c. 96, col. 669–70.

The Powers of the Pope

What had Pope Nicholas to gain or to lose from Lothar's divorce case? A high-born Roman, Nicholas had had a successful career in the papal bureaucracy before succeeding Benedict III (855–58) as bishop of Rome.[45] The bishops of Rome claimed precedence over other bishops, on the one hand, and a measure of independence and precedence with respect to secular powers, on the other. These were two different claims, but in practice they were often linked. Pope Nicholas pushed that double claim to lengths unheard of at the time.

Pope Nicholas and the Bishops

Nicholas interpreted "precedence" over other bishops to mean papal supremacy. According to him, all other bishops found the source and basis (the *principium*, says Nicholas) of their episcopal office in the see of the bishop of Rome, the head of the Church to whom the care of the whole Church had been entrusted.[46] On these grounds he had the power to dismiss them, as Nicholas in fact did. His authority, he claimed, exceeded even that of the councils. Stronger yet, he maintained that decisions of the bishop of Rome had the force of law and could overturn the current religious rules. Thus, this is Nicholas writing to the West Frankish bishops, after his dismissal of Archbishops Gunthar and Theutgaud:

> I ask you: what validity will your judgments have, if ours, which no man may revoke, are in one way or another enfeebled; and what force can your councils have, if the Apostolic See shall have lost its stability, without whose consent not one council can be accepted, as we read? Read the sacred canons and consult the synodal records and see that it was the custom that the Holy See has condemned and absolved not only certain metropolitans, whose cases were always reserved for the Holy See, but also patriarchs, according to the nature of the cases arising, and that the Holy See always had the right and the duty to judge all *sacerdotes*, because throughout the whole Church of

---

45. *Liber Pontificalis*, pp. 173, 175. Davis, *Lives of the Ninth-Century Popes*, pp. 205–6.

46. Council of Rome (October 863), c. 3, in *MGH Conc.* 4: p. 154; *Ep. Nic.* no. 31, to Adventius (17 September 864), p. 300; Nicholas made these claims to power in other cases too. His claim to authority in the matter of Bishop Rothad of Soissons brought him into conflict with Hincmar of Reims. In this case he employed similar arguments, for example, in *Ep. Nic.* no. 7 to the bishops in Gaul (865), pp. 392–400: the Apostolic See as Head of the Church (pp. 393, 398), the care for the whole Church (p. 397), the privileges of St. Peter's divinely instituted throne, the throne from which the apostolate and the episcopate take their origin (*exordium*) (pp. 398–99). For his clash with John, archbishop of Ravenna, see above, p. 106. For Nicholas's pretensions: Congar, *Ecclésiologie*, pp. 206–16, and Goetz, "Auctoritas."

Christ he has the right by a special prerogative to make laws, pronounce decrees, and announce decisions.[47]

In the letter he had circulated throughout the Frankish empire after the condemnation of the Lotharingian bishops he threatened anyone who might dare to disobey him: "If anyone disdains the dogmas, commands, prohibitions, measures, and decisions which are propagated regarding the true faith, religious discipline, the correction of the faithful, the punishment of offenders, and the interdiction of imminent or future ills by the Bishop of the Holy See for the welfare of all, he shall be excommunicated."[48] From 864 on Nicholas could underpin his claims to power by referring to the Pseudo-Isidorian decretals, which among other things leaned strongly toward an absolutist interpretation of papal authority. They were brought to Rome in May or June 864 by Rothad, bishop of Soissons. This Rothad had been deprived of his office at a synod of West Frankish bishops presided over by Hincmar of Reims. He contested their decision and appealed to the pope. To support his case he used the Pseudo-Isidorian decretals, which stated that the pope could dismiss bishops whose sees lay outside the Roman Church province or rescind council rulings dismissing bishops. Hincmar of Reims would in fact declare, in a different case some years later, that one of these decretals supporting the papal authority was false.[49] Nicholas—or the man who composed his letters and synodal texts, Anastasius—did make use of them, but only from 864 on, and thus not in sentencing Gunthar and Theutgaud in October 863.[50]

---

47. *Ep. Nic.* no. 29, to Rodulf of Bourges, p. 296: "Quam rogo validitatem vestra poterunt habere iudicia, si nostra quomodolibet infirmantur de quibus nec retractari licet, vel quod robur concilia vestra optinere valebunt, si suam perdiderit sedes apostolica firmitatem, sine cuius consensu nulla concilia vel accepta esse leguntur? Aut legite sacros (can) ones et sinodalia gesta revolvite et videte, quod sedi apostolicae (non) solum quoslibet metropolitanos, quorum causa eidem est sedi semper servanda, verum etiam patriarchas moris fuisse pro emergentium qualitate damnasse vel etiam absolvisse iusque semper et fas habuisse de omnibus sacerdotibus iudicare, utpote cui facultas est in tota Christi ecclesia leges speciali praerogativa ponere ac decreta statuere atque sententias promulgare."

48. Council of Rome (October 863), c. 5, in *MGH Conc.* 4: p. 155: "Si quis dogmata, mandata, interdicta, sanctiones vel decreta pro catholica fide, pro ecclesiastica disciplina, pro correctione fidelium, pro emendatione sceleratorum vel interdictione imminentium vel futurorum malorum a sedis apostolicae praesule salubriter promulgata contempserit, anathema sit."

49. On Hincmar's use of Pseudo-Isidore in this specific case, see Hincmar of Reims and Hincmar of Laon, *Streitschriften*, ed. Rudolf Schieffer, pp. 101–4. Hincmar, however, was confronted with a treatise using Pseudo-Isidoran decretals intertwined with others, and not with a complete volume consisting only of Pseudo-Isidoran decretals. It is not a verdict on Pseudo-Isidore as such. Nonetheless, he did spot the error.

50. Fuhrmann, *Einfluß* 2: pp. 247–72, 3: p. 664.

Gunthar and Theutgaud were convicted by Nicholas, at a synod Nicholas called in Rome, of multiple violations of the canonical and apostolic rules and of actions contrary to justice. They were dismissed as bishops and banned from carrying out their priestly functions.[51] The other bishops who had taken part in the Council of Metz could be granted forgiveness if they publicly accepted Nicholas's judgment. If they failed to do so, they too would lose their episcopal and priestly offices:

> The other bishops, however, of whom it is said that they are accomplices of Theutgaud and Gunthar, will like them be struck with damnation if they devise with them rebellions, plots, or conspiracies, or if they deviate from the head, that is the Seat of St. Peter, by following them. But if, either in person or in writing via their emissaries, they promise fidelity to the Apostolic See, in which their episcopal office has most evidently found its *principium*—its source and foundation—then they should know that forgiveness will not be denied them by us.[52]

Gunthar and Theutgaud reacted proportionately. They had traveled to Rome with the decisions of the Council of Metz to seek Nicholas's advice. Then, with the help of this advice, they would certainly have found a solution. But first Nicholas had made them wait for three weeks.[53] Then he had summoned them to his presence and they suddenly found themselves surrounded by "a hostile crowd of scoundrels"—the council called by Nicholas—totally alone and defenseless.[54] There they were immediately condemned, without charge, without proof, without being given the chance to put their case. The papal letter-writer Anastasius had suddenly produced a sheet of parchment and begun to read out the verdict.[55] Gunthar and

51. Council of Rome (October 863), c. 2, in *MGH Conc.* 4: pp. 152–53.

52. Ibid., c. 3, in *MGH Conc.* 4: p. 154: "Ceteri autem episcopi, qui complices horum, Theotgaudi scilicet et Guntharii, vel sectatores esse feruntur, si cum his coniuncti seditiones, coniurationes vel conspirationes fecerint vel si a capite id est a sede Petri, illis haerendo dissenserint, pari cum eis dampnatione teneantur constricti. Quod si cum sede apostolica, unde eos principium episcopatus sumpsisse manifestum est, sapere de cetero per semetipsos vel missis ad nos legatis cum scriptis suis, professi extiterint, noverint sibi a nobis veniam non negandam."

53. Letter from Gunthar and Theutgaud. Two versions of this exist: one by Hincmar in *AB* a° 863 and one in a single group of manuscripts of *AF* a° 863. In the latter, however, the beginning and end are missing. The *AF* version seems more reliable, so I shall use that by Hincmar only for the missing beginning. *AF* a° 863, p. 60, c. 1–2. For a comparison of Nicholas's account of events and that of Gunthar and Theutgaud, see Buc, *Danger*, pp. 67–72.

54. *AF* a° 863, c. 3, p. 61: "Ibique obseratis ostiis facta more latrocinali conspiratione ex clericis et laicis turba collecta et permixta, nos violenter inter tantos obprimere studuisti."

55. Ibid. Gunthar puts the blame on Anastasius, who also wrote Nicholas's letters. Hincmar's version of Gunthar's letter does not even mention Anastasius.

Theutgaud argued that Nicholas had so grossly exceeded his powers that really he was no pope any more. He was proud and arrogant and assumed powers he did not possess. "He is making himself into emperor of the world."[56] His actions were contrary to the canonical rules and the behavior of his predecessors.[57] The synod at which they had been condemned was made up of a motley bunch of laymen and clerics. None of their peers, that is, other "metropolitans," were present. The synod and Nicholas had no right to judge them in the absence of the other metropolitans and of their diocesan bishops. By his action Nicholas did violence to the episcopal class, the "*ordo*" of all bishops. As bishop of Rome, Nicholas belonged to the same class as they did. Gunthar and Theutgaud indignantly pointed out to him that "they are brothers and fellow-bishops, not his clergy."[58]

Some of Lothar's other bishops, though, chose to make the best of a bad job. Adventius of Metz, Franco of Liège, and Rathold of Strasbourg are known to have accepted Nicholas's judgment. At least, we know that they sent him letters in which they apologized for their behavior. In this Adventius was supported by—note well—Charles the Bald, who interceded for him with Nicholas. These displays of humility were enough to satisfy Nicholas, and he took no further action against Lothar's other bishops.[59]

Here two opposing views of papal authority were in violent collision: Nicholas's belief that bishops derived the "principle" of their office from the papal see and that he could dismiss them and rescind their judgments whenever he saw fit to do so. He thus made of them, as Gunthar and Theutgaud complained, "his clergy." Opposed to this was the opinion of the archbishops of Cologne and Trier, who believed in an order of bishops who should decide things in fraternal discussion. They put the emphasis on equality among bishops, including the bishop of Rome, though the latter did occupy a special place as a kind of paternal adviser. This stress on the equality of all bishops, Rome included, was not new to the Frankish bishops. As early as 833 Pope Gregory IV had lamented that the Frankish bishops addressed him as "Brother Pope" and not as "Father."[60]

56. Ibid. c. 4, p. 61. In Hincmar's version: *AB* a° 864, the introductory letter, p. 107: "Totiusque mundi imperatorem se facit."

57. *AF* a° 863, c. 5, p. 61.

58. Ibid., c. 6: "Sciesque nos non tuos esse . . . clericos, quos ut fratres et coepiscopos regnoscere . . . debueras."

59. Letters from Adventius, Rathold, and Charles to Nicholas, *Ep. Lot.* nos. 8 and 10 (Adventius), pp. 219–22, 223–24, no. 6 (a letter fragment from Rathold), p. 217, and no. 9 (Charles), pp. 222–23; letters from Nicholas to Franco and Adventius, *Ep. Nic.* nos. 30 and 31, pp. 297–300.

60. Letter from Pope Gregory IV, in *Ep. karol. aevi* 3: p. 218; for this letter, see Leupen, *Gods stad*, pp. 98–99.

Pope Nicholas and the Kings

The primacy of the power of the bishop of Rome derived, according to Nicholas's traditional interpretation, from the fact that the bishops—in Nicholas's view, his subordinates—held authority in matters of belief and morality. And matters of belief and morality ought to outweigh everything else.[61]

Nicholas condemned Lothar for immoral conduct, namely lasciviousness: "The crime that King Lothar committed with two women, namely Theutberga and Waldrada, is well known to all. That king, if at least he can truly be called a king, in no way restrains his fleshly appetites with salutary discipline but in ungoverned weakness gives himself over to the forbidden surges of that desire."[62] Lothar should keep his passions under control and not allow himself to be carried away by the unbridled upwellings of his lascivious desire. He who is not king of his passions can hardly be called a king.[63] Nicholas was providing Lothar's subjects and anyone ill-disposed toward him with a reason to withdraw obedience from Lothar and depose him as a tyrant:

> You say that you are subject to kings and princes. . . . But you must first check whether those kings and princes, to whom you are supposedly subject, truly are kings and princes. First look to see whether they are good rulers of themselves, and then of the people subject to them; for how can someone who is bad for himself be good for another? See if they rule according to the law. Otherwise we must regard them rather as tyrants than as kings; and those we must rather resist and rebel against than be subject to them.[64]

61. See also Nicholas's claims to papal authority regarding belief and morals in his letter quoted in *AB* a° 863, p. 103, and the Council of Rome (October 863), c. 5, in *MGH Conc.* 4: p. 155. On the pope's duty of pastoral care for his flock, in Lothar's matrimonial case, *Ep. Nic.* no. 3, p. 269. Nicholas instructed Bishop Ado to care for King Lothar like a shepherd, *Ep. Nic.* no. 25 (30 March 864), p. 289. Nicholas charged Adventius to carry out his episcopal function properly, that is, to make him obey the papal orders, *Ep. Nic.* no. 31, p. 300; the same in his letter to Franco of Liège, *Ep. Nic.* no. 30, p. 298; and in the letter to Lothar's bishops, *Ep. Nic.* no. 35, p. 306.

62. Letter from Nicholas in *AB* a° 863, p. 99: "Scelus quod Lotharius rex, si tamen rex veraciter dici possit, qui nullo salubri regimine corporis appetitus refrenat, sed lubrica enervatione magis ipsius illicitis motibus cedit, in duabus feminis, Theotberga scilicet et Waldrada, commisit, omnibus manifestum est."

63. This view was already common in patristic writings, inter alia in Augustine, Cassiodorus, Gregory the Great, and Isidore of Seville. And later also in Pseudo-Cyprian; see Anton, *Fürstenspiegel*, pp. 386–404.

64. *Ep. Nic.* no. 31, to Adventius (17 September 864), p. 299: "Illud vero quod dicitis regibus et principibus vos esse subiectos. . . . Verumtamen videte, utrum reges isti et principes, quibus vos subiectos esse dicitis, veraciter reges et principes sint. Videte, si primum se bene regunt, deinde subditum populum; nam qui sibi nequam est, cui alii bonus erit?

One way in which an obstinate sinner such as Lothar could be forced to toe the line was by excommunication. When Lothar refused to obey Nicholas's orders and amend his sinful life, Nicholas threatened to excommunicate him.[65] He would then be publicly branded a sinner and no one would be allowed to have anything to do with him. This was of course an impossible situation for a king who had to govern a kingdom, and it gave his opponents an unprecedented justification for a coup d'état.

Sometime in 866 Lothar had tried—at least so Nicholas writes in a letter to Charles the Bald—to resolve his matrimonial case by submitting it to a secular court, at which he sought to accuse Theutberga of adultery and settle the matter by a judicial duel. Nicholas rejected this maneuver. All parties in the case had turned to him for a judgment, and he personally had then ruled on the matter. Since there was no higher authority to review the case and his decision was irrevocable, that judgment was final: the marriage between Lothar and Theutberga was indissoluble. Nobody else had the right to pronounce on the matter, since everyone else occupied a lower position than he did. Moreover, he disapproved of judicial duels on principle, since there was not one divine authority that approved them and because in resorting to them people were attempting to importune God.[66]

A letter from Nicholas to Charles, archbishop of Mainz, also contains a point that shows how Nicholas saw the relative status of religious and secular rules in matrimonial cases. Asked whether it was permitted for a man to kill his wife because of her adultery, as the secular laws allowed, Nicholas answered with a categorical no, invoking the supremacy of the Church: "The Holy Church is never constrained by secular laws. She has no sword, save a spiritual and divine one; she does not kill, but brings to life."[67]

The Success of Nicholas's Claims to Power

Certainly, the powers Nicholas claimed were far from modest. But to what extent could he make good his claims? How did people react to Nicholas's demands, and why? In Lothar's case his claims mainly related to two areas.

Videte si iure principantur: alioquin potius tyranni credendi sunt quam reges habendi, quibus magis resistere et ex adverso ascendere quam subdi debemus."

65. Threats of excommunication are in *Ep. Nic.* no. 37, to Lothar (early 865), p. 308, and *AB* a° 865, p. 118. We have already seen the fear of excommunication in two letters from Adventius, pp. 132–33 above. And Lothar had evidently been excommunicated in 864, according to *Ep. Nic.* no. 32, to Ado (early 865), p. 301.

66. *Ep. Nic.* no. 45, to Charles the Bald (25 January 867), pp. 330–31.

67. Nicholas to Charles, archbishop of Mainz (858–63), in *Ep. Nic.*, pp. 674 and 677 (for this letter, see above, n. 38): "Sancta Dei ecclesia numquam mundanis constringitur legibus; gladium non habet nisi spiritalem atque divinum, non occidit sed vivificat."

On the one hand, he asserted his supremacy over the other bishops, a supremacy that made it possible for him to dismiss the archbishops of Cologne and Trier and overturn their decisions regarding Lothar. On the other hand, he considered himself authorized to judge the moral conduct of King Lothar and compel him to reinstate Theutberga as his wife.

Nicholas's Claims to Power vis-à-vis the Bishops

Initial reaction to the dismissal of Gunthar and Theutgaud, the two most important archbishops in the Lotharingian realm, scions of Frankish families of the highest nobility that had held these offices and helped to determine the empire's policy for generations, was violent. Gunthar and Theutgaud traveled to Rome with Emperor Louis II to call Nicholas to account and compel him, by force if necessary, to reconsider his decision, so Hincmar, at least, says. Nicholas countered this action, still according to Hincmar, "by proclaiming masses and a general fast for himself and the Romans, so that God with the aid of the apostles should give the aforementioned emperor a spirit of good will and respect for the divine service and the authority of the Apostolic See."[68] Then, says Hincmar, some of the emperor's followers violently assaulted the people walking in procession to St. Peter's. Blows were rained upon them, and some of the crosses and banners carried in the procession were broken. At this Nicholas fled into St. Peter's, where he remained fasting for two days and nights, taking neither food nor drink. Thereupon Emperor Louis fell sick and abandoned his attempt.[69]

A quite different version of events is to be found in the *Libellus de imperatoria potestate*, which describes what happened from the imperial side. This work dates from the beginning of the tenth century and so is certainly not to be trusted in every detail, but the change of perspective is illuminating. Here responsibility for the fight is laid squarely at the pope's door. Louis had come to Rome in all good faith to negotiate, but Nicholas provoked the emperor by having his monks and nuns hold processions and ordering masses to be sung "against ill-doing princes."[70] When some great nobles asked them to desist, their request was refused. Soon after, the same nobles encountered such a procession, flew into a rage, and gave the participants a good beating. "They took revenge out of loyalty to their lord," it

---

68. *AB* aᵒ 864, pp. 105–6: "Cum laetaniis generale ieiunium sibi et Romanis indixit ut Deus apostolorum suffragiis praefato imperatori mentem bonam et reverentiam erga divinum cultum et apostolicae sedis auctoritatem donaret."

69. *AB* aᵒ 864, p. 106.

70. *Libellus de imperatoria potestate*, pp. 203–4: "Contra principes male agentes." For the differing versions of these events, see Buc, *Danger*, pp. 72–79.

says in the *Libellus*.[71] In any case, according to the *Libellus* the cause of the quarrel between Louis and Nicholas was not the dismissal of Gunthar and Theutgaud—the book says nothing at all about the issue of Lothar—but the conflicting claims to power of Nicholas and John, archbishop of Ravenna, one of the most prominent bishops in the realm of Louis II.[72] Much of the struggle with John had taken place earlier; probably the author of the *Libellus* is blending a number of conflicts in his narrative. According to the *Liber pontificalis*, however, John was present in Rome with Gunthar and Theutgaud.[73]

A third, much less detailed version of events can be found in the *Liber pontificalis*. This recounts Nicholas's struggle with John and with Gunthar and Theutgaud from a papal perspective. It says absolutely nothing about the role of Louis II, who does not feature at all in the anti-Nicholas campaign in Rome. It does say, very briefly, that John had asked Louis for support, but no consequences are linked to this.[74]

Appearances suggest that after the initial violent but fruitless reaction of Gunthar, Theutgaud, and Louis II the majority of bishops and their kings acquiesced in the dismissal of the archbishops of Cologne and Trier. In practice, however, they pursued a dual strategy. The papal judgment was no longer openly contested. People said they accepted it, but at the same time they asked Nicholas to reconsider it. They were certainly not inclined to obey the pope's command to dismiss two of the most important archbishops north of the Alps. Passive resistance was the order of the day. No one was appointed to the sees of Cologne and Trier, and efforts were made to persuade the pope to reinstate the two archbishops. Louis the German and his bishops, in particular, exerted themselves on behalf of Theutgaud, who happened to be the brother of Louis' archchancellor, Grimald, abbot of St. Gall.[75] Trier would not have a bishop again until after Theutgaud's death in 868,[76] Cologne not until 870. In the meantime the bishopric was

71. *Libellus de imperatoria potestate*, p. 204: "Pro fidelitate sui senioris vindictam exercuerunt contra illos."

72. Ibid., pp. 200–201.

73. *Liber pontificalis* 2: pp. 160–161; Davis, *Lives of the Ninth-Century Popes*, p. 230.

74. *Liber pontificalis*, t. 2, pp. 155–61, on p. 155; Davis, *Lives of the Ninth-Century Popes*, pp. 213–31. A fourth, very brief, and fiercely anti-imperial version can be found in Erchempert, *Historia Langobardorum Beneventanorum* c. 37, p. 248.

75. Nicholas rebuked them for this, in *Ep. Nic.* no. 51, p. 336, no. 52, p. 339, no. 53, pp. 340–51 (Nicholas explains the whole affair and the offenses of Theutgaud and Gunthar yet again); no. 50, to Lothar, p. 334, on the refusal to appoint new bishops to Cologne and Trier.

76. The new bishop, in 869, was Bertulf, a nephew of Adventius of Metz, Regino aº 869, p. 98.

run by surrogates, from 866 on by Hilduin, who was none other than Gunthar's brother. In practice Gunthar still held the reins, except for the period 864–66 when he was in conflict with the other bishops and with Lothar and secular control of the bishopric came into the hands of Conrad's son Hugo.[77] During these years Gunthar was the only one actively to oppose the pope. At first he simply ignored his dismissal, until Lothar compelled him to surrender his bishopric.[78] After that he tried, without success, to have his dismissal rescinded at a synod called in Pavia on the orders of Emperor Louis II, but the bishops at this synod did write a letter in which they requested Pope Nicholas—vainly, as it turned out—to restore Gunthar and Theutgaud to their posts. Then Gunthar composed a letter that was clearly intended as propaganda. In it he claimed that at the urging of these bishops and of the emperor and empress Nicholas was inclined to restore him to his office. As proof he enclosed with the letter the decisions of the Pavia synod and its written request to Nicholas, together with a whole dossier of canon law arguments to support his reinstatement. The initial recipient of this letter, with the responsibility for its further dissemination, was Hincmar of Reims. Evidently at the time relations between Hincmar and Gunthar were such that Gunthar was content to entrust this task to him, possibly because they clearly had a common interest. Both were in conflict with Pope Nicholas, who had expressly meddled in matters that, according to them, infringed the authority of the metropolitans.[79]

The passive resistance of kings and bishops also found expression when Nicholas summoned the bishops from all the subkingdoms to Rome for a synod to be held in November 864. The subjects to be discussed included Lothar's matrimonial case, the dismissal of Gunthar and Theutgaud, and a few other important matters.[80] But the bishops did not turn up, and Nicholas had to cancel the synod. When he took them to task for their absence they came up with every conceivable excuse: the roads were unsafe, the bishops of Charles the Bald were needed to combat the Norsemen, and a

77. *AB* a° 864 and 866, pp. 111 and 126; *AX* a° 866, pp. 23–24.
78. *AB* a° 864, p. 111; *AX* a° 865, p. 22.
79. See Fuhrmann, "Propagandaschrift." The edition of the letter is in that work, pp. 36–51, and also in *MGH Conc.* 4: pp. 188–97. The original of this letter has been preserved, making it the oldest surviving original private letter from the middle ages. The dispute between Hincmar and Nicholas concerned the dismissal of Bishop Rothad of Soissons.
80. *AB* a° 864, p. 115; *Ep. Lot.* no. 8, Adventius to Nicholas, p. 224, confirms an invitation to all the archbishops from the realms of Charles, Louis, and Lothar to attend a second synod planned for 18 June (no year is mentioned, but it is probably 865); the participants could send two of their suffragans instead. For the dating of these proposed councils, see Fuhrmann, "Propagandaschrift," pp. 4–6.

few reprobates apparently even dared to say that for them there was not the slightest need to go to Rome.[81]

Theutberga's Reinstatement in the Political Power Play

Meanwhile, Lothar had been forced to accept Nicholas's decision and take Theutberga back because his uncles Charles and Louis were combining to threaten his kingdom. They were taking advantage of Nicholas's judgment, which cast doubts on Lothar's kingship. Nicholas had even threatened Lothar with excommunication, and an excommunicate, someone expelled from the Church and so forbidden to consort with other Christians, could not function as king. In any case, Lothar could not possibly ignore this threat of excommunication, since it gave his uncles a most powerful weapon. He had to deprive them of this weapon, and to this end he called on his remaining allies: he sent his uncle Liutfrid to his brother, Emperor Louis II. Louis talked Nicholas into sending an embassy to the northern subkingdoms to prevent a takeover by Charles the Bald and Louis the German and to restore proper marital relations between Lothar and Theutberga. This embassy was a weightier affair than its predecessor two years before. It was led by Arsenius, bishop of Orte, the uncle of Anastasius, the *apocrisiarus* (plenipotentiary) and secretary to Nicholas. This, then, was a man whose words carried authority, because people could be sure that what he said would have Nicholas's support.

Lothar had no alternative but to take Theutberga back. However, he was spared the humiliation of a public penance—to the great displeasure of Hincmar, in particular, who made no effort to hide his disappointment.[82]

---

81. *Ep. Nic.* no. 38 to the bishops of Charles and Louis (April 865), pp. 309–10. For the bishops' role in repelling the Norsemen by spiritual means, see Adventius's letter, published in Missone, "Mandement."

82. *AB* aº 865, p. 119. Flint, "Magic," argues that the so-called Lothar Crystal was made for this occasion. It would have been used in the ceremony at which Theutberga was reinstated, which would have had to have been during a mass held after the ceremony. According to Flint, the images on the crystal refer to Hincmar's work, the idea being that Hincmar would be appeased by this. But Hincmar was not appeased, as is clear from the above. Nor is there any evidence of Hincmar being involved in Theutberga's rehabilitation ceremony. On the contrary, during the period of Arsenius's embassy Hincmar tried to sabotage the mission. He could not block its decisions, however; all he could do was vent his spleen in his venomous commentary in the *Annales Bertiniani*. In any case, the Susanna symbolism is not unique to Hincmar. When writing *De divortio* he had borrowed it from a council text (*De raptu*), see *De divortio*, pp. 145–46, and Heidecker, *Kerk*, pp. 112–13. Besides, Flint is stretching possibilities in labeling the persons depicted on the crystal with the names of those concerned in Lothar's matrimonial case. The events shown on the crystal certainly do not correspond so exactly to Lothar's case. For a description and analysis of the crystal, see Kornbluth, *Engraved Gems*, pp. 27–48, with a pertinent critique of Flint's views on pp. 37–39.

The mission's diplomatic activities were not confined to Lothar, however. Both Louis the German and Charles the Bald were told by Arsenius to leave their nephews' kingdoms alone, while in Charles' realm Arsenius also settled the thorny problem of Rothad, the dismissed bishop of Soissons. He restored him to his office, to Hincmar's fury.[83] He also took it upon himself to take the two adulterous women, Engeltrude and Waldrada, back to Italy with him.[84] And finally he also transacted some business: he tried to take possession of properties claimed by the pope and he threatened some people who had stolen a sum of money from him some years before in a most undiplomatic way—according to Hincmar—"with a letter from Pope Nicholas which was full of the most terrible maledictions, such as had never before been heard from the Apostolic See" to make them return the money.[85]

In any event, Theutberga was queen again. She had been publicly received by Lothar, with the swearing of weighty oaths, as queen and consort. Robed and crowned as a queen she accompanied Lothar to mass.[86] She sat with him at table and he appeared to carry out his conjugal duties most willingly.[87]

It soon became apparent, though, that all this was no more than a pretty sham. Emotionally Lothar was still bound to Waldrada. True, when Waldrada came back from Italy she did not publicly return to his side, but she did resume her position as his favored mistress, with all the political influence that came with it.[88] The pope, who had excommunicated Waldrada, upbraided her for not having come to Rome to ask his forgiveness:

> Finally, while she ought to have come directly to us and asked the assent of the Throne of St. Peter, so that we, as had been arranged, should pronounce a judgment pleasing to God in her case, she then turned again to Satan and retraced her steps to the province, so that he should rule over her. This she did, even though by the exertions of our emissary she was immediately summoned back to Italy. And she behaved as though nothing had happened, by which a great scandal was wrought in the Church of Christ, and she strives after worldly honor and has dominion in matters of state; and worse yet, it is

83. *AB* aº 865, pp. 118–19.

84. *AB* aº 865, pp. 121–22. For Engeltrude, see also Arsenius's letter, *Ep. Lot.* no. 11, pp. 225–26. Engeltrude did at first go with Arsenius, but she never arrived in Italy. On the way she went to collect fresh horses from some relatives of hers, after which Arsenius never set eyes on her again.

85. *AB* aº 865, pp. 121–22: "Epistolam Nicolai pape plenam terribilibus et a modestia sedis apostolicae antea inauditis maledictionibus."

86. As confirmed by Arsenius himself, *AB* aº 865, p. 122.

87. As regards the latter, at least according to a letter from Adventius of Metz, *Ep. Lot.* no. 16, p. 235.

88. See above, p. 105.

even apparent that she has been placed at the head of pious institutions and of religious persons; and she is far from giving up her plans for the downfall of Queen Theutberga, as various persons bear witness, while she constantly strives to be in those places from which she can readily go to King Lothar and he to her. In short, from day to day she seeks for reasons to return to her old licentiousness.[89]

This letter of 13 June 866, addressed to all the bishops in all the subkingdoms, informs them of Waldrada's excommunication, which had been pronounced on 2 February 866. But Nicholas was not particularly successful in his efforts to enforce this excommunication. He had to confirm it several times, because not everyone received his letter and people did not abide by the excommunication. As late as 24 January 867 he wrote to Lothar and to Lothar's bishops saying that he had already written to them three times, but to no effect. Evidently a struggle was going on, with both sides spreading and withholding information. Nicholas suspected his opponents of suppressing his letters and spreading the rumor that Nicholas had given Waldrada permission to return.[90]

Quite soon after Theutberga's official reinstatement as queen and consort there was a radical shift in alliances. Lothar, Charles the Bald, and Theutberga now jointly appealed for her marriage to Lothar to be dissolved. The most striking new alliance here is that between Lothar and Theutberga. What could have persuaded Theutberga to seek a divorce from Lothar at this point? Officially she was now indeed the queen, but that did not give her much real influence. That influence belonged to Waldrada, because of her emotional bond with Lothar—a bond that was the stronger because Lothar had children by her. Theutberga, on the other hand, was childless. She may even have been incapable of bearing children after eleven years of marital upheavals. In any case, Lothar did not love her nor, very probably, did she love Lothar. She had no children on whom she could bestow a kingdom. One

89. *Ep. Nic.* no. 42, to all bishops of all the subkingdoms (13 June 866), p. 315: "Postremo cum recto itinere nos illi fuerat adeundum et sedis beati Petri suffragia requirenda, quatenus iuxta quod statutum fuerat nos de eius negotio Deo placita consideratione diffiniremus, postea retro est conversa post Satanam et in provinciam, ut principaretur in ea, iter reflexit; licet industria legati nostri ad Italiam denuo revocata sit et, quasi nihil fuerit operata, unde in Christi sit ecclesia non modicum scandalum generatum, gloriam mundi sectatur reique publicae dominatur ac, quod est gravius, etiam piis locis atque religiosis personis praeesse dinoscitur et a Theutbergae reginae coepta interitus meditatione, sicut nonnulli testantur, minime cessat, dum ea nimirum loca repetere affectat, in quibus facilis ipsius ad regem Hlotharium et eiusdem regis ad eam esse possit accessus. Et ut breviter cuncta complectar, de die in diem, qualiter ad pristinas voluptates redeat, variis argumentis exquirit."

90. *Ep. Nic.* nos. 46, p. 325, and 47, pp. 326–27, of 24 January 867 to Lothar and to his bishops. Nicholas had already written to them three times, he says, but without result.

of her brothers, Hucbert, was dead; the other, Boso, whose wife had run away from him years ago, wanted to marry someone else.[91] After eleven years of wrangling as Lothar's so-called wife, she had apparently had enough of being used as a pawn in her kinsmen's dynastic maneuvering. Now she could take advantage of a situation in which she had, officially at least, the power of a queen by selling the title as dear as possible and divorcing on her own terms.

This new attempt at divorce therefore looked very different from that of six years before. Naturally, there was no further mention of the terrible charges voiced against Theutberga at the previous synods. The grounds for divorce cited were that Lothar's marriage to Waldrada had taken place prior to that with Theutberga, that Theutberga was incapable of bearing children, and that she wished to lead a celibate life.[92] She made Lothar pay dearly for her support. She received a large number of estates in unrestricted ownership, and in addition all the confiscated possessions of her brother Hucbert.[93]

Charles the Bald too supported the plea for divorce. Lothar had concluded an alliance with him after mediation by Charles' wife, Ermentrude. Probably Queen Ermentrude played a key role in the double agreement between Lothar and Charles and between Lothar and Theutberga.[94] And Charles the Bald too was not doing this for nothing: he got the Abbey of St. Vaast,[95] and Lothar also made a donation to one of the most important West Frankish religious houses, St.-Denis, where his and Charles' kinsman Louis, a grandson of Charlemagne, was the abbot.[96]

There is absolutely no question of any fixed position or principled stance regarding the papal judgments concerning Lothar's marriage on the part

---

91. Nicholas to Louis the German, *Ep. Nic.* no. 49, p. 333.

92. See above, pp. 153–54.

93. *D Lot.II.* nos. 27 and 32, pp. 428–29 and 437–38. Both charters have also been edited by Dupraz, "Deux préceptes." The originals are in the *Archivio di Stato* in Parma, *Diplomi imperiali* 10 and 12. Opinions differ as to their dating. The first charter is dated by Theodor Schieffer, for convincing reasons, to 17 January 866, in *D Lot.II*, pp. 423–25, 428–29. Dupraz dates it exactly one year later, on unconvincing grounds. The second charter is dated by Theodor Schieffer to 24 November 868, *D Lot.II*, pp. 437–38, with no specific reasons given. Dupraz dates it to the same date, with his aforementioned unconvincing arguments. In my view this charter should be dated to 24 November 867. There is no need to correct the regnal year given in the document and the indiction then also fits. These datings match with the events. The first grant to Theutberga took place on 17 January 866, after the treaty between Charles the Bald and Lothar and before her planned, but never undertaken, journey to Rome; the second on 24 November 867, before her first completed journey to Rome, placed by Hincmar in late 867, *AB* a° 867, p. 140.

94. Ermentrude is recorded as being present at all the meetings: *AB*, a° 865, p. 121; *AB* a° 866, pp. 128 and 129–30. See also Hyam, "Ermentrude," p. 158.

95. *AB* a° 866, p. 128.

96. *D Lot.II.* no. 30 (12 June 866), pp. 433–35.

of those most involved. Charles the Bald and Theutberga initially declared that the pope's ruling forbidding the divorce of Lothar and Theutberga must definitely be implemented, only to request a little later that the pope pronounce that same divorce. And though Lothar himself had first asked the pope to rule on the divorce, after Nicholas's intervention and hearing his judgment he would successively ignore it, accept it, and—unsuccessfully— attempt to have it reconsidered. Quite plainly, papal judgments were ad- hered to mainly when one stood to gain by them or when one was forced to comply. As soon as the compulsion disappeared, though, or when a change of position was more to one's advantage, one's attitude changed. To ensure that his rulings were effective Pope Nicholas was obliged to resort to com- pulsion. In the immediate vicinity of Rome he could do this by mobilizing his followers. But outside this region his resources were very limited. North of the Alps he could only achieve anything by gaining the support of those who held power in those territories, in this case mainly the kings. And only when he had something to offer them or was able to play them off against each other was he successful.

Act VI

A New Pope and Lothar's
Last Battle, 867–869

Lothar wants to settle things once and for all with Nicholas, who has been con-
tinually bombarding him with accusations of misconduct and threatening to excommu-
nicate him. So long as Pope Nicholas is providing his uncles with reasons to accuse him
of being a bad king his political situation remains perilous. When Lothar learns in June
867 that his uncle Charles, with whom he concluded an alliance in 865, is holding talks
with Louis the German, he fears the worst.[1] He is chronically suspicious of Charles the
Bald. That this suspicion is well founded is clear from the text of the secret accord be-
tween Louis the German and Charles the Bald at Metz, in which they agree to divide
the realms of their nephews Lothar and Louis II between them.[2] Lothar reacts quickly
and goes to see Louis the German. He assigns to Louis the care of his kingdom and of his
son Hugo, saying that he himself intends to go to Rome.[3] But he does not go. Instead he
sends an embassy to Nicholas, headed by his chancellor, Grimland.[4] By not going to
Rome in person he probably saves himself a lot of trouble, for in the meantime Nicholas
has let it be known that he refuses to receive him so long as he fails to mend his ways.[5]

---

1. *AB* aº 867, pp. 136–37.

2. *MGH Cap.* 2: pp. 165–67. For this text, see above, p. 141. Opinions differ as to the
dating of this text: June 867 (Parisot, *Royaume*, pp. 296–99) or June 868 (Calmette, *Diplo-*
matie, appendix 3, pp. 195–200); see also Staubach, *Herrscherbild*, pp. 458–59.

3. *AB* aº 867, pp. 136–37; in *Ep. Lot.* no. 17, to Nicholas, p. 237, Lothar says that he
wants to come to Rome.

4. *Ep. Lot.* no. 17. The letter announcing Grimland's embassy is addressed to Nicholas.
The letters that Grimland brought back were from Nicholas's successor, Adrian. Grim-
land had returned by June 868, when he delivered letters from Adrian to Charles the Bald,
AB aº 868, p. 143.

5. *Ep. Nic.* no. 51 (30 October 867) to Louis the German, p. 336, forbids him to come.
In *Ep. Lot.* no. 18, to Adrian (February 868), p. 239, Lothar complains that Nicholas had
refused to receive him.

The ambassadors will not find Nicholas alive. On 13 November 867 Pope Nicholas dies, even on his deathbed still quarreling violently with the Byzantine emperor, with Lothar, and with innumerable bishops from both East and West.[6] Thereupon Lothar sends Theutberga too to Rome. Fate seems to be turning in his favor. The new Pope, Adrian II (867–872), is considerably more flexible than his predecessor. He grants Theutberga an audience and gives her leave to go and live in a place of her own choosing. She need not return to Lothar any more, and so is effectively divorced from him. Adrian also lifts Waldrada's excommunication and orders Louis the German and Charles the Bald to leave the realms of their nephews Lothar and Louis alone.[7]

In June 869 Lothar embarks on his decisive action and crosses the Alps. Once he reaches Italy, before anything else he wants to see his brother, Emperor Louis.[8] As usual, Louis is to mediate for him with Pope Adrian. But Louis is in Beneventum. He is at war with the Saracens and is busy besieging Bari, making it impossible for him to leave southern Italy. So he sends envoys to meet Lothar and tell him that for the time being it would be better for him to return home. They can discuss the matter at a more convenient time. But Lothar decides to continue and seeks out Louis. He now approaches Louis through his wife, Angilberga. With great difficulty, after many entreaties and numerous gifts, he gains a hearing. It is Angilberga, too, who is to lead the political mission. She accompanies Lothar to Monte Cassino, to which place Louis also summons Pope Adrian by imperial command. After Lothar has presented lavish gifts to the pope, Angilberga persuades him to have a mass celebrated for Lothar, at which he gives him Holy Communion. All this on one condition: that Lothar declare that since her excommunication he has had no contact at all with Waldrada. According to Hincmar, "the wretched man, like a true Judas, with a feigned clear conscience and brazen face, neither trembled nor refused to take Holy Communion on this condition."[9] His supporters also receive communion. Among their number is Gunthar of Cologne; he receives communion as a layman after promising to accept Nicholas's judgment.

As Hincmar continues the story, "Angilberga then returned to her Emperor and Pope Adrian left for Rome. Lothar followed in Adrian's tracks. And when Pope Adrian entered Rome Lothar came to St. Peter's; not one cleric came to meet him there, but he

6. *AB* a° 867, pp. 138–40, and Nicholas's letters of 30 and 31 October 867 to Louis the German and his bishops, *Ep. Nic.* nos. 51–53, pp. 334–51.

7. *Ep. Hadr.*, no. 1 to Lothar, pp. 695–97, no. 4 to Waldrada, p. 701, no. 5 to the bishops of Louis the German, p. 702, and no. 6 to Louis the German, pp. 702–4. *AB* a° 868, p. 143, report of the letters to Charles.

8. The following is based on *AB* a° 869, pp. 153–56.

9. *AB* a° 869, p. 154: "Ipse autem infelix more Iudae simulata bona conscientia et impudenti fronte eandem sacram communionem sub hac conventione accipere non pertimuit nec recusavit."

and his entourage did visit the tomb of St. Peter. Then he took lodgings in the squalid attic of a dwelling house, which had not even had a broom over it to clean it, but which was very close to St. Peter's. He expected that next day a mass would be held for him. That would after all be Sunday, for he had come to St. Peter's on a Saturday. But he did not receive this favor from the pope. Thereupon he went into Rome on the Monday and dined with the pope in the Lateran Palace. Lothar gave him many gifts: pitchers of gold and silver, by which he obliged Adrian to give gifts in return: a mantle, a palm branch, and a staff. These gifts were construed by himself and his people as follows: by the mantle he would again be invested with Waldrada. The palm would show that he had been victorious in the affairs he had embarked upon. By the staff he would coerce the bishops who opposed his will.[10]

"Lothar then left Rome in very good spirits and came to Lucca. There, however, he was struck down by a fever and an epidemic broke out among his followers, whom he saw die in large numbers before his eyes. But he refused to recognize the divine judgment (Iudicium Dei) and reached Piacenza on the sixth of August. There on Sunday around noon he suddenly fell almost lifeless and lost the power of speech. He died the following day at the second hour and was buried by those few of his followers who had survived the epidemic in a small monastery near that town."[11] *In their panic at the rapidly spreading deadly disease the survivors leave two important documents behind*

---

10. Ibid., p. 155: "Engelberga denique redeunte ad suum imperatorem, Adrianus papa Romam reversus est. Quem e vestigio Hlotharius est persecutus. Et Adriano papa Romam ingrediente, Hlotharius ad aecclesiam beati Petri venit. Ubi nullum clericum obvium habuit, sed tantum ipse usque ad sepulchrum sancti Petri cum suis pervenit, indeque solarium secus ecclesiam beati Petri mansionem habiturus intravit, quem nec etiam scopa mundatum invenit. Putavitque in crastina, subsequente videlicet domenica, nam sabbato ad basilicam sancti Petri pervenit, sibi cantari deberet missam. A praefato pontifice hoc obtinere non potuit. Inde secunda feria Romam ingrediens in palatio Lateranensi cum ipso apostolico prandidit, et datis ei muneribus in vasis aureis et argenteis obtinuit, ut ei ipse pontifex leenam et palmam ac ferulam daret. Sicut et fecit. Quae munera ita ipse et sui interpretati sunt, videlicet ut per leenam de Waldrada revestiretur, per palmam victorem se in his quae coeperat demonstraret, per ferulam episcopos suae voluntati resistentes obsistendo distringeret." The three papal gifts are probably pilgrim's tokens. It looks as though Hincmar is here putting a false interpretation of them into Lothar's mouth, one that already foreshadows his approaching doom. See also Buc, *Danger*, p. 80. My thanks to Mayke de Jong for her suggestions on the interpretation of this passage.

11. *AB*, a° 869, p. 156: "Hlotharius vero Roma laetus promovens, usque Lucam civitatem venit. Ubi febre corripitur, et grassante clade in suos, quos in oculos suos coacervatim mori conspiciebat, sed iudicium Dei intellegere nolens, usque Placentiam octavo idus augusti pervenit; ibique domenica die superdiurnans, circa horam nonam inopinate exanimis paene effectus est et obmutuit, atque in crastino hora diei secunda moritur et a paucis suorum qui a clade remanserant in quodam monasteriolo secus ipsam civitatem terrae mandatur." According to Ado of Vienne, he was buried in the basilica of St. Antoninus: Ado of Vienne, *Chronicon*, p. 323.

in Piacenza: Lothar's deeds of gift to Theutberga of 866 and 867 relating to their di-
vorce, which they had taken with them to the pope.[12]

Lothar's uncles Louis and Charles promptly fall upon his kingdom and divide it be-
tween them;[13] *this despite the protests of Emperor Louis II, Lothar's brother and heir*
apparent, and angry letters from Pope Adrian II.[14]

In the end Lothar's marriage strategy failed because of his untimely death.
The next Council of Rome was to have taken a fresh look at his case; what
it would have decided we shall never know. What is certain is that Pope
Adrian interpreted the rules on marriage rather differently from his predecessor Nicholas. In this case, though, a new pope meant a new political
setup but certainly not a reduction or modification of papal claims to
power, nor of the development of new means of enforcing them. For Lothar his journey to Rome was, in hindsight, his last battle. But Lothar
himself regarded it as a risky final attempt to secure his marriage to Waldrada and the future of his realm. Now we must look at Lothar's last opponents: first, Pope Adrian, and then, for the last time, his uncles Charles
and Louis.

Pope Adrian's Rules for Marriage
and His Claims to Power

In recent years Lothar had had no more implacable opponent than Pope
Nicholas. He had thrown his whole weight behind his judgment in Lothar's
matrimonial case, and by skillful use of the political situation had for the
most part succeeded in enforcing it. How did his successor Adrian apply
the rules on marriage, and how did this fit with the political situation in
the years following Nicholas's death?

Lothar's Attempt at Divorce and the Changed Political Situation

Initially Adrian confirmed Nicholas's rulings and his arguments: the
marriage of Lothar and Theutberga was valid in law; Lothar had not been

---

12. The original charters have been preserved and are now in the *Archivio di Stato* in
Parma. For datings and editions, see act 5 n. 93. According to Dupraz, "Deux préceptes,"
these charters are incomplete; before Theutberga's name a space has consistently been left
blank, in which her proper designation was later to be inserted, for instance "domna," "re-
gina," or "coniunx." Examination of the documents shows that there are indeed blank
spaces, but that these are not significantly larger than the spaces between other words.

13. *AB* a° 869–70, pp. 157–64, 167–75; *AF* a° 869–70, pp. 69–70.

14. *Ep. Hadr.* no. 16 to the magnates of Charles the Bald, pp. 717–19, no. 17 to the bishops
of Charles the Bald, pp. 719–20, no. 18 to Hincmar of Reims, pp. 720–21, no. 19 to the magnates of the realm of the late King Lothar, pp. 721–23. *AB* a° 869, pp. 167–68, a° 870, p. 175.

married to Waldrada first; barrenness and the woman's desire to enter a convent did not constitute reasons for a divorce; and Lothar had committed a grave sin by repudiating Theutberga and binding himself to Waldrada.[15] Nothing new so far, but Adrian was inclined to look at the case again. He received Theutberga in Rome, while Nicholas had specifically instructed her to remain with Lothar at all costs. When Theutberga appeared before him, "she swore that she would rather flee to the heathen than look upon Lothar's face again."[16] And Adrian complied with her request in a practical and ingenious way. He announced that he would convene a council to reconsider the case and in the meantime Theutberga need not return to Lothar. If she thought the return journey would be too long and too difficult, or if she was physically not fit for it, she had Adrian's permission to stay in one of the abbeys promised to her by Lothar. Thus, she was de facto separated from Lothar, something to which Nicholas had always been fiercely opposed.[17] Adrian also lifted Waldrada's excommunication and ordered the uncles of Lothar and Louis to leave their nephews' kingdoms alone.[18] Moreover, Adrian was prepared to receive Lothar, something Nicholas had always refused to do. Evidently his discussions with Adrian, when they dined together at the Lateran Palace in Rome, had given Lothar the impression that his case looked promising, for when he left for home he was in high spirits.

Nicholas's death and Adrian's succession had changed the political balance in Rome. Adrian was already an old man when he succeeded Nicholas. The Roman family from which he sprang had already produced two popes, namely Stephen V (816–17) and Sergius II (844–47). On top of that, he was married and had a daughter; his father too was a cleric.[19] Adrian had been elected with the backing of Emperor Louis II.[20] When Louis asked for support for himself and his brother Lothar against the aggressive policy of their uncles, his request was not refused. During these years two important figures who had helped to shape Nicholas's policy also

---

15. *Ep. Hadr.*, no. 1, pp. 695–96.

16. Synod of Rome or Monte Cassino (869), in *MGH Conc.* 4: pp. 369–70: "Cum iuramento dicebat, quod ante inter paganos aufugeret, quam faciem Lotharii gloriosi regis videret."

17. *Ep. Hadr.*, no. 1, pp. 695–96.

18. *Ep. Hadr.*, no. 4 to Waldrada, p. 701, no. 5 to the bishops of Louis the German, p. 702, and no. 6 to Louis the German, pp. 702–4. *AB* a° 868, report of the letters to Charles.

19. *Liber Pontificalis* 2: pp. 173–75, Davis, *Lives of the Ninth-Century Popes*, p. 259; see also Grotz, *Erbe*, pp. 16–24, who gives his birth date as 792.

20. *AB* a° 867, p. 140; *Liber Pontificalis* 2: pp. 174–75, Davis, *Lives of the Ninth-Century Popes*, pp. 262–63.

disappeared from the scene: Bishop Arsenius, who had reinstated the marriage of Lothar and Theutberga in 865, and his nephew Anastasius, the man who wrote Nicholas's letters.[21] Their downfall began in 868 when, at his father's urging, Arsenius's son Eleutherius had abducted Pope Adrian's daughter, though she was already betrothed to someone else. Arsenius fled from Adrian's rage, but on the way he fell sick and "after having—so they say—conversed with demons, he went without communion to the place where he belonged." So writes Hincmar, who had another score to settle with Arsenius.[22] What happened then is quite shocking and the exact events and their causes remain slightly obscure, but, again according to Hincmar, Eleutherius subsequently murdered Pope Adrian's daughter and wife at the instigation of his cousin Anastasius, after which he was himself killed by followers of Emperor Louis. Anastasius was excommunicated by Adrian.[23] Thus Lothar was free of these two clerical dignitaries, who had imposed on him a strict matrimonial morality.

Papal Claims to Power: Theory and Practice

Pope Nicholas had made great claims to power. Theoretically, those of Pope Adrian were no less great. He, too, like Nicholas, saw the pope as the supreme authority, whose decisions were not subject to review by any other authority.[24] Adrian was also the first to cite the Pseudo-Isidorian decretals word for word to support his claims.[25] In practice Adrian's

21. Quite soon after Nicholas's death Anastasius began to suspect that his successor would be inclined to decide Lothar's case in a different way from his predecessor. Consequently he wrote to Ado of Vienne seeking support for Nicholas's old policy, Anastasius, *Epistolae*, pp. 400–401. For the kinship of Arsenius and Anastasius, see p. 401, where Anastasius calls Arsenius *"avunculi mei"* (my maternal uncle). Hincmar of Reims, *AB* aº 868, p. 144, describes Arsenius as Anastasius's father.

22. *AB* aº 868, p. 144: "Arsenius . . . et, ut dicebatur, cum daemonibus confabulans, sine communione abiit in locum suum." For Arsenius's mission, during which among other things he reinstated the bishop of Soissons whom Hincmar had dismissed, and Hincmar's comments on this, see above, pp. 168–69.

23. *AB* aº 868, pp. 144–50. Hincmar is our only, very biased, source for this. However, he cannot have made up the events completely, since at least part of the intended audience of his Annals was also well informed. The silence in other sources is striking. The *Liber pontificalis*, for example, simply leaves out the entire episode. For a discussion of the episode, see *Annals of St.-Bertin*, trans. Nelson, p. 145 n. 8, Davis, *Lives of the Ninth-Century Popes*, pp. 250–51. Adrian became pope at an advanced age, having previously married and had a daughter. This was actually not uncommon among the clergy at that time; Nicholas I, for example, was the son of a cleric.

24. Synod of Rome or Monte Cassino (869), in *MGH Conc.* 4: pp. 366–79.

25. Fuhrmann, *Einfluß* 2: pp. 273–80; see the complete dossier with Pseudo-Isidorian texts accompanying the decisions of the above-mentioned synod: *MGH Conc.* 4: pp. 371–79.

claims to supremacy were not particularly effective, at least as regards the Carolingian kings and bishops. Politically speaking, he was in a weaker position than his predecessor, because he could not play the Frankish kings off against each other sufficiently. Whether the pope's commands were implemented north of the Alps in the realms of the Frankish kings depended entirely on the political situation. Usually people would politely promise obedience, and then if the particular commands suited them, as with the condemnations of Lothar, they would turn them to their own advantage. If they did not suit them, they simply ignored them. Only when there was no alternative, or when all parties had something to gain, as in Arsenius's mission in 865, were papal commands obeyed without question. Just how little effect the pope's demands sometimes had is shown by the fate of Adrian's expostulations about the carving up of Lothar's realm by Charles the Bald and Louis the German. His protests were completely ignored.[26] When there was plunder to be shared out, the Frankish kings were not susceptible to pious exhortations.

Political Power and the Preservation of Lothar's Realm

Lothar's policy consisted very largely of steering a middle course between his uncles Louis and Charles. He was in constant danger of losing his kingdom to one or the other of them. Invasions of other people's kingdoms by Carolingian kings were a common enough occurrence "because," says Regino, "the souls of the kings are acquisitive and ever insatiable."[27] The vicissitudes of Lothar's divorce and especially the papal judgments gave his uncles only too good reason to depose him as unworthy of being king. Lothar had to neutralize this threat as best he could. When both uncles combined against him he sought support from the pope and complied with his demands. When he had made an alliance with one of his uncles he tried to persuade the pope to let him divorce.

In 867 he wanted to settle things once and for all and decided to travel to Rome. Then, too, for the first time he took steps to regulate the succession. True, he was still young, but for the Carolingian rulers and their

26. *Ep. Hadr.* no. 16 to the magnates of Charles the Bald, pp. 717–19, no. 17 to the bishops of Charles the Bald, pp. 719–20, no. 18 to Hincmar of Reims, pp. 720–21, no. 19 to the magnates of the realm of the late King Lothar, pp. 721–23. *AB* a° 869.

27. Regino a° 866, p. 90: "Ut animi regum avidi et semper inexplebiles sunt," quoting from Justinus's compilation of Pompeius Trogus, *Historia*; on this, see Löwe, "Regino."

sons premature death was a constant possibility. There are numerous instances of them succumbing to accidents or disease, and the journey to
Rome was long and dangerous. A great many of Lothar's supporters would
accompany him to Rome, leaving his realm even more vulnerable. He
commended his kingdom and his son Hugo to the care of his uncle Louis
the German. Hugo was also given the duchy of Alsace.[28] In this way, should
anything happen to Lothar he would at least have something. Alsace was
evidently an area where Lothar and Waldrada enjoyed a great deal of support. Lothar's mother's family came from there, and Waldrada had relatives and property there.[29] But Lothar decided not to go to Rome in 867. In
869 he seems to have thought the situation safe enough. Pope Adrian had
sent letters ordering his uncles to leave his realm alone, but Lothar thought
that this was still not sufficient security. He asked his uncles to swear to
him that they would do his kingdom no harm during his absence. Louis
did so swear, "so it is said," the *Annales Bertiniani* maintain; Charles did
not.[30] Again, Lothar had to pay for this promise. On 22 January 869 he
made a gift to Bertha, a daughter of Louis the German, to reinforce his
friendship with her mother and father. Perhaps Bertha had intervened
with her father on Lothar's behalf. The intercessor's name is interesting:
Waldrada herself.[31] In any case, Lothar now decided to risk it and set out
for Rome.

Lothar's efforts to preserve his realm for himself and his son Hugo were
thwarted by his death. The epidemic also claimed the lives of most of his
loyal supporters, the men who were Hugo's potential followers. Charles
and Louis took advantage of the power vacuum and pounced on his kingdom. Then Louis fell ill, and Charles decided to make the most of this by
annexing the whole of Lothar's kingdom—contrary to the oaths he had
sworn in the pact of Metz in June 868, but what's an oath when there's a
kingdom to be gained? Louis took countermeasures and duly got his share
of the loot. Lothar's other possible heirs got nothing. Apart from Hugo—
who was still very young and, moreover, disqualified by the disastrous outcome of the marriage issue—the most serious legitimate contender was

28. *AB* a° 867, pp. 136–37.
29. The Alsatian count Eberhard was a kinsman of Waldrada's and would receive the
abbey of Lure from her when she retired to Remiremont after Lothar's death. Lure had
been given to her by Lothar, according to the *Vita Deicoli*, pp. 678–79.
30. *AB* a° 869, p. 153.
31. *D Lot.II.* no. 34, p. 441. "Waldrade" has been erased and changed to "Ruadrude."
See also the facsimile in Von Sybel and Sickel, *Kaiserurkunden in Abbildungen*, Lieferung
VII, Tafel 9.

Lothar's brother Louis II. However, his claims—as a brother he had greater rights than his uncles—came to nothing. Even the protests of Pope Adrian were to no avail. The succession was thus decided in favor of those who could mobilize the greatest political power; in this case, it was the two kings with the greatest military might who were able to attract new supporters by promising them a share of the booty: Lothar's kingdom.

Epilogue
Lothar's Reputation
and His Descendants

The annalists and chroniclers who wrote about it after the event approached Lothar's last attempt to sort out his marital affairs from one clear perspective: it was bound to fail, because Lothar's was a bad case. God would punish him for his sins. From this viewpoint his efforts to divorce Theutberga and marry Waldrada were obviously doomed to fail, and that failure at the same time served as a warning to readers and hearers not to try anything similar. Some writers told the tale briefly and rather inaccurately; it was the ending that counted. Some told it at length. The most detailed account is to be found in Hincmar's *Annales Bertiniani*, for which he almost certainly had the benefit of an eyewitness report.

Hincmar had already used the term *Iudicium Dei*, meaning divine judgment and hence also trial by ordeal. The deaths of Lothar and most of his loyal followers were seen as God's punishment for their wicked behavior. In particular, the false oath that Lothar swore before receiving communion weighed heavily against him. The whole setting of the account of the communion and the deaths of Lothar and his followers was that of a trial by ordeal. Regino's chronicle too makes this very clear, stating that Lothar and his supporters swore that they had complied with Nicholas's commands and the oath they had sworn earlier. "And the magnates who had come with him testified to this, and there was none who dared to engage in a legal conflict with the royal authority."[1] With a fine sense of the

---

1. Regino aᵒ 869, pp. 96–97: "Cumque proceres et optimates, qui cum eo venerant, eadem testificarentur nec ulla opposita persona inveniretur, quae adversus regiam auctoritatem legitimum auderet controversiae inire certamen."

dramatic, before they received communion Regino had Lothar and his men take a further oath on Adrian's orders, one which differs somewhat from Hincmar's account: if Lothar was sure that he was innocent of adultery and would never again sleep with Waldrada, he could receive communion. But if he knew that he had a guilty conscience and carried a mortal wound, or if he meant to return to his lascivious behavior, he could not do so, for then he would be judged and condemned. A similar question was put to Lothar's followers. They had to swear that they had not helped Lothar, acquiesced in his adultery, or had contact with Waldrada. "And thus each of those who, having given this false assurance, dared to take communion with a bad conscience was struck down by divine justice and died before the year was out. Only a very few, who absented themselves from communion, narrowly escaped death."[2]

It was clear to Regino that Lothar and his followers had been punished by God for their sins. And so Lothar went down in history as a sinner and an adulterer. God Himself had condemned him. A number of his contemporaries testified to this. The *Annales Xantenses* say: "Lothar, King of Ripuaria, came to Rome and spoke with Pope Adrian. He was commanded by the latter to put away his concubine and accept his lawful wife. He promised this, but did not keep his promise and on his way back from Rome was struck down in a terrible manner by the Lord, together with almost all his magnates."[3] The *Annales Fuldenses* say only that "Lothar died, without having gained any success in the matter for which he had traveled to Rome, near the town of Piacenza in Italy in the month of July when returning to his kingdom; and very many of his nobles perished on that same journey."[4] Ado of Vienne described the death of his former lord as follows: "He acted as he wished and dealt with the Church of Rome as seemed right to him at the time; but when he was returning, beguiled by false hope, by divine judgment he fell ill and came to Piacenza where he died and was buried in the church of the holy martyr Antoninus in the year from the

---

2. Regino a° 869, p. 97: "Igitur, quisquis in his se laesum sciens ausu temerario communionem sub tali contestatione porrectam sumere presumpsit, divino iudicio percussus ab hac luce subtractus est, antequam subsequentis anni rediret principium. Perpauci, qui se a communione subtraxerunt, vix mortis periculum evaserunt."

3. *AX* a° 870, p. 28: "Lotharius rex Ripuariae sepe vocatus tandem Romam venit, cum Adriano pontifice colloquium habuit. Et ab eo mandatum accepit pelicem eicere ac legitimam coniugem accipere. Qui ita se per omnia obtemperare velle promisit, sed minime implevit. Et idcirco eum Dominus Roma redeuntem terribiliter percussit cum omnibus pene suis optimatibus."

4. *AF* a° 869, p. 68: "Hlotharius rex infecto negotio, propter quod Romam venerat, in regnum suum redire volens apud Plasentiam Italiae urbem mense Iulio diem obiit, plurimique de optimatibus illius in eodem itinere consumpti sunt."

incarnation of the Lord 869."[5] In the words of the *Annales Lobienses,* "Lothar, who had repudiated his lawful spouse, Theutberga, sister of Abbot Hucbert, and had married Waldrada, having been summoned to Rome and excommunicated, died on the return journey at Piacenza."[6] Adrian's successor, Pope John VIII, saw Lothar's death as the prime example of a divine judgment requested by the Church: "You can ask for a divine judgment, for which the proof is provided by the body and blood of Christ, as our predecessor Adrian did with King Lothar in the matter of his concubine Waldrada."[7] Lothar's marriage policy had been condemned by God and by History.

Lothar's Descendants

Lothar's tragic death removed the main protagonist from the scene. After his demise both his wives retreated to convents: Theutberga to Metz[8] and Waldrada to Remiremont.[9] We are given a brief glimpse of Theutberga's later life in a testament of her kinsman Heccard, Count of Autun: dividing up his library, he left his book on medicine quite specifically to Theutberga, wife of Lothar.[10] Was Theutberga a literate and educated woman with an interest in medicine?

But what happened to Lothar's son Hugo? For the time being he had no chance of inheriting his father's kingdom. Lothar's efforts to have his marriage recognized as lawful and to preserve his realm had ended in total failure. He died in a foreign land, struck down "by God's hand"; and the timing of his death was unfortunate, since his underage son Hugo was still regarded as the child of an unlawful union.[11] When Hugo reached adult-

5. Ado of Vienne, *Chronicon,* p. 323: "Perrexit secundum libitum suum, egit apud ecclesiam Romanam quod ei pro tempore iustum visum est; sed cum rediret falsis spebus incitatus, divino iudicio infirmatus, usque Placentiam civitatem pervenit, ibique defunctus in ecclesia beati Antonini martyris sepelitur anno ab incarnatione Domini 869."

6. *Annales Lobienses* a° 870, pp. 232–33: "Lotharius, sicut iam supra dictum est, relicta uxore legitima nomine Tietbirga, sorore Hucberti abbatis, Waldrada superduxerat, . . . Lotharius vero Romam vocatus et excommunicatus in Placentia diem clausit extremam."

7. *Ep. Joh. VIII,* p. 331: "Divino examine, ut moris populi est, aut etiam corpore et sanguine Christi probetur, sicut noster decessor Adrianus fecit in Lothario rege pro Waldrada sua pellice."

8. *Ex translatione S. Glodesindis,* c. 28, p. 506 (edition in margin).

9. *Vita S. Deicoli,* p. 679.

10. *Recueil des chartes de l'abbaye de Saint-Benoît-sur-Loire* 1, testament of Heccard (876), p. 66.

11. Pope John VIII would later (878) call him "the son, not legitimate but natural, of the late King Lothar, born of an adulterous relationship." *Ep. Joh. VIII,* no. 98 (10 September 878), pp. 91–92: "Hlotharii regis quondam filium non legitimum sed naturalem, adulterina copula genitum."

hood, between 879 and 885 he made various attempts to seize power in his father's former kingdom; in these he had the support of a section of the area's nobility. One of his chief commanders was Theutbald, the son of Abbot Hucbert. Theutbald was married to Hugo's sister Bertha; so here we have a marriage alliance between the families of Lothar and Waldrada and that of Hucbert and Theutberga. Ten years on, evidently, the old feuds no longer mattered very much. Just as Bertha had been married to Theutbald with a view to gaining military support, so another daughter of Lothar II, Gisela, was married to the converted Norseman Godfried for the same reason. From time to time Hugo also managed to form an alliance with one of the Carolingian kings; he received fiefs from Louis the Younger and Charles the Fat.[12] But in the end his attempts had a grim outcome. In 885 he was taken prisoner. On the orders of Charles the Fat both his eyes were put out and he was shut up in a monastery. According to Regino, he died in the monastery of Prüm during the reign of King Zwentibold (895–900).[13]

A grandson of Lothar and Waldrada would indeed achieve kingship, however. This grandson, also named Hugo, became king of Italy in 926 (926–48). By a historical irony he was also the grandson of Hucbert, being born of the above-mentioned marriage of Theutbald and Bertha. It happened that this Hugo too had a turbulent married life, for he had at least four concubines and three lawful wives. His first relationship, in his youth, was with Wandelmoda, by whom he had a son whom he named after his grandfather Hucbert. His first "lawful" wife was Alda, and he named their son after his other grandfather, Lothar. Next, probably after Alda's death, Hugo married the notorious Marozia, daughter of the Roman patrician Theophylactus. Marozia had been married at least three times before: to Pope Sergius III (904–11), to Margrave Alberic of Spoleto, and to Wido of Tuscany, who was Hugo's half brother, being a son of their mother Bertha's second marriage.

At the time of his mother's marriage to Hugo, the son of Sergius and Marozia occupied the papal throne as John XI (931–35). Marozia had had a hand in his appointment: she had arranged for his predecessor to be murdered. The road to Rome ran through Marozia's bed, at least if we are to believe Liudprand of Cremona, who recounts the events of these years in his somewhat tendentious scandal sheet of a chronicle. The marriage of

---

12. *AB* aº 879, 880, 882, pp. 239, 242, 248–49; *AF* aº 879, 880, 881, 883, 885, pp. 93–96, 100, 103, 114; Regino aº 883 and 885, pp. 120–21, 123–25; *Annales Vedastini* aº 879, 885, pp. 45, 57; *Ep. Joh. VIII*, no. 98 (10 September 878), pp. 91–92.

13. Regino aº 885, p. 125.

Hugo and Marozia fell apart soon after Hugo's arrival in Rome, wrecked by Marozia's son Alberic. Hugo then married Bertha, the widow of Rudolf of Burgundy. But, says Liutprand, "Hugo was so bewitched by the charms of his many concubines that he was unable to love her and even began to hate her." [14] His most famous concubines were Pezola, Roza, and Stephania, popularly known as Venus (for her beauty), Juno (for her jealousy), and Semele. By Pezola he had a son, Boso (named for Hugo's great-grandfather), and a daughter, Bertha, whom he married to Romanos, the young son of the Byzantine emperor Constantine Porphyrogenitus—quite a step up for the daughter of a "concubine"! [15]

Should one be superstitious enough to think that Lothar and Waldrada and the life together that they so stoutly defended had been condemned by History, then that same History took its revenge through their descendants. Lothar went down in history as a bad, lascivious king who sought to set his ambitious "concubine" Waldrada on the throne. The hero's roles in the drama were reserved for clerics such as Pope Nicholas I and Archbishop Hincmar of Reims, who on the basis of their authority as spiritual shepherds rebuked the unprincipled lecher and his mistress. Right and Christian marital morality had triumphed. But Lothar's grandson Hugo had not just *one* wife and *one* concubine, but *three* wives and *four* concubines, without it causing him any great problems. And nobody used it as an excuse to depose him as king. The son to whom he left his kingdom was called Lothar. And the spiritual shepherds, for instance Pope Nicholas's successor, John XI? John was his kinsman by marriage.

"For the first time, a rule of private life—the prohibition against divorce—prevailed over reasons of state." [16] This is how Michel Rouche in his contribution to *A History of Private Life* describes the significance of the case of Lothar II. As the reader will have noticed, I take a very different view. The reasons of state prevailed because the prohibition against divorce was used to eliminate a political opponent. It was only political pressure that could make this prohibition of any importance, and that concerned only this particular interpretation of it, since this gave the best result in this situation.

14. This is based on Liutprand of Cremona, *Antapodosis*, pp. 59, 82, 95–98, 111–12: "Hugo denique multarum concubinarum deceptus inlecebris praefatam coniugem suam Bertam maritali non solum non coepit amore diligere, verum modis omnibus execrare." Liutprand's descriptions are invariably extremely biased, but among the Italian kings Hugo comes out relatively well; see Buc, *Danger*, pp. 18–50.

15. Liutprand of Cremona, *Antapodosis*, pp. 111–12, 141.

16. Rouche, "Early Middle Ages," p. 479.

Where there was no political pressure things were quite different, as is clear from the example of Hugo mentioned above.

However, there are aspects of the legal status of marriage and of competence to rule in matrimonial cases that came to the fore in Lothar's case and proved significant for the future. One is that the rules regarding them were increasingly systematized by learned clerics—we have seen a start made on this—and applied in religious courts. Important elements in this were the concept of indissoluble monogamy and, eventually, the notion that a marriage is based on the consensus of the partners. This latter point frequently came into conflict with the social, economic, and political functions of marriage. Not every parent was content that decisions on the marriages of his children, who would continue his line and inherit his property, would depend on a simple expression of will by his offspring while he himself had no say in the matter. But here too the usual conjunction of law and political power offered a way out, for if necessary these unions could be dissolved by a religious court provided that impediments to marriage or procedural errors could be found. Marriage continued to be a political matter and the Church's rules could still be interpreted with considerable freedom. Two ideas were plainly to persist, and are still dominant in our society to the present day. First, the view that a marriage rests on the personal will of the partners; in our modern Western society anything else is seen as almost immoral. And, second, the idea of marriage as monogamous and in principle indissoluble still dominates today. After all, despite the considerable number of divorces most people do not go into marriage with the idea that it is a temporary arrangement; and in most cases they even promise to be faithful to each other until death do them part.

Appendix 1

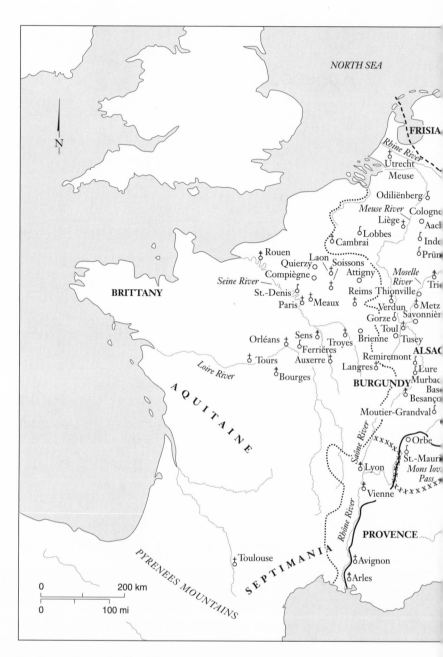

NORTH SEA

FRISIA

Rhine River
Utrecht
Meuse
Odiliënberg
Meuse River Cologne
Liège Aach
Lobbes Inde
Cambrai Prün
Rouen
Quierzy Laon Soissons
Compiègne Attigny *Moselle River* Tri
Seine River Reims Thionville
St.-Denis Verdun Metz
Paris Meaux Gorze Savonnièr
Toul
Sens Brienne Tusey
Orléans Troyes
Ferrières ALSAC
Tours Auxerre Remiremont
Bourges Langres Lure
Murbac
BURGUNDY Bas
Besanço
Moutier-Grandval

BRITTANY

Loire River

A Q U I T A I N E

Saône River
×××× Orbe
St.-Maur
Lyon *Mons Iov.*
Pass
Vienne ××××××

PROVENCE

Rhône River

Toulouse Avignon
Arles

PYRENEES MOUNTAINS S E P T I M A N I A

| 0 | | 200 km |
| 0 | 100 mi | |

N

Carolingian Europe in the ninth century

DANES

BALTIC
SEA

OBODRITES

Elbe River

archepiscopal see
episcopal see
monastery
FRISIA region
DANES neighboring people
)(mountain pass
other

········· 843 border (west)
- - - - 843 border (east)
x x x 855 border
——— 863 border

SAXONY

ünster

SORBS

Coblenz

THURINGIA

δ Fulda

Frankfurt
Mainz
Worms

Main River

BOHEMIANS

Wissembourg

Strasbourg

Regensburg

ALEMANNIA

Augsburg
Ottobeuren

BAVARIA

Salzburg

MORAVIANS

St. Gall
Zürich

Danube River

)(*Brenner Pass*

S

A L P S

P

FRIULI

L

Milan

LOMBARDY

Pavia

Piacenza

Lucca

Ravenna

*ADRIATIC
SEA*

Appendix 2
Genealogies

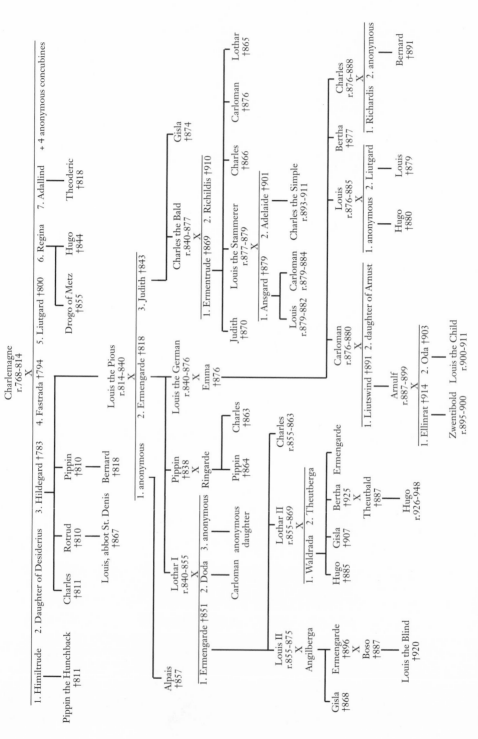

Genealogy 1: The Carolingians

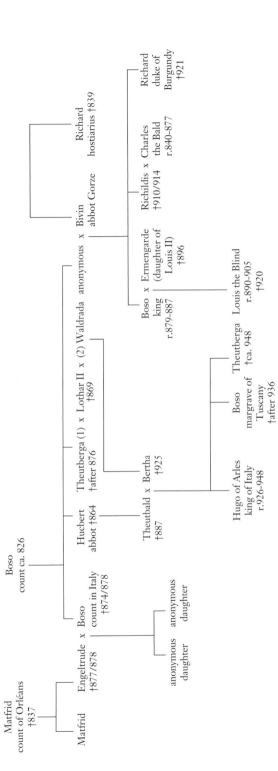

Genealogy 2: The Bosonids

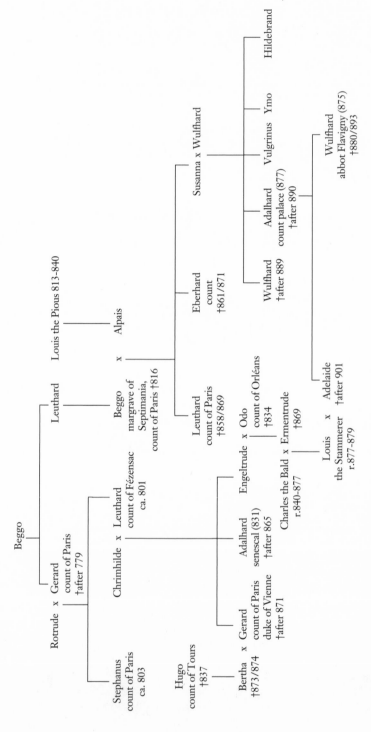

Genealogy 3: The descendants of Gerard, count of Paris, and Beggo

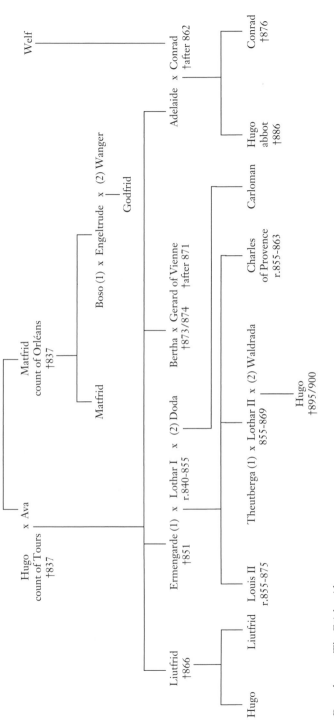

Genealogy 4: The Etichonids

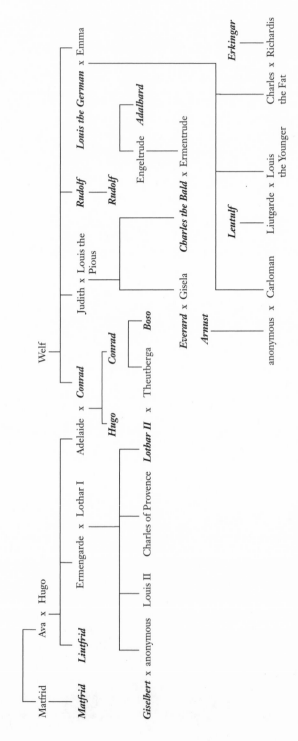

italic/bold: present

Genealogy 5: The Carolingians and their relatives, present at the treaty of Coblenz (860)

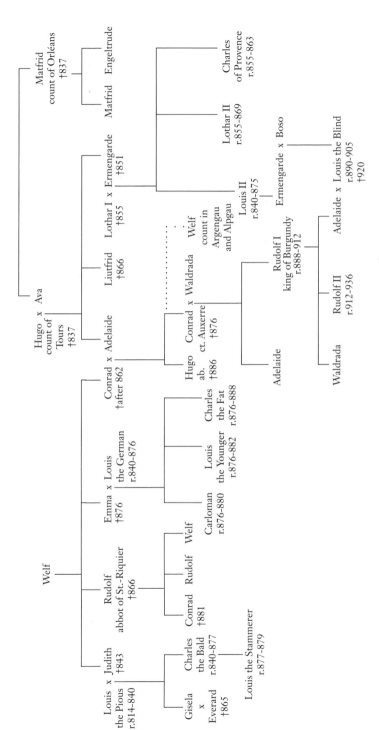

Genealogy 6: The Welfs

Appendix 3
Reigns of the Carolingian Kings

The years as subkings during their father's lifetime are not mentioned, nor are the years during which kings were temporarily deposed taken into account.

Pippin	751–768
Carloman	768–771
Charlemagne	768–814
Louis the Pious	814–840

Middle Kingdoms

Lothar I	840–855
Louis II of Italy	855–875
Lothar II of Lotharingia	855–869
Charles of Provence	855–863

Eastern Kingdoms

Louis the German	840–876
Carloman	876–879
Louis the Younger	876–882
Charles the Fat	876–887
Arnulf	887–899
Zwentibold of Lotharingia	895–900
Louis the Child	900–911

Western Kingdoms

Charles the Bald	840–877
Louis the Stammerer	877–879
Carloman	879–882
Louis III	879–884
Charles the Fat	(succession in all Carolingian kingdoms)
	884–888
Charles the Simple	893–925

Selected Bibliography

Manuscript Sources

Parma, Archivio di Stato. *Diplomatico, Diplomi imperiali* 10 and 12: Lothar II for Theut-
berga (866 and 867).
Rome, Biblioteca Apostolica Vaticana. *Ms. Palatina latina* 576.
Rome, Biblioteca Vallicelliana. *Ms.* I 76.

Printed Primary Sources

Ado of Vienne. *Chronicon*. Ed. Georg Heinrich Pertz. *MGH SS* 2: 315–23. Hanover,
1829.
Agobard of Lyon. *Opera Omnia*. Ed. Lieven van Acker. *CCCM* 52. Turnhout, 1981.
Alcuin. *De virtutibus et vitiis liber*. Ed. Jacques-Paul Migne. *PL* 101: col. 613–18.
Ambrosiaster. *Commentarius in epistulas ad Corinthios*. Ed. Henricus Josephus Vogels.
CSEL 81:2. Vienna, 1968.
Anastasius bibliothecarius. *Epistolae sive praefationes*. Ed. Ernst Perels and Gerhard
Laehr. *MGH Epp.* 7, *karol. aevi* 5: 395–442. Berlin, 1920.
Andreas of Bergamo. *Historiae*. Ed. Georg Waitz. *MGH SS rerum langobardorum*: 220–
30. Hanover, 1884.
Annales Bertiniani. Ed. Félix Grat, Jeanne Vieillard, and Susanne Clémencet, intro. and
notes by Léon Levillain. Société de l'histoire de France. Paris, 1964. English trans.:
The Annals of St.-Bertin, trans. Janet L. Nelson. Ninth Century Histories 1. Man-
chester, 1991.
Annales Fuldenses. Ed. Friedrich Kurze. *MGH SS rer. germ. i.u.s.* 7. Hanover, 1891. En-
glish trans., *The Annals of Fulda*. Trans. Timothy Reuter. Ninth Century Histories 2.
Manchester, 1992.
Annales Laubacenses. Ed. Georg Heinrich Pertz. *MGH SS* 1: 3–15. Hanover, 1826.
Annales Lobienses. Ed. Georg Waitz. *MGH SS* 13: 224–34. Hanover, 1881.
Annales Vedastini. Ed. Bernhard de Simson. *MGH SS rer. germ. i.u.s.* 12. Hanover, 1909.
Annales Xantenses. Ed. Bernhard de Simson. *MGH SS rer. germ. i.u.s.* 12. Hanover, 1909.

Ansegisus. *Collectio capitularium.* Ed. Gerhard Schmitz. *MGH Capitularia regum francorum nova series* 1. Hanover, 1996.

Astronomus. *Vita Hludowici imperatoris.* Ed. Ernst Tremp. *MGH SS rer. germ. i.u.s.* 64: 277–355. Hanover, 1995.

Augustine. *De bono conjugali, De conjugiis adulterinis.* Ed. and trans. Gustave Combes. *Oeuvres de Saint Augustin* 2. Paris, 1948.

——. *Contra Julianum.* Ed. Migne. *PL* 44.

——. *De fide et operibus.* Ed. Migne. *PL* 40.

——. *De nuptiis et concupiscentia.* Ed. and trans. François Joseph Thonnard, Emile Bleuzen, and Albert C. de Veer. *Oeuvres de Saint Augustin* 23. Paris, 1974.

——. *De sermone in monte habito.* Ed. Almut Mutzenbecher. *CCSL* 35. Turnhout, 1967.

Benedict III. *Epistola.* Ed. Ernst Dümmler. *MGH Epp. 5 epp. karol. aevi* 3: 612–14. Berlin, 1899.

Benedictus Levita. *Capitularia.* Ed. Georg Heinrich Pertz. *MGH LL* in f° II pars altera: 17–158. Hanover, 1837.

Breviarium Alaricianum. Ed. Max Conrat (= Cohn). Repr. Aalen, 1963.

Capitula Episcoporum 1. Ed. Peter Brommer. *MGH cap. episc.* 1. Hanover, 1984.

Capitula Episcoporum 2. Ed. Rudolf Pokorny and Martina Stratmann. *MGH cap. episc.* 2. Hanover, 1995.

Capitula Episcoporum 3. Ed. Rudolf Pokorny. *MGH cap. episc.* 3. Hanover, 1995.

Capitularia regum Francorum 1. Ed. Alfred Boretius. *MGH Cap.* 1. Hanover, 1883.

Capitularia regum Francorum 2. Ed. Alfred Boretius and Viktor Krause. *MGH Cap.* 2. Hanover, 1897.

Cartulaire de l'abbaye de Gorze, ms. 826 de la bibliothèque de Metz. Ed. Armand d'Herbomez. *Mémoires et Documents publiées par la Société nationale des antiquaires de France. Mettensia* 2. Paris, 1898.

Codex Canonum ecclesiasticorum Dionysii Exigui sive codex canonum vetus ecclesiae Romanae. Ed. Migne. *PL* 67: col. 135–346.

Codex Canonum Vetus Ecclesiae Romanae. Ed. Franciscus Pithoeus. Paris, 1687.

Codex Theodosianus. Ed. Paul Krüger. Berlin, 1923.

La collección canonica Hispana. Ed. Gonzalo Martinez Diez and Felix Rodriguez. *Monumenta Hispaniae Sacra,* Serie Canonica 1–4, 1982–84. 4 parts, divided into several vols.

Collectio antiqua canonum poenitentialium. In *Spicilegium sive collectio veterum aliquot scriptorum qui in Galliae Bibliothecis delituerant* 1. Ed. Lucas d'Achéry (editio nova Ludovicus F. J. De la Barre), 510–64. Paris, 1723.

Concilia aevi karolini 1–2. Ed. Albert Werminghoff. *MGH Conc.* 2. Hanover, 1906–08.

Concilia Galliae A.314–A.506. Ed. Charles Munier. *CCSL* 148. Turnhout, 1963.

Concilia Galliae A.511–A.695. Ed. Carlo de Clercq. *CCSL* 148A. Turnhout, 1963.

Corpus Iuris Canonici 1: *Decretum magistri Gratiani.* Ed. Emil Friedberg. Repr. Graz, 1959.

Corpus Iuris Civilis. Ed. Theodor Mommsen, Paul Krüger, Rudolfus Schöll, and Guilelmus Kroll. 3 vols. Berlin, 1906–11.

Corpus Iuris Civilis Institutionen. Ed. and trans. Okko Behrends, Rolf Knütel, Berthold Kupisch, and Hans Hermann Seiler. Heidelberg, 1993.

Decretales Pseudo-Isidoriani. Ed. Paul Hinschius. Leipzig, 1863.

Dhuoda. *Liber manualis. Manuel pour mon fils.* Ed. and trans. Pierre Riché. *Sources chrétiennes* 225 bis. Paris, 1991.

Dionysius Exiguus. *Codex canonum ecclesiasticum sive codex canonum vetus ecclesiae Romanae.* Ed. Migne. *PL* 67: col. 135–346.

Diplomata Karoli III. See: *Urkunden Karls III.*

Diplomata Lotharii I. See: *Urkunden Lothars I.*

Diplomata Lotharii II. See: *Urkunden Lothars II.*

Diplomata Ludowici Germanici. See: *Urkunden Ludwigs des Deutschen.*

Diplomata Ludowici Iunioris. See: *Urkunden Ludwigs des Jüngeren.*

Einhard. *Vita Karoli Magni.* Ed. Oswald Holder Egger. *MGH SS rer. germ. i.u.s.* 25. Hanover, 1911.

Epistolae ad divortium Lotharii II. regis pertinentes. Ed. Ernst Dümmler. *MGH Epp.* 6 *epp. karol. aevi* 4: 207–40. Berlin, 1925.

Epistolae Karolini Aevi 2. Ed. Ernst Dümmler. *MGH Epp.* 4. Berlin, 1895.

Epistolae Karolini Aevi 3. Ed. Ernst Dümmler. *MGH Epp.* 5. Berlin, 1899.

Epistolae Merowingici et Karolini Aevi 1. Ed. Ernst Dümmler. *MGH Epp.* 3. Berlin, 1892.

Epistolae variorum inde a saeculo nono medio usque ad mortem Karoli II (Calvi) imperatoris collectae. Ed. Ernst Dümmler. *MGH Epp.* 6, *epp. karol. aevi* 4: 127–206. Berlin, 1925.

Erchempert. *Historia Langobardorum Benevantanorum.* Ed. Georg Waitz. *MGH SS rerum langobardorum,* 231–64. Hanover, 1884.

Flodoard of Reims. *Die Geschichte der Reimser Kirche. Historia Remensis Ecclesiae.* Ed. Martina Stratmann. *MGH SS* 36. Hanover, 1998.

Folcuin. *Gesta Abbatum Lobiensium.* Ed. Georg Heinrich Pertz. *MGH SS* 4: 52–74. Hanover, 1841.

Formulae Merowingici et Karolini aevi. Ed. Karl Zeumer. *MGH LL Sectio V Formulae.* Hanover, 1886.

Die Gesetze der Angelsachsen. Ed. Felix Liebermann. 3 vols. Repr. Aalen, 1960.

Die Gesetze der Langobarden. Ed. Franz Beyerle. Weimar, 1947.

Hadrian II. *Epistolae.* Ed. Ernst Perels. *MGH Epp.* 6 *epp. karol. aevi* 4: 691–765. Berlin, 1924.

Hincmar of Reims. *De cavendis vitiis et virtutibus exercendis.* Ed. Doris Nachtmann. *MGH Quellen zur Geistesgeschichte des Mittelalters* 16. Munich, 1998.

——. *De divortio Lotharii regis et Theutbergae reginae.* Ed. Letha Böhringer. *MGH Concilia* 4, supplementum 1. Hanover, 1992.

——. *Epistolae* 1. Ed. Ernst Perels. *MGH Epp.* 8, 1 *epp. karol. aevi* 4. Berlin, 1939.

Hincmar of Reims and Hincmar of Laon. *Die Streitschriften Hinkmars von Reims und Hinkmars von Laon 869–871.* Ed. Rudolf Schieffer. *MGH Conc.* 4, supplementum 2. Hanover, 2003.

Hucbald of Saint-Amand. *Vita Rictrudis abbatissae Marchianensis.* Ed. Joannes Bollandus and Godofredus Henschenius. *Acta Sanctorum.* February t. I, p. 299 (excerpt). Antwerp, 1658.

Die Irische Kanonensammlung. Ed. Friedrich W. H. Wasserschleben. Leipzig, 1885.

Isidore of Sevilla. *De ecclesiasticis officiis.* Ed. Christopher Lawson. *CCSL* 113. Turnhout, 1989.

——. *Etymologiae sive origines.* Ed. Wallace Martin Lindsay. 2 vols. 2nd ed. Oxford, 1957.

Jerome. *Commentariorum in Matheum libri IV.* Ed. David Hurst and Marcus Adriaen. *CCSL* 77. Turnhout, 1969.

John VIII. *Epistolae.* Ed. Erich Casper. *MGH Epp.* 7, *karol. aevi* 5. Berlin, 1920.

John, abbot of St. Arnulf of Metz. *Ex miraculis S. Glodesindis.* Ed. Georg Heinrich Pertz. *MGH SS* 4: 235–38. Hanover, 1841.

——. *Ex translatione S. Glodesindis* c. 28. Ed. Georg Waitz. *MGH SS* 24: 506–7, n. 1. Hanover, 1879.

Jonas of Orléans. *De institutione laicali.* Ed. Migne. *PL* 106: col. 121–280.

Kaiserurkunden in Abbildungen. Ed. Heinrich von Sybel and Theodor Sickel. Berlin, 1880–91.

Die Konzilien der karolingischen Teilreiche (843–859). Ed. Wilfried Hartmann. *MGH Conc.* 3 Hanover, 1984.

Die Konzilien der karolingischen Teilreiche (860–874). Ed. Wilfried Hartmann. *MGH Conc.* 4 Hanover, 1998.

Leo the Great. *Epistolae.* Ed. Migne. *PL* 54: col. 582–1506.

Lex Baiwariorum. Ed. Ernestus de Schwind. *MGH LL* I, *Leges Nationum Germanicarum* V, 2. Hanover, 1926.

Lex Burgondionum. Ed. Ludovicus R. de Salis. *MGH LL* I, *Leges Nationum Germanicarum* II, 1. Hanover, 1892.

Lex Ribuaria. Ed. Franz Beyerle and Rudolf Buchner. *MGH LL* I, *Leges Nationum Germanicarum* III, 2. Hanover, 1954.

Lex Romana Visigothorum. Ed. Gustav Haenel. Repr. Aalen, 1962.

Lex Salica. Ed. Karl August Eckhardt. *MGH LL* I, *Leges Nationum Germanicarum* IV, 2. Hanover, 1969.

Lex Visigothorum. Ed. Karl Zeumer. *MGH LL* I, *Leges Nationum Germanicarum* I. Hanover, 1902.

Libellus de imperatoria potestate in urbe Roma. Ed. Giuseppe Zucchetti. *Fonti per la storia d'Italia* 55: 191–210. Rome, 1920.

Liber pontificalis. Ed. Louis Duchesne. 3 vols. 2nd ed. Paris, 1955. English trans. *The Book of Pontiffs (Liber Pontificalis). The Ancient Biographies of the First 190 Roman Bishops.* Trans. Raymond Davis. Liverpool, 1989; *The Lives of the Eighth-Century Popes (Liber Pontificalis).* Trans. Davis. Liverpool, 1992; *The Lives of the Ninth-Century Popes (Liber Pontificalis).* Trans. Davis. Liverpool, 1995.

Liber Sacramentarum Romanae Aecclesiae. Ed. Leo Cunibert Mohlberg, Leo Eisenhöfer, and Petrus Siffrin. *Rerum Ecclesiarum Documenta* 4. 3rd ed. Rome, 1981.

Liber Sacramentorum Gellonensis. Ed. A. Dumas. *CCSL* 159. Turnhout, 1989.

Liudprand of Cremona. *Antapodosis.* Ed. Josef Becker. *MGH SS rer. germ. i.u.s.* 41: 1–158. Hanover, 1915.

Lupus of Ferrières. *Correspondance.* Ed. Léon Levillain. 2 vols. *Les classiques de l'histoire de France au moyen age* 10/16. Paris, 1927–35.

Nicholas I. *Epistolae.* Ed. Ernst Perels. *MGH Epp.* 6, *epp. karol. aevi* 4: 257–690. Berlin, 1925.

Nithard. *Histoire des fils de Louis le Pieux.* Ed. Philippe Lauer. *Les classiques de l'histoire de France au moyen age* 7. Paris, 1926.

Oorkondenboek van het Sticht Utrecht tot 1301 1. Ed. Samuel Muller and Arie C. Bouman. Utrecht, 1920.

Pactus Legis Salicae. Ed. Karl August Eckhardt. *MGH LL* I, *Leges Nationum Germanicarum* IV, 1 Hanover, 1962.

Passio Maxellendis. In Yvonne Scherf, "De ontstaansgeschiedenis van de Passio Maxellendis en haar waarde als historische bron." MA thesis, Medieval History, University of Amsterdam, 1982. [Old edition in *AASSB* III: 580–87. Ed. Josephus Gesquierus. Brussels, 1785.]

Paulinus of Aquileia. *Liber exhortationis ad Henricum comitem seu ducem Forojuliensem.* Ed. Migne. *PL* 99: col. 197–281.

I Placiti del "Regnum Italiae." Ed. Cesare Manaresi. *Fonti per la storia d'Italia* 92. Rome, 1955.

Pseudo-Cyprianus. *De duodecim abusivis saeculi.* Ed. Siegmund Hellmann. *Texte und Untersuchungen zur altchristlichen Literatur* 34, 1 (1909): 32–60.

Rabanus Maurus. *De universo (De rerum naturis).* Ed. Migne. *PL* 111: col. 9–614.

Recueil des Actes de Charles II le Chauve, roi de France. Ed. George Tessier. *Chartes et diplômes relatifs à l'histoire de France.* 3 vols. Paris, 1943–55.

Recueil des Actes des rois de Provence. Ed. René Poupardin. *Chartes et diplômes relatifs à l'histoire de France.* Paris, 1920.

Recueil des chartes de l'abbaye de St.-Benoi't-sur-Loire 1. Ed. Maurice Prou and Alexandre Vidier. Paris, 1937.

Regino of Prüm. *Chronicon.* Ed. Friedrich Kurze. *MGH SS rer. germ. i.u.s.* 50. Hanover, 1890.

Regula Benedicti. Ed. Jean Neufville and Adalbert De Vogüë. 6 vols. *Sources chrétiennes* 181–86. Paris, 1971–72.

Le sacramentaire Grégorien. Ses principales formes d'après les plus anciens manuscrits. Ed. Jean Deshusses. 3 vols. Fribourg, 1971.
Das Sacramentarium Gregorianum nach dem Aachener Urexemplar. Ed. Hans Lietzmann. *Liturgiegeschichtliche Quellen* 3. Münster Westfalen, 1921.
Sacrorum conciliorum nova et amplissima collectio. Ed. Joannes Dominicus Mansi. 31 vols. Venice, 1759–89.
Thegan. *Die Taten Kaiser Ludwigs. Gesta Hludowici imperatoris.* Ed. Ernst Tremp. *MGH SS rer. germ. i.u.s.* 64: 166–277. Hanover, 1995.
Ex Translatione et Miraculis S. Reginae. Ed. Oswald Holder Egger. *MGH SS* 15, 1: 449–51. Hanover, 1887.
Die Urkunden Karls III. Ed. Paul Kehr. *MGH DD, Die Urkunden der deutschen Karolinger* 2. Berlin, 1937.
Die Urkunden Lothars I. Ed. Theodor Schieffer. *MGH DD, Die Urkunden der Karolinger* 3. Berlin, 1966.
Die Urkunden Lothars II. Ed. Theodor Schieffer. *MGH DD, Die Urkunden der Karolinger* 3. Berlin, 1966.
Die Urkunden Ludwigs II. Ed. Konrad Wanner. *MGH DD, Die Urkunden der Karolinger* 4. Munich, 1994.
Die Urkunden Ludwigs des Deutschen. Ed. Paul Kehr. *MGH DD, Die Urkunden der deutschen Karolinger* 1. Berlin, 1932–34.
Die Urkunden Ludwigs des Jüngeren. Ed. Paul Kehr. *MGH DD, Die Urkunden der deutschen Karolinger* 1. Berlin, 1932–34.
Das Verbrüderungsbuch der Abtei Reichenau. Einleitung, Register, Faksimile. Ed. Johanne Autenrieth, Dieter Geuenich, and Karl Schmid. *MGH Libri memoriales et Necrologia*, new series 1. Hanover, 1979.
Vita Sancti Deicoli. Ed. Georg Waitz. *MGH SS* 15, 2: 674–82. Hanover, 1888.

Secondary Sources

Affeldt, Werner, ed. *Frauen in Spätantike und Frühmittelalter. Lebensbedingungen-Lebensnormen-Lebensformen.* Sigmaringen, 1990.
Airlie, Stuart. "The Aristocracy." In McKitterick, *The New Cambridge Medieval History* 2: 431–50.
——. "Private Bodies and the Body Politic in the Divorce Case of Lothar II." *P&P* 161 (1998): 3–38.
——. " 'Semper fideles'? Loyauté envers les carolingiens comme constituant de l'identité aristocratique." In Le Jan, *La royauté et les élites*, 129–43.
Althoff, Gerd. *Verwandte, Freunde und Getreue. Zum politischen Stellenwert der Gruppenbindungen im früheren Mittelalter.* Darmstadt, 1990.
Angenendt, Arnold. *Das Frühmittelalter. Die abendländische Christenheit von 400 bis 900.* Stuttgart, 1990.
——. " 'Mit reinen Händen.' Das Motiv der kultischen Reinheit in der abendländischen Askese." In Jenal, *Herrschaft, Kirche, Kultur,* 297–316.
Anton, Hans Hubert. *Fürstenspiegel und Herrscherethos in der Karolingerzeit.* Bonner Historische Forschungen 32. Bonn, 1968.
——. *Studien zu den Klosterprivilegien der Päpste im frühen Mittelalter unter besonderer Berücksichtigung der Privilegierung von St. Maurice d'Agaune.* Beiträge zur Geschichte und Quellenkunde des Mittelalters 4. Berlin, 1975.
——. "Synoden, Teilreichepiskopat und die Herausbildung Lotharingiens (859–870)." In Jenal, *Herrschaft, Kirche, Kultur,* 83–124.
——. "Zum politischen Konzept karolingischer Synoden und zur karolingischen Brüdergemeinschaft." *HJ* 99 (1979): 55–132.

Ariès, Philippe, and Georges Duby, eds. *A History of Private Life* 1. *From Pagan Rome to Byzantium*. Ed. Paul Veyne. Cambridge, Mass., 1987.

Aurell, Martin. *Les noces du comte. Mariage et pouvoir en Catalogne (785–1213)*. Paris, 1995.

———. "Stratégies matrimoniales de l'aristocratie (IXe–XIII siècles)." In Rouche, *Mariage et sexualité au moyen age*, 185–202.

Bartlett, Robert. *Trial by Fire and Water: The Medieval Judicial Ordeal*. Oxford, 1986.

Bauer, Thomas. "Rechtliche Implikationen des Ehestreites Lothars II.: Eine Fallstudie zu Theorie und Praxis des geltenden Eherechts in der späten Karolingerzeit. Zugleich ein Beitrag zur Geschichte des frühmittelalterlichen Eherechts." *ZSRG KA* 80 (1994): 41–87.

Biget, Jean-Louis. "Hincmar de Reims, un archevêque dans son siècle." *MA* 87 (1981): 263–78.

Bischoff, Bernhard. "Die Karolingische Minuskel." In Bischoff, *Mittelalterliche Studien. Ausgewählte Aufsätze zur Schriftkunde und Literaturgeschichte* 3: 1–4. Stuttgart, 1981.

———. *Paläographie des römischen Altertums und des abendländischen Mittelalters*. 2nd ed. Berlin, 1981.

Bischoff, Bernhard, and Josef Hoffmann. *Libri Sancti Kyliani. Die Würzburger Schreibschule und die Dombibliothek im VIII. und IX. Jahrhundert*. Würzburg, 1952.

Bishop, Jane. "Bishops as Marital Advisors in the Ninth Century." In *Women of the Medieval World*, ed. Julius Kirshner and Suzanne F. Wemple, 53–84. Oxford, 1985.

Bitel, Lisa M. *Women in Early Medieval Europe*. Cambridge, 2002.

Bloch, Marc. *La société féodale* 1. *La formation des liens de dépendance* 2. *Les classes et le gouvernement des hommes*. Repr. Paris, 1968.

Böhringer, Letha. "Der eherechtliche Traktat im Paris. Lat. 12445, einer Arbeitshandschrift Hinkmars von Reims." *DA* 46 (1990): 18–47.

Borgolte, Michael. "Die Geschichte der Grafengewalt im Elsaß von Dagobert I bis Otto dem Großen." *Zeitschrift für die Geschichte des Oberrheins* 131 Neue Folge 92 (1983) (= Festgabe Tellenbach): 3–54.

———. *Geschichte der Grafschaften Alemanniens in fränkischer Zeit*. Vorträge und Forschungen Sonderband 31. Sigmaringen, 1984.

———. *Die Grafen Alemanniens in merowingischer und karolingischer Zeit. Eine Prosopografie*. Sigmaringen, 1986.

Bos, Marie Thérèse. "Wat is overspel?" In *Macht en gezag in de negende eeuw*, ed. Mayke de Jong, Marie-Thérèse Bos, and Carine van Rhijn, 133–45. Utrechtse historische cahiers 16. Hilversum, 1995.

Boschen, Lothar. *Die Annales Prumienses. Ihre nähere und ihre weitere Verwandtschaft*. Düsseldorf, 1972.

Bouchard, Constance Brittain. "The Bosonids or Rising to Power in the Late Carolingian Age." *French Historical Studies* 15 (1988): 407–31.

———. "Family Structure and Family Consciousness among the Aristocracy in the Ninth to Eleventh Centuries." *Francia* 14 (1986): 639–58.

———. "The Origins of the French Nobility: A Reassessment." *American Historical Review* 86 (1981): 501–32.

———. *Those of My Blood: Constructing Noble Families in Medieval Francia*. Philadelphia, 2001.

Bougard, François. "Anastase le Bibliothécaire ou Jean Diacre? Qui a récrit la *Vie* de Nicolas Ier et pourquoi?" In *Vaticana et medievalia. Études en l'honneur de Louis Duval-Arnould*, ed. Jean Marie Martin, Bernadette Martin-Hisard, and Agostino Paravicini Bagliani, 27–40. Florence, 2008.

———. "En marge du divorce de Lothaire II: Boson de Vienne, le cocu qui fut fait roi?" *Francia* 27, 1 (2000): 33–51.

Brekelmans, Antonius J. "Echtscheiding en hertrouwen in de oude kerk." In Van Eupen, *(On)ontbindbaarheid van het huwelijk*, 35–50.

Brown, Peter. "Society and the Supernatural: A Medieval Change." In Brown, *Society and the Holy in Late Antiquity*, 302–32. London, 1982.

Bruckner, Albert. *Regesta Alsatiae aevi merowingici et karolini. 496–918* 1. Quellenband. Strasbourg, 1949.

Brühl, Carlrichard. "Fränkischer Krönungsbrauch und das Problem der 'Festkrönungen.'" *HZ* 194 (1962): 265–326.

———. "Hincmariana II, Hinkmar im Widerstreit von kanonischem Recht und Politik in Ehefragen." *DA* 20 (1964): 55–77.

Brundage, James A. "Concubinage and Marriage in Medieval Canon Law." *Journal of Medieval History* 1 (1975): 1–17.

———. *Law, Sex, and Christian Society in Medieval Europe*. Chicago, 1987.

Brunhölzl, Franz. *Geschichte der lateinischen Literatur des Mittelalters 1. Von Cassiodor bis zum Ausklang der karolingischen Erneuerung*. Munich, 1975.

Brunner, Karl. *Oppositionelle Gruppen im Karolingerreich*. Veröffentlichungen des Instituts für Österreichische Geschichtsforschung 25. Vienna, 1979.

Buc, Philippe. *The Dangers of Ritual: Between Early Medieval Texts and Social Scientific Theory*. Princeton, 2001.

Buchner, Rudolf. *Die Rechtsquellen*. In WL, Beiheft. Weimar, 1953.

Bullough, Donald A. "Early Medieval Social Groupings: The Terminology of Kinship." *P&P* 45 (1969): 3–18.

Burguière, André, Christiane Klapisch-Zuber, Martine Segalen, and Françoise Zonabend, eds. *A History of the Family* 1. Cambridge, Mass., 1996.

Calmette, Joseph. *La diplomatie carolingienne du traité de Verdun à la mort de Charles le Chauve (843–877)*. Paris, 1901.

Chélini, Jean. *L'aube du moyen âge. Naissance de la chrétienté occidentale. La vie réligieuse des laics dans l'Europe carolingienne (750–900)*. Paris, 1991.

Classen, Peter, ed. *Recht und Schrift im Mittelalter*. Vorträge und Forschungen 23. Sigmaringen, 1977.

Congar, Yves. *L'ecclésiologie du haut Moyen Age de Saint Grégoire le Grand à la désunion entre Byzance et Rome*. Paris, 1968.

Conrat, Max (= Cohn). *Geschichte der Quellen und Literatur des Römischen Rechts im frühen Mittelalter* 1. Leipzig, 1891, repr. Aalen, 1963.

Constable, Giles. *Letters and Letter-collections*. Typologie des sources du Moyen Age occidental 17. Turnhout, 1976.

Daudet, Pierre. *Études sur l'histoire de la juridiction matrimoniale. Les origines de la compétence exclusive de l'église (France et Germanie)*. Paris, 1933.

Davis, Raymond. *The Book of Pontiffs* (Liber Pontificalis)*: The Ancient Biographies of the First 190 Roman Bishops*. Trans. Davis. Liverpool, 1989.

———. *The Lives of the Eighth-Century Popes* (Liber Pontificalis). Trans. Davis. Liverpool, 1992.

———. *The Lives of the Ninth-Century Popes* (Liber Pontificalis). Trans. Davis. Liverpool, 1995.

De Bruin, Lucie A. "Een levende schakel. De Frankische bruidsgift in de formulieren van Marculf." In Mostert, *Vrouw, familie en macht*, 79–98.

De Clercq, Carlo. *La législation réligieuse franque 1: De Clovis à Charlemagne (507–814)*. Louvain, 1936.

———. *La législation réligieuse franque 2: De Louis le Pieux à la fin du IXe siècle*. Antwerp, 1958.

De Jong, Mayke B. "Power and Humility in Carolingian Society: The Public Penance of Louis the Pious." *EME* 1 (1992): 29–52.

——. "To the Limits of Kinship: Anti-Incest Legislation in the Early Medieval West (500–900)." In *From Sappho to De Sade: Moments in the History of Sexuality*, ed. Jan Bremmer, 36–59. London, 1989.

——. "An Unsolved Riddle: Early Medieval Incest Legislation." In *Franks and Alamanni in the Merovingian Period: An Ethnographic Perspective*, ed. Ian Wood, 107–40. Woodbridge, 1998.

——. "Wat bedoelde paus Gregorius III?" In *Convivium aangeboden aan prof. jkvr. dr. J. M. van Winter bij haar afscheid als hoogleraar aan de Rijksuniversiteit te Utrecht*, 177–200. Hilversum, 1988.

Demyttenaere, Albrecht L. W. "The Cleric, Women, and the Stain: Some Beliefs and Ritual Practices concerning Women in the Early Middle Ages." In Affeldt, *Frauen in Spätantike und Frühmittelalter*, 141–65, 171–72.

——. "De God van Augustinus en het geheim van de gesluierde vrouw. Enkele passages in een traktaat over de Drieëenheid." In Mostert, *Vrouw, familie en macht*, 195–234.

——. "Mentaliteit in de twaalfde eeuw en de benauwenis van Galbert van Brugge." In *Middeleeuwse cultuur: Verscheidenheid, spanning en verandering*, ed. Marco Mostert, Rudi E. Künzel, and Albrecht L. W. Demyttenaere, 77–129. Hilversum, 1994.

——. "Over het ware christendom." In *De betovering van het middeleeuwse christendom*, ed. Marco Mostert and Albrecht L. W. Demyttenaere, 11–60. Hilversum, 1995.

——. "Vrouw en sexualiteit. Een aantal kerkideologische standpunten in de vroege middeleeuwen." *TvG* 86 (1973): 236–61.

——. "Wat weet men over vrouwen? De vrouw in de duistere Middeleeuwen." In Mostert, *Vrouw, familie en macht*, 11–45.

Depreux, Philippe. "Le comte Matfrid d'Orléans (av. 815–836)." *Bibliothèque de l'École des Chartes* 152 (1994): 331–74.

——. *Prosopographie de l'entourage de Louis le Pieux (781–840)*. Instrumenta herausgegeben vom Deutschen Historischen Institut Paris 1. Sigmaringen, 1997.

Deshusses, Jean. *Le sacramentaire Grégorien. Ses principales formes d'après les plus anciens manuscrits*. 3 vols. Fribourg, 1971.

Devisse, Jean. *Hincmar, Archevêque de Reims (845–882)*. 3 vols. Geneva, 1976.

——. *Hincmar et la loi*. Dakar, 1962.

Dhondt, Jan. "Élection et hérédité sous les Carolingiens et les premiers Capétiens." *Revue Belge de Philologie et d'Histoire* 18 (1939): 913–53 [= "Königswahl und Thronerbrecht zur Zeit der Karolinger und der ersten Kapetinger." In Hlawitschka, *Königswahl und Thronfolge in fränkisch-karolingischer Zeit*, 144–89].

——. *Das frühe Mittelalter*. Fischer Weltgeschichte 10. Frankfurt am Main, 1968.

——. "Groepsvorming in de verre middeleeuwen: Vlaanderen in 1127–1128, een maatschappij die van uitzicht verandert." In Dhondt, *Geschiedkundige opstellen*, 47–83. Antwerp, 1963. (= rev. version of "Les 'solidarités' médiévales. Une société en transition: La Flandre en 1127–1128." *AESC* 12 (1957): 529–60.

Dierkens, Alain. *Abbayes et chapitres entre Sambre et Meuse (VIIe–XIe siècles. Contribution à l'histoire réligieuse des campagnes du Haut Moyen Age)*. Beihefte der Francia 14. Sigmaringen, 1985.

——. "La production hagiographique à Lobbes au Xème siècle." *RB* 93 (1983): 245–59.

Dilcher, Gerhard, Heiner Lück, Reiner Schulze, Elmar Wadle, et al., eds. *Gewohnheitsrecht und Rechtsgewohnheiten im Mittelalter*. Schriften zur Europäischen Rechts- und Verfassungsgeschichte 6. Berlin, 1992.

Dilcher, Gerhard, and Eva-Marie Distler, eds. *Leges-Gentes-Regna. Zur Rolle von germanischen Rechtsgewohnheiten und lateinischer Schrifttradition bei der Ausbildung der frühmittelalterlichen Rechtskultur*. Berlin, 2006.

Drew, Katherine Fischer. "The Family in Frankish Law." In Drew, *Law and Society*, VI.

——. "The Family in Visigothic Law." In Drew, *Law and Society*, VII.

——. "The Germanic Family of the Leges Burgundionum." In Drew, *Law and Society*, V.

——. "The Law of the Family in the Germanic Barbarian Kingdoms: A Synthesis." In Drew, *Law and Society*, VIII.

——. *Law and Society in Early Medieval Europe: Studies in Legal History*. Variorum Reprints. London, 1988.

——. "Notes on Lombard Institutions." In Drew, *Law and Society*, IV.

Duby, Georges, and Jacques Le Goff, eds. *Famille et parenté dans l'occident médiéval*. Collection de l'École française de Rome 30. Rome, 1977.

Duchesne, Louis. *Fastes episcopaux de l'ancienne Gaule*. 3 vols. Paris, 1907–15.

Dümmler, Ernst. *Geschichte des ostfränkischen Reiches*. 2 vols. Jahrbücher der Deutschen Geschichte. Leipzig, 1887–88.

Dupraz, Louis. "Le capitulaire de Lothaire I, empereur 'De expeditione contra Sarracenos facienda' et la Suisse romande (847)." *Zeitschrift für schweizerische Geschichte* 16 (1936): 241–93.

——. "Deux préceptes de Lothaire II (867 et 868) ou les vestiges diplomatiques d'un divorce manqué." *Zeitschrift für schweizerische Kirchengeschichte* 59 (1965): 193–236.

——. "Un domaine royal carolingien en transjurane." *Schweizerische Zeitschrift für Geschichte* 18 (1968): 1–22.

Ebel, Else. "Die sog. 'Friedelehe' im Island der Saga- und Freistaatzeit (870–1264)." In *Staat, Kirche, Wissenschaft in einer pluralistischen Gesellschaft. Festschrift zum 65. Geburtstag von Paul Mikat*, ed. Dieter Schwab, Dieter Giesch, Joseph Listl, and Hans-Wolfgang Strätz, 243–58. Berlin, 1989.

——. *Der Konkubinat nach altwestnordischen Quellen. Philologische Studien zur sogenannten "Friedelehe."* Ergänzungsband zum Reallexikon der Germanischen Altertumskunde 8. Berlin, 1993.

Edwards, Charles, and Thomas Mowbray. "Kinship, Status and the Origins of the Hide." *P&P* 56 (1972): 3–33.

Ertl, Nelly. "Diktatoren frühmittelalterlicher Papstbriefe." *Archiv für Urkundenforschung* 15 (1938): 56–132.

Esmein, Adhémar. *Le mariage en droit canonique*. Paris, 1891.

Felten, Franz J. *Äbte und Laienäbte im Frankenreich. Studie zum Verhältnis van Staat und Kirche im früheren Mittelalter*. Monographien zur Geschichte des Mittelalters 20. Stuttgart, 1980.

——. "Konzilsakten als Quellen für die Gesellschaftsgeschichte des 9. Jahrhunderts." In Jenal, *Herrschaft, Kirche, Kultur*, 177–202.

——. "Laienäbte in der Karolingerzeit. Ein Beitrag zum Problem der Adelsherrschaft über die Kirche." In *Mönchtum, Episkopat und Adel zur Gründungszeit des Klosters Reichenau*, ed. Arno Borst, 397–431. Vorträge und Forschungen 20. Sigmaringen, 1974.

Firey, Abigail. "Ghostly Recensions in Early Medieval Canon Law: The Problem of the *Collectio Dacheriana* and Its Shades." *Tijdschrift voor rechtsgeschiedenis* 68 (2000): 63–82.

——. "Toward a History of Carolingian Legal Culture: Canon Law Collections of Early Medieval Southern Gaul." PhD thesis, Toronto, 1995.

Fleckenstein, Josef. "Über die Herkunft der Welfen und ihre Anfänge in Süddeutschland." In Tellenbach, *Studien und Vorarbeiten*, 71–136.

Flint, Valery I. J. "Magic and Marriage in Ninth-Century Francia: Lothar, Hincmar—and Susanna." In *The Culture of Christendom: Essays in Medieval History in Commemoration of Denis L. T. Bethell*, ed. Marc Anthony Meyer, 61–74. London, 1993.

——. "Susanna and the Lothar Crystal: A Liturgical Perspective." *EME* 4 (1995): 61–86.

Folz, Robert. *Le couronnement impérial de Charlemagne. 25 décembre 800*. Repr. Paris, 1989.

Fournier, Paul, and Gabriel Le Bras. *Histoire des collections canoniques en Occident depuis les fausses décrétales jusqu'au Décret de Gratien*. 2 vols. Paris, 1931–32.

Fransen, Gérard. *Les décrétales et les collections des décrétales*. Typologie des sources 21. Turnhout, 1972.

———. "La lettre d'Hincmar de Reims au sujet du mariage d'Étienne. Une relecture." In *Pascua mediaevalia. Studien voor Josef Maria De Smet*, ed. Robrecht Lievens, Erik van Mingroot, and Werner Verbeke, 133–46. Mediaevalia Lovaniensia series I studia X. Louvain, 1983.

———. "La rupture du mariage." In *Il matrimonio nella società altomedievale*, 603–32.

Freisen, Joseph. *Geschichte des canonischen Eherechts bis zum Verfall der Glossenliteratur*. Tübingen, 1888.

Fried, Johannes. "Der Karolingische Herrschaftsverband im 9. Jahrhundert zwischen 'Kirche' und 'Königshaus.'" *HZ* 235, 2 (1982): 1–43.

Friedberg, Emil. *Das Recht der Eheschliessung in seiner geschichtlichen Entwicklung*. Leipzig, 1865.

———. *Verlobung und Trauung. Zugleich als Kritik von Sohm. Das Recht der Eheschliessung*. Leipzig, 1876.

Fuhrmann, Horst. *Einfluß und Verbreitung der Pseudoisidorischen Fälschungen von ihrem Auftauchen bis in die neuere Zeit*. 2 vols. Schriften der *MGH* 24. Stuttgart, 1972–74.

———. "Eine im Original erhaltene Propagandaschrift des Erzbischofs Gunthar von Köln." *Archiv für Diplomatik, Schriftgeschichte, Siegel- und Wappenkunde* 4 (1958): 1–51.

———. "Fälscher unter sich: Zum Streit zwischen Hinkmar von Reims und Hinkmar von Laon." In Gibson and Nelson, *Charles the Bald: Court and Kingdom*, 224–34.

———. "Das Papsttum und das kirchliche Leben im Frankenreich." In *Nascita dell'Europa ed Europa Carolingia*, 419–56.

Gaillard, Michèle. *D'une réforme à l'autre. 816–934: Les communauteés réligieuses en Lorraine à l'époque carolingienne*. Paris, 2006.

———. "Un évêque et son temps, Advence de Metz (858–875)." In *Lotharingia—une région au centre de l'Europe autour de l'an Mil*, 89–119. Veröffentlichungen der Kommission für saarländische Geschichte 26. Saarbrücken, 1995.

Ganshof, François. *Droit romain dans les capitulaires*. Jus Romanum Medii Aevi I, 2bcc A-ß. Milan, 1969.

———. "La preuve dans le droit franc." In *La Preuve*, 71–98. Recueils de la société Jean Bodin 17, 2. Brussels, 1965.

———. "Le statut de la femme dans la monarchie franque." In *La Femme*, 5–58. Recueils de la société Jean Bodin 12, 2. Brussels, 1962.

———. *Wat waren de capitularia?* Verhandelingen van de Koninklijke Vlaamse Academie voor wetenschappen, letteren en schone kunsten van België, Klasse der Letteren 22. Brussels, 1955.

Ganz, David. "Book Production in the Carolingian Empire and the Spread of Caroline Minuscule." In McKitterick, *The New Cambridge Medieval History* 2: 786–808.

———. "The Preconditions for Caroline Minuscule." *Viator. Medieval and Renaissance Studies* 18 (1987): 23–44.

———. Review of *Hincmar, Archevêque de Reims (845–882)*. *Revue belge de philologie et d'Histoire/ Belgisch Tijdschrift voor Filologie en Geschiedenis* 59 (1979): 711–718.

Garrison, Mary. "'Send More Socks': On Mentality and the Preservation Context of Medieval Letters." In *New Approaches to Medieval Communication*, ed. Marco Mostert, 69–100. Turnhout, 1999.

Gaudemet, Jean. "Indissolubilité et consommation du mariage, l'apport d'Hincmar de Reims." *RDC* 30 (1980): 28–40.

——. "L'interprétation du principe d'indissolubilité du mariage chrétien au cours du premier millénaire." *Bullettino dell'Istituto di diritto romano "Vittorio Scialoja"* 81, 3rd series, vol. 20 (1978): 11–70.

——. "Le legs du droit romain en matière matrimoniale." In *Il matrimonio nella società altomedievale*, 139–79.

——. *Le mariage en occident: Les moeurs et le droit.* Paris, 1987.

——. *Sociétés et mariage.* Paris, 1980.

Genzmer, Fritz. "Die germanische Sippe als Rechtsgebilde." *ZSRG GA* 67 (1950): 34–49.

Geuenich, Dieter. "Beobachtungen zu Grimald von St. Gallen, Erzkapellan und Oberkanzler Ludwigs des Deutschen." In *Litterae Medii Aevi. Festschrift für Johanne Autenrieth*, ed. Michael Borgolte and Herrad Spilling, 55–68. Sigmaringen, 1988.

Gibson, Margaret T., and Janet L. Nelson, eds. *Charles the Bald: Court and Kingdom.* Rev. ed. Aldershot, 1990.

La giustizia nell'alto medioevo. Secoli IX–XI. Settimane di studio del centro italiano di studi sull'alto medioevo 44. Spoleto, 1997.

Godman, Peter, and Roger Collins, eds. *Charlemagne's Heir: New Perspectives on the Reign of Louis the Pious (814–840).* Oxford, 1990.

Goetz, Hans-Werner. "Auctoritas et Dilectio. Zum päpstlichen Selbstverständnis im späteren 9. Jahrhundert." In *Gedenkreden auf Ludwig Buisson (1918–1992). Ansprachen auf der Akademischen Gedenkfeier am 7. Januar 1993*, 27–58. Hamburg, 1993.

——. "Frauenbild und weibliche Lebensgestaltung im Fränkischen Reich." In Goetz, *Weibliche Lebensgestaltung im frühen Mittelalter*, 7–44.

——. "Social and Military Institutions." In McKitterick, *The New Cambridge Medieval History* 2: 451–80.

——. ed. *Weibliche Lebensgestaltung im frühen Mittelalter.* Cologne, 1991.

Goldberg, Eric J. *Struggle for Empire: Kingship and Conflict under Louis the German, 817–876.* Ithaca, 2006.

Goody, Jack. *Comparative Studies in Kinship.* London, 1969.

——. *The Development of the Family and Marriage in Europe.* Cambridge, 1983.

——. *The Oriental, the Ancient and the Primitive: Systems of Marriage and the Family in the Pre-industrial Societies of Eurasia.* Cambridge, 1990.

Gradowicz-Pancer, Nira. "Honneur féminin et pureté sexuelle: Équation ou paradoxe?" In Rouche, *Mariage et sexualité au moyen age*, 37–51.

Grotz, Hans. *Erbe wider Willen. Hadrian II. (867–872) und seine Zeit.* Vienna, 1970.

Guerrau-Jalabert, Anita. "La désignation des relations et des groupes de parenté en latin médiéval." *Archivum latinitatis Medii Aevi (Bulletin Du Cange)* 16–17 (1986–87): 65–108.

——. "Sur les structures de parenté dans l'Europe médiévale." *AESC* 36 (1981): 1028–49.

Guichard, Pierre, and Jean-Pierre Cuvillier. "Barbarian Europe." In Burguière, *A History of the Family* 1: 318–78.

Haller, Johannes. *Nikolaus I. und Pseudoisidor.* Stuttgart, 1936.

Halphen, Louis. *Charlemagne et l'empire carolingien.* Paris, 1947.

Hampe, Karl. "Reise nach Frankreich und Belgien im Frühjahr 1897. II Beilagen. Erster Theil, VIII." *NA* 23 (1898): 603–11.

Hartmann, Wilfried. "Fälschungsverdacht und Fälschungsnachweis im früheren Mittelalter." In *Fälschungen im Mittelalter. Internationaler Kongreß der MGH München, 16–19. September 1986* 2: 111–27. MGH Schriften 33. Hanover, 1988.

——. *Das Konzil von Worms 868: Überlieferung und Bedeutung.* Abhandlungen der Akademie der Wissenschaften in Göttingen. Philologisch-historische Klasse 3. Folge 105. Göttingen, 1977.

——. "Laien auf Synoden der Karolingerzeit." *AHC* 10 (1978): 249–69.

——. *Die Synoden der Karolingerzeit im Frankenreich und in Italien*. Konziliengeschichte: Reihe A. Darstellungen. Paderborn, 1989.

——. "Vetera et Nova. Altes und neues Kirchenrecht in den Beschlüssen karolingischer Konzilien." *AHC* 15 (1983): 79–95.

——. "Zu einigen Problemen der karolingischen Konzilsgeschichte." *AHC* 9 (1977): 6–28.

Heene, Katrien. *The Legacy of Paradise: Marriage, Motherhood, and Woman in Carolingian Edifying Literature*. Frankfurt am Main, 1997.

Heidecker, Karl. "Gathering and recycling authoritative texts. The use of marginalia in Hincmar of Rheims' *De divortio Lotharii*." In *Organizing the Written Word*, ed. Marco Mostert. Utrecht studies in medieval literacy 2. Turnhout, forthcoming.

——. *Kerk, huwelijk en politieke macht. De zaak Lotharius II (855–869)*. Amsterdam, 1997.

Heidrich, Ingrid. "Besitz und Besitzverfügung verheirateter und verwitweter freier Frauen im merowingischen Frankenreich." In Goetz, *Weibliche Lebensgestaltung im frühen Mittelalter*, 119–38.

Hellmann, Siegmund. "Die Annales Fuldenses." *NA* 37 (1912): 53–65.

——. "Die Entstehung und Überlieferung der Annales Fuldenses." *NA* 33 (1908): 695–742.

——. "Die Heiraten der Karolinger." In *Festgabe für Karl Theodor von Heigel*, 1–99. Munich, 1903.

Hennebicque (= Le Jan), Régine. "Prosopographica Neustrica. Les agents du roi en Neustrie de 639 à 840." In *La Neustrie. Le pays au nord de la Loire de 650 à 850*, ed. Hartmut Atsma, 231–69. Sigmaringen, 1989.

——. "Structures familiales et politiques au IXe siècle: Un groupe familial de l'aristocratie franque." *RH* 265 (1981) 288–333.

Hlawitschka, Eduard. *Franken, Alemannen, Bayern und Burgunder in Oberitalien (774–962). Zum Verständnis der fränkischen Königsherrschaft in Italien*. Forschungen zur oberrheinischen Landesgeschichte 8. Freiburg im Breisgau, 1960.

——. *Lotharingien und das Reich an der Schwelle der deutschen Geschichte*. Schriften der MGH 21. Stuttgart, 1968.

——. "Waren die Kaiser Wido und Lambert Nachkommen Karls des Großen?" *QFIAB* 49 (1969): 366–86.

——. ed. *Königswahl und Thronfolge in fränkisch-karolingischer Zeit*. Wege der Forschung 247. Darmstadt, 1975.

Hoffmann, Hartmut. *Untersuchungen zur Karolingischen Annalistik*. Bonn, 1958.

Hübner, Rudolf. *Grundzüge des deutschen Privatrechts*. 5th ed. Leipzig, 1930.

Hughes, Diane Owen. "From Brideprice to Dowry in Mediterranean Europe." *Journal of Family History* 3 (1978): 262–96.

Hyam, Jane. "Ermentrude and Richildis." In Gibson and Nelson, *Charles the Bald: Court and Kingdom*, 154–68.

Jarnut, Jörg. "Ein Bruderkampf und seine Folgen: Die Krise des Frankenreiches (768–771)." In Jenal, *Herrschaft, Kirche, Kultur*, 165–76.

Jarnut, Jörg, Ulrich Nonn, and Michael Richter, eds. *Karl Martell in seiner Zeit*. Sigmaringen, 1994.

Jenal, Georg, ed. *Herrschaft, Kirche, Kultur. Beiträge zur Geschichte des Mittelalters. Festschrift für Friedrich Prinz zu seinem 65. Geburtstag*. Monographien zur Geschichte des Mittelalters 37. Stuttgart, 1993.

Joch, Waltraut. "Karl Martell—ein minderberechtigter Erbe Pippins?" In Jarnut, Nonn, and Richter, eds., *Karl Martell in seiner Zeit*, 149–69.

Keller, Hagen. "Zum Sturz Karls III." *DA* 22 (1966): 333–84.

Kennedy, K. "The Permanence of an Idea: The Ninth-Century Frankish Ecclesiastics and the Authority of the Roman See." In Mordek, *Aus Kirche und Reich*, 105–26.

Kern, Fritz. *Gottesgnadentum und Widerstandsrecht im früheren Mittelalter. Zur Entwicklungsgeschichte der Monarchie.* Münster, 1954.

Konecny, Sylvia. "Eherecht und Ehepolitik unter Ludwig dem Frommen." *MIÖG* 85 (1977): 1–21.

——. *Die Frauen des karolingischen Königshauses. Die politische Bedeutung der Ehe und die Stellung der Frau in der fränkischen Herrscherfamilie vom 7. bis zum 10. Jahrhundert.* Vienna, 1976.

Kornbluth, Genevra. *Engraved Gems of the Carolingian Empire.* University Park, Pennsylvania, 1996.

Kottje, Raymund. "Einheit und Vielfalt des kirchlichen Lebens in der Karolingerzeit." *Zeitschrift für Kirchengeschichte* 4. Folge 76 (1965): 323–42.

——. "Eherechtliche Bestimmungen der germanischen Volksrechte (5.–8. Jahrhundert)." In Affeldt, *Frauen in Spätantike und Frühmittelalter,* 212–20.

——. "Ehe und Eheverständnis in den vorgratianischen Bußbüchern." In *Love and Marriage in the Twelfth Century,* ed. Willy van Hoecke and Andreas Welkenhuysen, 18–40. Louvain, 1981.

——. "Kirchliches Recht und päpstlicher Autoritätsanspruch. Zu den Auseinandersetzungen über die Ehe Lothars II." In Mordek, *Aus Kirche und Reich,* 97–103.

Kroeschell, Karl. "Die Sippe im germanischen Recht." *ZSRG GA* 77 (1960): 1–25.

Krüger, Karl Heinrich. *Die Universalchroniken.* Typologie des sources 16. Turnhout, 1976.

Kurze, Friedrich. "Die Annales Fuldenses." *NA* 36 (1911): 343–93 and 37 (1912): 778–85.

——. "Die Annales Laubacenses und ihre nähere Verwandtschaft." *NA* 39 (1914): 13–41.

——. "Die Annales Lobienses." *NA* 37 (1912): 587–614.

——. "Handschriftliche Überlieferung und Quellen der Chronik Reginos und seines Fortsetzers." *NA* 15 (1890): 293–330.

——. "Über die Annales Fuldenses." *NA* 17 (1892): 83–158.

Laiou, Angeliki E. "Consensus facit nuptias—et non. Pope Nicholas I's Response to the Bulgarians as a Source for Byzantine Marriage Customs." *Rechtshistorisches Journal* 4 (1985): 189–201.

Lauranson-Rosaz, Christian. "Douaire et sponsalicium durant le haut moyen âge." In Parisse, *Veuves et veuvages dans le haut moyen age,* 99–105.

Le Jan, Régine. "Douaires et pouvoirs des reines en Francie et en Germanie (VIe–Xe siècle)." In Le Jan, *Femmes, pouvoir et société dans le haut Moyen Age,* 68–88.

——. *Famille et pouvoir dans le monde franc (VIIe–Xe siècle), essai d'anthropologie sociale.* Paris, 1995.

——. *Femmes, pouvoir et société dans le haut Moyen Age.* Paris, 2001.

——. ed. *La royauté et les élites dans l'Europe carolingienne (début IXe siècle aux environs de 920).* Lille, 1998.

Le Jan-Hennebicque, Régine. "Aux origines du douaire médiéval (6e–10e siècle)." In Parisse, *Veuves et veuvages dans le haut moyen age,* 107–22 (= Le Jan, *Femmes, pouvoir et société*), 53–67.

Lemaire, André. "Aux origines de la règle 'Nullum sine dote fiat conjugium.'" In *Mélanges Paul Fournier,* 415–24. Paris, 1929.

——. "La dotation de l'épouse de l'époque mérovingienne au XIIIe siècle." *Revue historique de droit français et étranger,* 4th series, 8 (1929): 569–80.

Lendi, Walter. *Untersuchungen zur Frühalemannischen Annalistik. Die Murbacher Annalen mit Edition.* Freiburg/Schweiz, 1971.

Leupen, Piet H. D. *De bisschoppen en de moraal. Gezag en macht in de vroege en volle middeleeuwen.* Hilversum, 1985.

——. "'Ecclesia et Imperium.' De visie van de Frankische bisschoppen op de verhouding tussen kerk en staat in het midden van de negende eeuw." In *Geschiedenis, godsdienst, letterkunde. Opstellen aangeboden aan Sigfried B. J. Zilverberg*, ed. Elidius K. Grootes and Johannes den Haan, 12–16. Roden, 1989.

——. *Gods stad op aarde. Eenheid van kerk en staat in het eerste millennium na Christus. Een kerkelijke ideologie*. Amsterdam, 1996.

——. "De Karolingische villa Beek en de stamvader van de Bosoniden." *BMGN* 92 (1977): 373–93.

——. "Nogmaals Beek en de stamvader van de Bosoniden." *BMGN* 93 (1978): 446–49.

Levillain, Léon. "Girart comte de Vienne." *MA* 55 (1949): 225–45.

Leyser, Karl. "The German Aristocracy from the Ninth to the Early Twelfth Century: A Historical and Cultural Sketch." *P&P* 41 (1968): 126–38.

——. "Maternal Kin in Early Medieval Germany: A Reply." *P&P* 49 (1970): 126–38.

——. *Rule and Conflict in Early Medieval Society: Ottonian Saxony*. London, 1979.

Louis, René. *Girart, comte de Vienne (. . . 819–877) et ses fondations monastiques*. Auxerre, 1946.

Löwe, Heinz. "Regino von Prüm und das historische Weltbild der Karolingerzeit." In *Geschichtsdenken und Geschichtsbild im Mittelalter*, 91–134. Wege der Forschung 21: Darmstadt, 1961. (= in Löwe, *Von Cassiodor zu Dante. Ausgewählte Aufsätze zur Geschichtsschreibung und politischen Ideenwelt des Mittelalters*, 149–79. Berlin, 1973).

——. "Studien zu den Annales Xantenses." *DA* 8 (1950): 59–99.

Lynch, Joseph. *Godparents and Kinship in Early Medieval Europe*. Princeton, 1986.

——. *The Medieval Church: A Brief History*. London, 1992.

Maassen, Friedrich. *Eine burgundische Synode vom Jahr 855*. (repr. from *Sitzungsberichte der Akademie für Wissenschaften Wien 1878*). Vienna, 1879.

Maccioni, P. A. " 'It is allowed neither to Husband nor Wife . . .' The Ideas of Jonas of Orléans on Marriage." In Mostert, *Vrouw, familie en macht*, 99–125

Il matrimonio nella società altomedievale. Settimane di studio del centro italiano di studi sull' alto medioevo 24. Spoleto, 1977.

McCormick, Michael. *Les Annales du haut moyen âge*. Typologie des sources 14. Turnhout, 1975.

McKeon, Peter R. "The Carolingian Councils of Savonnières (859) and Tusey (860) and Their Background: A Study in the Ecclesiastical and Political History of the Ninth Century." *RB* 84 (1974): 75–110.

McKitterick, Rosamond. *The Carolingians and the Written Word*. Cambridge, 1989.

——. *The Frankish Church and the Carolingian Reforms 789–895*. Royal Historical Society. Studies in History. London, 1977.

——. ed. *The New Cambridge Medieval History*, vol. 2, c.700–c.900. Cambridge, 1995.

McNamara, Jo-Ann, and Suzanne F. Wemple. "Marriage and Divorce in the Frankish Kingdom." In *Women in Medieval Society*, ed. Susan M. Stuard, 95–124. Philadelphia, 1976.

Mayer-Maly, Th. "Morgengabe." In Aldalbert Erler and Ekkehard Kaufmann, eds., *Handwörterbuch zur deutschen Rechtsgeschichte* 3: col. 678–83. Berlin, 1984.

Meens, Rob. *Het tripartite boeteboek. Overlevering en betekenis van vroegmiddeleeuwse biechtvoorschriften*. Hilversum, 1994.

Metzger, Marcel. *Les sacramentaires*. Typologie des sources 70. Turnhout, 1994.

Meyer, Herbert. "Friedelehe und Mutterrecht." *ZSRG GA* 27 (1927): 198–286.

Meyer-Gebel, Marlene. "Zur annalistischen Arbeitsweise Hinkmars von Reims." *Francia* 15 (1987): 75–108.

Migne, Jacques-Paul, ed. *Patrologia Cursus Completus, series latina*. 221 vols. Paris, 1841–64.

Mikat, Paul. *Dotierte Ehe, rechte Ehe. Zur Entwicklung des Eheschliessungsrechts in fränkischer Zeit*. Rheinisch-Westfälische Akademie für Wissenschaften. Geisteswissenschaften. Vorträge G 227. Opladen, 1978.

——. "Zu den Voraussetzungen der Begegnung von fränkischer und kirchlicher Eheauffassung in Gallien." In *Diaconia et Ius: Festgabe für Heinrich Flatten zum 65. Geburtstag*, ed. Heribert Heinemann, Horst Herrmann, and Paul Mikat, 1–26. Munich, 1973.

Missone, David. "Mandement inédit d'Adventius de Metz à l'occasion d'une incursion normande (mai–juin 867)." *RB* 93 (1983): 71–79.

Mordek, Hubert, ed. *Aus Archiven und Bibliotheken. Festschrift für Raymund Kottje zum 65. Gebuhrtstag.* Freiburger Beiträge zur Mittelalterlichen Geschichte 3. Frankfurt am Main, 1992.

——. *Bibliotheca capitularium regum Francorum manuscripta. Überlieferung und Traditionszusammenhang der fränkischen Herrschererlasse.* MGH Hilfsmittel 15: Munich, 1995.

——. "Kapitularien." In *Lexikon des Mittelalters* 5: col. 943–46. Munich, 1991.

——. *Kirchenrecht und Reform im Frankenreich. Die Collectio Vetus Gallica, die älteste systematische Kanonessammlung des Fränkischen Gallien. Studien und Edition.* Beiträge zur Geschichte und Quellenkunde des Mittelalters 1. Berlin, 1975.

——. "Kirchenrechtliche Autoritäten im Frühmittelalter." In Classen, *Recht und Schrift im Mittelalter*, 237–55.

——. "Zur handschriftlichen Überlieferung der Dacheriana." *QFIAB* 47 (1967): 574–95.

——. ed. *Aus Kirche und Reich. Studien zu Theologie, Politik und Recht im Mittelalter. Festschrift für Friedrich Kempf.* Sigmaringen, 1983.

Morelle, Laurent. "La main du roi et le nom de Dieu: La validation de l'acte royal selon Hincmar, d'après un passage de son *De divortio*." In *Foi chrétienne et églises dans la société politique de l'Occident du haut moyen âge, IVe–XIIe siècle*, ed. Jacqueline Hoareau-Dodinau and Pascal Texier, 287–318. Limoges, 2004.

Morrison, Karl F. *The Two Kingdoms: Ecclesiology in Carolingian Political Thought.* Princeton, 1964.

——. "'Unum ex multis': Hincmar of Rheims' Medical and Aesthetic Rationales for Unification." In *Nascita dell' Europa ed Europa Carolingia*, 583–712.

Mostert Marco, Albrecht L. W. Demyttenaere, Edward O. Van Hartingsveldt, and Rudi E. Künzel, eds. *Vrouw, familie en macht. Bronnen over vrouwen in de Middeleeuwen.* Hilversum, 1990.

Murray, Alexander C. *Germanic Kinship Structure: Studies in Law and Society in Antiquity and the Early Middle Ages.* Pontifical Institute of Medieval Studies, Studies and Texts 65. Toronto, 1983.

Nascita dell' Europa ed Europa Carolingia: Un equazione da verificare. Settimane di studio del Centro Italiano di Studi sull' alto medioevo 27. Spoleto, 1981.

Nehlsen, Hermann. "Zur Aktualität und Effektivität der ältesten germanischen Rechtsaufzeichnungen." In Classen, *Recht und Schrift im Mittelalter*, 449–502.

Nelson, Janet L. *Charles the Bald.* London, 1992.

——. "Inauguration Rituals." In *Early Medieval Kingship*, ed. Peter Sawyer and Ian Wood, 50–71. Leeds, 1977. (= Nelson, *Politics and Ritual*, 283–307).

——. "Kingship and Empire." In *The Cambridge History of Medieval Political Thought c.350–c.1450*, ed. James Henderson Burns, 211–51. Cambridge, 1988.

——. "Kingship and Royal Government." In McKitterick, *The New Cambridge Medieval History* 2: 383–430.

——. "Kingship, Law and Liturgy in the Political Thought of Hincmar of Rheims." *English Historical Review* 92 (1977): 241–79 (= Nelson, *Politics and Ritual*, 133–71).

——. "Legislation and Consensus in the Reign of Charles the Bald." In Nelson, *Politics and Ritual in Early Medieval Europe*, 91–116.

——. "National Synods, Kingship as Office, and Royal Anointing: An Early Medieval Syndrome." In Nelson, *Politics and Ritual in Early Medieval Europe*, 239–57

——. *Politics and Ritual in Early Medieval Europe.* London, 1986.

——. Review of Wemple, *Women in Frankish Society.* In *History: Journal of the Historical Association* 69 (1984): 449–50.

——. "Symbols in Context: Rulers' Inauguration Rituals in Byzantium and the West in the Early Middle Ages." In Nelson, *Politics and Ritual in Early Medieval Europe,* 259–81.

Noonan, John T. "An Almost Absolute Value in History." In *The Morality of Abortion: Legal and Historical Perspectives,* ed. Noonan, 1–59. Cambridge, Mass., 1970.

Nottarp, Hermann. *Gottesurteilstudien.* Munich, 1956.

Oexle, Otto Gerhard. "Die Karolinger und die Stadt des heiligen Arnulf." *FS* 1 (1967): 250–364.

Ogris, Werner. "Friedelehe." In Aldalbert Erler and Ekkehard Kaufmann, eds., *Handwörterbuch zur deutschen Rechtsgeschichte* 1: col. 1293–96. Berlin, 1971.

Parisot, Robert. *Le royaume de Lorraine sous les carolingiens (843–923).* Paris, 1898.

Parisse, Michel, ed. *Veuves et veuvages dans le haut moyen age. Table ronde organisée à Göttingen par la Mission Historique Française en Allemagne.* Paris, 1993.

Penndorf, Ursula. *Das Problem der "Reichseinheitsidee" nach der Teilung von Verdun (843). Untersuchungen zu den späten Karolingern.* Münchener Beiträge zur Mediävistik und Renaissance-Forschung 20. Munich, 1974.

Perels, Ernst. *Papst Nikolaus I. und Anastasius Bibliothecarius. Ein Beitrag zur Geschichte des Papsttums im neunten Jahrhundert.* Berlin, 1920.

Pohl-Resl, Brigitte. "'Quod me legibus contanget auere': Rechtsfähigkeit und Landbesitz langobardischer Frauen." *MIÖG* 101 (1993): 201–27.

——. "Vorsorge, Memoria und soziales Ereignis: Frauen als Schenkerinnen in den bayerischen und alemannischen Urkunden des 8. und 9. Jahrhunderts." *MIÖG* 103 (1995): 265–87.

Poupardin, René. "Les grandes familles comtales à l'époque carolingienne." *RH* 72 (1900): 72–95.

Prinz, Joseph. "Ein unbekanntes Aktenstück zum Ehestreit König Lothars II." *DA* 21 (1965): 249–63.

Reuter, Timothy, ed. *The Medieval Nobility: Studies on the Ruling Classes of France and Germany from the Sixth to the Twelfth Century.* Amsterdam, 1979.

Reynolds, Philip Lyndon. *Marriage in the Western Church: The Christianization of Marriage during the Patristic and Early Medieval Periods.* Supplements to Vigilae Christanae. Texts and Studies of Early Christian Life and Language 24. Leiden, 1994.

Reynolds, Roger E. "Canon Law to Gratian." In Joseph R. Strayer, ed., *Dictionary of the Middle Ages* 7: 395–413. New York, 1986.

——. "The Organisation, Law and Liturgy of the Western Church, 700–900." In McKitterick, *The New Cambridge Medieval History* 2: 587–621.

Riché, Pierre. *Les carolingiens. Une famille qui fit l'Europe.* Paris, 1983.

——. *Les écoles et l'enseignement dans l'occident chrétien de la fin de Ve siècle au milieu du XIe siècle.* Paris, 1979.

Ritzer, Korbinian. *Formen, Riten und religiöses Brauchtum der Eheschliessung in den christlichen Kirchen des Ersten Jahrtausends.* Liturgiewissenschaftliche Quellen und Forschungen 38. 2nd ed. Münster, 1981.

Rösener, Werner. "Strukturformen der adeligen Grundherrschaft in der Karolingerzeit." In *Strukturen der Grundherrschaft im Frühen Mittelalter,* ed. Rösener, 126–80. Veröffentlichungen des Max-Planck-Instituts für Geschichte 92. Göttingen, 1989.

Rouche, Michel. "The Early Middle Ages in the West." In Ariès and Duby, *A History of Private Life* 1: 415–549.

——. "Des mariages païens au mariage chrétien. Sacré et sacrement." In *Segni e riti nella chiesa altomedievale occidentale,* 835–873. Settimane di studio del centro italiano di studi sull'alto medioevo 33. Spoleto, 1987.

——. ed. *Mariage et sexualité au moyen age. Accord ou crise?* Cultures et civilisations médiévales 21. Paris, 2000.

Schieffer, Rudolf. "Hinkmar von Reims." In *Theologische Realenzyklopädie* 15: 355–60. Berlin, 1986.

——. "Karl Martell und seine Familie." In Jarnut, Nonn, and Richter, eds., *Karl Martell in seiner Zeit*, 305–15.

——. "Karolingische Töchter." In Jenal, *Herrschaft, Kirche, Kultur*, 125–40.

——. "Möglichkeiten und Grenzen der biographischen Darstellung frühmittelalterlicher Persönlichkeiten. Zu dem neuen Hinkmar-Buch von J. Devisse." *HZ* 229 (1979): 85–95.

Schieffer, Theodor. "Eheschließung und Ehescheidung im Hause der karolingischen Kaiser und Könige." *Theologisch-Praktische Quartalschrift, herausgegeben von den Professoren der Philosophisch-theologischen Diözesan Lehranstalt Linz/Donau* 116 (1968): 37–43.

——. "Die Krise des karolingischen Imperiums." In *Aus Mittelalter und Neuzeit. Festschrift für Gerhard Kallen*, ed. Josef Engel, 1–15. Bonn, 1975.

Schlesinger, Walter. "Karlingische Königswahlen." In Hlawitschka, *Königswahl und Thronfolge in fränkisch-karolingischer Zeit*, 190–266.

Schmid, Karl. "Ein karolingischer Königseintrag im Gedenkbuch von Remiremont." *FS* 2 (1968): 96–134.

——. "Programmatisches zur Erforschung der mittelalterlichen Personen und Personengruppen." *FS* 8 (1974): 116–30.

——. "Über die Struktur des Adels im früheren Mittelalter." *Jahrbuch für fränkische Landesforschung* 19 (1959): 1–23.

——. "Zur Problematik von Familie, Sippe und Geschlecht, Haus und Dynastie beim mittelalterlichen Adel." *Zeitschrift für die Geschichte des Oberrheins* 105 (1957): 1–62.

Schmidt-Wiegand, Ruth. "Lex Salica." In Aldalbert Erler and Ekkehard Kaufmann, eds., *Handwörterbuch zur deutschen Rechtsgeschicht* 2: col. 1944–62. Berlin, 1998.

Schmitz, Gerhard. "Concilium Perfectum. Überlegungen zum Konzilsverständnis Hinkmars von Reims." *ZSRG KA* 66 (1979): 26–54.

——. "Wucher in Laon. Eine neue Quelle zu Karl dem Kahlen und Hinkmar von Reims." *DA* 37 (1981): 529–58.

Schneider, Reinhard. *Brüdergemeine und Schwurfreundschaft. Der Auflösungsprozeß des Karlingerreiches im Spiegel der Caritas-Terminologie in den Verträgen der Karlingischen Teilkönige des 9. Jahrhunderts*. Historische Studien 388. Lübeck, 1964.

——. "Schriftlichkeit und Mündlichkeit im Bereich der Kapitularien." In Classen, *Recht und Schrift im Mittelalter*, 257–79.

Schott, Clausdieter. "Der Stand der Leges-Forschung." *FS* 13 (1979): 29–55.

Schrörs, Heinrich. *Hinkmar, Erzbischof von Reims. Sein Leben und seine Schriften*. Freiburg im Breisgau, 1884.

Seckel, Emil. "Studien zu Benedictus Levita VII." *NA* 35 (1910): 105–91, 433–539.

Sickel, Wilhelm. "Das Thronfolgerecht der unehelichen Karolinger." In Hlawitschka, *Königswahl und Thronfolge in fränkisch-karolingischer Zeit*, 106–43.

Sieben, Hermann Josef. "Konzilien in Leben und Lehre des Hinkmar von Reims (†882)." *Theologie und Philosophie* 55 (1980): 44–77.

Sohm, Rudolf. *Das Recht der Eheschliessung aus dem deutschen und canonischen Recht geschichtlich entwickelt. Eine Antwort auf die Frage nach dem Verhältniss der kirchlichen Trauung zur Zivilehe*. Weimar, 1875.

——. *Trauung und Verlobung. Eine Entgegnung auf Friedberg: Verlobung und Trauung*. Weimar, 1876.

Staab, Franz. "Jugement moral et propagande. Boson de Vienne vu par les élites du royaume de l'est." In Le Jan, *La royauté et les élites dans l'Europe carolingienne*, 365–82.

Stafford, Pauline. "La mutation familiale: A Suitable Case for Caution." In *The Community, the Family and the Saint: Patterns of Power in Early Medieval Europe*, ed. Joyce Hil and Mary Swan, 103–26. Turnhout, 1998.

———. *Queens, Concubines and Dowagers: The King's Wife in the Early Middle Ages.* London, 1983.

Staubach, Nikolaus. "Das Herrscherbild Karls des Kahlen. Formen und Funktionen monarchischer Repräsentation im früheren Mittelalter" 1. Diss. Münster, 1982.

———. *Rex Christianus: Hofkultur und Herrschaftspropaganda im Reich Karls des Kahlen.* 2. *Die Grundlegung der "religion royale."* Pictura et Poesis 2.2. Cologne, 1993.

Stevenson, Kenneth. *Nuptial Blessing: A Study of Christian Marriage Rites.* London, 1982.

Störmer, Werner. *Früher Adel. Studien zur politischen Führungsschicht im fränkisch-deutschen Reich vom 8. bis 11. Jahrhundert.* Monographien zur Geschichte des Mittelalters 6. Stuttgart, 1973.

Stratmann, Martina. *Hinkmar von Reims als Verwalter von Bistum und Kirchenprovinz.* Quellen und Forschungen zum Recht im Mittelalter 6. Sigmaringen, 1991.

Tellenbach, Gerd. *Ausgewählte Abhandlungen und Aufsätze.* 4 vols. Stuttgart, 1988.

———. "Der großfränkische Adel und die Regierung Italiens in der Blütezeit des Karolingerreiches." In Tellenbach, *Studien und Vorarbeiten,* 40–70.

———. "Die geistigen und politischen Grundlagen der karolingischen Thronfolge. Zugleich eine Studie über kollektive Willensbildung und kollektives Handeln im neunten Jahrhundert." *FS* 13 (1979): 184–302.

———. "Zur Erforschung des mittelalterlichen Adels (9.–12. Jahrhundert)." In *XIIe Congrès international des sciences historiques* 1, *Grands Thèmes,* 318–36. Vienna, 1965. (= "Internationaler Historikerkongreß Wien 1965." In Tellenbach, *Ausgewählte Abhandlungen* 3, 868–88).

———. ed., *Studien und Vorarbeiten zur Geschichte des großfränkischen und frühdeutschen Adels.* Forschungen zur oberrheinischen Landesgeschichte 4. Freiburg im Breisgau, 1957.

Tellenbach, Gerd, Josef Fleckenstein, and Karl Schmid. "Kritische Studien zur großfränkischen und alemannischen Adelsgeschichte." *Zeitschrift für würtembergische Landesgeschichte* 15 (1956): 169–90.

Thomas, Heinz. "Der Mönch Theoderich von Trier und die Vita Deicoli." *Rheinische Vierteljahrblätter* 31 (1966–67): 42–63.

Toubert, Pierre. "The Carolingian Moment: Eighth–Tenth Century." In Burguière, *A History of the Family* 1: 379–406.

———. "L'institution du mariage chrétien, de l'antiquité tardive à l'an mil." In *Morfologie sociali e culturali in Europa fra tarda antichità e alto medioevo,* 503–49. Settimane di studio del centro italiano di studi sull'alto medioevo 45. Spoleto, 1998.

———. "La théorie du mariage chez les moralistes carolingiens." In *Il matrimonio nella società altomedievale,* 233–82.

Van Caenegem, Raoul C. "Reflexions on Rational and Irrational Modes of Proof in Medieval Europe." *Tijdschrift voor rechtsgeschiedenis* 58 (1990): 263–79.

Van Eupen, Th. A. G., ed. *(On)ontbindbaarheid van het huwelijk.* Annalen van het Thijmgenootschap 58.1. Hilversum, 1970.

———. "De (on)ontbindbaarheid van het huwelijk in de middeleeuwen." In Van Eupen, *(On)ontbindbaarheid van het huwelijk,* 51–90.

———. "De onverbreekbaarheid van de huwelijksband: een eenstemmige traditie?" In *Alternatief kerkelijk huwelijksrecht,* ed. Josephus H. A. van Tilborg, Th. A. G. Van Eupen, and Petrus J. M Huizing, 24–37. *Annalen van het Thijmgenootschap* 62, 4. Bilthoven, 1974.

Van Tilborg, Josephus H. A. "Mattheüs 19, 3–12 en het onontbindbare huwelijk." In Van Eupen, *(On)ontbindbaarheid van het huwelijk,* 23–34.

Van Vliet, Kaj. *In kringen van kanunniken. Munsters en kapittels in het bisdom Utrecht, 695–1227.* Zutphen, 2002.

Van Winter, Johanna Maria. "Adel en Aristocratie in de Middeleeuwen." *TvG* 93 (1980): 357–76.

———. "The First Centuries of the Episcopal See at Utrecht." In *Utrecht, Britain and the Continent: Archaeology, Art and Architecture*, ed. Elisabeth de Bièvre. British Archaeological Association conference transactions 18 (1996): 22–29.

Veyne, Paul. "La famille et l'amour sous le haut-empire romain." *AESC* 33, 1 (1978): 35–63.

———. "The Roman Empire." In Ariès and Duby, *A History of Private Life* 1: 5–233.

Vogel, Cyril. *Introduction aux sources de l'histoire du culte chrétien au moyen âge.* Biblioteca degli Studi Medievali 1. Spoleto, 1966. (= *Medieval Liturgy: An Introduction to the Sources.* Rev. and trans. William G. Storey and Niels K. Rasmussen. Washington, 1986).

———. "Les rites de la célébration du mariage: Leur signification dans la formation du lien durant le haut moyen âge." In *Il matrimonio nella società altomedievale*, 397–465.

———. "Le rôle du liturge dans la formation du lien conjugal." *RDC* 30 (1980): 7–27.

Vollmer, Franz. "Die Etichonen. Ein Beitrag zur Frage der Kontinuität früher Adelsfamilien." In Tellenbach, *Studien und Vorarbeiten*, 137–84.

Von Pölnitz-Kehr, Gudila. "Kaiserin Angilberga: Ein Exkurs zur Diplomatik Kaiser Ludwigs von Italien." *HJ* 60 (1940): 429–40.

Voss, Ingrid. *Herrschertreffen im frühen- und hohen Mittelalter Untersuchungen zu den Begegnungen der ostfränkischen und westfränkischen Herrscher im 9. und 10. Jahrhundert sowie der deutschen und französischen Könige vom 11. bis 12. Jahrhundert.* Beihefte zum Archiv für Kulturgeschichte 26. Cologne, 1987.

Wallace-Hadrill, John Michael. *The Frankish Church.* Oxford History of the Christian Church. Oxford, 1983.

Wattenbach, Wilhelm, and Ernst Dümmler. *Deutschlands Geschichtsquellen im Mittelalter. Frühzeit und Karolinger.* Rev. Franz Huf, 2 vols. Kettwig, 1991.

Wattenbach, Wilhelm, and Robert Holtzmann. *Deutschlands Geschichtsquellen im Mittelalter. Die Zeit der Sachsen und Salier* 1: *Das Zeitalter des Ottonischen Staates (900–1050).* Rev. Franz Josef Schmale. Cologne, 1967.

Wattenbach, Wilhelm, and Wilhelm Levison. *Deutschlands Geschichtsquellen im Mittelalter. Vorzeit und Karolinger* 2: *Die Karolinger vom Anfang des 8. Jahrhunderts bis zum Tode Karls des Großen.* Rev. Heinz Löwe. Weimar, 1953.

———. *Deutschlands Geschichtsquellen im Mittelalter. Vorzeit und Karolinger* 3: *Die Karolinger vom Tode Karls des Großen bis zum Vertrag von Verdun.* Rev. Heinz Löwe. Weimar, 1957.

———. *Deutschlands Geschichtsquellen im Mittelalter. Vorzeit und Karolinger* 4: *Die Karolinger vom Vertrag von Verdun bis zum Herrschaftsantritt der Herrscher aus dem sächsischen Hause. Italien und das Papsttum.* Rev. Heinz Löwe. Weimar, 1963.

———. *Deutschlands Geschichtsquellen im Mittelalter. Vorzeit und Karolinger* 5: *Die Karolinger vom Vertrag von Verdun bis zum Herrschaftsantritt der Herrscher aus dem sächsischen Hause. Das Westfränkische Reich.* Rev. Heinz Löwe. Weimar, 1973.

———. *Deutschlands Geschichtsquellen im Mittelalter. Vorzeit und Karolinger* 6: *Die Karolinger vom Vertrag von Verdun bis zum Herrschaftsantritt der Herrscher aus dem sächsischen Hause. Das Ostfränkische Reich.* Rev. Heinz Löwe. Weimar, 1990.

Wegman, Herman A. J. *Riten en mythen. Liturgie in de geschiedenis van het christendom.* Kampen, 1991.

Weinfurter, Stefan, and Odilo Engels. *Series Episcoporum Ecclesiae Catholicae occidentalis V, Germania I Archiepiscopatus Coloniensis.* Stuttgart, 1982.

Wemple, Suzanne F., *Women in Frankish Society: Marriage and the Cloister, 500–900.* Philadelphia, 1981.

Werminghoff, Albert. "Reise nach Italien im Jahre 1901." *NA* 27 (1902): 565–675.

Werner, Karl Ferdinand. "Bedeutende Adelsfamilien im Reich Karls des Grossen." In *Karl der Große. Lebenswerk und Nachleben* 1, ed. Helmut Beumann, 83–142. Düsseldorf, 1965.

———. "Les femmes, le pouvoir et la transmission du pouvoir." In *La femme au moyen-âge*, ed. Michel Rouche and Jean Heuclin, 365–77. Maubeuge, 1990.

———. "Hludovicus Augustus: Gouverner l'empire chrétien—Idées et réalités." In Godman and Collins, *Charlemagne's Heir*, 3–124.

———. "Liens de parenté et noms de personne." In Duby and Le Goff, *Famille et parenté dans l'occident médiéval*, 13–18, 25–34.

———. "Die Nachkommen Karls des Grossen." In *Karl der Große: Lebenswerk und Nachleben* 4, ed. Wolfgang Braunfels and Percy Ernst Schramm, 403–82. Düsseldorf, 1967.

———. "Untersuchungen zur Frühzeit des französischen Fürstentums (9.–10. Jahrhundert)." *Die Welt als Geschichte. Eine Zeitschrift für Universalgeschichte* 18 (1958): 256–89; 19 (1959): 146–93; 20 (1960): 87–119.

———. "Zur Arbeitsweise des Regino von Prüm." *Die Welt als Geschichte. Eine Zeitschrift für Universalgeschichte* 9 (1959): 96–116.

Wilsdorf, Christian. "Les Etichonides aux temps carolingiens et ottoniens." *Bulletin philologique et historique (jusquà 1610) du comité des travaux historiques et scientifiques* (1964): 1–33.

———. "Le monasterium scottorum de Honau et la famille des ducs d'Alsace au 8ème siècle. Vestiges d'un cartulaire perdue." *Francia* 3 (1975): 1–87.

Winterer, Hermann. "Die Stellung des unehelichen Kindes in der langobardischen Gesetzgebung." *ZSRG GA* 87 (1970): 32–56.

Wollasch, Joachim. "Eine adlige Familie des frühen Mittelalters. Ihr Selbstverständnis und ihre Wirklichkeit." *Archiv für Kulturgeschichte* 39 (1957): 150–88.

Zechiel-Eckes, Klaus. "Ein Blick in Pseudoisidors Werkstatt. Studien zum Entstehungsprozess der falschen Dekretalen." *Francia* 28 (2000): 37–90.

———. "Verecundus oder Pseudoisidor? Zur Genese der Excerptiones de gestis Chalcedonensis concilii." *DA* 56 (2001): 413–46.

Index

Aachen
  first council of (860), 15, 43, 46, 63–64,
    74–78, 82, 92, 94, 104
  second council of (860), 43, 46–47,
    63–64, 68, 75, 78, 82, 94–95, 102
  third council of (862), 43, 68, 102–10,
    119, 127–33
abbots, 4, 6, 15, 45, 47, 73–75, 80, 98, 166,
  171
  See also lay abbots
abduction, 17n20, 21, 25–26, 29, 30, 78,
  80–81, 86, 101–2, 114, 117, 137n163,
  142, 148, 178
acclamation, 103
Adalhard, seneschal to Louis the Pious,
  60, 60n51, 61n46, 136–37, 143
Adelaide, daughter of Hugo of Tours, 70
Adelaide, wife of Louis the Stammerer,
  60, 61n46, 98, 115
Ado, archbishop of Vienne, 40, 157,
  163n61, 175n11, 178n21, 183
Adrian II, pope, 40, 44, 173n4, 174–81,
  183–84
Adventius, bishop of Metz
  political activities of, 42–43nn, 63n3,
    72n49, 74–75, 92–95, 102, 110–12,
    114–15, 128n127, 131–34, 162–63
  upbringing of, 74n8, 147n202
adultery, 12–14, 17–20, 22–25, 29, 31–32,
  34, 65, 69, 79–81, 83–86, 88, 96,
  105–8, 149, 156, 164, 183
Alcuin, 23

allods. *See under* properties
Ambrosiaster, 14n9, 106–7
Anastasius, papal librarian, 40n17, 42,
  160–61, 168, 178
Angilberga, wife of Louis II of Italy, 117,
  126, 150, 174
Annales Bertiniani, 37–38, 40, 43–44, 48,
  57–58, 98, 110, 168, 180, 182
Annales Fuldenses, 38, 40, 43, 48, 110n58, 183
Annales Laubacenses, 39–40, 48
Annales Lobienses, 39, 48, 184
Annales Xantenses, 39, 40, 43, 48, 183
annals, 37, 42
  See also specific annals
anointment, 55–56, 92
Ansgard, wife of Louis the Stammerer,
  98, 114–15
Arnulf, bishop of Toul, 76n20, 102,
  107n46
Arnust, father-in-law of Louis the
  German's son Carloman, 137, 143
Arsenius, bishop of Orte, 150, 153,
  168–69, 178–79
Atto. *See* Hatto
Augustine, 12, 14, 23, 31, 79, 83, 84n62,
  85, 97, 106–8, 163n63
Ava, wife of Hugo of Tours, 70, 104n28,
  138

Baldwin, husband of Judith, daughter of
  Charles the Bald, 101–2, 104, 114,
  142, 158

Beggo, 60–61

Benedict III, pope, 40, 59n38, 68n34, 159

Benedict Levita (Benedict the Deacon), 29–33, 97n128

Berengar, son of Count Gebhard, 137

Bertha, daughter of Hugo of Italy, 186

Bertha, daughter of Hugo of Tours, 70

Bertha, daughter of Lothar II, 52n5, 61, 139, 185–86

Bertha, daughter of Louis the German, 180

betrothal, 26–27, 31–34, 78, 81, 83–86, 111–12, 115–17, 120, 124–27, 131, 137, 155–57

bishops
  competencies of, 5–6, 86–92, 129–30, 132–35, 161–62
  See also specific bishops

Bivin, *hostiarius* to Louis the Pious, 60–61, 72, 134

blessing of marriage, 14, 20, 25, 27–28, 30–35, 67, 78, 86, 88–89, 91, 124, 152–53, 155–56, 158

Boso, father of Hucbert and Theutberga, 59–60, 152

Boso, son of Bivin, 53–54, 61, 114–15, 126

Boso, son of Boso, 47, 59, 71, 77, 97, 138, 171

Boso, son of Hugo of Italy, 186

bridal gift, 27, 30–34, 78, 81, 83, 86, 111, 115–17, 125–27, 131, 152, 155–57

canon law collections, 16–19, 21–22, 25–26, 28–35, 81, 158
  See also specific collections

Capitula episcoporum, 22, 33

capitularies, 15–17, 19, 21, 28–30, 33

Carloman, son of Charles the Bald, 126

Carloman, son of Lothar I, 126n120, 131n170

Carloman, son of Louis the German, 54, 101, 137, 142

Carloman, son of Louis the Stammerer, 54

Charlemagne, 4–5, 16–20, 27, 54, 57, 122, 126, 131, 140, 171

Charles, archbishop of Mainz, 156–57, 164

Charles, son of Charles the Bald, 55, 101–2, 114, 126, 157–58

Charles of Provence, 44, 51, 53–55, 57, 70, 73, 75, 101, 136–37, 139–42, 150

Charles the Bald
  and his brothers and nephews, 4, 55–57, 64, 91, 94, 96, 101, 133, 139–42, 147, 150–51, 153, 168–71, 179–81. (*See also* Coblenz, Treaty of; Metz, Treaty of; Savonnières, Treaty of)
  and his children, 28, 55, 98, 101–3, 114–15, 126, 142, 157–58
  government and ecclesiastical politics of, 25, 37–38, 40, 47, 73, 75–77, 131, 162, 167, 171–72
  marriage of, 28, 60–61, 126, 136

Charles the Fat, 53, 117, 137, 185

charters, 36, 45, 59, 72, 116–17, 127, 148, 171, 176

chastity, 22, 30, 32–34, 79, 81, 107–8

chronicles, 37
  See also Ado; Regino

Coblenz, Treaty of (860), 45, 47, 58–59, 73–74, 100–101, 135–38, 145–56

Collectio Dacheriana, 21–22, 25, 33, 35, 81

Collectio Dionysio-Hadriana, 17–21, 25

concubine, 24–27, 29, 83–85, 103, 110–13, 119, 123–27, 130, 137, 157, 183–86

Conrad, son of Conrad, 69, 136–38, 146–47, 150

Conrad, son of Welf, 70, 104, 136–37, 143–48

consent
  of parents, 33–34, 111–17, 131, 155–58
  of partners, 33–34, 64, 86, 120–21, 155–56, 158

coronation
  of kings, 56, 98
  of queens, 28, 98, 103, 126–27, 153, 169

councils, 7, 13–33, 42–43, 87, 89–95, 157, 159–60
  See also specific councils

Dhuoda, 23

diplomatic missions, 73–75, 92–95, 100–103, 149–51, 153, 168–69, 173

divisions of kingdoms, 4–5, 45, 51, 53–55, 58, 60, 140–42, 150, 173, 176, 179

divorce
  permission for, 11–13, 17–20, 22–24, 29–31, 65, 74–82, 85–86, 88–89, 97–98, 105–6, 109–10, 148, 157–58, 171
  prohibition against, 12–14, 34, 46, 63–65, 68, 77–81, 97–98, 107–9, 153–54, 157–58, 176–77, 186–87

Doda, concubine of Lothar I, 126n120, 139n170
Drogo, bishop of Metz, 134, 138
Drogo, son of Charles the Bald, 139n170

Egilo. *See* Heigil
election of kings. *See* succession of kings
Engelberga. *See* Angilberga
Engeltrude, daughter of Matfrid Count of Orléans, 47, 59, 71, 77, 97, 104, 169
Erkingar (Erchanger), father-in-law of Charles the Fat, 137
Ermengarde, daughter of Lothar II, 52n5
Ermengarde, daughter of Louis II of Italy, 53–54, 61
Ermengarde, wife of Lothar I, 69, 117, 137
Ermengarde, wife of Louis the Pious, 126
Ermentrude, wife of Charles the Bald, 28, 60, 126, 136, 158, 171
Ernst. *See* Arnust
excommunication, 83, 85, 101, 104–5, 133, 151, 154, 160, 164, 168–70, 173–74, 177–78, 184

fiefs. *See under* properties
fornication, 12, 14, 22–23, 32, 83, 98, 109, 121–22, 153
Franco, bishop of Liège, 74, 102, 138, 147, 162
Friedelehe, 2, 119–23

Gerard, Count of Paris, 60–61
Gerard, Count of Vienne, 70, 104
Germanic law, 2, 30, 65, 113, 116–17, 119–23
    See also *Lex Ribuaria*; *Lex Salica*
Gisela, daughter of Lothar II, 52n5, 185
Gisela, daughter of Louis the Pious, 138n165
Giselbert, son-in-law of Lothar I, 137
Gorze, 45, 60, 72, 134
Grimald, archchancellor of Louis the German, 38, 166
Grimland, archchancellor of Lothar II, 173
Gunthar, archbishop of Cologne
    kindred of, 74, 143
    political activities of, 48, 74, 93, 102, 110, 112–13, 118–19, 132, 149–53, 159–62, 165–67, 174

Hadrian II. *See* Adrian II
Harduic, archbishop of Besançon, 76n20, 102n17, 156–57

Hatto, bishop of Verdun, 75n14, 102, 133
Heigil, abbot of Prüm, abbot of Flavigny, archbishop of Sens, 74, 76n20
Hildegar, bishop of Meaux, 94–95
Hilduin, bishop-elect of Cambrai, 74n5, 167
Hincmar, archbishop of Reims
    political activities of, 46–48, 66, 73–77, 92–99, 146–47, 160, 167–69, 186
    writings of, 5–6, 23, 35–36, 38, 41, 43–44, 46–48, 54, 63, 66–69, 71, 77–92, 95–99, 106–7, 109–10, 113–14, 130, 150, 158, 165, 174–76, 178, 182–83
Hucbert, son of Boso
    accusations against, 63, 68, 75, 106
    political activities of, 51–52, 59–62, 65, 69, 71–73, 82, 100, 134, 143, 147, 151, 171, 185
Hugo, Count of Tours, 69–70
Hugo, king of Italy, 185–87
Hugo, son of Conrad, 136, 146, 167
Hugo, son of Liutfrid, 70
Hugo, son of Lothar II, 45, 54, 127, 147, 173, 180, 184–85
Hunger, bishop of Utrecht, 102

incest, 17–20, 22–25, 29, 63, 68, 81–86, 103, 105–6, 109–10, 157
infertility, 29, 79, 98, 154, 158, 177
Ingilberga. *See* Angilberga
Ingiltrude. *See* Engeltrude
inheritance, 125, 148
    See also divisions of kingdoms; succession of kings
Isidore of Seville, 12–13, 21n33, 116n83, 125n16, 163n63

Jerome, 12–14, 31, 106, 154
John, archbishop of Ravenna, 159n46, 166
John VIII, pope, 98, 125n116, 184
Jonas, bishop of Orléans, 23, 27, 29, 118n95, 124–25
Judith, daughter of Charles the Bald, 28, 37, 101–4, 114, 142, 157–58
Judith, daughter of Welf, 70, 145

kings
    authority of, 89–91, 95–96, 128–29, 163–64
    See also individual kings

lay abbots, 52, 59–60, 69–72, 134–37, 171

Leo the Great, pope, 13, 26–27, 30, 78–79, 83–85, 97, 99, 112n66, 119n98, 124n114

letters, 36, 38–39, 41–44, 48, 95, 102, 110–11, 118, 128–29, 132, 152, 156, 160, 162, 170, 176–178, 180

Leutulf, father-in-law of Louis III (Louis the Younger), 137

Lex Ribuaria, 65n17, 116n86

Lex Salica, 65n17, 112n16, 113n68, 121, 139n173

Liber pontificalis, 40, 43, 149n2, 166, 178n23

Liutbert, archbishop of Mainz, 39, 125n116

Liutfrid, son of Hugo, 69–71, 104, 111, 125, 137, 143, 168

Liutfrid, son of Liutfrid, 70

Lobbes, 39, 41n18, 59n38, 134, 151n16

Lothar I
  and his brothers, 4, 57
  and his children, 51, 54–55, 58, 76, 111–16, 137, 141
  marriage of, 59–60, 69–71, 126

Louis II, king of Italy
  ecclesiastical politics of, 149–50, 165–67, 174, 177–78
  government of, 59, 70, 147
  marriage of, 117, 126
  and his uncles and brothers, 44, 51, 54–55, 64, 69, 104, 141–42, 150, 168, 174, 176, 181

Louis III (Louis the Younger), son of Louis the German, 54, 99, 115, 137, 142, 185

Louis III, son of Louis the Stammerer, 54

Louis, abbot of St.-Denis, 75n13, 139n170, 171

Louis the German
  and his brothers and nephews, 54, 56–57, 64, 91, 94, 96, 101, 133, 139–42, 150, 168–69, 174, 176, 179. (*See also* Coblenz, Treaty of; Metz, Treaty of; Savonnières, Treaty of)
  and his children, 101, 115, 142
  diplomatic missions of, 101, 115, 142
  government and ecclesiastical politics of, 25, 39
  marriage of, 136

Louis the Pious

and his children, 4, 37, 54, 60, 70, 140, 154
  ecclesiastical politics of, 21, 87, 127
  government of, 47, 60, 70
  marriage of, 126, 136, 145

Louis the Stammerer, 54, 56, 60, 98–99, 102–3, 114–15, 126, 134, 142, 157

love, conjugal, 8, 29, 80–81, 111–12, 118, 120, 127, 158, 170, 186

Lure, 41n18, 180n29

Magingoz, bishop of Würzburg, 11–14, 35

marriage
  impediments to, 17–22, 24–25, 29, 31, 34, 78–79, 81, 84–86, 97–98, 105–6, 157–58, 171
  publicity of, 17, 30–34, 152
  and religious vows, 17–18, 22, 25, 78–79, 81, 154, 171
  remarriage, 11–14, 17, 19–23, 25, 29, 31, 78, 81, 84, 97, 105–6, 109, 157
  of unfree persons, 17, 22, 25–27, 78, 112–13, 123–24
  validity of, 32–34, 78–79, 81, 86, 97, 107, 110–19, 152–54, 158, 176
  See also divorce

Matfrid, Count of Orléans, 59, 70–71

Matfrid, son of Matfrid, 59–60, 138

Metz, Council of (859), 73, 75, 91n98

Metz, Council of (863), 43, 149, 152, 161

Metz, Treaty of (867/868), 44–45, 58, 173, 180

Monte Cassino, Council of (869), 44, 174, 177–78

Moutier-Grandval, 70

Muntehe, 119–20

Nicholas I, pope
  and Frankish kings, 4, 41, 44, 100–102, 104, 131, 133, 149–54, 163–64, 168–70, 172–74
  government of, 40–42, 44
  ideology of, 6, 42, 159–162

nobility
  factions among, 71n44, 143–44
  marital alliances of, 59–62, 69–72, 97–98, 136–38, 143–48
  power of, 52–58

oaths, 66–67, 77n24, 98, 114, 133, 141, 169, 180–83

Odelingus, abbot of Inden (Kornelimünster), 74

Odiliënberg, 102n15
offices. *See under* properties
ordeal (*iudicium Dei*), 63, 65–67, 75–77,
    82, 93, 98, 175, 182

Paris, Council of (829), 23–24, 29
Paulinus, archbishop of Aquileia, 23
penance, 67, 76, 80, 83–88, 90–92, 103,
    110, 129, 132–34, 157, 168
Pippin, son of Charles the Bald,
    139n170
Pippin II, Mayor of the Palace, 127
Pippin III, Mayor of the Palace, (King
    Pippin I), 15–19
popes. *See* Adrian II; Benedict III; John
    VIII; Leo the Great; Nicholas I
properties
    allods, 145–46
    fiefs (*beneficia*), 101, 143
    offices (*honores*), 56–60, 69–70, 136–38,
        145–47
Pseudo-Isidore, 28–35, 44n32, 81, 160,
    178

Rathold, bishop of Strasbourg, 102, 162
rebellions, 47, 56, 101, 126, 142
Regino, abbot of Prüm, 39, 51, 53–54,
    68n34, 93n103, 114–15, 140, 179,
    182–83, 185
Remiremont, 69n38, 101n6, 127n120,
    147n203, 180n29, 184
Richardis, wife of Charles the Fat, 117
Richildis, wife of Charles the Bald,
    60–61, 126
Roman law, 24, 26–27, 29–30, 88, 112,
    117–18, 120, 124, 156, 158
Rome, Council of (863), 44, 149–50,
    159–63
Rudolf, son of Conrad and king of
    Burgundy, 148
Rudolf, son of Rudolf the abbot of
    St.-Riquier, 136
Rudolf, son of Welf, 136

sacramentaries, 14–15, 20, 27–28, 30–31,
    34–35
Savonnières, Council of (859), 14, 73, 75,
    91
Savonnières, Treaty of (862), 44, 58, 103,
    139–40, 146
Sigeard, Count, 137

sodomy, 63, 68, 82–86
St.-Maurice, 59, 134
Stephan, Count of Auvergne, 97–99
succession of kings, 4, 17, 53–55, 57,
    114–15, 127, 140
    See also divisions of kingdoms

T(h)eoderic, bishop of Cambrai, 6n9,
    102n17
T(h)eutbald, son of Hucbert, 185
T(h)eutberga
    accusations against, 63–64, 66–68,
        74–76, 82–86, 92–96, 106, 110, 131,
        164, 171
    kindred of, 51, 59–61, 69, 104, 138,
        184–85
    marriage of, 51–52, 64, 103, 105,
        107–9, 151–54, 157, 164–65, 176
    political activities of, 100, 104, 110,
        123, 130–32, 150–53, 168–72, 174,
        177
T(h)eutgaud, archbishop of Trier
    kindred of, 38, 74n6
    political activities of, 74, 102–3, 110,
        112–14, 118–19, 133, 149–53,
        164–67
Tusey
    Council of (860), 47–48, 91
    Treaty of (865), 44, 139

Ungarius. *See* Hunger

Waldrada, wife of Conrad, 136n154
Waldrada, wife of Lothar II
    concubinage of, 52, 64, 110, 113, 119,
        123, 125, 127, 133, 184
    kindred of, 71n47, 113n67, 180n29
    marriage of, 45, 76, 82, 95, 102–5,
        110–12, 115–18, 127, 130–34,
        152–54, 171, 176–77
    political activities of, 104, 151, 154,
        169–70, 174, 180, 183
Walther, count of Lothar II, 71
wedding, 27–28, 30–34, 83, 86, 113,
    115–16, 120, 152, 155–56
Welf, father of Conrad,
    136, 144–46
Wenilo, bishop of Rouen, 94–95
Wicpert, nephew of Lothar II, 147

Zwentibold, son of Arnulf, 56, 185